THE F.A. *Complete* GUIDE TO

ENGLAND PLAYERS

SINCE 1945

THE F.A. *Complete* GUIDE TO
ENGLAND PLAYERS
SINCE 1945

STANLEY PAUL
LONDON

Statistical information up to and
including June 1993

First published 1993

1 3 5 7 9 10 8 6 4 2

Stanley Paul & Co Ltd
Random House, 20 Vauxhall Bridge Road,
London SW1V 2SA

Random House Australia (Pty) Limited
20 Alfred Street, Milsons Point, Sydney,
New South Wales 2061, Australia

Random House New Zealand Limited
18 Poland Road, Glenfield,
Auckland 10, New Zealand

Random House South Africa (Pty) Limited
PO Box 337, Bergvlei, South Africa

Random House UK Limited Reg. No. 954009

A CIP catalogue record for this book
is available from the British Library

ISBN 0 09 177294 X

Typeset in Helvetica and Sabon by
Textype Typesetters, Cambridge

Printed and bound in Great Britain by
Butler & Tanner Ltd, Frome, Somerset

CONTENTS

SIR WALTER WINTERBOTTOM

The Victoria Station Hotel, Sheffield, in 1946 was my first eye-opening experience of the England Selection Committee. The chairman of the Committee was present plus eight others, including myself, the newly appointed manager of England.

We all sat around the table putting forward our nominations for each position. There were something like four or five players nominated for the goalkeeping position alone. The list was reduced by a process of votes until it was down to the final two and a straight majority vote.

I was fascinated by the whole rigmarole and when it was all over I asked: 'How many of the Committee have actually seen these goalkeepers this season, or in fact any of the other players?'

The reply astonished me: 'None.'

But let's be fair. This system was in operation around the world – no-one knew any better at the time. The Argentinians, the Brazilians and West Germany all adopted a similar selection approach. You've also got to remember that club football was vastly differently organised from what it is today. Club sides were run by the players. The captain had a huge say in selection, being involved in discussions with the manager, and would often pick his friends.

Selection for the England side was not based on pure ability or merit alone. Quite often a player would be awarded an England cap in recognition of his services to the game. It might even have been treated as a reward for long service, for example. You would hear the Selection Committee say: 'It's really time we gave this deserving chap a cap.'

Leslie Compton was doing so well for Arsenal during the season that the Committee felt it was right to honour him with an international cap. 'Why not give him a chance?' one of them suggested.

I could see that the system needed to be refined and it helped my cause when matches involving the Football League were used to honour players with representative appearances. That left me with the main task to mould a side fit to represent the nation in the World Cup.

The selectors agreed to go out and watch players. The chairmen and myself in particular were allocated specific matches to watch certain individuals.

Selectors were chairmen or directors of clubs and they would previously only see a player if he appeared on their own home ground. Now they went to see them perform at other venues. At last the selectors were observing players in matches other than against their own teams. They could pick up more information and learn more about the players on their travels. There were clashes within the Selection Committee but I wouldn't say there were any vicious arguments.

However, there were vast differences over the way I felt we should be preparing the team for World Cups. I wanted to start a policy of developing a young team that would play together, mature together, and be ready within a four-year cycle.

Brian Clough was summoned to the team in 1959 along with a group of other outstanding young players. Fundamentally most of the team were 21 or under. Unfortunately we lost to Sweden in our second match, England's second home defeat by overseas opposition, our first home defeat having been inflicted by Hungary in 1953. The Selection Committee objected strongly to the policy of promoting young players and went back to the old regime.

As for the selection of Brian Clough, it is interesting that a member of the Committee just happened to be the Middlesbrough chairman! It didn't really matter for a friendly match. I didn't have any strong objections to players being tried out in those circumstances.

I suppose in my time as England manager, I presided over two of the most talked about defeats in England's international history – by the USA in the World Cup and by Hungary at Wembley in 1953.

Certainly, the defeat by the USA hurt very badly, while defeat by Hungary was to be expected. I appreciate that England's first defeat at home seemed to have a devastating effect, but I could foresee it. I didn't foresee the defeat by the USA.

It would be silly to give excuses for the Hungary result, but it still irks me to this very day that the structure of our game set it all up. The Hungarians had two powerful club teams, one had the entire star forward line, the other the whole of the international defence. Their national side came together twice a week for training over a two-year period. Although they were classified as amateurs they were clearly professionals, yet they were entitled to enter their best players for the Olympics. They won gold medals with ease. It was a resounding Olympic triumph for the Hungarians. Their players were together for a long time, their moves well rehearsed. They played together instinctively.

In contrast I would pick a team for one match and then find myself with a completely different side for the next. More often than not my 11 players came from 11 different clubs.

I travelled out to Budapest 10 days before our Wembley match to watch Hungary scrape a lucky draw with Sweden. The English press were convinced it would be a pushover for England. But the Hungarians travelled through Europe playing club sides, keeping their fitness and team pattern. I picked a team on Wednesday, but on Saturday several were injured playing for their clubs. By the following Wednesday, the day of the match, I had to put out a severely weakened side, with no pre-match training.

Tom Finney was among the casualties. In came George Robb, an amateur with Tottenham Hotspur, for his first international cap. He was poleaxed. He didn't know how to handle it, and why should he? It takes time to settle a new player into the England side and certainly it would be difficult for anyone to replace Finney.

It was no surprise to me what happened next. Even with our weakened team we played ever so well. But the Hungarians were far superior, notably in their clinical finishing. And they rammed home that aspect of their game.

To lose our first international match at home, and in such comprehensive fashion, was bound to be viewed as a watershed for English football. But, in my view, it's sheer codswallop to believe that we were the only nation capable of playing good football. Just ask the Scots in those days!

But it did gall me that other countries were able to draw their players from one or two teams, or at least the bulk of their sides. I would go along to watch Arsenal versus Manchester City, two of our leading clubs at that time, and only five out of the 22 players on show would be English; the rest were Scots, Northern Irish, Southern Irish, or Welsh. And it's still going on today!

Yet just look at the World Cup in Spain. There were 11 Juventus players in the Italy squad of 22 and the West Germans had seven from Bayern Munich. In the 1974 Finals in Germany, the hosts had six from Bayern Munich while the Dutch had six from Ajax. Even when Liverpool were consistently winning the Championship, most of their players were not English.

However, nothing upset me more than that defeat by the USA. I just couldn't believe it when they beat us 1–0 in the World Cup Finals.

Maurice Smith compiled statistics on the game and told me that England had hit the woodwork 11 times! That's impossible to believe.

We also scored what I thought was a perfectly good goal, but it was disallowed, and their goal was just stupid; a deflection that sent our 'keeper the wrong way. Then we went out of the World Cup because we lost 1–0 to Spain and that riled me even more!

At that time we were experiencing a lot of problems with referees and their interpretation of the rules. What's more, I was appalled by the tactics of some of the Spanish players. There must have been half a dozen deliberate handballs; they just caught the ball at the merest sign of danger. Their attitude was cynical and they would not hesitate in blocking our players at any threat of an attack.

But it's the defeat by America that no-one will forget.

When I returned to the States, they were determined to remind me of that day. They presented me with an enlarged 'colour' photograph of the winning goal . . . they'd actually painted a black and white picture!

I've received letters from all over the world for many years now to nominate my greatest ever England team, my greatest world team and so on. But that's a game I don't believe in playing. I've stuck solidly all through my life to the principle that I won't nominate one great player above another, because I never wanted to create favourites.

I'm also continually asked whether I would choose between Stanley Matthews and Tom Finney, as I was fortunate enough to have them both in my England team.

For undiluted entertainment Matthews was superb. He made things look so easy, yet they were so clever. Tom would score far more goals and for efficiency he was actually the better of the two. He would provide more assists than even Matthews.

Yet for entertainment and wizardry there was none better than Matthews. I'll never forget one match in Belgium. We were losing by 2–1 at half-time. But the second half belonged to Stan. He took over and we won 5–2. The remainder of the goals were down to his extraordinary wizardry. One was amazing. He took off on one of his dribbles from the half-way line and the centre half, who was wearing gloves, dived at him to try to rugby tackle him to the ground. Instead, he pulled Stan's shorts down. Stan never flinched, went on with his mazy dribble even with his shorts round his knees. He ended this breathtaking run with a delicate chip for Tom Finney to score. Everyone in the ground rose to their feet, in stages, as the run went on. By the time the goal was scored, both sets of players were applauding Stan.

Who would I choose? I would have them *both* in my side and on one occasion, with the two of them, we beat

Portugal 10–0.

I don't like making comparisons between my players and the current generation because the game is so vastly different now. It is all about speed and fitness these days. Physically, all sportsmen throughout the world are getting stronger and bigger, able to jump further, swim faster, and run quicker. It is a faster game in every respect and the modern-day player needs a high level of fitness as well as skill. It has reached the stage where a player no longer has time and space to deliberate. The game is played instinctively.

Every country is better organised. They all play with the sweeper system and that makes even the minnows hard to beat. In our day it was five forwards against five and five defenders against five. Now when a team loses the ball it's everybody between the ball and the goal, and the skilful players are confronted with defensive blocks. But that is not to say I am opposed to the modern game. In fact I like it, but only when it's a good game. In my time it was bound to be more entertaining because the play was more open and there were more attacks on goal. But some of the recent Wembley play-offs have been outstanding matches, with the emphasis on attacking football.

One aspect of the game never changes, but this is one that the current England manager would dearly love to change. It has never been fully appreciated how much advantage the other top nations have over England in the way they prepare for internationals, particularly the competitive games.

We only had one competition – the World Cup – otherwise we would go on tour. At the end of one season I wanted Tom Finney in our touring party, but his club doctor insisted that he needed an operation on varicose veins. In those days the Brazilians and Argentinians would suspend their league seasons for six months to prepare for the World Cup. It's not quite so bad now, but still those nations take their international sides far more seriously than we do.

SOME PLAYER PROFILES

TONY ADAMS

The Arsenal defender was nominated as a future England captain by Bobby Robson when he made his breakthrough into the side against Spain in 1987.

That label became like a millstone to the tall defender and, after England's disappointing and abortive challenge for the European Championship in 1988, he was selected only three times the following season when his reputation suffered through a three-match ban for a professional foul and a short prison sentence for a drink-driving offence.

But Adams is recognised as an outstanding defender and captain who has collected two Championship medals with Arsenal and he was recalled by Graham Taylor to play in all of the World Cup qualifying matches in the 1992–93 season.

VIV ANDERSON

Came into the England side as the international career of Phil Neal neared its end. Anderson was the first black player to wear the England shirt.

A tall, leggy defender with an infectious personality, he was selected first by Ron Greenwood but played the bulk of his 30 internationals for Bobby Robson. He was a member of the 1986 World Cup squad in Mexico, though didn't play in any of the finals series, being kept out by Gary Stevens.

Enjoyed an exceptional club career and is still enjoying his football as player/ manager of Barnsley.

JIMMY ARMFIELD

The Blackpool full back was one of the most distinguished defenders in the history of international football, coming to the fore during the 1962 World Cup in Chile, after which he was voted the finest right back in the world. He was still a squad member when England won the competition four years later, though by then he had been replaced in the side by George Cohen.

Armfield had pace and was an overlapping full back before they were fashionable. He never lost his stylish and composed manner as he chalked up nearly 600 League appearances with his hometown club.

He had the distinction of an extended run of 31 consecutive matches and skippered the side in his last 14 internationals before Bobby Moore took over the role.

Jimmy subsequently went into management with Bolton Wanderers and Leeds United but now divides his time between writing on soccer for the *Daily Express* and as a match analyst with the BBC Radio 5 team.

ALAN BALL

Will be forever remembered for his energy and example during extra-time of the 1966 World Cup final when he was the youngest member of the successful England side.

Indeed, Ball made his debut for England three days before his 20th birthday and was an England regular for over a decade.

'Ballie' had a temperament to match his red hair and though he was sent off twice in England colours (once in an Under-23 game) he was rarely left out, for he was a skilful and energetic midfielder who could inspire by example.

Towards the end of his career he returned as player-manager to the club where it had begun, Blackpool, but it was not a successful homecoming and he took up playing again for Lawrie McMenemy at Southampton.

Ball had a spell in charge at Portsmouth, ran a pub and acted as one of Graham Taylor's coaches during the European Championship in 1992. Since 1991 he has been manager of Exeter City.

GORDON BANKS

Always included in any goalkeeping Hall of Fame, the phlegmatic 'Banksie' compiled a number of distinguished records in his 73-match international career.

He was the first England goalkeeper to keep more than 10 clean sheets (he finished with 35) and still holds the record for the most consecutive clean sheets at seven – broken only by Eusebio's semi-final penalty during the 1966 World Cup in which Banks was the outstanding 'keeper.

He will forever be remembered for his save against Pelé during the 1970 World Cup game against Brazil in Mexico. But great saves were Banks's forte until his career was brought tragically to an end in 1972 by a car accident in which he lost an eye.

He remains a cheerful character and has worked for various clubs over the years as a goalkeeping coach.

JOHN BARNES

John Barnes made his debut for England as a 19-year-old when it seemed he could take on the world. But in 73 games to date he has never really transported excellent club form into the international arena.

His statistics show that he did not really score enough goals (11) and not enough matches were won, although one of his goals, against Brazil in the Maracana in 1984, remains one of the most exhilarating ever scored by an England forward.

Barnes, the son of a Jamaican diplomat, has always been angered by suggestions that his heart was not in winning for England – a claim that is certainly not substantiated by his effort.

He remains in Graham Taylor's squad when fit and is very much part of Liverpool's plans to regain their status as England's top club side.

PETER BEARDSLEY

Beardsley was another England forward whose ratio of goals scored to appearances made was perhaps disappointing. But his importance to the side over the six seasons he played, mostly under Bobby Robson, should not be underestimated.

He came to the fore just three months before the World Cup of 1986 and had played only three full games for England

when he was brought in after the first game of the finals in Mexico.

Peter retained his place for the rest of the tournament where his partnership with Gary Lineker began to flourish. He was the perfect foil for the rapier-like Lineker and, of all the partners he had, Gary always maintained Beardsley was the best.

He played alongside Lineker in the 1990 World Cup in Italy but was discarded by Graham Taylor after four games, some suggest prematurely. Has now rejoined Newcastle United where he was playing when he first won international recognition.

COLIN BELL

Bell was an indefatigable worker who came to real prominence at the start of the seventies.

With Francis Lee and Mike Summerbee he was the hub of Manchester City's Championship success in 1968 under Joe Mercer and Malcolm Allison and brought an energy to England's midfield. Was an important figure in Mercer's brief caretaker period as manager.

Bell scored twice in Don Revie's opening game as manager against Czechoslovakia but suffered a serious injury and was unable to play nine matches later.

ROY BENTLEY

Bentley had the misfortune to play in the side which lost to the USA in the 1950 World Cup in Belo Horizonte. But that should not obscure his talent as a centre forward of real pedigree.

Though he won only 12 caps they were spread over seven seasons during which he was a prolific goalscorer for Chelsea. He was the first England centre forward to score all three goals in a match (v Wales in 1954) and scored in each of his last four appearances for his country.

PETER BONETTI

It is sad that Bonetti is best remembered for his final, disastrous appearance when he was clearly struck by nerves as England fell in extra-time to West Germany in the 1970 World Cup after being in front.

He had been brought into the side at the last minute when Gordon Banks was taken ill.

That disaster obscured his earlier appearances when in six other matches he kept five clean sheets. His international career was restricted by the excellence of Banks for whom he understudied season after season.

Bonetti is still involved with England as a goalkeeping coach.

TREVOR BROOKING

One of the more elegant midfield players, Brooking made up for being one-paced with intelligence and a supreme range of passing combined with the ability to cross the ball accurately.

Had been a centre-forward at international youth level but it was as a provider that he became famous. He made his England debut in Sir Alf Ramsey's final match but went on to play under Joe Mercer and Ron Greenwood.

Trevor scored only five goals for England but two of those came in a 3–1 victory over Hungary in Budapest which ensured England's qualification for the 1982 World Cup finals in Spain. He was affected by injury in the final stages of the tournament, along with his great friend and partner Kevin Keegan, losses that were largely responsible for England not advancing beyond the second stage. Brooking's final England appearance, in fact, was as a sub against Spain.

TERRY BUTCHER

Undoubtedly one of the foremost defenders in English international history along with Billy Wright, Jack Charlton and Roy McFarland, Butcher was also a great patriot.

Another player who found himself playing in a World Cup tournament after only four previous matches, he was given the vote for the 1982 side in Spain when he took over from Dave Watson and made

the centre back position his by right.

Butcher did not often miss a match under Bobby Robson, who had been his club manager at Ipswich, but Terry broke a leg just before the European Championship in Germany in 1988, which was to prove a disastrous loss for England.

He captained the side on seven occasions, usually as stand-in for Bryan Robson, and climaxed an excellent career by playing a significant role in England's assault on the 1990 World Cup in Italy, his third World Cup.

Has remained in football as player-manager at Coventry and then Sunderland.

IAN CALLAGHAN

Ian Callaghan set up a record that is unlikely ever to be broken by any other England player – that of having the longest gap between selections.

He played in the 1966 World Cup – having just one match against France at Wembley in the second match of the victorious campaign – but was not picked again for 11 years and 49 days when Ron Greenwood selected him in *his* very first international against Switzerland. Five other Liverpool players took part in that 0–0 draw – Ray Clemence, Phil Neal, Terry McDermott, Emlyn Hughes and Ray Kennedy.

MICK CHANNON

Mick Channon, now a highly successful racehorse trainer, was himself a thoroughbred. He is joint-12th leading goalscorer in the history of England internationals with 21 goals from 46 games, a better strike rate than some of those ahead of him.

Tall, and with a deceptive turn of pace, he had a strength belied by his slim physique. It was a pity for Channon that he was around only during the barren period when England failed to qualify for either the 1974 or 1978 World Cups. In the 1975–76 season, Channon scored nine goals in as many games for England, an excellent return.

The good humour with which he played the game was used for a time in his role as a match summariser for TV and radio. But he now concentrates on horse racing.

BOBBY CHARLTON

Perhaps the best loved of all English footballers, Bobby is a legend in the global game. Along with Pelé he is perhaps the best known player of all time. There are numerous reasons for Charlton's fame – the fact that he survived the Munich air disaster, his unassuming personality and not least his ability as a midfield player, winger or centre forward.

There were few finer sights in the game than Charlton in motion, with those explosions of pace towards the penalty area and a shot that was the dread of goalkeepers across the world.

He scored crucial goals against Portugal in the World Cup semi-final of 1966, the second of his three World Cups, and was a principal figure in England's victory.

It was his substitution by Colin Bell in the game in Leon against West Germany in 1970 which swung the game away from England. Ramsey was saving him for a potential semi-final but Charlton's departure served only to give the Germans fresh impetus.

That game marked the end of his 13-season international career, in which he had played 106 times for his country and scored 49 goals, a record that Gary Lineker challenged but never managed to overtake.

Bobby kept his connections with Manchester United where he is a director. He also runs soccer coaching schools and is in demand the world over for personal appearances and coaching engagements.

JACK CHARLTON

Jack Charlton didn't make his international breakthrough until he was almost 30 and the fact that he went on to win 35 caps is testimony to his fitness and determination.

Alf Ramsey brought him in when the career of Maurice Norman was drawing to a close, although in fact there was exactly one year's difference in their ages.

It is well chronicled that Jack went on to be an important member of the glorious 1966 World Cup side where his defensive partnership with Bobby Moore was so vital.

He actually stayed in the side well into his thirties, playing one match in the 1970 World Cup, but by then Brian Labone was making a strong claim for the place of central defender. Jack and Bobby Charlton were the last brothers to play for England.

Jack now mixes his life as a country gentleman with managing the Republic of Ireland side, a job he has done with outstanding success.

BOBBY CHARLTON

It was 'a golden age'. And I'm not alone in feeling that way about the English game in the years before and after the 1966 World Cup win.

English clubs were enjoying regular success in Europe, gates were up, and of course winning the World Cup has been unsurpassed. It was simply a pure pleasure just to play. I was lucky enough to play in a club side with such gifted individuals as Denis Law and George Best and every game was an adventure. Fantastic. Players were tough, even dirty – yet, paradoxically, there was a fairness about it that doesn't seem to exist these days. Most important was the philosophy; players wanted to express themselves, were keen to try things, experiment, and if you failed nobody booed you!

I now run soccer schools and I tell my kids that if you succeed at this sport, every day is Christmas Day. That's how I felt in those days. The hooligan element had not reared its ugly head – and I am pleased that it has almost disappeared now. The game was played in a terrific atmosphere, every ground was full, or at least it seemed that way!

In 1962 the international side reached the World Cup quarter-finals in Chile and I fancied our chances to win the World Cup in '66. I felt we had a superb chance because it was being played in England, and by the end we justified being the best team in the world. In 1970 we had a really good run and we might have retained the World Championship. We were certainly good enough.

They were sensational times, really, and I for one did not want to change them. But the rest of the world started to catch up to such an extent that the power base is no longer restricted to the obvious areas. England now find it harder to qualify for the major tournaments. Off the field it has been even worse. Changes have occurred . . . and not for the better.

Money, commercialism, television have increasingly taken a stranglehold on the game. There is so much money changing hands between clubs, players and agents nowadays, that I regret to say the game itself has lost the people's sympathy.

In my time the game was very adventurous; it provided value for money. That's no longer the case, with the cost of going to a football match always increasing. I would exclude my own club from that criticism because I feel that Manchester United place the emphasis on exciting, attacking football and at a relatively low cost to the supporters. Most fans, however, would not forgive their clubs if they considered they were subsidising the game.

There can be no doubt that standards have declined. We had a

good team in '66 and good players, and we played in a way that football should be played in this country. The often used excuse that we now play in the big competitions after a very long, hard season has some merit. Without question our players are stale by the time they are asked to perform in the European Championship or the World Cup and that is one of the reasons for our poor performances.

However, I also feel that we no longer have the right philosophy for the game. I believe that the general public still want to see adventurous football; they would love to see an England team *going forward*. Instead, we are apprehensive and the Europeans consider us to be technically naïve. I would agree with that. I am afraid that we have jeopardised some of the characteristics that once made us repected throughout the world. The British game was always feared because it was tough, brave and adventurous. We have tried to maintain those qualities, but sometimes to our detriment.

Basically, our youngsters still come too late into the game. When they are at an impressionable age they are not allowed to be part of a professional club, unless they have written permission from their headmaster and parents. We shoot ourselves in the foot.

The 1966 World Cup side would form the basis of the best players I have played with. My squad would include Gordon Banks, without question the best goalkeeper England have ever had. Ray Wilson would definitely be in.

I would select Cohen, Armfield and Howe as the best three full backs I've ever seen in my time but George Cohen would just have the edge. Nobody liked playing against him and he also provided an extra dimension by supporting the attack.

Bobby Moore and Alan Ball would be certainties for inclusion, and the incomparable Duncan Edwards, who was simply sensational. Tom Finney, despite the fact that I played only one or two matches with him. Johnny Haynes, who was a fantastic passer of the ball. Nobby Stiles, the best of all the ball winners. Nat Lofthouse was not a regular in the England side during my time, but I would still pick him. Jimmy Greaves, the greatest striker I've played with. He was so unlucky not to play in the World Cup winning side, but none the less still the greatest finisher.

Of the most recent generation of footballers I would go for Bryan Robson as the one individual who would get nearest to that side – a really brave player who can impose himself on any match.

What about Gazza? Well, maybe, but he is still only a baby in terms of international football. There is still a lot to be fulfilled, but there can be no doubt that he has quality.

Basically I am just one of those people who are proud of the English game and I am sympathetic to the problems of trying to bridge the gap. But I do not like the modern idea of the long ball game. We should really be trying to keep up with developments in the world game and produce better-quality individuals. I hate the slow build-up and the offside game. I love *adventure* and I would like to see a return to the type of football that we thrived on in our prime.

MARTIN CHIVERS

Chivers achieved a strike rate of almost a goal every two games, and three times achieved a two-goal haul – no mean achievement at international level.

He was a nimble mover for a big man and was highly regarded not just in this country but extensively abroad. He could be a moody player and is another who suffered the disappointment of failing to qualify for the 1974 World Cup finals.

He played in both the matches against Poland (0–2 away, 1–1 home) which cost England a place in the 1974 West German World Cup and ultimately lost Alf Ramsey his job.

RAY CLEMENCE

Clemence followed in the tradition of the great English goalkeepers and was without doubt one of the finest. He and Peter Shilton contested the England No. 1 jersey over the ten years following the accident that put Gordon Banks out of the game.

More athletic than Shilton but perhaps marginally less reliable, Clemence was, none the less, among the world's best. It was Ron Greenwood who decided to alternate his goalkeepers, promising to make a decisive choice for the 1982 World Cup finals.

When that decision came it was Shilton who got the vote and as a result 'Clem' played only twice more for his country. He stayed in the game as coach at Spurs until the end of the 1992–93 season and is now a television summariser.

STEVE COPPELL

A player who exemplified the art of combining wing play with the ability to work back and defend when the situation demanded. Despite experiments with numerous players since, none has achieved the excellence Coppell displayed for the job.

However, he is perhaps best remembered as a winger who could get forward and score goals (four in the 1978–79 season). His career ended prematurely in 1983, as the result of an injury suffered in an horrendous tackle in the game against Hungary at Wembley 18 months earlier.

JIMMY DICKINSON

Won 48 caps in 9 seasons following the Second World War and was renowned for his unflustered efficiency and consistency without being conspicuous. A model professional, he was never cautioned throughout his career.

Dickinson played in 25 consecutive matches in the early fifties when he was the driving force behind Portsmouth's Championship seasons of 1948–49 and 1949–50.

MARTIN DOBSON

Dobson played only five games for his country, yet appeared under three managers. He made his debut in Alf Ramsey's final game, played for Joe Mercer in his caretaker period and made his last appearance in Don Revie's first game before being replaced by Trevor Brooking.

BRYAN DOUGLAS

The Blackburn Rovers winger cut an unusual sight since he stood only just over 5ft 5in. It was felt that he might be a natural successor to Stanley Matthews for Douglas, too, had uncanny dribbling skills.

Bryan's artistry made him an automatic selection for the 1958 World Cup, and in 1960–61 he played in three of England's biggest-ever victories – 9–0 against Luxembourg, 9–3 against Scotland and 8–0 against Mexico, when he scored twice.

He played in all England's World Cup games in 1962 in Chile and scored in each of his last three appearances the following season.

DUNCAN EDWARDS

At the age of 18 years and 183 days Duncan Edwards was the youngest player this century to wear the England shirt – a mark of his exceptional talent and maturity as a powerful wing half.

He had played 18 times before his 21st birthday and was only 21 when he lost his life in the Munich air crash in 1958, in which his fellow internationals Roger Byrne, David Pegg and Tommy Taylor were also killed.

TOM FINNEY

Whenever there is debate about the merits and greatness of England players you will inevitably find the name of Tom Finney mentioned, for either as winger or centre forward he was a formidable player.

Tom, the 'Preston Plumber', remains fourth (along with Nat Lofthouse) in the list of all-time England goalscorers behind Charlton, Lineker and Greaves.

His England career – one of the longest – spanned 12 years and included one memorable four-goal performance in the 5–3 victory over Portugal in Lisbon in 1950.

It is to his credit that he shone in the era when Stanley Matthews was at his peak and many would argue that Finney was the better player. Certainly he was a more prolific scorer and there wasn't much wrong with his dribbling ability, either.

GERRY FRANCIS

The player Don Revie chose to be his England captain, Gerry Francis played 12 matches for his country. He was Revie's skipper in eight of those games and it was only injury that curtailed his appearances.

His final game was an excellent 4–1 World Cup qualifying victory against Finland in Helsinki, but he was injured for the remaining 10 matches of Revie's management. When Ron Greenwood took over there was no place for the man who now manages Queens Park Rangers.

TREVOR FRANCIS

After a blistering rise to fame which included exemplary performances at Youth and Under-23 level Trevor Francis never quite fulfilled expectations at senior level.

As with John Barnes, he didn't always scintillate in the England shirt in the way he could for his clubs. However, he seemed to be acclimatising to the international demands when he was struck by an Achilles tendon injury which certainly jeopardised England's chances in the 1980 European Championship.

He continued to be a regular in the side under Bobby Robson and was bitterly disappointed when he didn't make the squad for the 1986 World Cup finals, an omission which still rankles.

Francis had a spell as player-manager at QPR and has been successful as manager of Sheffield Wednesday, taking them to two Wembley finals in 1993.

NEIL FRANKLIN

The first of the distinguished post-war central defenders, Franklin won 27 consecutive caps in the immediate post-war period.

He is notable as the first England international to seek fame abroad, in Bogota, Colombia, thus writing himself out of England consideration. He came home only to find that his desertion had left him out in the cold.

PAUL GASCOIGNE

One of the most talented yet one of the most frustrating of all players to wear the England shirt, Gascoigne continues to be an enigma of English soccer.

He was nursed towards international stardom by Bobby Robson who rationed his appearances during 1988 and '89 from fear of over-exposure too early, which he felt might inflict long-term damage. His timing in bringing 'Gazza' in for the 1990 World Cup was immaculate.

The tears shed by Gascoigne after England's penalty shoot-out defeat by West Germany, which were shown to a world-wide TV audience, made him an international name and each teardrop turned out to be worth millions!

His career was shattered by a serious knee injury sustained in the 1991 FA Cup final and which jeopardised his £5.5 million transfer to Lazio of Italy. His complete recovery has been slow and he found himself substituted in many club matches in 1992–93.

Yet the fact that he demands so much attention is in itself an indication of the high regard in which his skill is held. He can still be a matchwinner in his own right, exciting and capable of scoring great goals.

JIMMY GREAVES

Another player to make his England debut before the age of 20, against Peru in Lima in 1959, Greaves went on to score 44 goals in 57 matches – a phenomenal strike rate. He still holds the record for the most international goals scored in one season

(13 in 1960–61), which included hat-tricks against Scotland and Luxembourg.

In all he notched six international hat-tricks and twice scored four, against Northern Ireland at Wembley in 1963 and Norway in Oslo in the build-up tour to the 1966 World Cup finals.

There seemed little doubt he would be in the World Cup side and so he was for the first-stage matches. But then he was left out of the quarter-final because of injury, Geoff Hurst scored and Greaves could not win back his place.

It remained one of the major disappointments of his life that he was not in the winning side and in fact he only played three more times for his country in the season that followed the famous victory.

He has a new career as a television pundit and an author of soccer books.

MARK HATELEY

England seemed to have found the perfect 'old-fashioned centre forward' in the tall, willowy Hateley, who was with Portsmouth when Bobby Robson introduced him into his side to act as foil to Tony Woodcock.

Hateley joined AC Milan the next season, becoming a cult figure in Northern Italy and acquiring the nickname 'Attila' as he climbed to head some memorable goals.

He settled in with Trevor Francis as his England partner when Robson experimented with players in the build-up to the 1986 World Cup and when Francis was omitted he linked up with Gary Lineker.

They began the finals together for the first two matches in Monterrey, but after a defeat and a draw Hateley was replaced by Peter Beardsley.

He failed to score in 13 appearances between 1986–88 though he only came on as a sub in the last seven of them. After a three-season break he was recalled for one match by Graham Taylor in recognition of his performances for Rangers, but he failed to score and has not been selected since.

JOHNNY HAYNES

Will be forever labelled as the country's first £100 a week footballer because the Fulham chairman Tommy Trinder was at great pains to advertise the fact. But in the context of players' wages at the time, he was probably worth it.

Haynes embroidered the history of England international football with his passes and was often mentioned affectionately by Bobby Robson as being a delight to play alongside.

He captained his country in the last 22 of his 56 appearances, including the abortive assault on the World Cup in Chile in 1962 which marked the end of his international career.

Haynes was still only 28 when Alf Ramsey took over the England managership. But despite some clamour by the newspapers of the day, he was never recalled.

GLENN HODDLE

Glenn Hoddle scored a spectacular goal on his England debut against Bulgaria but was then dropped for the next match by Ron Greenwood.

Hoddle's philosophy was based on precise, long-range passing, unsurpassed in the modern game. But that failed to make him an automatic choice and he became the centre of debate about the priorities of English football – flair versus fight.

Ossie Ardiles considered Hoddle's talents to be second only to those of Diego Maradona, but lacking the pace to reach the pinnacle of world fame. Glenn finally discovered his ideal in France with Monaco, after an illustrious career with Spurs. Now player-manager of Chelsea after breaking into management at Swindon and taking the Wiltshire club into the Premier League.

DON HOWE

Taking over as England right back from Birmingham City's Jeff Hall, Howe enjoyed a run of 23 consecutive matches as a dependable and intelligent right back with the crunching tackles of Tommy Banks of Bolton on the opposite flank.

It was this full back pairing that Walter Winterbottom took to the 1958 World Cup in Sweden without any resounding success (three draws and a defeat) and Howe played in the summer tour to South America a year later where England lost every match.

He gave way to Jimmy Armfield in 1960 and perhaps enjoyed more fame as an England coach under Ron Greenwood and Bobby Robson than he had done as an England player. Still involved in coaching he has had a succession of clubs.

EMLYN HUGHES

One of the stars of the most successful Liverpool era and a Bill Shankly disciple. 'Crazy Horse' was the epitome of the English player, a dynamo in defence with a 'thou shalt not pass' attitude. All heart and passion, his commitment to the flag was unflinching.

Hughes failed in his switch to football management and is now uncompromising in his denunciation of the perceived faults in the England teams via his newspaper column.

EMLYN HUGHES

My 12 years as an England player spanned several different eras, from the end of the great '66 side, the '70s, and the early '80s. I was captain 23 times under four different managers; skipper in only Sir Alf's under-23 side, but senior captain under Joe Mercer, Don Revie and Ron Greenwood. I am very proud of that record.

I have always felt that the 1966 side was a wonderful team and were deservedly World Champions. But they won it because the tournament was played in Europe, in England at Wembley. Only Brazil have won the World Cup playing on a different continent.

I consider the 1970 side superior to the team that actually won the Cup for the first and only time in England's history. It was better balanced, there were better players, it had more vitality, more energy, more workers, more skill. That's my opinion!

This was a 'funny' era for English football. Joe Mercer was a super, super fellow. I remember once he came up to me and asked: 'Hey, Emlyn, what do you think about Mickey Pejic?'

I didn't know what to say about the England left back at that time. 'Why, Joe?' I replied.

Mercer wouldn't leave it alone. 'Just tell me your opinion.'

'He's miserable,' I said.

'Bloody right. I'm not having him in my team!'

I was astounded. I asked Joe why he'd asked my opinion.

'While I am England manager, you will be my England captain,' he replied.

Joe was one of the funniest men I have ever come across in the game. He had a bit of style, he made the players laugh and relax, and it worked when we went on a tour of the Eastern bloc countries and returned unbeaten. But Joe wasn't long in charge of the team. Then it went to the other extreme with Don Revie and back again to a more relaxed atmosphere with Ron Greenwood.

The Revie era was one to forget. He was the type of manager who wouldn't let his players out of his sight. He wouldn't let them out to enjoy themselves, but tried to enforce entertainment on them.

The Liverpool regime under Shankly and Paisley was well organised, but well organised because we were bloody good players who knew what everyone else was going to do on the field, a perfect machine for European football. It worked like a dream for the best part of a decade. Yet we were never taught to be organised. Everyone searched for the Liverpool secret. But there was no real mystery. Shanks would simply tell us to 'go out and play'. That was Joe Mercer's philosophy, too. He wanted us to express ourselves and he would tell us that we were the best in the country and that we had the ability to do just that. If you were a midfield player he wanted you to perform to the full extent of your talents, knowing that the defenders behind you were of the highest calibre who could make up for any mistakes.

It was so vastly different under Revie. It was a total, unflinching commitment to the point of being boring. It was a 'do as I tell you' regime . . . 3 o'clock was rub down time . . . 4 o'clock hot bath . . . 4.30 another rub . . . 6 o'clock meal time . . . 7 o'clock pictures . . . 9 o'clock another rub before going to sleep. It was a poor era!

I scored one goal in my England career. Unfortunately it was against Wales at Ninian Park and it upset my dad. We won 3–0 in 1972 and as I walked off the park I looked up in the stand and saw my mum and dad; I knew they would be in the crowd. I got washed and changed and was desperate for a drink in the players' lounge, but I saw my dad in the car park and I thought I would get a big hug and kiss and congratulations from him. I was his son and had just scored for England. Instead he bellowed: 'Oh, boyo, anybody else but Wales.' Of course he's Welsh and all his brothers and relations were there, too!

For my best XI I would select most of the players from the 1966 and 1970 sides as they proved themselves the best. I'd go for the more flamboyant players. Certainly I would choose the likes of Moore, Bobby Charlton, Peters, Hurst, Wilson, Cohen and Banks from the World Cup winning side.

Banks was the world's best goalkeeper of his time. Wilson and Cohen – the World Cup winning full backs were both superb players, and hard workers in a team that really did work hard. Moore – you were guaranteed a superb performance from him. The best ever right-sided defender, the only one to get near him, was Franz Beckenbauer.

I'm sorry, but I was not impressed with Jack Charlton even though he was in the World Cup winning side and I would go for Roy McFarland instead. A class defender as well as a big influence in any side. Bobby Charlton, you couldn't pick a side without him! Martin Peters – I rated him highly. He had that little bit of extra flair. West Ham provided three superb players for the 1966 World Cup winning side.

I played a couple of times with Bryan Robson late on in my international career. He has proved to be one of England's best ever players with 90 caps. Hurst, who scored a hat-trick in the World Cup Final. What more can you do?

Kevin Keegan – simply a superb player for both Liverpool and England. Jimmy Greaves – the best goalscorer I have ever seen. Lethal in and around the penalty box. It was such a shame that he was never the same for England after being left out of the World Cup

winning side of '66.

No current players. Not even Gascoigne. Don't get me wrong, he's very talented, Paul's got bags of skill, but he is not a team player.

I might have gone for Gary Lineker, but he is just behind Jimmy Greaves as a goalscorer. Greaves was a more naturally gifted goalscorer, while Lineker runs into spaces trying to create his own chances. David Platt came the closest because he is a natural goalscorer.

I don't particularly like the modern game because it is based on running, rather than skill. You might say that's a bit rich, as Liverpool's game was based on running. But Liverpool also had gifted players. There are precious few of those talents around these days who the fans would really want to go and watch, the type of player who can go past an opponent. Instead it's all about power and speed, the sprinter and the marathon runner.

Graham Taylor has a thankless task. Whoever was in charge of the national team would have the same problems with the current England set up. No-one can make it any better. Since Alf Ramsey every England manager has come out and made the identical assessment . . . England must be rated about eighth in the world. When we come up against the Germanys, Brazils and Argentinas of this world in the big competitions we *are* second best, we can't beat them any more. We don't possess the flair players for that level and that's a sad fact of life.

ROGER HUNT

A supreme goalscorer who was in at the start of Liverpool's takeover of English football. Hunt was a typical hard-working English centre forward with a high work rate and sharpness in front of goal. A member of the 1966 World Cup winning team.

GEOFF HURST

TV commentator Kenneth Wolstenholme's famous line, 'They think it's all over . . . it is now,' refers to Geoff Hurst blasting the final goal against West Germany in the 1966 World Cup final, completing his remarkable hat-trick. Hurst was England's hero in the triumvirate of West Ham players, which also included Bobby Moore and Martin Peters, the scorer of the 'other' goal on that historic day for English football. Hurst's performance in the final justified manager Alf Ramsey's decision to leave out ace goalscorer Jimmy Greaves.

Hurst later tried his hand at management with Chelsea, and has since become a successful businessman.

KEVIN KEEGAN

Keegan was twice voted European Footballer of the Year and was one of the most respected England captains of his generation. Often referred to as a self-made player, he applied professionalism in the extreme to make the most of his talents. An outstanding goalscorer in his own right, Kevin starred for Liverpool, SV Hamburg, Southampton and Newcastle.

He quit the game for a long period as he went into retirement in Spain, lowering his golfing handicap, before being lured back as manager of Newcastle and leading them into the Premier League.

RAY KENNEDY

A member of the glorious Arsenal double squad, who later converted from attack to midfield for a second spell of success with Liverpool. Ray made the progression to the England team without becoming a regular.

He tragically contracted Parkinson's disease which affected him towards the end of his playing career.

CYRIL KNOWLES

One of the toughest and most exciting full backs in the English game, Knowles played for Spurs in an era when the country had a crop of talented players in that position. 'Nice one, Cyril' was the song named in his honour as he became a cult figure on the White Hart Lane terraces. He was one of the original 'bite yer legs' type of defender, yet possessed great quality and skill.

Tragedy closely followed Cyril's success on the field. His young son was killed by a stone through the windscreen of his car. Then, when manager of Hartlepool, a brain tumour claimed Knowles, one of the game's great characters.

KEVIN KEEGAN

When I look back on my England career the greatest thing was the actual honour bestowed upon me simply to play for my country. Nothing in my professional life has come anywhere near it. That feeling never changed from the first game I played under Sir Alf Ramsey to the last under Ron Greenwood in the World Cup in Spain. I never lost that buzz. In retrospect even the darkest days weren't so bad. There is no higher achievement for an individual than to play for his country, it's the summit of any career.

Not only that, but to captain your country, walking out in front of the team – I might only be five foot eight but I felt ten foot tall. What a privilege!

Naturally, I coveted the biggest prize of them all – the World Cup – but it

wasn't to be. Had the 1982 finals been played a month earlier or a month later, there would have been no problem. But they don't delay the World Cup for anyone!

I went to Spain with a back injury, and it went in the first England training session. I was lying in the bath and my room-mate Trevor Brooking went down to breakfast. When he returned I was still there, stuck in the same position: I couldn't move. Naturally he reacted instantly – he laughed!

But it was no laughing matter. Years and years of heading balls from long goal kicks had taken their toll and my back had lodged out of line. It had been clicked back into place from time to time and sometimes I suffered with a stiff neck. Usually treatment put it right, but never was it serious enough to put me out of a game.

I came on as a late substitute against Spain when England were virtually out of the World Cup and that turned out to be my farewell international appearance.

I had a great deal of empathy with Ron Greenwood – especially at the time he decided to quit as England manager on the way home from Hungary.

We lost in Norway in a World Cup qualifying tie in 1981 when it was far more of a shock than the 1993 defeat in Oslo. Then, Norway were nowhere near as highly rated as they are these days. Ron was under tremendous pressure when we went to Hungary. As the manager you pick the team and take the flak and it was all being aimed at Ron.

We came out of Hungary with England's first win in the Nep Stadium and that made him feel proud. On the plane back, it all became too much for him. We were playing cards and he strolled over to us and announced: 'I've quit.' It was a hasty decision and one that he probably wouldn't have made had he had the chance to analyse it with his trusted friends and family. Perhaps he wanted to go out with a good victory.

But it was a wrong decision in the opinion of the players. A group of players represented the squad including myself, Ray Wilkins and Mick Mills. I was the captain but it was a universal view that we should talk Ron out of it. We went to the front of the plane and suggested that it wasn't the right time to go. We still had to ensure our World Cup qualification and we felt we should prove wrong the people who said we wouldn't get there.

There was a lot of affection for Ron. Even among those players who didn't have anything to gain by him staying.

There was a unanimous view that he should remain the manager. We could understand why he had had enough, but we all wanted him to see the job through.

If ever 'player power' had some use, this was it. Common sense prevailed. Ron changed his mind and I felt we had a reasonably good World Cup, although naturally we could have done a lot better.

I suppose my most memorable goal for England was against the Scots. I picked the ball up in our half and at that time I had no idea I would be scoring such a satisfying goal – probably the best I managed for England. I played a one-two with Trevor Brooking before finishing it off and it must be one of the best goals that didn't even warrant a cheer . . . those were the days of 90,000 crowds at Wembley and most of them Scots for an England game!

I shall always consider my headed goal against Italy to be one of those rare 'perfect goals'. Once again it was provided by a Trevor Brooking cross and I was able to do everything I wanted to. I guessed right that Dino Zoff would go for the near post as every goalkeeper wants to protect the position where it would be worse to let in a goal. I flicked it to the area he was coming from. Everything went right. It was a special one for me.

Finally, I would select my chip against Ireland. I had returned from Hamburg and there was a campaign in the press to keep me out of the national team. That was the time when it was felt that anyone who played abroad should not be allowed back into the national side. You were then considered some sort of traitor to have played on the Continent. Little wonder that it gave me so much pleasure to score a quality goal with a left foot chip.

'My Greatest Team' is not a game I want to play because, to tell the truth, there were far too many players used in my time in the England side.

I would not want to choose between goalkeepers Ray Clemence and Peter Shilton. I would have had Colin Todd as one of my first choices, yet he hardly got a look in. Trevor Brooking would be the only player guaranteed a place from my personal point of view. If I picked an England XI one day, I'd wake up the next and select a different one.

At that time England could have fielded three separate teams, all of the same level; each side as good as the others. That was the problem . . . there wasn't a special team capable of winning the World Cup. There were precious few exceptional players. Nothing seems to have changed.

FRANCIS LEE

'Franny' Lee was a member of an outstanding Manchester City side, and the squat, diminutive yet powerful winger made the transformation into a highly entertaining England player. He chose a post-football career in business and has since become a millionaire businessman and, like Mike Channon, a successful racehorse trainer.

GARY LINEKER

'Captain Courteous' was the England skipper who was never booked in his entire career.

Gary came so close to equalling Bobby Charlton's long-standing record of 49 international goals, but finished his England career just one short. He retired from international football at the top after the 1992 European Championship, while in his early thirties. But the final chapter failed to follow the script. After he had been substituted by manager Graham Taylor before the end of the match with Sweden, it proved to be a sad farewell as England failed to progress any further in the tournament.

Lineker enjoyed an outstanding career with Leicester City, Everton, Barcelona and Spurs before joining Grampus Eight in the newly formed professional 'J' League in Japan.

NAT LOFTHOUSE

The 'Lion of Vienna' was another England centre forward who enjoyed a remarkable strike rate – 30 goals in 33 internationals – and who, given as many matches as Lineker, might have set a record never to be beaten.

Remarkably, he never scored a hat-trick for England but his goals came consistently and he scored twice in a match on 12 occasions, a record equalled only by Bobby Charlton.

Earned his nickname for a stirring performance against Austria in Vienna in 1952 when England won 3–2 and he came closest to getting that elusive hat-trick.

Lofthouse was another player recalled to the colours after his career had apparently finished, playing two matches in the winter of 1958 at the age of 33.

GARY MABBUTT

Against All Odds was an appropriate title for Gary Mabbutt's autobiography. When diabetes was first diagnosed he promised himself that he would overcome the condition and one day play for England. He achieved that ambition in a variety of positions and has also become a well respected skipper of Spurs. He has given his club 10 years of loyal service and his courage in continuing to play football at the top level for so long is an inspiration to thousands of diabetic youngsters.

MALCOLM MACDONALD

'SuperMac' scored in only two of his 14 internationals but will be remembered always as the man who got all *five* goals in a European Championship qualifying game against Cyprus at Wembley in April 1975.

Only four England players before and none since have achieved five in a game and in the barren seventies Macdonald was the only England international player to score a hat-trick.

WILF MANNION

Found his place in the history books by scoring a hat-trick in the first post-war international, against Northern Ireland in Belfast, after Raich Carter had scored in the first minute.

His Middlesbrough team-mate George Hardwick captained England in that 7–2 victory. Mannion was to score a further four goals that season. Sturdy and fair-haired he was an old-fashioned scheming inside forward.

PAUL MARINER

Mariner starred for Ipswich Town under Bobby Robson who then capped him for England. A towering, highly talented central striker, he was an all-purpose player who led Ipswich to glory in Europe.

STANLEY MATTHEWS

The man they termed the 'wizard of the dribble' stands out among the most gifted of all England players over a career spanning a staggering 23 years.

He made his first appearance for England as a 19-year-old in 1934 in a 4–0 win over Wales and played his last in 1957 at the age of 42. Seventeen of his 54 caps were won before the war and his only England hat-trick, against Czechoslovakia, was scored pre-war.

He remains the only footballer to have received a knighthood while still playing and had a fine World Cup in 1954, where his name in the programme was misprinted as 'St Matthews' – those who marvelled at his performance in winning the 1953 FA

Cup final for Blackpool would have claimed it was no printer's error! Unquestionably the finest right-footed dribbler in the history of the game.

ROY McFARLAND

Many would claim McFarland as the best centre half England have ever produced, though he played far fewer internationals than he should have because of recurring injuries which eventually curtailed his playing career.

It is no coincidence that England failed to lose in any of his first 16 appearances, winning the first seven and conceding only six goals.

McFarland was one of those rare defenders who was also a good footballer, able to bring the ball out from the back comfortably. Still involved in football as manager of Derby County.

MICK MILLS

An accomplished and stylish full back for both club and country, and another of Bobby Robson's boys at Ipswich Town who went on to captain his country and play in the World Cup finals. Mick now works as a BBC Radio 5 summariser.

BOBBY MOORE

The fact that Bobby captained his country in 91 of his 108 internationals is testimony enough to his remarkable ability to lead by example.

From his earliest days he had a presence which earned respect and his own unflappable temperament was an inspiration to those around him. He took over the captain's armband a month after his 22nd birthday when Jimmy Armfield missed the game against Czechoslovakia in May 1963, and he was to make it his own in the seasons that followed.

As a player it is well-known that Moore had weaknesses, lacking the pace of a Beckenbauer and not being strong in the air. Whatever the shortcomings in his game, however, he compensated for them with an untouchable sense of timing and an ability to see situations earlier than anyone else.

He led England to their moment of World Cup glory in 1966, when he was voted Player of the Tournament, and to the World Cup finals in 1970. Certain Colombians in Bogota attempted to sabotage his impeccable reputation by trumping up a theft charge and Bobby was under house arrest while the team prepared for the World Cup.

Yet he rose above that trauma to perform brilliantly in Mexico and the picture of him and Pelé after England's defeat by Brazil says all there is to say about his sportsmanship and the respect he won from the best forwards in the game.

His death from cancer in 1993 was a blow to the game.

STANLEY MORTENSEN

You can't do much better than score four goals on your debut which is what 'Morty' achieved in England's 10-goal thrashing of Portugal in Lisbon in May 1947.

He was a quick striker who fed off the service supplied by his club and international colleague Stanley Matthews. Mortensen played in the 1950 World Cup in Brazil, scoring against Chile.

In all, he netted 23 in 25 matches and his last goal in his last game was against Hungary in the 6–3 defeat of 1953.

ALAN MULLERY

'Mullers' took over the role of destroyer from Nobby Stiles, though there was perhaps a broader base to his game since he combined tenacity with an ability to pass the ball accurately (which is what persuaded Spurs to buy him from Fulham).

Like Stiles he was shortsighted and occasionally his timing was adrift. This led to him being the first player ever to be sent off in an England shirt, against Yugoslavia in the European Championship in 1968.

But Mullery proved an excellent competitor in the 1970 World Cup in Mexico and the following season he had the distinction of captaining his country

for a one and only time (against Malta).

He still commentates on the game, having tried his hand at management with QPR, Crystal Palace and Brighton, whom he led to promotion to the old Division One.

BILL NICHOLSON

Nicholson, the former Tottenham manager, won just one cap for England, but in that game he carved a little niche in history. The match was against Portugal at Goodison Park and Bill scored a goal inside 30 seconds, still the fastest international debut goal ever.

He might have avoided the list of one-cap wonders had he not been injured on a couple of occasions when selected and had he not been around at the same time as Billy Wright, the defender no one could budge.

RUSSELL OSMAN

Osman's partnership with Terry Butcher at Ipswich Town was one of the most profitable in football and it was Ron Greenwood who decided they should do the same for England.

It was thought that here was a partnership to last and when Robson took over from Greenwood that likelihood seemed to increase.

But Osman performed indifferently when it really mattered and after playing in the fateful 0–1 defeat by Denmark which put England out of the 1984 European Championship, he was not selected again.

Osman can still claim to have represented his country at both soccer and rugby union, for he was a schoolboy international with the oval ball before taking up football when he was 15, the age most promising youngsters are joining their first professional club.

He is still in the game, as player-manager of Bristol City.

TERRY PAINE

Terry Paine was an old-fashioned winger who can claim to be one of the few flank men ever to score a hat-trick for his country – against Northern Ireland in an 8–3 victory in 1963.

Like Ian Callaghan he was tried in the first phase of the 1966 World Cup, playing just one game against Mexico. But then Ramsey decided there was no point in playing wide men if they were not effective in that role and Paine and Callaghan sat out the rest of the competition as Alf played his team of 'Wingless Wonders'. Not much consolation for Paine but he was a bouncy lad from Winchester and took it in his stride. Finished his career with Hereford.

PAUL PARKER

Paul's role at right back in the sweeper system adopted by Bobby Robson for the later stages of the 1990 campaign was crucial and he played in all but the first match of that memorable competition.

Although he prefers to play in central defence, it is as a number 2 that he settled at Manchester United where he won a Premier League Championship medal in 1992–93. A versatile player, he can operate across the back four or in midfield.

STUART PEARCE

'Psycho' to his pals, Pearce is an uncompromising left back in the mould of Ray Wilson and Kenny Sansom who preceded him.

Brian Clough thought the world of him at Nottingham Forest and though his public image may be one of sullen moodiness he can, in fact, be bright and amusing company.

Pearce was overlooked as skipper for a time because of this reputation but he took over the armband on the retirement of Gary Lineker. Unfortunately injury restricted those occasions to three games in '92–93 though he did captain twice in Lineker's absence in 1992, and returned with a vengeance to lead England to a vital World Cup victory over Poland in September 1993.

MARTIN PETERS

Had to live with the tag of being '10 years ahead of his time', a description Alf Ramsey gave to the tall, slim and unassuming Peters – a reference to his ability to read the game and think his way through a football match.

His role in the winning the 1966 World Cup cannot be understated, for he had an ability to 'ghost' into positions – a knack that earned him a goal in the final.

His intelligence as a player was to win him 67 caps and he was skipper on four occasions, including Sir Alf's final game in Portugal on 3 April 1974.

Peters's own last appearance was to come under Joe Mercer the following month by which time the captaincy had passed to Emlyn Hughes. Still looks as if he could step out and play today but instead works in insurance.

DAVID PLATT

In the long term, and fitness permitting, Platt is almost certainly the 'next Bryan Robson' of the England side. He has looked every inch the right man to lead the side through the nineties.

As a player his strengths are his indefatigable ability to shuttle from one penalty area to another and the Robson-like knack of arriving late in the area to score vital goals.

Platt's strike rate of 20 in 42 games for England is even more remarkable when you consider that most of the games he has played have been in midfield.

He can, however, play effectively as a forward. In that capacity he scored four against San Marino and nine in nine games during the 1992–93 season. He was the natural choice as captain once Stuart Pearce was injured and fulfilled those duties splendidly when taking over in February 1993.

Has now been involved in a record £17.4 million in transfer moves, not bad for a lad whose career looked to be on a downward curve when he was released by Manchester United and went to play for

Crewe. Success could not have come to a more personable young man.

ALF RAMSEY

His role in managing the victorious boys of '66 tends to obscure the fact that Alf Ramsey was himself a distinguished international footballer in the late forties and early fifties, making his debut as a Southampton player but winning his remaining 31 caps as a Tottenham full back.

In his playing days he was known as 'The General' for his quiet assurance and determination, qualities that were to re-surface when he had charge of the national

SIR ALF RAMSEY

When I look back on what I achieved, I still have the unshakeable belief that it couldn't have been done without the right players. The blend may have been perfect, but it was the ingredients that were so important.

During those heady months leading up to 1966 and England's victory in the World Cup Final, I became very close to my team. We became as one, a unit, bonded together in a cloudless search for perfection.

It was built around Bobby Moore, with leading roles played by Nobby Stiles, Alan Ball and Bobby Charlton. They were my men, those I had gambled upon.

It is still sometimes said that when I suggested England could win the World Cup, I had been misquoted. But I meant it; I believed it, and that wasn't difficult when I had yeomen like Bobby Moore around me. He was a great footballer and an inspiring captain, also a lucid, clear thinker about how to play the game. With Bobby to support my ideas we had no trouble convincing the team of the destiny we believed in.

I'd have private chats with Moore because he was a fellow who could laugh with you in company, yet be icily single-minded when a job had to be done.

I remember him leading England from the dressing-room on the afternoon of the Final against West Germany. There were no fist clenching exhortations, no shouting, back slapping, or fierce gestures of intent. He just picked up the ball and said: 'Okay . . . let's go.' I saw by his eyes he had already retreated into his cocoon of concentration; had already buckled on his breastplate for the fight to come.

We'd talk about football, tactics. He always understood and would sometimes finish a sentence for me. We both were on the same wavelength to an uncanny degree.

Of course when socialising with the players I knew he would get my message across and soon I had a band of disciples ready to lay down their lives for their country.

I picked Bobby as my man for all moments because of his composure, coolness, his brilliance as a footballer, and because he was a nice person.

He tried to get me drunk many times, aided and abetted by little Alan Ball. Sometimes I'd pretend I was a little merry, to see if there was any unfamiliarity towards me. There were jokes, yes. Leg pulls . . . so many times. But the respect from them all remained intact on many boisterous evenings.

I admired the way Moore survived his ordeal in Bogota when wrongly accused of stealing a bracelet. How he calmed the team in Mexico when Gordon Banks went down with illness (to this day, I will swear, Banks was got at in some form or another, with drug or potion).

Moore's own incarceration was in my opinion a deliberate plot to discredit English football, hatched by those who wanted him out at any cost.

We were never friends. I was too reserved, deliberately, to let him too far into my world. He was too cool and cautious to let his own guard drop.

But, days before his tragic death, there was Bobby on the telephone, setting up a little business arrangement that might help me. He thought of others until the very end.

When Bobby Moore died I was desperately saddened. Football had lost a magnificent ambassador; my right hand man in glory.

Of all the players I used during my time in international management, he became the epicentre of the plans that saw England conquer the world.

I was also proud to manage Bobby Charlton, a world class footballer of marvellous talent. Proud, sometimes prickly, he was so gloriously blessed that I doubt if English football will see his equal again.

And then there was Nobby Stiles, the man I was prepared to resign over, and Alan Ball, a red-haired bundle of mischief and magnificence.

If Bobby Moore was the essence of that World Cup triumph, then Stiles was the spice. We have never had anyone who has come near to him since. The role he played, sitting just in front of the back four, was tailored for his talent. He did it so effectively, with such a hunger and a belief, that he went beyond my wildest dreams.

Nobby was a vastly under-rated player both for Manchester United and England. I had asked Sir Matt Busby about him, then watched him. It didn't take me long to realise he was the linchpin of my plan. Funny, in his short-sighted way with an engaging toothless smile, Nobby was as important to me as Bobby was. And when I told him so, I have never known a little fellow so genuinely proud.

Alan Ball was tremendous, and a great competitor to have around. His heart beat for the colours of his country. He loved to play, loved to learn and listen. He would sit at my feet, literally sometimes, taking it all in, freckles and fierceness on his face.

I knew I could rely on him to run and play and fight and inspire. At 21, he had the attitude and homespun wisdom of someone twice his age.

The passion of Ball was fire to Moore's ice, but Bobby could never dampen his enthusiasm. They were a marvellous combination and forged a friendship that was deep and lasting to the day Bobby died.

My memories of my era must always surround those men. I will treasure what they achieved for always. And I was a lucky man to manage them.

side from February 1963 until April 1974.

Few can claim to have been close to Ramsey either in his playing days or subsequently when he managed the side. But what he did have in both phases of his career was the respect of his fellow professionals.

His inscrutable look as the World Cup was won summed up a man who kept his emotions hidden. Knighted for his achievement in 1966, Sir Alf subsided from the picture after finishing as manager.

Still seen in the Royal Box when England play at Wembley, Sir Alf now imparts his views in a daily newspaper and still lives in Ipswich where his club managerial career had climaxed with a Championship win.

DON REVIE

It could be said that Revie's England playing career was no more distinguished than his management of the side, which ended with his defection to the Middle East halfway through a World Cup qualifying competition.

As a player he won a mere six caps between 1954 and 1956 but it was as manager of Leeds that his flair for building successful soccer teams was developed. The Leeds side of Bremner, Giles, Charlton, Lorimer *et al.* was an outstanding one.

His reputation for detail was well earned. He would present each of his players with a dossier on their direct opponent before an international (although it is said there were those who used to toss them in the wastepaper basket unread).

He was a meticulous man who stayed in charge for 29 internationals, winning 14 and drawing eight. But he found a world of difference between managing the national team and a club side.

Without prior warning and during a tour to South America in 1977 he announced his resignation to take up a lucrative post as manager of the UAE national side.

BOBBY ROBSON

A fine wing half of the late fifties and early sixties, Robson was a member of England's 1958 World Cup side in Sweden and played in the following three seasons as partner to his ex-Fulham club-mate Johnny Haynes.

His international playing career was less eventful than his tenure as the team's manager from 1982 to 1990 when he had to contend with media who were not always kind to him.

But Bobby took it all in his stride because he was, first and foremost, a gentleman. He did tend to wear his heart on his sleeve but it was a heart full of passion for his country and compassion for his fellow man.

Like Ramsey before him he was appointed to run the England team after huge success at Ipswich Town where he won the FA Cup and the UEFA Cup.

During his time at Portman Road he turned down numerous bigger clubs (Leeds, Everton, Barcelona etc.) out of loyalty.

Robson came closer than anyone to winning the World Cup outside England, beaten in the semi-final against West Germany in Italy only on a penalty shoot-out.

When his contract was not renewed in 1990 he took a club job with PSV Eindhoven in Holland and promptly led them to the Dutch Championship. He currently manages Sporting Lisbon and still enjoys his coaching.

BRYAN ROBSON

'Captain Marvel' played 90 times for England, but had he not been so often injured there is little doubt that his total would have broken the record for an outfield player.

Robson was a world-class midfield player, a fierce ball winner, supreme goal taker and a born leader. At his peak he was indispensable to the national side.

He was often too brave for his own welfare and many of the injuries he sustained were inflicted through making challenges that few other players in the world could have aspired to.

There have been almost two dozen fractures, breaks or dislocations and some of them cost England mightily, not least in Mexico and Italy. His playing in the latter tournament could have meant the difference between defeat and history-making victory.

Slight of build but with supreme physical courage and strength, he captained his side on 65 occasions, fewer than either Moore or Wright. He would, without doubt, have passed both but for crucial matches missed.

He has enjoyed his life in the game and, at the age of 36, continues to inspire Manchester United with his appetite for the game quite undiminshed. There have been few better or more inspiring players to pull on the England shirt.

KENNY SANSOM

England's most-capped full back with 86 appearances between 1979 and 1988 including one run of 37 consecutive matches. For most of those years there was no-one in England to challenge his right to the number 3 shirt. Certainly, he kept Stuart Pearce waiting.

Short and stocky and with a dogged attitude in the tackle he was at his best sweeping forward, his short legs pumping like pistons.

With Peter Shilton, Bryan Robson, Ray Wilkins, Chris Waddle and Gary Lineker, he was the backbone of Bobby Robson's side in the eighties and was rated at that time as the best left back in Europe.

PETER SHILTON

In an England career spanning almost 20 years, it is not surprising that Peter Shilton set records along the way. He is the most capped player in history with 125 appearances, played in more World Cup finals games (17) than any England player and kept 10 clean sheets, a record for any country.

Shilton used to hang from beams in his Leicester home to stretch his arms and it was that kind of determination and ambition that was to help him carry on winning the last of his caps in his 41st year.

Peter was a ferocious trainer, a habit that has been handed down to his successors, and he worked as hard as he trained. He learned his trade under Gordon Banks and put it to good use.

'Shilts' might have made even more appearances if Ron Greenwood had not decided to alternate his 'keepers to give Ray Clemence his share of the responsibility.

Peter missed out on the 1974 and '78 World Cup finals because of England's failure to qualify, but still managed to play in three tournaments – '82, '86 and '90, when he was peerless. There was a time when Bobby Robson contemplated replacing him, but Shilton went on and on. We are unlikely to see his kind again.

NOBBY STILES

Who could ever forget that toothless grin of the little Manchester United scrapper, Nobby Stiles, the most unlikely looking of professional athletes – unless you played against him?

He had much more to his game than the aggression that was his hallmark. Surely, it was argued, someone that small could not instil that amount of fear in forwards. But he did and his role in 1966 cannot be underestimated.

It was said that his poor eyesight (he wore contact lenses during matches) was responsible for a number of mis-timed tackles, although it may have been more down to Nobby's fierce competitiveness.

TOMMY TAYLOR

Who can say how many inroads Tommy Taylor would have made into the list of all-time scorers but for his tragic death in the Munich air disaster at the age of 26?

He was already making his mark, scoring 10 goals in four games – including hat-tricks against Denmark and the Irish Republic in World Cup qualifying games.

Those games were to help England reach the 1958 World Cup finals in Sweden but Taylor, Roger Byrne and Duncan Edwards, all Munich victims, were sorely missed.

Tommy's 16 goals in 19 appearances stand as testimony to his strength and ability in the air.

COLIN TODD

A player who was perhaps not appreciated as much as his talent deserved, although this might have been because he was said not to be as proud of pulling on the white shirt of England as some players were.

This was a pity because he had all the requisite qualities for the job of international defender: quick, bright, an excellent ball winner and cool under pressure. McFarland and Todd were a defensive unit that was respected everywhere.

CHRIS WADDLE

Few players have created as much debate as Chris Waddle. Should he be retained or should he be discarded? He could, indeed, be a frustrating player. But he would also excite in a way that few others in the England record book could emulate.

He seemed equally at home on either right or left side, but the feeling still persists that he and Barnes ought to have achieved a good deal more for their country than they did.

RAY WILKINS

As good an example for aspiring young players as you could find, Ray Wilkins was conspicuous in his teens when he was skipper of the England youth side and of Chelsea.

All kinds of criticisms were laid at his feet – he didn't score enough goals, too many square passes etc., but a succession of managers in England, Italy and Scotland were more than happy to have him in their sides.

Internationally he played in midfield with Bryan Robson and they were a formidable combination both on and off the field. There are those who expect great things from Ray as a coach, but at the age of 37 he is still playing in the Premier League with QPR, a tribute to the way he conducts and looks after himself.

RAY WILSON

One of those players who arguably played better for his country than he did for his club, Wilson was England's oldest player

in the World Cup final team of 1966. His 63 caps remained a record for a full back until Kenny Sansom overtook him.

There were few better defensive full backs then or now and he unobtrusively got on with his job without seeking the limelight. After retiring from the game he took over his family's undertaking business which he still runs.

BILLY WRIGHT

The first player to win 100 caps for England (he finished with 105), Billy Wright is thought of as a long-serving centre half, though his first 59 caps were won playing as a wing half.

He became synonymous with the long management term of Walter Winterbottom in the way that Bobby Moore is linked with Alf Ramsey and Bryan Robson with Bobby Robson.

Wright was a dependable number 5, good in the air and sure on the ground. He won his 100th cap against Scotland in 1959, with two heavy defeats by the 'Mighty Magyars' from Hungary a distant if painful memory.

He led his country through three World Cups, ran up a score of 70 consecutive internationals, all of them as skipper. He tried his hand at management with Arsenal but he was perhaps too kind a man to make it in such a cut-throat business. Instead he went into another – television – where he became a top executive.

FULL ENGLAND APPEARANCES 1945–1993

A'COURT, ALAN *Born:* 30.9.34 (Rainhill) *Club:* Liverpool *Caps:* 5 *Goals:* 1

1957–58

6 Nov 1957	*v* Northern Ireland	Wembley	2–3 (1 goal)
11 June 1958	*v* Brazil (WC)	Gothenburg	0–0
15 June 1958	*v* Austria (WC)	Boras	2–2
17 June 1958	*v* USSR (WC)	Gothenburg	0–1

1958–59

26 Nov 1958	*v* Wales	Aston Villa	2–2

ADAMS, TONY A. *Born:* 10.10.66 (London) *Club:* Arsenal *Caps:* 26 *Goals:* 4

1986–87

18 Feb 1987	*v* Spain	Madrid	4–2
29 April 1987	*v* Turkey (ECQ)	Izmir	0–0
19 May 1987	*v* Brazil (RC)	Wembley	1–1

1987–88

9 Sept 1987	*v* West Germany	Düsseldorf	1–3
14 Oct 1987	*v* Turkey (ECQ)	Wembley	8–0
11 Nov 1987	*v* Yugoslavia (ECQ)	Belgrade	4–1 (1 goal)
23 March 1988	*v* Holland	Wembley	2–2 (1 goal)
27 April 1988	*v* Hungary	Budapest	0–0
21 May 1988	*v* Scotland (RC)	Wembley	1–0
24 May 1988	*v* Colombia (RC)	Wembley	1–1
28 May 1988	*v* Switzerland	Lausanne	1–0
12 June 1988	*v* Eire (EC)	Stuttgart	0–1
15 June 1988	*v* Holland (EC)	Düsseldorf	1–3
18 June 1988	*v* USSR (EC)	Frankfurt	1–3 (1 goal)

1988–89

14 Sept 1988	*v* Denmark	Wembley	1–0
19 Oct 1988	*v* Sweden (WCQ)	Wembley	0–0
16 Nov 1988	*v* Saudi Arabia	Riyadh	1–1 (1 goal)

1990–91

14 Nov 1990	*v* Eire (ECQ)	Dublin	1–1
27 March 1991	*v* Eire (ECQ)	Wembley	1–1

1992–93

14 Oct 1992	*v* Norway (WCQ)	Wembley	1–1

*	captain	SFAC	Scottish FA Centenary
BJT	Brazilian Jubilee Tournament	USABT	USA Bicentenary Tournament
ECQ	European Championship Qualifier	USC	United States Cup 1993
EC	European Championship Finals	WCQ	World Cup Qualifier
FAWC	FA of Wales Centenary	WC	World Cup Finals
RC	Rous Cup	WCF	World Cup Final 1966
		†	abandoned after 23 mins

18 Nov 1992	*v* Turkey (WCQ)	Wembley	4–0
17 Feb 1993	*v* San Marino (WCQ)	Wembley	6–0
31 March 1993	*v* Turkey (WCQ)	Izmir	2–0
28 April 1993	*v* Holland (WCQ)	Wembley	2–2
29 May 1993	*v* Poland (WCQ)	Chorzow	1–1
2 June 1993	*v* Norway (WCQ)	Olso	0–2

ALLEN, ANTHONY *Born:* 27.11.39 (Stoke) *Club:* Stoke City *Caps:* 3

1959–60
17 Oct 1959	*v* Wales	Cardiff	1–1
28 Oct 1959	*v* Sweden	Wembley	2–3
18 Nov 1959	*v* Northern Ireland	Wembley	2–1

ALLEN, CLIVE D. *Born:* 20.5.61 (London) *Clubs:* Queens Park Rangers, Tottenham Hotspur *Caps:* 5

1983–84 (with Queens Park Rangers)
10 June 1984	*v* Brazil (sub)	Rio de Janeiro	2–0
13 June 1984	*v* Uruguay	Montevideo	0–2
17 June 1984	*v* Chile	Santiago	0–0

1986–87 (with Tottenham Hotspur)
29 April 1987	*v* Turkey (ECQ)	Izmir	0–0

1987–88
17 Feb 1988	*v* Israel	Tel Aviv	0–0

ALLEN, RONNIE *Born:* 15.1.29 (Fenton) *Club:* West Bromwich Albion *Caps:* 5 *Goals:* 2

1951–52
28 May 1952	*v* Switzerland	Zurich	3–0

1953–54
3 April 1954	*v* Scotland (WCQ)	Glasgow	4–2 (1 goal)
16 May 1954	*v* Yugoslavia	Belgrade	0–1

1954–55
10 Nov 1954	*v* Wales	Wembley	3–2
1 Dec 1954	*v* West Germany	Wembley	3–1 (1 goal)

ANDERSON, STAN *Born:* 27.2.34 (Hordern) *Club:* Sunderland *Caps:* 2

1961–62
4 April 1962	*v* Austria	Wembley	3–1
14 April 1962	*v* Scotland	Glasgow	0–2

ANDERSON, VIV A. *Born:* 29.8.56 (Nottingham) *Clubs:* Nottingham Forest, Arsenal, Manchester United *Caps:* 30 *Goals:* 2

1978–79 (with Nottingham Forest)
29 Nov 1978	*v* Czechoslovakia	Wembley	1–0
10 June 1979	*v* Sweden	Stockholm	0–0

1979–80
22 Nov 1979	*v* Bulgaria (ECQ)	Wembley	2–0

18 June 1980	*v* Spain (EC)	Naples	2–1

1980–81

10 Sept 1980	*v* Norway (WCQ)	Wembley	4–0
29 April 1981	*v* Romania (WCQ)	Wembley	0–0
20 May 1981	*v* Wales	Wembley	0–0
23 May 1981	*v* Scotland	Wembley	0–1

1981–82

23 Feb 1982	*v* Northern Ireland	Wembley	4–0
2 June 1982	*v* Iceland	Reykjavik	1–1

1983–84

4 April 1984	*v* Northern Ireland	Wembley	1–0

1984–85 (with Arsenal)

14 Nov 1984	*v* Turkey (WCQ)	Istanbul	8–0 (1 goal)
27 Feb 1985	*v* Northern Ireland (WCQ)	Belfast	1–0
26 March 1985	*v* Eire	Wembley	2–1
1 May 1985	*v* Romania (WCQ)	Bucharest	0–0
22 May 1985	*v* Finland (WCQ)	Helsinki	1–1
25 May 1985	*v* Scotland (RC)	Glasgow	0–1
9 June 1985	*v* Mexico	Mexico City	0–1
16 June 1985	*v* USA	Los Angeles	5–0

1985–86

26 March 1986	*v* USSR	Tbilisi	1–0
17 May 1986	*v* Mexico	Los Angeles	3–0

1986–87

10 Sept 1986	*v* Sweden	Stockholm	0–1
15 Oct 1986	*v* Northern Ireland (ECQ)	Wembley	3–0
12 Nov 1986	*v* Yugoslavia (ECQ)	Wembley	2–0 (1 goal)
18 Feb 1987	*v* Spain	Madrid	4–2
1 April 1987	*v* Northern Ireland (ECQ)	Belfast	2–0
29 April 1987	*v* Turkey (ECQ)	Izmir	0–0

1987–88 (with Manchester United)

9 Sept 1987	*v* West Germany	Düsseldorf	1–3
27 April 1988	*v* Hungary	Budapest	0–0
24 May 1988	*v* Colombia (RC)	Wembley	1–1

ANGUS, JOHN *Born:* 2.9.38 (Amble) *Club:* Burnley *Caps:* 1

1960–61

27 May 1961	*v* Austria	Vienna	1–3

ARMFIELD, JIMMY *Born:* 21.9.35 (Blackpool) *Club:* Blackpool *Caps:* 43

1958–59

13 May 1959	*v* Brazil	Rio de Janeiro	0–2
17 May 1959	*v* Peru	Lima	1–4
24 May 1959	*v* Mexico	Mexico City	1–2
28 May 1959	*v* USA	Los Angeles	8–1

1959–60

19 April 1960	*v* Scotland	Glasgow	1–1

11 May 1960	v Yugoslavia	Wembley	3–3
15 May 1960	v Spain	Madrid	0–3
22 May 1960	v Hungary	Budapest	0–2

1960–61

8 Oct 1960	v Northern Ireland	Belfast	5–2
19 Oct 1960	v Luxembourg (WCQ)	Luxembourg	9–0
26 Oct 1960	v Spain	Wembley	4–2
23 Nov 1960	v Wales	Wembley	5–1
15 April 1961	v Scotland	Wembley	9–3
10 May 1961	v Mexico	Wembley	8–0
21 May 1961	v Portugal (WCQ)	Lisbon	1–1
24 May 1961	v Italy	Rome	3–2
27 May 1961	v Austria	Vienna	1–3

1961–62

28 Sept 1961	v Luxembourg*(WCQ)	Arsenal	4–1
14 Oct 1961	v Wales	Cardiff	1–1
25 Oct 1961	v Portugal (WCQ)	Wembley	2–0
22 Nov 1961	v Northern Ireland	Wembley	1–1
4 April 1962	v Austria	Wembley	3–1
14 April 1962	v Scotland	Glasgow	0–2
9 May 1962	v Switzerland	Wembley	3–1
20 May 1962	v Peru	Lima	4–0
31 May 1962	v Hungary (WC)	Rancagua	1–2
2 June 1962	v Argentina (WC)	Rancagua	3–1
7 June 1962	v Bulgaria (WC)	Rancagua	0–0
10 June 1962	v Brazil (WC)	Vina del Mar	1–3

1962–63

3 Oct 1962	v France* (ECQ)	Sheffield Wednesday	1–1
20 Oct 1962	v Northern Ireland*	Belfast	3–1
21 Nov 1962	v Wales*	Wembley	4–0
27 Feb 1963	v France*(ECQ)	Paris	2–5
6 April 1963	v Scotland*	Wembley	1–2
8 May 1963	v Brazil*	Wembley	1–1
2 June 1963	v East Germany*	Leipzig	2–1
5 June 1963	v Switzerland*	Basle	8–1

1963–64

12 Oct 1963	v Wales*	Cardiff	4–0
23 Oct 1963	v Rest of the World*	Wembley	2–1
20 Nov 1963	v Northern Ireland*	Wembley	8–3
11 April 1964	v Scotland*	Glasgow	0–1

1965–66

| 4 May 1966 | v Yugoslavia* | Wembley | 2–0 |
| 26 June 1966 | v Finland* | Helsinki | 3–0 |

ARMSTRONG, DAVID *Born:* 26.12.54 (Durham) *Clubs:* Middlesbrough, Southampton
Caps: 3

1979–80 (with Middlesbrough)

| 31 May 1980 | v Australia | Sydney | 2–1 |

1982–83 (with Southampton)
13 Oct 1982	*v* West Germany	Wembley	1–2

1983–84
2 May 1984	*v* Wales	Wrexham	0–1

ARMSTRONG, KEN *Born:* 3.6.24 (Bradford) *Club:* Chelsea *Caps:* 1

1954–55
2 April 1955	*v* Scotland	Wembley	7–2

ASTALL, GORDON *Born:* 22.9.27 (Horwich) *Club:* Birmingham City *Caps:* 2 *Goals:* 1

1955–56
20 May 1956	*v* Finland	Helsinki	5–1 (1 goal)
26 May 1956	*v* West Germany	Berlin	3–1

ASTLE, JEFF *Born:* 13.5.42 (Eastwood) *Club:* West Bromwich Albion *Caps:* 5

1968–69
7 May 1969	*v* Wales	Wembley	2–1

1969–70
10 Dec 1969	*v* Portugal	Wembley	1–0
25 April 1970	*v* Scotland	Glasgow	0–0
7 June 1970	*v* Brazil (sub) (WC)	Guadalajara	0–1
11 June 1970	*v* Czechoslovakia (WC)	Guadalajara	1–0

ASTON, JOHN *Born:* 3.9.21 (Manchester) *Club:* Manchester United *Caps:* 17

1948–49
26 Sept 1948	*v* Denmark	Copenhagen	0–0
10 Nov 1948	*v* Wales	Aston Villa	1–0
1 Dec 1948	*v* Switzerland	Arsenal	6–0
9 April 1949	*v* Scotland	Wembley	1–3
13 May 1949	*v* Sweden	Stockholm	1–3
18 May 1949	*v* Norway	Oslo	4–1
22 May 1949	*v* France	Paris	3–1

1949–50
21 Sept 1949	*v* Eire	Everton	0–2
15 Oct 1949	*v* Wales (WCQ)	Cardiff	4–1
16 Nov 1949	*v* Northern Ireland (WCQ)	Manchester City	9–2
30 Nov 1949	*v* Italy	Tottenham	2–0
15 April 1950	*v* Scotland (WCQ)	Glasgow	1–0
14 May 1950	*v* Portugal	Lisbon	5–3
18 May 1950	*v* Belgium	Brussels	4–1
15 June 1950	*v* Chile (WC)	Rio de Janeiro	2–0
29 June 1950	*v* USA (WC)	Belo Horizonte	0–1

1950–51
7 Oct 1950	*v* Northern Ireland	Belfast	4–1

ATYEO, JOHN P. *Born:* 7.2.32 (Dilton) *Club:* Bristol City *Caps:* 6 *Goals:* 5

1955–56
30 Nov 1955	*v* Spain	Wembley	4–1 (1 goal)
9 May 1956	*v* Brazil	Wembley	4–2
16 May 1956	*v* Sweden	Stockholm	0–0

1956–57
8 May 1957	*v* Eire (WCQ)	Wembley	5–1 (2 goals)
15 May 1957	*v* Denmark (WCQ)	Copenhagen	4–1 (1 goal)
19 May 1957	*v* Eire (WCQ)	Dublin	1–1 (1 goal)

BAILEY, GARY R. *Born:* 9.8.58 (Ipswich) *Club:* Manchester United *Caps:* 2

1984–85
26 March 1985	*v* Eire	Wembley	2–1
9 June 1985	*v* Mexico	Mexico City	0–1

BAILEY, MIKE A. *Born:* 27.2.42 (Wisbech) *Club:* Charlton Athletic *Caps:* 2

1963–64
27 May 1964	*v* USA	New York	10–0

1964–65
18 Nov 1964	*v* Wales	Wembley	2–1

BAILY, EDDIE F. *Born:* 6.8.25 (Clapton) *Club:* Tottenham Hotspur *Caps:* 9 *Goals:* 5

1949–50
2 July 1950	*v* Spain (WC)	Rio de Janeiro	0–1

1950–51
7 Oct 1950	*v* Northern Ireland	Belfast	4–1 (2 goals)
15 Nov 1950	*v* Wales	Sunderland	4–2 (2 goals)
22 Nov 1950	*v* Yugoslavia	Arsenal	2–2

1951–52
20 Oct 1951	*v* Wales	Cardiff	1–1 (1 goal)
28 Nov 1951	*v* Austria	Wembley	2–2
25 May 1952	*v* Austria	Vienna	3–2
28 May 1952	*v* Switzerland	Zurich	3–0

1952–53
4 Oct 1952	*v* Northern Ireland	Belfast	2–2

BAKER, JOE H. *Born:* 17.7.40 (Liverpool) *Clubs:* Hibernian, Arsenal *Caps:* 8 *Goals:* 3

1959–60 (with Hibernian)
18 Nov 1959	*v* Northern Ireland	Wembley	2–1 (1 goal)
19 April 1960	*v* Scotland	Glasgow	1–1
11 May 1960	*v* Yugoslavia	Wembley	3–3
15 May 1960	*v* Spain	Madrid	0–3
22 May 1960	*v* Hungary	Budapest	0–2

1965–66 (with Arsenal)
10 Nov 1965	*v* Northern Ireland	Wembley	2–1 (1 goal)

| 8 Dec 1965 | *v* Spain | Madrid | 2–0 (1 goal) |
| 5 Jan 1966 | *v* Poland | Everton | 1–1 |

BALL, ALAN J. *Born:* 12.5.45 (Farnworth) *Clubs:* Blackpool, Everton, Arsenal *Caps:* 72 *Goals:* 8

1964–65 (with Blackpool)

9 May 1965	*v* Yugoslavia	Belgrade	1–1
12 May 1965	*v* West Germany	Nuremberg	1–0
16 May 1965	*v* Sweden	Gothenburg	2–1 (1 goal)

1965–66

8 Dec 1965	*v* Spain	Madrid	2–0
5 Jan 1966	*v* Poland	Everton	1–1
23 Feb 1966	*v* West Germany	Wembley	1–0
2 April 1966	*v* Scotland	Glasgow	4–3
26 June 1966	*v* Finland	Helsinki	3–0
3 July 1966	*v* Denmark	Copenhagen	2–0
5 July 1966	*v* Poland	Chorzow	1–0
11 July 1966	*v* Uruguay (WC)	Wembley	0–0
23 July 1966	*v* Argentina (WC)	Wembley	1–0
26 July 1966	*v* Portugal (WC)	Wembley	2–1
30 July 1966	*v* West Germany (WCF)	Wembley	4–2 (aet)

1966–67 (with Everton)

22 Oct 1966	*v* Northern Ireland (ECQ)	Belfast	2–0
2 Nov 1966	*v* Czechoslovakia	Wembley	0–0
16 Nov 1966	*v* Wales (ECQ)	Wembley	5–1
15 April 1967	*v* Scotland (ECQ)	Wembley	2–3
24 May 1967	*v* Spain	Wembley	2–0
27 May 1967	*v* Austria	Vienna	1–0 (1 goal)

1967–68

21 Oct 1967	*v* Wales (ECQ)	Cardiff	3–0 (1 goal)
6 Dec 1967	*v* USSR	Wembley	2–2 (1 goal)
24 Feb 1968	*v* Scotland (ECQ)	Glasgow	1–1
3 April 1968	*v* Spain (ECQ)	Wembley	1–0
8 May 1968	*v* Spain (ECQ)	Madrid	2–1
1 June 1968	*v* West Germany	Hanover	0–1
5 June 1968	*v* Yugoslavia (EC)	Florence	0–1

1968–69

6 Nov 1968	*v* Romania	Bucharest	0–0
15 Jan 1969	*v* Romania	Wembley	1–1
3 May 1969	*v* Northern Ireland	Belfast	3–1
7 May 1969	*v* Wales	Wembley	2–1
10 May 1969	*v* Scotland	Wembley	4–1
1 June 1969	*v* Mexico	Mexico City	0–0
8 June 1969	*v* Uruguay	Montevideo	2–1
12 June 1969	*v* Brazil	Rio de Janeiro	1–2

1969–70

| 10 Dec 1969 | *v* Portugal | Wembley | 1–0 |
| 25 Feb 1970 | *v* Belgium | Brussels | 3–1 (2 goals) |

18 April 1970	*v* Wales	Cardiff	1–1
25 April 1970	*v* Scotland	Glasgow	0–0
20 May 1970	*v* Colombia	Bogota	4–0 (1 goal)
24 May 1970	*v* Ecuador	Quito	2–0
2 June 1970	*v* Romania (WC)	Guadalajara	1–0
7 June 1970	*v* Brazil (WC)	Guadalajara	0–1
11 June 1970	*v* Czechoslovakia (sub) (WC)	Guadalajara	1–0
14 June 1970	*v* West Germany (WC)	Leon	2–3 (aet)

1970–71

25 Nov 1970	*v* East Germany	Wembley	3–1
3 Feb 1971	*v* Malta (ECQ)	Valletta	1–0
21 April 1971	*v* Greece (ECQ)	Wembley	3–0
12 May 1971	*v* Malta (sub) (ECQ)	Wembley	5–0
15 May 1971	*v* Northern Ireland	Belfast	1–0
22 May 1971	*v* Scotland	Wembley	3–1

1971–72 (with Arsenal)

10 Nov 1971	*v* Switzerland (ECQ)	Wembley	1–1
1 Dec 1971	*v* Greece (ECQ)	Athens	2–0
29 April 1972	*v* West Germany (ECQ)	Wembley	1–3
13 May 1972	*v* West Germany (ECQ)	Berlin	0–0
27 May 1972	*v* Scotland	Glasgow	1–0 (1 goal)

1972–73

11 Oct 1972	*v* Yugoslavia	Wembley	1–1
15 Nov 1972	*v* Wales (WCQ)	Cardiff	1–0
24 Jan 1973	*v* Wales (WCQ)	Wembley	1–1
14 Feb 1973	*v* Scotland (SFAC)	Glasgow	5–0
12 May 1973	*v* Northern Ireland	Everton	2–1
15 May 1973	*v* Wales	Wembley	3–0
19 May 1973	*v* Scotland	Wembley	1–0
27 May 1973	*v* Czechoslovakia	Prague	1–1
6 June 1973	*v* Poland (WCQ)	Chorzow	0–2

1973–74

3 April 1974	*v* Portugal (sub)	Lisbon	0–0

1974–75

12 March 1975	*v* West Germany*	Wembley	2–0
16 April 1975	*v* Cyprus* (ECQ)	Wembley	5–0
11 May 1975	*v* Cyprus* (ECQ)	Limassol	1–0
17 May 1975	*v* Northern Ireland*	Belfast	0–0
21 May 1975	*v* Wales*	Wembley	2–2
24 May 1975	*v* Scotland*	Wembley	5–1

BANKS, GORDON *Born:* 20.12.37 (Sheffield) *Clubs:* Leicester City, Stoke City *Caps:* 73

1962–63 (with Leicester City)

6 April 1963	*v* Scotland	Wembley	1–2
8 May 1963	*v* Brazil	Wembley	1–1
20 May 1963	*v* Czechoslovakia	Bratislava	4–2
2 June 1963	*v* East Germany	Leipzig	2–1

1963–64

12 Oct 1963	v Wales	Cardiff	4–0
23 Oct 1963	v Rest of the World	Wembley	2–1
20 Nov 1963	v Northern Ireland	Wembley	8–3
11 April 1964	v Scotland	Glasgow	0–1
6 May 1964	v Uruguay	Wembley	2–1
17 May 1964	v Portugal	Lisbon	4–3
27 May 1964	v USA	New York	10–0
4 June 1964	v Portugal (BJT)	Sao Paulo	1–1
6 June 1964	v Argentina (BJT)	Rio de Janeiro	0–1

1964–65

3 Oct 1964	v Northern Ireland	Belfast	4–3
10 April 1965	v Scotland	Wembley	2–2
5 May 1965	v Hungary	Wembley	1–0
9 May 1965	v Yugoslavia	Belgrade	1–1
12 May 1965	v West Germany	Nuremberg	1–0
16 May 1965	v Sweden	Gothenburg	2–1

1965–66

10 Nov 1965	v Northern Ireland	Wembley	2–1
8 Dec 1965	v Spain	Madrid	2–0
5 Jan 1966	v Poland	Liverpool	1–1
23 Feb 1966	v West Germany	Wembley	1–0
2 April 1966	v Scotland	Glasgow	4–3
4 May 1966	v Yugoslavia	Wembley	2–0
26 June 1966	v Finland	Helsinki	3–0
5 July 1966	v Poland	Chorzow	1–0
11 July 1966	v Uruguay (WC)	Wembley	0–0
16 July 1966	v Mexico (WC)	Wembley	2–0
20 July 1966	v France (WC)	Wembley	2–0
23 July 1966	v Argentina (WC)	Wembley	1–0
26 July 1966	v Portugal (WC)	Wembley	2–1
30 July 1966	v West Germany (WCF)	Wembley	4–2 (aet)

1966–67

22 Oct 1966	v Northern Ireland (ECQ)	Belfast	2–0
2 Nov 1966	v Czechoslovakia	Wembley	0–0
16 Nov 1966	v Wales (ECQ)	Wembley	5–1
15 April 1967	v Scotland (ECQ)	Wembley	2–3

1967–68 (with Stoke City)

21 Oct 1967	v Wales (ECQ)	Cardiff	3–0
22 Nov 1967	v Northern Ireland (ECQ)	Wembley	2–0
6 Dec 1967	v USSR	Wembley	2–2
24 Feb 1968	v Scotland (ECQ)	Glasgow	1–1
3 April 1968	v Spain (ECQ)	Wembley	1–0
1 June 1968	v West Germany	Hanover	0–1
5 June 1968	v Yugoslavia (EC)	Florence	0–1
8 June 1968	v USSR (EC)	Rome	2–0

1968–69

6 Nov 1968	v Romania	Bucharest	0–0

15 Jan 1969	*v* Romania	Wembley	1–1
12 March 1969	*v* France	Wembley	5–0
3 May 1969	*v* Northern Ireland	Belfast	3–1
10 May 1969	*v* Scotland	Wembley	4–1
8 June 1969	*v* Uruguay	Montevideo	2–1
12 June 1969	*v* Brazil	Rio de Janeiro	1–2

1969–70

14 Jan 1970	*v* Holland	Wembley	0–0
25 Feb 1970	*v* Belgium	Brussels	3–1
18 April 1970	*v* Wales	Cardiff	1–1
21 April 1970	*v* Northern Ireland	Wembley	3–1
25 April 1970	*v* Scotland	Glasgow	0–0
20 May 1970	*v* Colombia	Bogota	4–0
24 May 1970	*v* Ecuador	Quito	2–0
2 June 1970	*v* Romania (WC)	Guadalajara	1–0
7 June 1970	*v* Brazil (WC)	Guadalajara	0–1
11 June 1970	*v* Czechoslovakia (WC)	Guadalajara	1–0

1970–71

3 Feb 1971	*v* Malta (ECQ)	Valletta	1–0
21 April 1971	*v* Greece (ECQ)	Wembley	3–0
12 May 1971	*v* Malta (ECQ)	Wembley	5–0
15 May 1971	*v* Northern Ireland	Belfast	1–0
22 May 1971	*v* Scotland	Wembley	3–1

1971–72

13 Oct 1971	*v* Switzerland (ECQ)	Basle	3–2
1 Dec 1971	*v* Greece (ECQ)	Athens	2–0
29 April 1972	*v* West Germany (ECQ)	Wembley	1–3
13 May 1972	*v* West Germany (ECQ)	Berlin	0–0
20 May 1972	*v* Wales	Cardiff	3–0
27 May 1972	*v* Scotland	Glasgow	1–0

BANKS, TOMMY *Born:* 10.11.29 (Farnworth) *Club:* Bolton Wanderers *Caps:* 6

1957–58

18 May 1958	*v* USSR	Moscow	1–1
8 June 1958	*v* USSR (WC)	Gothenburg	2–2
11 June 1958	*v* Brazil (WC)	Gothenburg	0–0
15 June 1958	*v* Austria (WC)	Boras	2–2
17 June 1958	*v* USSR (WC)	Gothenburg	0–1

1958–59

4 Oct 1958	*v* Northern Ireland	Belfast	3–3

BARDSLEY, DAVID *Born:* 11.9.64 (Manchester) *Club:* Queens Park Rangers *Caps:* 2

1992–93

9 Sept 1992	*v* Spain (sub)	Santander	0–1
29 May 1993	*v* Poland (WCQ)	Chorzow	1–1

BARHAM, MARK *Born:* 12.7.62 (Folkestone) *Club:* Norwich City *Caps:* 2

1982–83

12 June 1983	*v* Australia	Sydney	0–0
15 June 1983	*v* Australia	Brisbane	1–0

BARLOW, RAY J. *Born:* 17.8.26 (Swindon) *Club:* West Bromwich Albion *Caps:* 1

1954–55

2 Oct 1954	*v* Northern Ireland	Belfast	2–0

BARNES, JOHN *Born:* 7.9.63 (Jamaica) *Clubs:* Watford, Liverpool *Caps:* 73 *Goals:* 11

1982–83 (with Watford)

28 May 1983	*v* Northern Ireland (sub)	Belfast	0–0
12 June 1983	*v* Australia (sub)	Sydney	0–0
15 June 1983	*v* Australia	Brisbane	1–0
19 June 1983	*v* Australia	Melbourne	1–1

1983–84

21 Sept 1983	*v* Denmark (ECQ)	Wembley	0–1
16 Nov 1983	*v* Luxembourg (sub) (ECQ)	Luxembourg	4–0
29 Feb 1984	*v* France (sub)	Paris	0–2
26 May 1984	*v* Scotland	Glasgow	1–1
2 June 1984	*v* USSR	Wembley	0–2
10 June 1984	*v* Brazil	Rio de Janeiro	2–0 (1 goal)
13 June 1984	*v* Uruguay	Montevideo	0–2
17 June 1984	*v* Chile	Santiago	0–0

1984–85

12 Sept 1984	*v* East Germany	Wembley	1–0
17 Oct 1984	*v* Finland (WCQ)	Wembley	5–0
14 Nov 1984	*v* Turkey (WCQ)	Istanbul	8–0 (2 goals)
27 Feb 1985	*v* Northern Ireland (WCQ)	Belfast	1–0
1 May 1985	*v* Romania (WCQ)	Bucharest	0–0
22 May 1985	*v* Finland (WCQ)	Helsinki	1–1
25 May 1985	*v* Scotland (RC)	Glasgow	0–1
6 June 1985	*v* Italy (sub)	Mexico City	1–2
9 June 1985	*v* Mexico	Mexico City	0–1
12 June 1985	*v* West Germany (sub)	Mexico City	3–0
16 June 1985	*v* USA (sub)	Los Angeles	5–0

1985–86

11 Sept 1985	*v* Romania (sub) (WCQ)	Wembley	1–1
26 Feb 1986	*v* Israel (sub)	Tel Aviv	2–1
17 May 1986	*v* Mexico (sub)	Los Angeles	3–0
24 May 1986	*v* Canada (sub)	Vancouver	1–0
22 June 1986	*v* Argentina (sub) (WC)	Mexico City	1–2

1986–87

10 Sept 1986	*v* Sweden	Stockholm	0–1
29 April 1987	*v* Turkey (sub) (ECQ)	Izmir	0–0
19 May 1987	*v* Brazil (RC)	Wembley	1–1

1987–88 (with Liverpool)

9 Sept 1987	*v* West Germany	Düsseldorf	1–3
14 Oct 1987	*v* Turkey (ECQ)	Wembley	8–0 (2 goals)
11 Nov 1987	*v* Yugoslavia (ECQ)	Belgrade	4–1 (1 goal)
17 Feb 1988	*v* Israel	Tel Aviv	0–0
23 March 1988	*v* Holland	Wembley	2–2
21 May 1988	*v* Scotland (RC)	Wembley	1–0
24 May 1988	*v* Colombia (RC)	Wembley	1–1
28 May 1988	*v* Switzerland	Lausanne	1–0
12 June 1988	*v* Eire (EC)	Stuttgart	0–1
15 June 1988	*v* Holland (EC)	Düsseldorf	1–3
18 June 1988	*v* USSR (EC)	Frankfurt	1–3

1988–89

19 Oct 1988	*v* Sweden (WCQ)	Wembley	0–0
8 Feb 1989	*v* Greece	Athens	2–1 (1 goal)
8 March 1989	*v* Albania (WCQ)	Tirana	2–0 (1 goal)
3 June 1989	*v* Poland (WCQ)	Wembley	3–0 (1 goal)
7 June 1989	*v* Denmark	Copenhagen	1–1

1989–90

6 Sept 1989	*v* Sweden (WCQ)	Stockholm	0–0
15 Nov 1989	*v* Italy	Wembley	0–0
28 March 1990	*v* Brazil	Wembley	1–0
15 May 1990	*v* Denmark	Wembley	1–0
22 May 1990	*v* Uruguay	Wembley	1–2 (1 goal)
2 June 1990	*v* Tunisia	Tunis	1–1
11 June 1990	*v* Eire (WC)	Cagliari	1–1
16 June 1990	*v* Holland (WC)	Cagliari	0–0
21 June 1990	*v* Egypt (WC)	Cagliari	1–0
26 June 1990	*v* Belgium (WC)	Bologna	1–0 (aet)
1 July 1990	*v* Cameroon (WC)	Naples	3–2 (aet)

1990–91

12 Sept 1990	*v* Hungary	Wembley	1–0
17 Oct 1990	*v* Poland (ECQ)	Wembley	2–0
6 Feb 1991	*v* Cameroon	Wembley	2–0
27 March 1991	*v* Eire (ECQ)	Wembley	1–1
1 May 1991	*v* Turkey (ECQ)	Izmir	1–0
21 May 1991	*v* USSR	Wembley	3–1
25 May 1991	*v* Argentina	Wembley	2–2

1991–92

25 March 1992	*v* Czechoslovakia	Prague	2–2
3 June 1992	*v* Finland	Helsinki	2–1

1992–93

17 Feb 1993	*v* San Marino (WCQ)	Wembley	6–0
31 March 1993	*v* Turkey (WCQ))	Izmir	2–0
28 April 1993	*v* Holland (WCQ)	Wembley	2–2 (1 goal)
29 May 1993	*v* Poland (WCQ)	Chorzow	1–1
9 June 1993	*v* USA (USC)	Boston	0–2
19 June 1993	*v* Germany (USC)	Detroit	1–2

BARNES, PETER S. *Born:* 10.6.57 (Manchester) *Clubs:* Manchester City, West Bromwich Albion, Leeds United *Caps:* 22 *Goals:* 4

1977–78 (with Manchester City)
16 Nov 1977	*v* Italy (WCQ)	Wembley	2–0
22 Feb 1978	*v* West Germany	Munich	1–2
19 April 1978	*v* Brazil	Wembley	1–1
13 May 1978	*v* Wales	Cardiff	3–1 (1 goal)
20 May 1978	*v* Scotland	Glasgow	1–0
24 May 1978	*v* Hungary	Wembley	4–1 (1 goal)

1978–79
20 Sept 1978	*v* Denmark (ECQ)	Copenhagen	4–3
25 Oct 1978	*v* Eire (ECQ)	Dublin	1–1
29 Nov 1978	*v* Czechoslovakia	Wembley	1–0
7 Feb 1979	*v* Northern Ireland (ECQ)	Wembley	4–0
19 May 1979	*v* Northern Ireland	Belfast	2–0
26 May 1979	*v* Scotland	Wembley	3–1 (1 goal)
6 June 1979	*v* Bulgaria (ECQ)	Sofia	3–0 (1 goal)
13 June 1979	*v* Austria	Vienna	3–4

1979–80 (with West Bromwich Albion)
12 Sept 1979	*v* Denmark (ECQ)	Wembley	1–0
17 May 1980	*v* Wales	Wrexham	1–4

1980–81
25 March 1981	*v* Spain (sub)	Wembley	1–2
12 May 1981	*v* Brazil	Wembley	0–1
20 May 1981	*v* Wales	Wembley	0–0
30 May 1981	*v* Switzerland (sub) (WCQ)	Basle	1–2

1981–82 (with Leeds United)
9 Sept 1981	*v* Norway (sub) (WCQ)	Oslo	1–2
25 May 1982	*v* Holland (sub)	Wembley	2–0

BARRASS, MALCOLM W. *Born:* 13.12.24 (Blackpool) *Club:* Bolton Wanderers *Caps:* 3

1951–52
20 Oct 1951	*v* Wales	Cardiff	1-1
14 Nov 1951	*v* Northern Ireland	Aston Villa	2–0

1952–53
18 April 1953	*v* Scotland	Wembley	2–2

BARRETT, EARL D. *Born:* 28.4.67 (Rochdale) *Clubs:* Oldham Athletic, Aston Villa *Caps:* 3

1990–91 (with Oldham Athletic)
3 June 1991	*v* New Zealand	Auckland	1–0

1992–93 (with Aston Villa)
13 June 1993	*v* Brazil (USC)	Washington	1–1
19 June 1993	*v* Germany (USC)	Detroit	1–2

BATTY, DAVID *Born:* 2.12.68 (Leeds) *Club:* Leeds United *Caps:* 14

1990–91

21 May 1991	*v* USSR (sub)	Wembley	3–1
25 May 1991	*v* Argentina	Wembley	2–2
1 June 1991	*v* Australia	Sydney	1–0
3 June 1991	*v* New Zealand	Auckland	1–0
12 June 1991	*v* Malaysia	Kuala Lumpur	4–2

1991–92

11 Sept 1991	*v* Germany	Wembley	0–1
16 Oct 1991	*v* Turkey (ECQ)	Wembley	1–0
12 May 1992	*v* Hungary (sub)	Budapest	1–0
14 June 1992	*v* France (EC)	Malmo	0–0
17 June 1992	*v* Sweden (EC)	Stockholm	1–2

1992–93

14 Oct 1992	*v* Norway (WCQ)	Wembley	1–1
17 Feb 1993	*v* San Marino (WCQ)	Wembley	6–0
9 June 1993	*v* USA (USC)	Boston	0–2
13 June 1993	*v* Brazil (USC)	Washington	1–1

BAYNHAM, RON L. *Born:* 10.6.29 (Birmingham) *Club:* Luton Town *Caps:* 3

1955–56

2 Oct 1955	*v* Denmark	Copenhagen	5–1
2 Nov 1955	*v* Northern Ireland	Wembley	3–0
30 Nov 1955	*v* Spain	Wembley	4–1

BEARDSLEY, PETER A. *Born:* 18.1.61 (Newcastle) *Clubs:* Newcastle United, Liverpool
Caps: 49 *Goals:* 8

1985–86 (with Newcastle United)

29 Jan 1986	*v* Egypt (sub)	Cairo	4–0
26 Feb 1986	*v* Israel	Tel Aviv	2–1
26 March 1986	*v* USSR	Tbilisi	1–0
17 May 1986	*v* Mexico	Los Angeles	3–0 (1 goal)
24 May 1986	*v* Canada (sub)	Vancouver	1–0
3 June 1986	*v* Portugal (WC) (sub)	Monterrey	0–1
11 June 1986	*v* Poland (WC)	Monterrey	3–0
18 June 1986	*v* Paraguay (WC)	Mexico City	3–0 (1 goal)
22 June 1986	*v* Argentina (WC)	Mexico City	1–2

1986–87

15 Oct 1986	*v* Northern Ireland (ECQ)	Wembley	3–0
12 Nov 1986	*v* Yugoslavia (ECQ)	Wembley	2–0
18 Feb 1987	*v* Spain	Madrid	4–2
1 April 1987	*v* Northern Ireland (EC)	Belfast	2–0
19 May 1987	*v* Brazil (RC)	Wembley	1–1
23 May 1987	*v* Scotland (RC)	Glasgow	0–0

1987–88 (with Liverpool)

9 Sept 1987	*v* West Germany	Düsseldorf	1–3
14 Oct 1987	*v* Turkey (ECQ)	Wembley	8–0 (1 goal)

11 Nov 1987	*v* Yugoslavia (ECQ)	Belgrade	4–1 (1 goal)
17 Feb 1988	*v* Israel*	Tel Aviv	0–0
23 March 1988	*v* Holland	Wembley	2–2
27 April 1988	*v* Hungary	Budapest	0–0
21 May 1988	*v* Scotland (RC)	Wembley	1–0 (1 goal)
24 May 1988	*v* Colombia (RC)	Wembley	1–1
28 May 1988	*v* Switzerland	Lausanne	1–0
12 June 1988	*v* Eire (EC)	Stuttgart	0–1
15 June 1988	*v* Holland (EC)	Düsseldorf	1–3

1988–89

14 Sept 1988	*v* Denmark	Wembley	1–0
19 Oct 1988	*v* Sweden (WCQ)	Wembley	0–0
16 Nov 1988	*v* Saudi Arabia	Riyadh	1–1
8 Feb 1989	*v* Greece (sub)	Athens	2–1
8 March 1989	*v* Albania (sub) (WCQ)	Tirana	2–0
26 April 1989	*v* Albania (WCQ)	Wembley	5–0 (2 goals)
3 June 1989	*v* Poland (WCQ)	Wembley	3–0
7 June 1989	*v* Denmark	Copenhagen	1–1

1989–90

6 Sept 1989	*v* Sweden (WCQ)	Stockholm	0–0
11 Oct 1989	*v* Poland (WCQ)	Katowice	0–0
15 Nov 1989	*v* Italy	Wembley	0–0
28 March 1990	*v* Brazil	Wembley	1–0
22 May 1990	*v* Uruguay (sub)	Wembley	1–2
2 June 1990	*v* Tunisia (sub)	Tunis	1–1
11 June 1990	*v* Eire (WC)	Cagliari	1–1
21 June 1990	*v* Egypt (sub) (WC)	Cagliari	1–0
1 July 1990	*v* Cameroon (sub) (WC)	Naples	3–2 (aet)
4 July 1990	*v* West Germany (WC)	Turin	1–1 (aet)
7 July 1990	*v* Italy (WC)	Bari	1–2

1990–91

17 Oct 1990	*v* Poland (sub) (ECQ)	Wembley	2–0 (1 goal)
14 Nov 1990	*v* Eire (ECQ)	Dublin	1–1
27 March 1991	*v* Eire (ECQ)	Wembley	1–1
21 May 1991	*v* USSR (sub)	Wembley	3–1

BEASANT, DAVID J. *Born:* 20.3.59 (Willesden) *Club:* Chelsea *Caps:* 2

1989–90

15 Nov 1989	*v* Italy (sub)	Wembley	0–0
13 Dec 1989	*v* Yugoslavia (sub)	Wembley	2–1

BEATTIE, T. KEVIN *Born:* 18.12.53 (Carlisle) *Club:* Ipswich Town *Caps:* 9 *Goals:* 1

1974–75

16 April 1975	*v* Cyprus (ECQ)	Wembley	5–0
11 May 1975	*v* Cyprus (ECQ)	Limassol	1–0
24 May 1975	*v* Scotland	Wembley	5–1 (1 goal)

1975–76

3 Sept 1975	*v* Switzerland	Basle	2–1
19 Nov 1975	*v* Portugal (ECQ)	Lisbon	1–1

1976–77

13 Oct 1976	*v* Finland (WCQ)	Wembley	2–1
17 Nov 1976	*v* Italy (sub) (WCQ)	Rome	0–2
9 Feb 1977	*v* Holland	Wembley	0–2

1977–78

12 Oct 1977	*v* Luxembourg (sub) (WCQ)	Luxembourg	2–0

BELL, COLIN *Born:* 26.2.46 (Heselden) *Club:* Manchester City *Caps:* 48 *Goals:* 9

1967–68

22 May 1968	*v* Sweden	Wembley	3–1
1 June 1968	*v* West Germany	Hanover	0–1

1968–69

11 Dec 1968	*v* Bulgaria	Wembley	1–1
12 March 1969	*v* France	Wembley	5–0
7 May 1969	*v* Wales	Wembley	2–1
8 June 1969	*v* Uruguay	Montevideo	2–1
12 June 1969	*v* Brazil	Rio de Janeiro	1–2 (1 goal)

1969–70

5 Nov 1969	*v* Holland	Amsterdam	1–0 (1 goal)
10 Dec 1969	*v* Portugal	Wembley	1–0
14 Jan 1970	*v* Holland	Wembley	0–0
21 April 1970	*v* Northern Ireland (sub)	Wembley	3–1
7 June 1970	*v* Brazil (sub) (WC)	Guadalajara	0–1
11 June 1970	*v* Czechoslovakia (WC)	Guadalajara	1–0
14 June 1970	*v* West Germany (sub) (WC)	Leon	2–3 (aet)

1971–72

1 Dec 1971	*v* Greece (ECQ)	Athens	2–0
29 April 1972	*v* West Germany (ECQ)	Wembley	1–3
13 May 1972	*v* West Germany (ECQ)	Berlin	0–0
20 May 1972	*v* Wales	Cardiff	3–0 (1 goal)
23 May 1972	*v* Northern Ireland*	Wembley	0–1
27 May 1972	*v* Scotland	Glasgow	1–0

1972–73

11 Oct 1972	*v* Yugoslavia	Wembley	1–1
15 Nov 1972	*v* Wales (WCQ)	Cardiff	1–0 (1 goal)
24 Jan 1973	*v* Wales (WCQ)	Wembley	1–1
14 Feb 1973	*v* Scotland (SFAC)	Glasgow	5–0
12 May 1973	*v* Northern Ireland	Everton	2–1
15 May 1973	*v* Wales	Wembley	3–0
19 May 1973	*v* Scotland	Wembley	1–0
27 May 1973	*v* Czechoslovakia	Prague	1–1
6 June 1973	*v* Poland (WCQ)	Chorzow	0–2

1973–74

26 Sept 1973	*v* Austria	Wembley	7–0 (1 goal)

17 Oct 1973	*v* Poland (WCQ)	Wembley	1–1
14 Nov 1973	*v* Italy	Wembley	0–1
11 May 1974	*v* Wales	Cardiff	2–0
15 May 1974	*v* Northern Ireland	Wembley	1–0
18 May 1974	*v* Scotland	Glasgow	0–2
22 May 1974	*v* Argentina	Wembley	2–2
29 May 1974	*v* East Germany	Leipzig	1–1
1 June 1974	*v* Bulgaria	Sofia	1–0
5 June 1974	*v* Yugoslavia	Belgrade	2–2

1974–75

30 Oct 1974	*v* Czechoslovakia (ECQ)	Wembley	3–0 (2 goals)
20 Nov 1974	*v* Portugal (ECQ)	Wembley	0–0
12 March 1975	*v* West Germany	Wembley	2–0 (1 goal)
16 April 1975	*v* Cyprus (ECQ)	Wembley	5–0
11 May 1975	*v* Cyprus (ECQ)	Limassol	1–0
17 May 1975	*v* Northern Ireland	Belfast	0–0
24 May 1975	*v* Scotland	Wembley	5–1 (1 goal)

1975–76

3 Sept 1975	*v* Switzerland	Basle	2–1
30 Oct 1975	*v* Czechoslovakia (ECQ)	Bratislava	1–2

BENTLEY, ROY T. F. *Born:* 17.5.24 (Bristol) *Club:* Chelsea *Caps:* 12 *Goals:* 9

1948–49

13 May 1949	*v* Sweden	Stockholm	1–3

1949–50

15 April 1950	*v* Scotland (WCQ)	Glasgow	1–0 (1 goal)
14 May 1950	*v* Portugal	Lisbon	5–3
18 May 1950	*v* Belgium	Brussels	4–1 (1 goal)
25 June 1950	*v* Chile (WC)	Rio de Janeiro	2–0
29 June 1950	*v* USA (WC)	Belo Horizonte	0–1

1952–53

12 Nov 1952	*v* Wales	Wembley	5–2 (1 goal)
26 Nov 1952	*v* Belgium	Wembley	5–0

1954–55

10 Nov 1954	*v* Wales	Wembley	3–2 (3 goals)
1 Dec 1954	*v* West Germany	Wembley	3–1 (1 goal)
18 May 1955	*v* Spain	Madrid	1–1 (1 goal)
22 May 1955	*v* Portugal	Oporto	1–3 (1 goal)

BERRY, JOHNNY J. *Born:* 1.6.26 (Aldershot) *Club:* Manchester United *Caps:* 4

1952–53

17 May 1953	*v* Argentina	Buenos Aires	0–0 †
24 May 1953	*v* Chile	Santiago	2–1
31 May 1953	*v* Uruguay	Montevideo	1–2

1955–56

16 May 1956	*v* Sweden	Stockholm	0–0

BIRTLES, GARRY *Born:* 27.7.56 (Nottingham) *Club:* Nottingham Forest *Caps:* 3

1979–80
13 May 1980	*v* Argentina (sub)	Wembley	3–1
15 June 1980	*v* Italy (EC)	Turin	0–1

1980–81
15 Oct 1980	*v* Romania (WCQ)	Bucharest	1–2

BLISSETT, LUTHER *Born:* 1.2.58 (Jamaica) *Clubs:* Watford, AC Milan *Caps:* 14 *Goals:* 3

1982–83 (with Watford)
13 Oct 1982	*v* West Germany (sub)	Wembley	1–2
15 Dec 1982	*v* Luxembourg (ECQ)	Wembley	9–0 (3 goals)
23 Feb 1983	*v* Wales	Wembley	2–1
30 March 1983	*v* Greece (sub) (ECQ)	Wembley	0–0
27 April 1983	*v* Hungary (ECQ)	Wembley	2–0
28 May 1983	*v* Northern Ireland	Belfast	0–0
1 June 1983	*v* Scotland (sub)	Wembley	2–0
12 June 1983	*v* Australia	Sydney	0–0
19 June 1983	*v* Australia (sub)	Melbourne	1–1

1983–84 (with AC Milan)
21 Sept 1983	*v* Denmark (sub) (ECQ)	Wembley	0–1
12 Oct 1983	*v* Hungary (ECQ)	Budapest	3–0
2 May 1984	*v* Wales (sub)	Wrexham	0–1
26 May 1984	*v* Scotland	Glasgow	1–1
2 June 1984	*v* USSR	Wembley	0–2

BLOCKLEY, JEFF *Born:* 12.9.49 (Leicester) *Club:* Arsenal *Caps:* 1

1972–73
11 Oct 1972	*v* Yugoslavia	Wembley	1–1

BLUNSTONE, FRANK *Born:* 17.10.34 (Crewe) *Club:* Chelsea *Caps:* 5

1954–55
10 Nov 1954	*v* Wales	Wembley	3–2
2 April 1955	*v* Scotland	Wembley	7–2
15 May 1955	*v* France	Paris	0–1
22 May 1955	*v* Portugal	Oporto	1–3

1956–57
28 Nov 1956	*v* Yugoslavia	Wembley	3–0

BONETTI, PETER P. *Born:* 27.9.41 (Putney) *Club:* Chelsea *Caps:* 7

1965–66
3 July 1966	*v* Denmark	Copenhagen	2–0

1966–67
24 May 1967	*v* Spain	Wembley	2–0
27 May 1967	*v* Austria	Vienna	1–0

1967–68

8 May 1968	v Spain (ECQ)	Madrid	2–1

1969–70

5 Nov 1969	v Holland	Amsterdam	1–0
10 Dec 1969	v Portugal	Wembley	1–0
14 June 1970	v West Germany (WC)	Leon	2–3 (aet)

BOWLES, STAN *Born:* 24.12.48 (Manchester) *Club:* Queens Park Rangers *Caps:* 5
Goals: 1

1973–74

3 April 1974	v Portugal	Lisbon	0–0
11 May 1974	v Wales	Cardiff	2–0 (1 goal)
15 May 1974	v Northern Ireland	Wembley	1–0

1976–77

17 Nov 1976	v Italy (WCQ)	Rome	0–2
9 Feb 1977	v Holland	Wembley	0–2

BOYER, PHILIP J. *Born:* 25.1.49 (Nottingham) *Club:* Norwich City *Caps:* 1

1975–76

24 March 1976	v Wales (FAWC)	Wrexham	2–1

BRABROOK, PETER *Born:* 8.11.37 (East Ham) *Club:* Chelsea *Caps:* 3

1957–58

17 June 1958	v USSR (WC)	Gothenburg	0–1

1958–59

4 Oct 1958	v Northern Ireland	Belfast	3–3

1959–60

15 May 1960	v Spain	Madrid	0–3

BRACEWELL, PAUL W. *Born:* 19.7.62 (Stoke) *Club:* Everton *Caps:* 3

1984–85

12 June 1985	v West Germany (sub)	Mexico City	3–0
16 June 1985	v USA	Los Angeles	5–0

1985–86

13 Nov 1985	v Northern Ireland (WCQ)	Wembley	0–0

BRADFORD, GEOFF R.W. *Born:* 18.7.27 (Bristol) *Club:* Bristol Rovers *Caps:* 1 *Goals:* 1

1955–56

2 Oct 1955	v Denmark	Copenhagen	5–1 (1 goal)

BRADLEY, WARREN *Born:* 20.6.33 (Hyde) *Club:* Manchester United *Caps:* 3 *Goals:* 2

1958–59

6 May 1959	*v* Italy	Wembley	2–2 (1 goal)
24 May 1959	*v* Mexico (sub)	Mexico City	1–2
28 May 1959	*v* USA	Los Angeles	8–1 (1 goal)

BRIDGES, BARRY J. *Born:* 29.4.41 (Norwich) *Club:* Chelsea *Caps:* 4 *Goals:* 1

1964–65

10 April 1965	*v* Scotland	Wembley	2–2
5 May 1965	*v* Hungary	Wembley	1–0
9 May 1965	*v* Yugoslavia	Belgrade	1–1 (1 goal)

1965–66

20 Oct 1965	*v* Austria	Wembley	2–3

BROADBENT, PETER F. *Born:* 15.5.33 (Ellerington) *Club:* Wolverhampton Wanderers *Caps:* 7 *Goals:* 2

1957–58

17 June 1958	*v* USSR (WC)	Gothenburg	0–1

1958–59

4 Oct 1958	*v* Northern Ireland	Belfast	3–3
26 Nov 1958	*v* Wales	Aston Villa	2–2 (2 goals)
11 April 1959	*v* Scotland	Wembley	1–0
6 May 1959	*v* Italy	Wembley	2–2
13 May 1959	*v* Brazil	Rio de Janeiro	0–2

1959–60

19 April 1960	*v* Scotland	Glasgow	1–1

BROADIS, IVOR A. *Born:* 18.12.22 (Poplar) *Clubs:* Manchester City, Newcastle United *Caps:* 14 *Goals:* 8

1951–52 (with Manchester City)

28 Nov 1951	*v* Austria	Wembley	2–2
5 April 1952	*v* Scotland	Glasgow	2–1
18 May 1952	*v* Italy	Florence	1–1 (1 goal)

1952–53

18 April 1953	*v* Scotland	Wembley	2–2 (2 goals)
17 May 1953	*v* Argentina	Buenos Aires	0–0†
24 May 1953	*v* Chile	Santiago	2–1
31 May 1953	*v* Uruguay	Montevideo	1–2
8 June 1953	*v* USA	New York	6–3 (1 goal)

1953–54 (with Newcastle United)

3 April 1954	*v* Scotland (WCQ)	Glasgow	4–2 (1 goal)
16 May 1954	*v* Yugoslavia	Belgrade	0–1
23 May 1954	*v* Hungary	Budapest	1–7 (1 goal)
17 June 1954	*v* Belgium (WC)	Basle	4–4 (2 goals)
20 June 1954	*v* Switzerland (WC)	Berne	2–0
26 June 1954	*v* Uruguay (WC)	Basle	2–4

BROOKING, TREVOR D. *Born:* 2.10.48 (Barking) *Club:* West Ham United *Caps:* 47
Goals: 5

1973–74

3 April 1974	*v* Portugal	Lisbon	0–0
22 May 1974	*v* Argentina	Wembley	2–2
29 May 1974	*v* East Germany	Leipzig	1–1
1 June 1974	*v* Bulgaria	Sofia	1–0
5 June 1974	*v* Yugoslavia	Belgrade	2–2

1974–75

30 Oct 1974	*v* Czechoslovakia (sub) (ECQ)	Wembley	3–0
20 Nov 1974	*v* Portugal (ECQ)	Wembley	0–0

1975–76

19 Nov 1975	*v* Portugal (ECQ)	Lisbon	1–1
24 March 1976	*v* Wales (FAWC)	Wrexham	2–1
23 May 1976	*v* Brazil (USABT)	Los Angeles	0–1
28 May 1976	*v* Italy (USABT)	New York	3–2
13 June 1976	*v* Finland (WCQ)	Helsinki	4–1

1976–77

8 Sept 1976	*v* Eire	Wembley	1–1
13 Oct 1976	*v* Finland (WCQ)	Wembley	2–1
17 Nov 1976	*v* Italy (WCQ)	Rome	0–2
9 Feb 1977	*v* Holland	Wembley	0–2
28 May 1977	*v* Northern Ireland	Belfast	2–1
31 May 1977	*v* Wales	Wembley	0–1

1977–78

16 Nov 1977	*v* Italy (WCQ)	Wembley	2–0 (1 goal)
22 Feb 1978	*v* West Germany	Munich	1–2
13 May 1978	*v* Wales	Cardiff	3–1
20 May 1978	*v* Scotland (sub)	Glasgow	1–0
24 May 1978	*v* Hungary	Wembley	4–1

1978–79

20 Sept 1978	*v* Denmark (ECQ)	Copenhagen	4–3
25 Oct 1978	*v* Eire (ECQ)	Dublin	1–1
7 Feb 1979	*v* Northern Ireland (ECQ)	Wembley	4–0
23 May 1979	*v* Wales (sub)	Wembley	0–0
26 May 1979	*v* Scotland	Wembley	3–1
6 June 1979	*v* Bulgaria (ECQ)	Sofia	3–0
10 June 1979	*v* Sweden (sub)	Stockholm	0–0
13 June 1979	*v* Austria	Vienna	3–4

1979–80

12 Sept 1979	*v* Denmark (ECQ)	Wembley	1–0
17 Oct 1979	*v* Northern Ireland (ECQ)	Belfast	5–1
13 May 1980	*v* Argentina (sub)	Wembley	3–1
17 May 1980	*v* Wales	Wrexham	1–4
20 May 1980	*v* Northern Ireland	Wembley	1–1
24 May 1980	*v* Scotland	Glasgow	2–0 (1 goal)
12 June 1980	*v* Belgium (EC)	Turin	1–1

18 June 1980	*v* Spain (EC)	Naples	2–1 (1 goal)

1980–81

19 Nov 1980	*v* Switzerland (WCQ)	Wembley	2–1
25 March 1981	*v* Spain	Wembley	1–2
29 April 1981	*v* Romania (WCQ)	Wembley	0–0
6 June 1981	*v* Hungary (WCQ)	Budapest	3–1 (2 goals)

1981–82

18 Nov 1981	*v* Hungary (WCQ)	Wembley	1–0
29 May 1982	*v* Scotland	Glasgow	1–0
3 June 1982	*v* Finland	Helsinki	4–1
5 July 1982	*v* Spain (sub) (WC)	Madrid	0–0

BROOKS, JOHNNY *Born:* 23.12.31 (Reading) *Club:* Tottenham Hotspur *Caps:* 3
Goals: 2

1956–57

14 Nov 1956	*v* Wales	Wembley	3–1 (1 goal)
28 Nov 1956	*v* Yugoslavia	Wembley	3–0 (1 goal)
5 Dec 1956	*v* Denmark (WCQ)	Wolverhampton	5–2

BROWN, ANTHONY *Born:* 3.10.45 (Oldham) *Club:* West Bromwich Albion *Caps:* 1

1970–71

19 May 1971	*v* Wales	Wembley	0–0

BROWN, KEN *Born:* 16.2.34 (London) *Club:* West Ham United *Caps:* 1

1959–60

18 Nov 1959	*v* Northern Ireland	Wembley	2–1

BULL, STEVE G. *Born:* 28.3.65 (Tipton) *Club:* Wolverhampton Wanderers *Caps:* 13
Goals: 4

1988–89

27 May 1989	*v* Scotland (sub) (RC)	Glasgow	2–0 (1 goal)
7 June 1989	*v* Denmark (sub)	Copenhagen	1–1

1989–90

13 Dec 1989	*v* Yugoslavia	Wembley	2–1
25 April 1990	*v* Czechoslovakia	Wembley	4–2 (2 goals)
15 May 1990	*v* Denmark (sub)	Wembley	1–0
22 May 1990	*v* Uruguay (sub)	Wembley	1–2
2 June 1990	*v* Tunisia (sub)	Tunis	1–1 (1 goal)
11 June 1990	*v* Eire (sub) (WC)	Cagliari	1–1
16 June 1990	*v* Holland (sub) (WC)	Cagliari	0–0
21 June 1990	*v* Egypt (WC)	Cagliari	1–0
26 June 1990	*v* Belgium (sub) (WC)	Bologna	1–0 (aet)

1990–91

12 Sept 1990	*v* Hungary	Wembley	1–0
17 Oct 1990	*v* Poland (ECQ)	Wembley	2–0

BUTCHER, TERRY *Born:* 28.12.58 (Singapore) *Clubs:* Ipswich Town, Rangers *Caps:* 77
Goals: 3

1979–80 (with Ipswich Town)

31 May 1980	*v* Australia	Sydney	2–1

1980–81

25 March 1981	*v* Spain	Wembley	1–2

1981–82

27 April 1982	*v* Wales	Cardiff	1–0
29 May 1982	*v* Scotland	Glasgow	1–0
16 June 1982	*v* France (WC)	Bilbao	3–1
20 June 1982	*v* Czechoslovakia (WC)	Bilbao	2–0
29 June 1982	*v* West Germany (WC)	Madrid	0–0
5 July 1982	*v* Spain (WC)	Madrid	0–0

1982–83

22 Sept 1982	*v* Denmark (ECQ)	Copenhagen	2–2
13 Oct 1982	*v* West Germany	Wembley	1–2
15 Dec 1982	*v* Luxembourg (ECQ)	Wembley	9–0
23 Feb 1983	*v* Wales	Wembley	2–1 (1 goal)
30 March 1983	*v* Greece (ECQ)	Wembley	0–0
27 April 1983	*v* Hungary (ECQ)	Wembley	2–0
28 May 1983	*v* Northern Ireland	Belfast	0–0
1 June 1983	*v* Scotland	Wembley	2–0
12 June 1983	*v* Australia	Sydney	0–0
15 June 1983	*v* Australia	Brisbane	1–0
19 June 1983	*v* Australia	Melbourne	1–1

1983–84

21 Sept 1983	*v* Denmark (ECQ)	Wembley	0–1
12 Oct 1983	*v* Hungary (ECQ)	Budapest	3–0
16 Nov 1983	*v* Luxembourg (ECQ)	Luxembourg	4–0 (1 goal)
29 Feb 1984	*v* France	Paris	0–2
4 April 1984	*v* Northern Ireland	Wembley	1–0

1984–85

12 Sept 1984	*v* East Germany	Wembley	1–0
17 Oct 1984	*v* Finland (WCQ)	Wembley	5–0
14 Nov 1984	*v* Turkey (WCQ)	Istanbul	8–0
27 Feb 1985	*v* Northern Ireland (WCQ)	Belfast	1–0
26 March 1985	*v* Eire	Wembley	2–1
1 May 1985	*v* Romania (WCQ)	Bucharest	0–0
22 May 1985	*v* Finland (WCQ)	Helsinki	1–1
25 May 1985	*v* Scotland (RC)	Glasgow	0–1
6 June 1985	*v* Italy	Mexico City	1–2
12 June 1985	*v* West Germany	Mexico City	3–0
16 June 1985	*v* USA	Los Angeles	5–0

1985–86

26 Feb 1986	*v* Israel	Tel Aviv	2–1
26 March 1986	*v* USSR	Tbilisi	1–0
23 April 1986	*v* Scotland (RC)	Wembley	2–1 (1 goal)

17 May 1986	*v* Mexico	Los Angeles	3–0
24 May 1986	*v* Canada	Vancouver	1–0
3 June 1986	*v* Portugal (WC)	Monterrey	0–1
6 June 1986	*v* Morocco (WC)	Monterrey	0–0
11 June 1986	*v* Poland (WC)	Monterrey	3–0
18 June 1986	*v* Paraguay (WC)	Mexico City	3–0
22 June 1986	*v* Argentina (WC)	Mexico City	1–2

1986–87 (with Rangers)

10 Sept 1986	*v* Sweden	Stockholm	0–1
15 Oct 1986	*v* Northern Ireland (ECQ)	Wembley	3–0
12 Nov 1986	*v* Yugoslavia* (ECQ)	Wembley	2–0
18 Feb 1987	*v* Spain	Madrid	4–2
1 April 1987	*v* Northern Ireland	Belfast	2–0
19 May 1987	*v* Brazil (RC)	Wembley	1–1
23 May 1987	*v* Scotland (RC)	Glasgow	0–0

1987–88

14 Oct 1987	*v* Turkey (ECQ)	Wembley	8–0
11 Nov 1987	*v* Yugoslavia (ECQ)	Belgrade	4–1

1988–89

14 Sept 1988	*v* Denmark	Wembley	1–0
19 Oct 1988	*v* Sweden (WCQ)	Wembley	0–0
8 Feb 1989	*v* Greece	Athens	2–1
8 March 1989	*v* Albania (WCQ)	Tirana	2–0
26 April 1989	*v* Albania (WCQ)	Wembley	5–0
23 May 1989	*v* Chile (RC)	Wembley	0–0
27 May 1989	*v* Scotland (RC)	Glasgow	2–0
3 June 1989	*v* Poland (WCQ)	Wembley	3–0
7 June 1989	*v* Denmark	Copenhagen	1–1

1989–90

6 Sept 1989	*v* Sweden* (WCQ)	Stockholm	0–0
11 Oct 1989	*v* Poland (WCQ)	Katowice	0–0
15 Nov 1989	*v* Italy	Wembley	0–0
13 Dec 1989	*v* Yugoslavia	Wembley	2–1
28 March 1990	*v* Brazil*	Wembley	1–0
25 April 1990	*v* Czechoslovakia	Wembley	4–2
15 May 1990	*v* Denmark*	Wembley	1–0
22 May 1990	*v* Uruguay	Wembley	1–2
2 June 1990	*v* Tunisia	Tunis	1–1
11 June 1990	*v* Eire (WC)	Cagliari	1–1
16 June 1990	*v* Holland (WC)	Cagliari	0–0
26 June 1990	*v* Belgium* (WC)	Bologna	1–0 (aet)
1 July 1990	*v* Cameroon* (WC)	Naples	3–2 (aet)
4 July 1990	*v* West Germany* (WC)	Turin	1–1 (aet)

BYRNE, GERRY *Born:* 29.8.38 (Liverpool) *Club:* Liverpool *Caps:* 2

1962–63

6 April 1963	*v* Scotland	Wembley	1–2

1965–66

29 June 1966	*v* Norway	Oslo	6–1

BYRNE, JOHN J. *Born:* 13.5.39 (West Horsley) *Clubs:* Crystal Palace, West Ham United
Caps: 11 *Goals:* 8

1961–62 (with Crystal Palace)

22 Nov 1961	*v* Northern Ireland	Wembley	1–1

1962–63 (with West Ham United)

5 June 1963	*v* Switzerland	Basle	8–1 (2 goals)

1963–64

11 April 1964	*v* Scotland	Glasgow	0–1
6 May 1964	*v* Uruguay	Wembley	2–1 (2 goals)
17 May 1964	*v* Portugal	Lisbon	4–3 (3 goals)
24 May 1964	*v* Eire	Dublin	3–1 (1 goal)
30 May 1964	*v* Brazil (BJT)	Rio de Janeiro	1–5
4 June 1964	*v* Portugal (BJT)	Sao Paulo	1–1
6 June 1964	*v* Argentina (BJT)	Rio de Janeiro	0–1

1964–65

18 Nov 1964	*v* Wales	Wembley	2–1
10 April 1965	*v* Scotland	Wembley	2–2

BYRNE, ROGER W. *Born:* 8.2.29 (Manchester) *Club:* Manchester United *Caps:* 33

1953–54

3 April 1954	*v* Scotland (WCQ)	Glasgow	4–2
16 May 1954	*v* Yugoslavia	Belgrade	0–1
23 May 1954	*v* Hungary	Budapest	1–7
17 June 1954	*v* Belgium (WC)	Basle	4–4
20 June 1954	*v* Switzerland (WC)	Berne	2–0
26 June 1954	*v* Uruguay (WC)	Basle	2–4

1954–55

2 Oct 1954	*v* Northern Ireland	Belfast	2–0
10 Nov 1954	*v* Wales	Wembley	3–2
1 Dec 1954	*v* West Germany	Wembley	3–1
2 April 1955	*v* Scotland	Wembley	7–2
15 May 1955	*v* France	Paris	0–1
18 May 1955	*v* Spain	Madrid	1–1
22 May 1955	*v* Portugal	Oporto	1–3

1955–56

2 Oct 1955	*v* Denmark	Copenhagen	5–1
22 Oct 1955	*v* Wales	Cardiff	1–2
2 Nov 1955	*v* Northern Ireland	Wembley	3–0
30 Nov 1955	*v* Spain	Wembley	4–1
14 April 1956	*v* Scotland	Glasgow	1–1
9 May 1956	*v* Brazil	Wembley	4–2
16 May 1956	*v* Sweden	Stockholm	0–0
20 May 1956	*v* Finland	Helsinki	5–1
26 May 1956	*v* West Germany	Berlin	3–1

1956–57

6 Oct 1956	v Northern Ireland	Belfast	1–1
14 Nov 1956	v Wales	Wembley	3–1
28 Nov 1956	v Yugoslavia	Wembley	3–0
5 Dec 1956	v Denmark (WCQ)	Wolverhampton	5–2
6 April 1957	v Scotland	Wembley	2–1
8 May 1957	v Eire (WCQ)	Wembley	5–1
15 May 1957	v Denmark (WCQ)	Copenhagen	4–1
19 May 1957	v Eire (WCQ)	Dublin	1–1

1957–58

19 Oct 1957	v Wales	Cardiff	4–0
6 Nov 1957	v Northern Ireland	Wembley	2–3
27 Nov 1957	v France	Wembley	4–0

CALLAGHAN, IAN R. *Born:* 10.4.42 (Liverpool) *Club:* Liverpool *Caps:* 4

1965–66

26 June 1966	v Finland	Helsinki	3–0
20 July 1966	v France (WC)	Wembley	2–0

1977–78

7 Sept 1977	v Switzerland	Wembley	0–0
12 Oct 1977	v Luxembourg (WCQ)	Luxembourg	2–0

CARTER, HORATIO S. *Born:* 21.12.13 (Sunderland) *Club:* Derby County *Caps:* 13 (including 6 Pre-war) *Goals:* 5

1946–47

28 Sept 1946	v Northern Ireland	Belfast	7–2 (1 goal)
30 Sept 1946	v Eire	Dublin	1–0
19 Oct 1946	v Wales	Manchester City	3–0
27 Nov 1946	v Holland	Huddersfield	8–2 (2 goals)
12 April 1947	v Scotland	Wembley	1–1 (1 goal)
3 May 1947	v France	Arsenal	3–0 (1 goal)
18 May 1947	v Switzerland	Zurich	0–1

CHAMBERLAIN, MARK *Born:* 19.11.61 (Stoke) *Club:* Stoke City *Caps:* 8 *Goals:* 1

1982–83

15 Dec 1982	v Luxembourg (sub) (ECQ)	Wembley	9–0 (1 goal)

1983–84

21 Sept 1983	v Denmark (sub) (ECQ)	Wembley	0–1
26 May 1984	v Scotland	Glasgow	1–1
2 June 1984	v USSR	Wembley	0–2
10 June 1984	v Brazil	Rio de Janeiro	2–0
13 June 1984	v Uruguay	Montevideo	0–2
17 June 1984	v Chile	Santiago	0–0

1984–85

17 Oct 1984	v Finland (sub) (WCQ)	Wembley	5–0

CHANNON, MICHAEL R. *Born:* 28.11.48 (Orcheston) *Clubs:* Southampton, Manchester City *Caps:* 46 *Goals:* 21

1972–73 (with Southampton)

11 Oct 1972	*v* Yugoslavia	Wembley	1–1
14 Feb 1973	*v* Scotland (SFAC)	Glasgow	5–0 (1 goal)
12 May 1973	*v* Northern Ireland	Everton	2–1
15 May 1973	*v* Wales	Wembley	3–0 (1 goal)
19 May 1973	*v* Scotland	Wembley	1–0
27 May 1973	*v* Czechoslovakia	Prague	1–1
10 June 1973	*v* USSR	Moscow	2–1
14 June 1973	*v* Italy	Turin	0–2

1973–74

26 Sept 1973	*v* Austria	Wembley	7–0 (2 goals)
17 Oct 1973	*v* Poland (WCQ)	Wembley	1–1
14 Nov 1973	*v* Italy	Wembley	0–1
3 April 1974	*v* Portugal	Lisbon	0–0
11 May 1974	*v* Wales	Cardiff	2–0
15 May 1974	*v* Northern Ireland	Wembley	1–0
18 May 1974	*v* Scotland	Glasgow	0–2
22 May 1974	*v* Argentina	Wembley	2–2 (1 goal)
29 May 1974	*v* East Germany	Leipzig	1–1 (1 goal)
1 June 1974	*v* Bulgaria	Sofia	1–0
5 June 1974	*v* Yugoslavia	Belgrade	2–2 (1 goal)

1974–75

30 Oct 1974	*v* Czechoslovakia (ECQ)	Wembley	3–0 (1 goal)
20 Nov 1974	*v* Portugal (ECQ)	Wembley	0–0
12 March 1975	*v* West Germany	Wembley	2–0
16 April 1975	*v* Cyprus (ECQ)	Wembley	5–0
11 May 1975	*v* Cyprus (ECQ)	Limassol	1–0
17 May 1975	*v* Northern Ireland (sub)	Belfast	0–0
21 May 1975	*v* Wales	Wembley	2–2
24 May 1975	*v* Scotland	Wembley	5–1

1975–76

3 Sept 1975	*v* Switzerland	Basle	2–1 (1 goal)
30 Oct 1975	*v* Czechoslovakia (ECQ)	Bratislava	1–2 (1 goal)
19 Nov 1975	*v* Portugal (ECQ)	Lisbon	1–1 (1 goal)
24 March 1976	*v* Wales (FAWC)	Wrexham	2–1
11 May 1976	*v* Northern Ireland	Wembley	4–0 (2 goals)
15 May 1976	*v* Scotland	Glasgow	1–2 (1 goal)
23 May 1976	*v* Brazil (USABT)	Los Angeles	0–1
28 May 1976	*v* Italy* (USABT)	New York	3–2 (2 goals)
13 June 1976	*v* Finland (WCQ)	Helsinki	4–1 (1 goal)

1976–77

13 Oct 1976	*v* Finland (WCQ)	Wembley	2–1
17 Nov 1976	*v* Italy (WCQ)	Rome	0–2
30 March 1977	*v* Luxembourg (WCQ)	Wembley	5–0 (2 goals)
28 May 1977	*v* Northern Ireland	Belfast	2–1 (1 goal)
31 May 1977	*v* Wales	Wembley	0–1

4 June 1977	v Scotland	Wembley	1–2 (1 goal)
8 June 1977	v Brazil (sub)	Rio de Janeiro	0–0
12 June 1977	v Argentina	Buenos Aires	1–1
15 June 1977	v Uruguay	Montevideo	0–0

1977–78 (with Manchester City)

| 7 Sept 1977 | v Switzerland | Wembley | 0–0 |

CHARLES, GARY A. *Born:* 13.4.70 (London) *Club:* Nottingham Forest *Caps:* 2

1990–91

| 8 June 1991 | v New Zealand | Wellington | 2–0 |
| 12 June 1991 | v Malaysia | Kuala Lumpur | 4–2 |

CHARLTON, JACK *Born:* 8.5.35 (Ashington) *Club:* Leeds United *Caps:* 35 *Goals:* 6

1964–65

10 April 1965	v Scotland	Wembley	2–2
5 May 1965	v Hungary	Wembley	1–0
9 May 1965	v Yugoslavia	Belgrade	1–1
12 May 1965	v West Germany	Nuremberg	1–0
16 May 1965	v Sweden	Gothenburg	2–1

1965–66

2 Oct 1965	v Wales	Cardiff	0–0
20 Oct 1965	v Austria	Wembley	2–3
10 Nov 1965	v Northern Ireland	Wembley	2–1
8 Dec 1965	v Spain	Madrid	2–0
5 Jan 1966	v Poland	Everton	1–1
23 Feb 1966	v West Germany	Wembley	1–0
2 April 1966	v Scotland	Glasgow	4–3
4 May 1966	v Yugoslavia	Wembley	2–0
26 June 1966	v Finland	Helsinki	3–0 (1 goal)
3 July 1966	v Denmark	Copenhagen	2–0 (1 goal)
5 July 1966	v Poland	Chorzow	1–0
11 July 1966	v Uruguay (WC)	Wembley	0–0
16 July 1966	v Mexico (WC)	Wembley	2–0
20 July 1966	v France (WC)	Wembley	2–0
23 July 1966	v Argentina (WC)	Wembley	1–0
26 July 1966	v Portugal (WC)	Wembley	2–1
30 July 1966	v West Germany (WCF)	Wembley	4–2 (aet)

1966–67

22 Oct 1966	v Northern Ireland (ECQ)	Belfast	2–0
2 Nov 1966	v Czechoslovakia	Wembley	0–0
16 Nov 1966	v Wales (ECQ)	Wembley	5–1 (1 goal)
15 April 1967	v Scotland (ECQ)	Wembley	2–3 (1 goal)

1967–68

| 21 Oct 1967 | v Wales (ECQ) | Cardiff | 3–0 |
| 3 April 1968 | v Spain (ECQ) | Wembley | 1–0 |

1968–69

| 15 Jan 1969 | v Romania | Wembley | 1–1 (1 goal) |

| 12 March 1969 | v France | Wembley | 5–0 |
| 7 May 1969 | v Wales | Wembley | 2–1 |

1969–70

5 Nov 1969	v Holland	Amsterdam	1–0
10 Dec 1969	v Portugal	Wembley	1–0 (1 goal)
14 Jan 1970	v Holland	Wembley	0–0
11 June 1970	v Czechoslovakia (WC)	Guadalajara	1–0

CHARLTON, ROBERT (BOBBY) *Born:* 11.10.37 (Ashington) *Club:* Manchester United
Caps: 106 *Goals:* 49

1957–58

19 April 1958	v Scotland	Glasgow	4–0 (1 goal)
7 May 1958	v Portugal	Wembley	2–1 (2 goals)
11 May 1958	v Yugoslavia	Belgrade	0–5

1958–59

4 Oct 1958	v Northern Ireland	Belfast	3–3 (2 goals)
22 Oct 1958	v USSR	Wembley	5–0 (1 goal)
26 Nov 1958	v Wales	Aston Villa	2–2
11 April 1959	v Scotland	Wembley	1–0 (1 goal)
6 May 1959	v Italy	Wembley	2–2 (1 goal)
13 May 1959	v Brazil	Rio de Janeiro	0–2
17 May 1959	v Peru	Lima	1–4
24 May 1959	v Mexico	Mexico City	1–2
28 May 1959	v USA	Los Angeles	8–1 (3 goals)

1959–60

17 Oct 1959	v Wales	Cardiff	1–1
28 Oct 1959	v Sweden	Wembley	2–3 (1 goal)
19 April 1960	v Scotland	Glasgow	1–1 (1 goal)
11 May 1960	v Yugoslavia	Wembley	3–3
15 May 1960	v Spain	Madrid	0–3
22 May 1960	v Hungary	Budapest	0–2

1960–61

8 Oct 1960	v Northern Ireland	Belfast	5–2 (1 goal)
19 Oct 1960	v Luxembourg (WCQ)	Luxembourg	9–0 (3 goals)
26 Oct 1960	v Spain	Wembley	4–2
23 Nov 1960	v Wales	Wembley	5–1 (1 goal)
15 April 1961	v Scotland	Wembley	9–3
10 May 1961	v Mexico	Wembley	8–0 (3 goals)
21 May 1961	v Portugal (WCQ)	Lisbon	1–1
24 May 1961	v Italy	Rome	3–2
27 May 1961	v Austria	Vienna	1–3

1961–62

28 Sept 1961	v Luxembourg (WCQ)	Arsenal	4–1 (2 goals)
11 Oct 1961	v Wales	Cardiff	1–1
25 Oct 1961	v Portugal (WCQ)	Wembley	2–0
22 Nov 1961	v Northern Ireland	Wembley	1–1 (1 goal)
4 April 1962	v Austria	Wembley	3–1
14 April 1962	v Scotland	Glasgow	0–2

9 May 1962	*v* Switzerland	Wembley	3–1
20 May 1962	*v* Peru	Lima	4–0
31 May 1962	*v* Hungary (WC)	Rancagua	1–2
2 June 1962	*v* Argentina (WC)	Rancagua	3–1 (1 goal)
7 June 1962	*v* Bulgaria (WC)	Rancagua	0–0
10 June 1962	*v* Brazil (WC)	Vina del Mar	1–3

1962–63

27 Feb 1963	*v* France (ECQ)	Paris	2–5
6 April 1963	*v* Scotland	Wembley	1–2
8 May 1963	*v* Brazil	Wembley	1–1
20 May 1963	*v* Czechoslovakia	Bratislava	4–2 (1 goal)
2 June 1963	*v* East Germany	Leipzig	2–1 (1 goal)
5 June 1963	*v* Switzerland	Basle	8–1 (3 goals)

1963–64

12 Oct 1963	*v* Wales	Cardiff	4–0 (1 goal)
23 Oct 1963	*v* Rest of the World	Wembley	2–1
20 Nov 1963	*v* Northern Ireland	Wembley	8–3
11 April 1964	*v* Scotland	Glasgow	0–1
6 May 1964	*v* Uruguay	Wembley	2–1
17 May 1964	*v* Portugal	Lisbon	4–3 (1 goal)
24 May 1964	*v* Eire	Dublin	3–1
27 May 1964	*v* USA (sub)	New York	10–0 (1 goal)
30 May 1964	*v* Brazil (BJT)	Rio de Janeiro	1–5
6 June 1964	*v* Argentina (BJT)	Rio de Janeiro	0–1

1964–65

3 Oct 1964	*v* Northern Ireland	Belfast	4–3
9 Dec 1964	*v* Holland	Amsterdam	1–1
10 April 1965	*v* Scotland	Wembley	2–2 (1 goal)

1965–66

2 Oct 1965	*v* Wales	Cardiff	0–0
20 Oct 1965	*v* Austria	Wembley	2–3 (1 goal)
10 Nov 1965	*v* Northern Ireland	Wembley	2–1
8 Dec 1965	*v* Spain	Madrid	2–0
23 Feb 1966	*v* West Germany	Wembley	1–0
2 April 1966	*v* Scotland	Glasgow	4–3 (1 goal)
4 May 1966	*v* Yugoslavia	Wembley	2–0 (1 goal)
26 June 1966	*v* Finland	Helsinki	3–0
29 June 1966	*v* Norway	Oslo	6–1
5 July 1966	*v* Poland	Chorzow	1–0
11 July 1966	*v* Uruguay (WC)	Wembley	0–0
16 July 1966	*v* Mexico (WC)	Wembley	2–0 (1 goal)
20 July 1966	*v* France (WC)	Wembley	2–0
23 July 1966	*v* Argentina (WC)	Wembley	1–0
26 July 1966	*v* Portugal (WC)	Wembley	2–1 (2 goals)
30 July 1966	*v* West Germany (WCF)	Wembley	4–2 (aet)

1966–67

22 Oct 1966	*v* Northern Ireland (ECQ)	Belfast	2–0
2 Nov 1966	*v* Czechoslovakia	Wembley	0–0

| 16 Nov 1966 | *v* Wales (ECQ) | Wembley | 5–1 (1 goal) |
| 15 April 1967 | *v* Scotland (ECQ) | Wembley | 2–3 |

1967–68

21 Oct 1967	*v* Wales (ECQ)	Cardiff	3–0 (1 goal)
22 Nov 1967	*v* Northern Ireland (ECQ)	Wembley	2–0 (1 goal)
6 Dec 1967	*v* USSR	Wembley	2–2
24 Feb 1968	*v* Scotland (ECQ)	Glasgow	1–1
3 April 1968	*v* Spain (ECQ)	Wembley	1–0 (1 goal)
8 May 1968	*v* Spain (ECQ)	Madrid	2–1
22 May 1968	*v* Sweden	Wembley	3–1 (1 goal)
5 June 1968	*v* Yugoslavia (EC)	Florence	0–1
8 June 1968	*v* USSR (EC)	Rome	2–0 (1 goal)

1968–69

6 Nov 1968	*v* Romania*	Bucharest	0–0
11 Dec 1968	*v* Bulgaria	Wembley	1–1
15 Jan 1969	*v* Romania	Wembley	1–1
3 May 1969	*v* Northern Ireland	Belfast	3–1
7 May 1969	*v* Wales	Wembley	2–1 (1 goal)
10 May 1969	*v* Scotland	Wembley	4–1
1 June 1969	*v* Mexico	Mexico City	0–0
12 June 1969	*v* Brazil	Rio de Janeiro	1–2

1969–70

5 Nov 1969	*v* Holland	Amsterdam	1–0
10 Dec 1969	*v* Portugal	Wembley	1–0
14 Jan 1970	*v* Holland*	Wembley	0–0
18 April 1970	*v* Wales	Cardiff	1–1
21 April 1970	*v* Northern Ireland	Wembley	3–1 (1 goal)
20 May 1970	*v* Colombia	Bogota	4–0 (1 goal)
24 May 1970	*v* Ecuador	Quito	2–0
2 June 1970	*v* Romania (WC)	Guadalajara	1–0
7 June 1970	*v* Brazil (WC)	Guadalajara	0–1
11 June 1970	*v* Czechoslovakia (WC)	Guadalajara	1–0
14 June 1970	*v* West Germany (WC)	Leon	2–3 (aet)

CHARNLEY, RAY O. *Born:* 29.5.35 (Lancaster) *Club:* Blackpool *Caps:* 1

1962–63

| 3 Oct 1962 | *v* France (ECQ) | Sheffield Wednesday | 1–1 |

CHERRY, TREVOR *Born:* 23.2.48 (Huddersfield) *Club:* Leeds United *Caps:* 27

1975–76

24 March 1976	*v* Wales (FAWC)	Wrexham	2–1
15 May 1976	*v* Scotland (sub)	Glasgow	1–2
23 May 1976	*v* Brazil (USABT)	Los Angeles	0–1
13 June 1976	*v* Finland (WCQ)	Helsinki	4–1

1976–77

8 Sept 1976	*v* Eire	Wembley	1–1
17 Nov 1976	*v* Italy (WCQ)	Rome	0–2
30 March 1977	*v* Luxembourg (WCQ)	Wembley	5–0

28 May 1977	v Northern Ireland	Belfast	2–1
4 June 1977	v Scotland (sub)	Wembley	1–2
8 June 1977	v Brazil	Rio de Janeiro	0–0
12 June 1977	v Argentina	Buenos Aires	1–1
15 June 1977	v Uruguay	Montevideo	0–0

1977–78

7 Sept 1977	v Switzerland	Wembley	0–0
12 Oct 1977	v Luxembourg (WCQ)	Luxembourg	2–0
16 Nov 1977	v Italy (WCQ)	Wembley	2–0
19 April 1978	v Brazil	Wembley	1–1
13 May 1978	v Wales	Cardiff	3–1

1978–79

29 Nov 1978	v Czechoslovakia	Wembley	1–0
23 May 1979	v Wales	Wembley	0–0
10 June 1979	v Sweden	Stockholm	0–0

1979–80

6 Feb 1980	v Eire (ECQ)	Wembley	2–0
13 May 1980	v Argentina	Wembley	3–1
17 May 1980	v Wales	Wrexham	1–4
20 May 1980	v Northern Ireland	Wembley	1–1
24 May 1980	v Scotland	Glasgow	2–0
31 May 1980	v Australia*	Sydney	2–1
18 June 1980	v Spain (sub)(EC)	Naples	2–1

CHILTON, ALLENBY C. *Born:* 16.9.18 (South Hylton) *Club:* Manchester United *Caps:* 2

1950–51

7 Oct 1950	v Northern Ireland	Belfast	4–1

1951–52

3 Oct 1951	v France	Arsenal	2–2

CHIVERS, MARTIN *Born:* 27.4.45 (Southampton) *Club:* Tottenham Hotspur *Caps:* 24 *Goals:* 13

1970–71

3 Feb 1971	v Malta (ECQ)	Valletta	1–0
21 April 1971	v Greece (ECQ)	Wembley	3–0 (1 goal)
12 May 1971	v Malta (ECQ)	Wembley	5–0 (2 goals)
15 May 1971	v Northern Ireland	Belfast	1–0
22 May 1971	v Scotland	Wembley	3–1 (2 goals)

1971–72

13 Oct 1971	v Switzerland (ECQ)	Basle	3–2 (1 goal)
10 Nov 1971	v Switzerland (sub) (ECQ)	Wembley	1–1
1 Dec 1971	v Greece (ECQ)	Athens	2–0 (1 goal)
29 April 1972	v West Germany (ECQ)	Wembley	1–3
13 May 1972	v West Germany (ECQ)	Berlin	0–0
23 May 1972	v Northern Ireland (sub)	Wembley	0–1
27 May 1972	v Scotland	Glasgow	1–0

1972–73

15 Nov 1972	*v* Wales (WCQ)	Cardiff	1–0
24 Jan 1973	*v* Wales (WCQ)	Wembley	1–1
14 Feb 1973	*v* Scotland (SFAC)	Glasgow	5–0 (1 goal)
12 May 1973	*v* Northern Ireland	Everton	2–1 (2 goals)
15 May 1973	*v* Wales	Wembley	3–0 (1 goal)
19 May 1973	*v* Scotland	Wembley	1–0
27 May 1973	*v* Czechoslovakia	Prague	1–1
6 June 1973	*v* Poland (WCQ)	Chorzow	0–2
10 June 1973	*v* USSR	Moscow	2–1 (1 goal)
14 June 1973	*v* Italy	Turin	0–2

1973–74

26 Sept 1973	*v* Austria	Wembley	7–0 (1 goal)
17 Oct 1973	*v* Poland (WCQ)	Wembley	1–1

CLAMP, EDDIE *Born:* 14.9.34 (Coalville) *Club:* Wolverhampton Wanderers *Caps:* 4

1957–58

18 May 1958	*v* USSR	Moscow	1–1
8 June 1958	*v* USSR (WC)	Gothenburg	2–2
11 June 1958	*v* Brazil (WC)	Gothenburg	0–0
15 June 1958	*v* Austria (WC)	Boras	2–2

CLAPTON, DANNY R. *Born:* 22.7.34 (London) *Club:* Arsenal *Caps:* 1

1958–59

26 Nov 1958	*v* Wales	Aston Villa	2–2

CLARKE, ALLAN J. *Born:* 31.7.46 (Willenhall) *Club:* Leeds United *Caps:* 19 *Goals:* 10

1969–70

11 June 1970	*v* Czechoslovakia (WC)	Guadalajara	1–0 (1 goal)

1970–71

25 Nov 1970	*v* East Germany	Wembley	3–1 (1 goal)
12 May 1971	*v* Malta (ECQ)	Wembley	5–0 (1 goal)
15 May 1971	*v* Northern Ireland	Belfast	1–0 (1 goal)
19 May 1971	*v* Wales (sub)	Wembley	0–0
22 May 1971	*v* Scotland (sub)	Wembley	3–1

1972–73

14 Feb 1973	*v* Scotland (SFAC)	Glasgow	5–0 (2 goals)
15 May 1973	*v* Wales	Wembley	3–0
19 May 1973	*v* Scotland	Wembley	1–0
27 May 1973	*v* Czechoslovakia	Prague	1–1 (1 goal)
6 June 1973	*v* Poland (WCQ)	Chorzow	0–2
10 June 1973	*v* USSR	Moscow	2–1
14 June 1973	*v* Italy	Turin	0–2

1973–74

26 Sept 1973	*v* Austria	Wembley	7–0 (2 goals)
17 Oct 1973	*v* Poland (WCQ)	Wembley	1–1 (1 goal)
14 Nov 1973	*v* Italy	Wembley	0–1

1974–75
20 Nov 1974	*v* Portugal (ECQ)	Wembley	0–0

1975–76
30 Oct 1975	*v* Czechoslovakia (ECQ)	Bratislava	1–2
19 Nov 1975	*v* Portugal (sub) (ECQ)	Lisbon	1–1

CLARKE, HARRY A. *Born:* 23.2.23 (Woodford)　*Club:* Tottenham Hotspur　*Caps:* 1

1953–54
3 April 1954	*v* Scotland (WCQ)	Glasgow	4–2

CLAYTON, RONNIE *Born:* 5.8.34 (Preston)　*Club:* Blackburn Rovers　*Caps:* 35

1955–56
2 Nov 1955	*v* Northern Ireland	Belfast	3–0
30 Nov 1955	*v* Spain	Wembley	4–1
9 May 1956	*v* Brazil	Wembley	4–2
16 May 1956	*v* Sweden	Stockholm	0–0
20 May 1956	*v* Finland	Helsinki	5–1
26 May 1956	*v* West Germany	Berlin	3–1

1956–57
6 Oct 1956	*v* Northern Ireland	Belfast	1–1
14 Nov 1956	*v* Wales	Wembley	3–1
28 Nov 1956	*v* Yugoslavia	Wembley	3–0
5 Dec 1956	*v* Denmark (WCQ)	Wolverhampton	5–2
6 April 1957	*v* Scotland	Wembley	2–1
8 May 1957	*v* Eire (WCQ)	Wembley	5–1
15 May 1957	*v* Denmark (WCQ)	Copenhagen	4–1
19 May 1957	*v* Eire (WCQ)	Dublin	1–1

1957–58
19 Oct 1957	*v* Wales	Cardiff	4–0
6 Nov 1957	*v* Northern Ireland	Wembley	2–3
27 Nov 1957	*v* France	Wembley	4–0
19 April 1958	*v* Scotland	Glasgow	4–0
7 May 1958	*v* Portugal	Wembley	2–1
11 May 1958	*v* Yugoslavia	Belgrade	0–5
17 June 1958	*v* USSR (WC)	Gothenburg	0–1

1958–59
4 Oct 1958	*v* Northern Ireland	Belfast	3–3
22 Oct 1958	*v* USSR	Wembley	5–0
26 Nov 1958	*v* Wales	Aston Villa	2–2
11 April 1959	*v* Scotland	Wembley	1–0
6 May 1959	*v* Italy	Wembley	2–2
13 May 1959	*v* Brazil	Rio de Janeiro	0–2
17 May 1959	*v* Peru	Lima	1–4
24 May 1959	*v* Mexico	Mexico City	1–2
28 May 1959	*v* USA	Los Angeles	8–1

1959–60
17 Oct 1959	*v* Wales*	Cardiff	1–1

28 Oct 1959	v Sweden*	Wembley	2–3
18 Nov 1959	v Northern Ireland*	Wembley	2–1
19 April 1960	v Scotland*	Glasgow	1–1
11 May 1960	v Yugoslavia*	Wembley	3–3

CLEMENCE, RAY N. *Born:* 5.8.48 (Skegness) *Clubs:* Liverpool, Tottenham Hotspur *Caps:* 61

1972–73 (with Liverpool)
| 15 Nov 1972 | v Wales (WCQ) | Cardiff | 1–0 |
| 24 Jan 1973 | v Wales (WCQ) | Wembley | 1–1 |

1973–74
29 May 1974	v East Germany	Leipzig	1–1
1 June 1974	v Bulgaria	Sofia	1–0
5 June 1974	v Yugoslavia	Belgrade	2–2

1974–75
30 Oct 1974	v Czechoslovakia (ECQ)	Wembley	3–0
20 Nov 1974	v Portugal (ECQ)	Wembley	0–0
12 March 1975	v West Germany	Wembley	2–0
11 May 1975	v Cyprus (ECQ)	Limassol	1–0
17 May 1975	v Northern Ireland	Belfast	0–0
21 May 1975	v Wales	Wembley	2–2
24 May 1975	v Scotland	Wembley	5–1

1975–76
3 Sept 1975	v Switzerland	Basle	2–1
30 Oct 1975	v Czechoslovakia (ECQ)	Bratislava	1–2
19 Nov 1975	v Portugal (ECQ)	Lisbon	1–1
24 March 1976	v Wales (FAWC)	Wrexham	2–1
8 May 1976	v Wales	Cardiff	1–0
11 May 1976	v Northern Ireland	Wembley	4–0
15 May 1976	v Scotland	Glasgow	1–2
23 May 1976	v Brazil (USABT)	Los Angeles	0–1
13 June 1976	v Finland (WCQ)	Helsinki	4–1

1976–77
8 Sept 1976	v Eire	Wembley	1–1
13 Oct 1976	v Finland (WCQ)	Wembley	2–1
17 Nov 1976	v Italy (WCQ)	Rome	0–2
9 Feb 1977	v Holland	Wembley	0–2
30 March 1977	v Luxembourg (WCQ)	Wembley	5–0
4 June 1977	v Scotland	Wembley	1–2
8 June 1977	v Brazil	Rio de Janeiro	0–0
12 June 1977	v Argentina	Buenos Aires	1–1
15 June 1977	v Uruguay	Montevideo	0–0

1977–78
7 Sept 1977	v Switzerland	Wembley	0–0
12 Oct 1977	v Luxembourg (WCQ)	Luxembourg	2–0
16 Nov 1977	v Italy (WCQ)	Wembley	2–0
22 Feb 1978	v West Germany	Munich	1–2
16 May 1978	v Northern Ireland	Wembley	1–0
20 May 1978	v Scotland	Glasgow	1–0

1978–79

20 Sept 1978	v Denmark (ECQ)	Copenhagen	4–3
25 Oct 1978	v Eire (ECQ)	Dublin	1–1
7 Feb 1979	v Northern Ireland (ECQ)	Wembley	4–0
19 May 1979	v Northern Ireland	Belfast	2–0
26 May 1979	v Scotland	Wembley	3–1
6 June 1979	v Bulgaria (ECQ)	Sofia	3–0
13 June 1979	v Austria (sub)	Vienna	3–4

1979–80

12 Sept 1979	v Denmark (ECQ)	Wembley	1–0
22 Nov 1979	v Bulgaria (ECQ)	Wembley	2–0
6 Feb 1980	v Eire (ECQ)	Wembley	2–0
13 May 1980	v Argentina	Wembley	3–1
17 May 1980	v Wales	Wrexham	1–4
24 May 1980	v Scotland	Glasgow	2–0
12 June 1980	v Belgium (EC)	Turin	1–1
18 June 1980	v Spain (EC)	Naples	2–1

1980–81

15 Oct 1980	v Romania (WCQ)	Bucharest	1–2
25 March 1981	v Spain	Wembley	1–2
12 May 1981	v Brazil*	Wembley	0–1
30 May 1981	v Switzerland (WCQ)	Basle	1–2
6 June 1981	v Hungary (WCQ)	Budapest	3–1

1981–82 (with Tottenham Hotspur)

9 Sept 1981	v Norway (WCQ)	Oslo	1–2
23 Feb 1982	v Northern Ireland	Wembley	4–0
3 June 1982	v Finland	Helsinki	4–1

1982–83

15 Dec 1982	v Luxembourg (ECQ)	Wembley	9–0

1983–84

16 Nov 1983	v Luxembourg (ECQ)	Luxembourg	4–0

CLEMENT, DAVE T. *Born:* 2.2.48 (Battersea) *Club:* Queens Park Rangers *Caps:* 5

1975–76

24 March 1976	v Wales (sub) (FAWC)	Wrexham	2–1
8 May 1976	v Wales	Cardiff	1–0
28 May 1976	v Italy (USABT)	New York	3–2

1976–77

17 Nov 1976	v Italy (WCQ)	Rome	0–2
9 Feb 1977	v Holland	Wembley	0–2

CLOUGH, BRIAN H. *Born:* 21.3.35 (Middlesbrough) *Club:* Middlesbrough *Caps:* 2

1959–60

17 Oct 1959	v Wales	Cardiff	1–1
28 Oct 1959	v Sweden	Wembley	2–3

CLOUGH, NIGEL H. *Born:* 19.3.66 (Sunderland) *Club:* Nottingham Forest *Caps:* 14

1988–89

23 May 1989	*v* Chile (RC)	Wembley	0–0

1990–91

25 May 1991	*v* Argentina (sub)	Wembley	2–2
1 June 1991	*v* Australia	Sydney	1–0
12 June 1991	*v* Malaysia	Kuala Lumpur	4–2

1991–92

19 Feb 1992	*v* France	Wembley	2–0
25 March 1992	*v* Czechoslovakia	Prague	2–2
29 April 1992	*v* CIS (sub)	Moscow	2–2

1992–93

9 Sept 1992	*v* Spain	Santander	0–1
31 March 1993	*v* Turkey (sub) (WCQ)	Izmir	2–0
29 May 1993	*v* Poland (sub) (WCQ)	Chorzow	1–1
2 June 1993	*v* Norway (sub) (WCQ)	Oslo	0–2
9 June 1993	*v* USA (USC)	Boston	0–2
13 June 1993	*v* Brazil (USC)	Washington	1–1
19 June 1993	*v* Germany (USC)	Detroit	1–2

COATES, RALPH *Born:* 26.4.46 (Hetton) *Clubs:* Burnley, Tottenham Hotspur *Caps:* 4

1969–70 (with Burnley)

21 April 1970	*v* Northern Ireland	Wembley	3–1

1970–71

21 April 1971	*v* Greece (sub) (ECQ)	Wembley	3–0
	(with Tottenham Hotspur)		
12 May 1971	*v* Malta (ECQ)	Wembley	5–0
19 May 1971	*v* Wales	Wembley	0–0

COCKBURN, HENRY *Born:* 14.9.23 (Ashton) *Club:* Manchester United *Caps:* 13

1946–47

28 Sept 1946	*v* Northern Ireland	Belfast	7–2
30 Sept 1946	*v* Eire	Dublin	1–0
19 Oct 1946	*v* Wales	Manchester City	3–0

1947–48

10 April 1948	*v* Scotland	Glasgow	2–0
16 May 1948	*v* Italy	Turin	4–0

1948–49

26 Sept 1948	*v* Denmark	Copenhagen	0–0
9 Oct 1948	*v* Northern Ireland	Belfast	6–2
1 Dec 1948	*v* Switzerland	Arsenal	6–0
9 April 1949	*v* Scotland	Wembley	1–3
13 May 1949	*v* Sweden	Stockholm	1–3

1950–51

9 May 1951	*v* Argentina	Wembley	2–1
19 May 1951	*v* Portugal	Everton	5–2

1951–52

3 Oct 1951	*v* France	Arsenal	2–2

COHEN, GEORGE R. *Born:* 22.10.39 (Kensington) *Club:* Fulham *Caps:* 37

1963–64

6 May 1964	*v* Uruguay	Wembley	2–1
17 May 1964	*v* Portugal	Lisbon	4–3
24 May 1964	*v* Eire	Dublin	3–1
27 May 1964	*v* USA	New York	10–0
30 May 1964	*v* Brazil (BJT)	Rio de Janeiro	1–5

1964–65

3 Oct 1964	*v* Northern Ireland	Belfast	4–3
21 Oct 1964	*v* Belgium	Wembley	2–2
18 Nov 1964	*v* Wales	Wembley	2–1
9 Dec 1964	*v* Holland	Amsterdam	1–1
10 April 1965	*v* Scotland	Wembley	2–2
5 May 1965	*v* Hungary	Wembley	1–0
9 May 1965	*v* Yugoslavia	Belgrade	1–1
12 May 1965	*v* West Germany	Nuremberg	1–0
16 May 1965	*v* Sweden	Gothenburg	2–1

1965–66

2 Oct 1965	*v* Wales	Cardiff	0–0
20 Oct 1965	*v* Austria	Wembley	2–3
10 Nov 1965	*v* Northern Ireland	Wembley	2–1
8 Dec 1965	*v* Spain	Madrid	2–0
5 Jan 1966	*v* Poland	Everton	1–1
23 Feb 1966	*v* West Germany	Wembley	1–0
2 April 1966	*v* Scotland	Glasgow	4–3
29 June 1966	*v* Norway	Oslo	6–1
3 July 1966	*v* Denmark	Copenhagen	2–0
5 July 1966	*v* Poland	Chorzow	1–0
11 July 1966	*v* Uruguay (WC)	Wembley	0–0
16 July 1966	*v* Mexico (WC)	Wembley	2–0
20 July 1966	*v* France (WC)	Wembley	2–0
23 July 1966	*v* Argentina (WC)	Wembley	1–0
26 July 1966	*v* Portugal (WC)	Wembley	2–1
30 July 1966	*v* West Germany (WCF)	Wembley	4–2 (aet)

1966–67

22 Oct 1966	*v* Northern Ireland (ECQ)	Belfast	2–0
2 Nov 1966	*v* Czechoslovakia	Wembley	0–0
16 Nov 1966	*v* Wales (ECQ)	Wembley	5–1
15 April 1967	*v* Scotland (ECQ)	Wembley	2–3
24 May 1967	*v* Spain	Wembley	2–0

1967–68

21 Oct 1967	*v* Wales (ECQ)	Cardiff	3–0
22 Nov 1967	*v* Northern Ireland (ECQ)	Wembley	2–0

COMPTON, LESLIE H. *Born:* 12.9.12 (Woodford) *Club:* Arsenal *Caps:* 2

1950–51

15 Nov 1950	*v* Wales	Sunderland	4–2
22 Nov 1950	*v* Yugoslavia	Arsenal	2–2

CONNELLY, JOHN *Born:* 18.7.38 (St. Helens) *Clubs:* Burnley, Manchester United *Caps:* 20 *Goals:* 7

1959–60 (with Burnley)

17 Oct 1959	*v* Wales	Cardiff	1–1
28 Oct 1959	*v* Sweden	Wembley	2–3 (1 goal)
18 Nov 1959	*v* Northern Ireland	Wembley	2–1
19 April 1960	*v* Scotland	Glasgow	1–1

1961–62

14 Oct 1961	*v* Wales	Cardiff	1–1
25 Oct 1961	*v* Portugal (WCQ)	Wembley	2–0 (1 goal)
4 April 1962	*v* Austria	Wembley	3–1
9 May 1962	*v* Switzerland	Wembley	3–1 (1 goal)

1962–63

21 Nov 1962	*v* Wales	Wembley	4–0 (1 goal)
27 Feb 1963	*v* France (ECQ)	Paris	2–5

1964–65 (with Manchester United)

5 May 1965	*v* Hungary	Wembley	1–0
9 May 1965	*v* Yugoslavia	Belgrade	1–1
16 May 1965	*v* Sweden	Gothenburg	2–1 (1 goal)

1965–66

2 Oct 1965	*v* Wales	Cardiff	0–0
20 Oct 1965	*v* Austria	Wembley	2–3 (1 goal)
10 Nov 1965	*v* Northern Ireland	Wembley	2–1
2 April 1966	*v* Scotland	Glasgow	4–3
29 June 1966	*v* Norway	Oslo	6–1 (1 goal)
3 July 1966	*v* Denmark	Copenhagen	2–0
11 July 1966	*v* Uruguay (WC)	Wembley	0–0

COOPER, TERRY *Born:* 12.7.44 (Castleford) *Club:* Leeds United *Caps:* 20

1968–69

12 March 1969	*v* France	Wembley	5–0
7 May 1969	*v* Wales	Wembley	2–1
10 May 1969	*v* Scotland	Wembley	4–1
1 June 1969	*v* Mexico	Mexico City	0–0

1969–70

14 Jan 1970	*v* Holland	Wembley	0–0
25 Feb 1970	*v* Belgium	Brussels	3–1
20 May 1970	*v* Colombia	Bogota	4–0
24 May 1970	*v* Ecuador	Quito	2–0
2 June 1970	*v* Romania (WC)	Guadalajara	1–0
7 June 1970	*v* Brazil (WC)	Guadalajara	0–1

11 June 1970	v Czechoslovakia (WC)	Guadalajara	1–0
14 June 1970	v West Germany (WC)	Leon	2–3 (aet)

1970–71

25 Nov 1970	v East Germany	Wembley	3–1
12 May 1971	v Malta (ECQ)	Wembley	5–0
15 May 1971	v Northern Ireland	Belfast	1–0
19 May 1971	v Wales	Wembley	0–0
22 May 1971	v Scotland	Wembley	3–1

1971–72

13 Oct 1971	v Switzerland (ECQ)	Basle	3–2
10 Nov 1971	v Switzerland (ECQ)	Wembley	1–1

1974–75

20 Nov 1974	v Portugal (ECQ)	Wembley	0–0

COPPELL, STEVE J. *Born:* 9.7.55 (Liverpool) *Club:* Manchester United *Caps:* 42 *Goals:* 7

1977–78

16 Nov 1977	v Italy (WCQ)	Wembley	2–0
22 Feb 1978	v West Germany	Munich	1–2
19 April 1978	v Brazil	Wembley	1–1
13 May 1978	v Wales	Cardiff	3–1
16 May 1978	v Northern Ireland	Wembley	1–0
20 May 1978	v Scotland	Glasgow	1–0 (1 goal)
24 May 1978	v Hungary	Wembley	4–1

1978–79

20 Sept 1978	v Denmark (ECQ)	Copenhagen	4–3
25 Oct 1978	v Eire (ECQ)	Dublin	1–1
29 Nov 1978	v Czechoslovakia˙	Wembley	1–0 (1 goal)
7 Feb 1979	v Northern Ireland (ECQ)	Wembley	4–0
19 May 1979	v Northern Ireland	Belfast	2–0 (1 goal)
23 May 1979	v Wales (sub)	Wembley	0–0
26 May 1979	v Scotland	Wembley	3–1 (1 goal)
6 June 1979	v Bulgaria (ECQ)	Sofia	3–0
13 June 1979	v Austria	Vienna	3–4 (1 goal)

1979–80

12 Sept 1979	v Denmark (ECQ)	Wembley	1–0
17 Oct 1979	v Northern Ireland (ECQ)	Belfast	5–1
6 Feb 1980	v Eire (sub) (ECQ)	Wembley	2–0
26 Mar 1980	v Spain	Barcelona	2–0
13 May 1980	v Argentina	Wembley	3–1
17 May 1980	v Wales	Wrexham	1–4
24 May 1980	v Scotland	Glasgow	2–0 (1 goal)
12 June 1980	v Belgium (EC)	Turin	1–1
15 June 1980	v Italy (EC)	Turin	0–1

1980–81

15 Oct 1980	v Romania (sub) (WCQ)	Bucharest	1–2
19 Nov 1980	v Switzerland (WCQ)	Wembley	2–1
29 April 1981	v Romania (WCQ)	Wembley	0–0
12 May 1981	v Brazil	Wembley	0–1

20 May 1981	*v* Wales	Wembley	0–0
23 May 1981	*v* Scotland	Wembley	0–1
30 May 1981	*v* Switzerland (WCQ)	Basle	1–2
6 June 1981	*v* Hungary (WCQ)	Budapest	3–1

1981–82

18 Nov 1981	*v* Hungary (WCQ)	Wembley	1–0
29 May 1982	*v* Scotland	Glasgow	1–0
3 June 1982	*v* Finland	Helsinki	4–1
16 June 1982	*v* France (WC)	Bilbao	3–1
20 June 1982	*v* Czechoslovakia (WC)	Bilbao	2–0
25 June 1982	*v* Kuwait (WC)	Bilbao	1–0
29 June 1982	*v* West Germany (WC)	Madrid	0–0

1982–83

15 Dec 1982	*v* Luxembourg (ECQ)	Wembley	9–0 (1 goal)
30 Mar 1983	*v* Greece (ECQ)	Wembley	0–0

CORRIGAN, JOE T. *Born:* 18.11.48 (Manchester) *Club:* Manchester City *Caps:* 9

1975–76

28 May 1976	*v* Italy (sub) (USABT)	New York	3–2

1977–78

19 April 1978	*v* Brazil	Wembley	1–1

1978–79

23 May 1979	*v* Wales	Wembley	0–0

1979–80

20 May 1980	*v* Northern Ireland	Wembley	1–1
31 May 1980	*v* Australia	Sydney	2–1

1980–81

20 May 1981	*v* Wales	Wembley	0–0
23 May 1981	*v* Scotland	Wembley	0–1

1981–82

27 April 1982	*v* Wales	Cardiff	1–0
2 June 1982	*v* Iceland	Reykjavik	1–1

COTTEE, TONY R. *Born:* 11.7.65 (West Ham) *Clubs:* West Ham United, Everton *Caps:* 7

1986–87 (with West Ham United)

10 Sept 1986	*v* Sweden (sub)	Stockholm	0–1
15 Oct 1986	*v* N. Ireland (sub) (ECQ)	Wembley	3–0

1987–88

27 April 1988	*v* Hungary (sub)	Budapest	0–0

1988–89 (with Everton)

14 Sept 1988	*v* Denmark (sub)	Wembley	1–0
19 Oct 1988	*v* Sweden (sub) (WCQ)	Wembley	0–0
23 May 1989	*v* Chile (sub) (RC)	Wembley	0–0
27 May 1989	*v* Scotland (RC)	Glasgow	2–0

COWANS, GORDON S. *Born:* 27.10.58 (Durham) *Clubs:* Aston Villa, Bari *Caps:* 10
Goals: 2

1982–83 (with Aston Villa)

23 Feb 1983	*v* Wales	Wembley	2–1
27 April 1983	*v* Hungary (ECQ)	Wembley	2–0
28 May 1983	*v* Northern Ireland	Belfast	0–0
1 June 1983	*v* Scotland	Wembley	2–0 (1 goal)
12 June 1983	*v* Australia	Sydney	0–0
15 June 1983	*v* Australia	Brisbane	1–0
19 June 1983	*v* Australia	Melbourne	1–1

1985–86 (with Bari)

29 Jan 1986	*v* Egypt	Cairo	4–0 (1 goal)
26 March 1986	*v* USSR	Tbilisi	1–0

1990–91 (with Aston Villa)

14 Nov 1990	*v* Eire (ECQ)	Dublin	1–1

CRAWFORD, RAY *Born:* 13.7.36 (Portsmouth) *Club:* Ipswich Town *Caps:* 2 *Goals:* 1

1961–62

22 Nov 1961	*v* Northern Ireland	Wembley	1–1
4 April 1962	*v* Austria	Wembley	3–1 (1 goal)

CROWE, CHRIS *Born:* 11.6.39 (Newcastle) *Club:* Wolverhampton Wanderers *Caps:* 1

1962–63

3 Oct 1962	*v* France (ECQ)	Sheffield Wednesday	1–1

CUNNINGHAM, LAURIE *Born:* 8.3.56 (Archway) *Clubs:* West Bromwich Albion, Real Madrid *Caps:* 6

1978–79 (with West Bromwich Albion)

23 May 1979	v Wales	Wembley	0–0
10 June 1979	*v* Sweden	Stockholm	0–0
13 June 1979	*v* Austria (sub)	Vienna	3–4

1979–80 (with Real Madrid)

6 Feb 1980	*v* Eire (ECQ)	Wembley	2–0
26 March 1980	*v* Spain (sub)	Barcelona	2–0

1980–81

15 Oct 1980	*v* Romania (sub) (WCQ)	Bucharest	1–2

CURLE, KEITH. *Born:* 14.11.63 (Bristol) *Club:* Manchester City *Caps:* 3

1991–92

29 April 1992	*v* CIS (sub)	Moscow	2–2
12 May 1992	*v* Hungary	Budapest	1–0
11 June 1992	*v* Denmark (EC)	Malmo	0–0

CURRIE, ANTHONY W. *Born:* 1.1.50 (Edgware) *Clubs:* Sheffield United, Leeds United
Caps: 17 *Goals:* 3

1971–72 (with Sheffield United)
23 May 1972	*v* Northern Ireland	Wembley	0–1

1972–73
10 June 1973	*v* USSR	Moscow	2–1
14 June 1973	*v* Italy	Turin	0–2

1973–74
26 Sept 1973	*v* Austria	Wembley	7–0 (1 goal)
17 Oct 1973	*v* Poland (WCQ)	Wembley	1–1
14 Nov 1973	*v* Italy	Wembley	0–1

1975–76
3 Sept 1975	*v* Switzerland	Basle	2–1

1977–78 (with Leeds United)
19 April 1978	*v* Brazil	Wembley	1–1
13 May 1978	*v* Wales (sub)	Cardiff	3–1 (1 goal)
16 May 1978	*v* Northern Ireland	Wembley	1–0
20 May 1978	*v* Scotland	Glasgow	1–0
24 May 1978	*v* Hungary (sub)	Wembley	4–1 (1 goal)

1978–79
29 Nov 1978	*v* Czechoslovakia	Wembley	1–0
7 Feb 1979	*v* Northern Ireland (ECQ)	Wembley	4–0
19 May 1979	*v* Northern Ireland	Belfast	2–0
23 May 1979	*v* Wales	Wembley	0–0
10 June 1979	*v* Sweden	Stockholm	0–0

DALEY, ANTHONY M. *Born:* 18.10.67 (Birmingham) *Club:* Aston Villa *Caps:* 7

1991–92
13 Nov 1991	*v* Poland (sub) (ECQ)	Poznan	1–1
29 April 1992	*v* CIS	Moscow	2–2
12 May 1992	*v* Hungary	Budapest	1–0
17 May 1992	*v* Brazil	Wembley	1–1
3 June 1992	*v* Finland (sub)	Helsinki	2–1
11 June 1992	*v* Denmark (sub) (EC)	Malmo	0–0
17 June 1992	*v* Sweden (EC)	Stockholm	1–2

DAVENPORT, PETER *Born:* 24.3.61 (Birkenhead) *Club:* Nottingham Forest *Caps:* 1

1984–5
25 March 1985	*v* Eire (sub)	Wembley	2–1

DEANE, BRIAN C. *Born:* 17.2.68 (Leeds) *Club:* Sheffield United: *Caps:* 3

1990–91
3 June 1991	*v* New Zealand (sub)	Auckland	1–0
8 June 1991	*v* New Zealand	Wellington	2–0

1992–93
9 Sept 1992	*v* Spain (sub)	Santander	0–1

DEELEY, NORMAN V. *Born:* 30.11.33 (Wednesbury) *Club:* Wolverhampton Wanderers
Caps: 2

1958–59			
13 May 1959	*v* Brazil	Rio de Janeiro	0–2
17 May 1959	*v* Peru	Lima	1–4

DEVONSHIRE, ALAN *Born:* 13.4.56 (London) *Club:* West Ham United *Caps:* 8

1979–80			
20 May 1980	*v* Northern Ireland	Wembley	1–1
31 May 1980	*v* Australia (sub)	Sydney	2–1
1981–82			
25 May 1982	*v* Holland	Wembley	2–0
2 June 1982	*v* Iceland	Reykjavik	1–1
1982–83			
13 Oct 1982	*v* West Germany	Wembley	1–2
23 Feb 1983	*v* Wales	Wembley	2–1
30 March 1983	*v* Greece (ECQ)	Wembley	0–0
1983–84			
16 Nov 1983	*v* Luxembourg (ECQ)	Luxembourg	4–0

DICKINSON, JIMMY W. *Born:* 24.4.25 (Alton) *Club:* Portsmouth *Caps:* 48

1948–49			
18 May 1949	*v* Norway	Oslo	4–1
22 May 1949	*v* France	Paris	3–1
1949–50			
21 Sept 1949	*v* Eire	Everton	0–2
15 Oct 1949	*v* Wales (WCQ)	Cardiff	4–1
15 April 1950	*v* Scotland (WCQ)	Glasgow	1–0
14 May 1950	*v* Portugal	Lisbon	5–3
18 May 1950	*v* Belgium	Brussels	4–1
25 June 1950	*v* Chile (WC)	Rio de Janeiro	2–0
29 June 1950	*v* USA (WC)	Belo Horizonte	0–1
2 July 1950	*v* Spain (WC)	Rio de Janeiro	0–1
1950–51			
7 Oct 1950	*v* Northern Ireland	Belfast	4–1
15 Nov 1950	*v* Wales	Sunderland	4–2
22 Nov 1950	*v* Yugoslavia	Arsenal	2–2
1951–52			
20 Oct 1951	*v* Wales	Cardiff	1–1
14 Nov 1951	*v* Northern Ireland	Aston Villa	2–0
28 Nov 1951	*v* Austria	Wembley	2–2
5 April 1952	*v* Scotland	Glasgow	2–1
18 May 1952	*v* Italy	Florence	1–1
25 May 1952	*v* Austria	Vienna	3–2
28 May 1952	*v* Switzerland	Zurich	3–0

1952–53

4 Oct 1952	v Northern Ireland	Belfast	2–2
12 Nov 1952	v Wales	Wembley	5–2
26 Nov 1952	v Belgium	Wembley	5–0
18 April 1953	v Scotland	Wembley	2–2
17 May 1953	v Argentina	Buenos Aires	0–0†
24 May 1953	v Chile	Santiago	2–1
31 May 1953	v Uruguay	Montevideo	1–2
8 June 1953	v USA	New York	6–3

1953–54

10 Oct 1953	v Wales (WCQ)	Cardiff	4–1
21 Oct 1953	v FIFA (Rest of Europe)	Wembley	4–4
11 Nov 1953	v Northern Ireland (WCQ)	Everton	3–1
25 Nov 1953	v Hungary	Wembley	3–6
3 April 1954	v Scotland (WCQ)	Glasgow	4–2
16 May 1954	v Yugoslavia	Belgrade	0–1
23 May 1954	v Hungary	Budapest	1–7
17 June 1954	v Belgium (WC)	Basle	4–4
20 June 1954	v Switzerland (WC)	Berne	2–0
26 June 1954	v Uruguay (WC)	Basle	2–4

1954–55

18 May 1955	v Spain	Madrid	1–1
22 May 1955	v Portugal	Oporto	1–3

1955–56

2 Oct 1955	v Denmark	Copenhagen	5–1
22 Oct 1955	v Wales	Cardiff	1–2
2 Nov 1955	v Northern Ireland	Wembley	3–0
30 Nov 1955	v Spain	Wembley	4–1
14 April 1956	v Scotland	Glasgow	1–1

1956–57

14 Nov 1956	v Wales	Wembley	3–1
28 Nov 1956	v Yugoslavia	Wembley	3–0
5 Dec 1956	v Denmark (WCQ)	Wolverhampton	5–2

DITCHBURN, EDWARD G. *Born:* 24.10.21 (Gillingham) *Club:* Tottenham Hotspur
Caps: 6

1948–49

2 Dec 1948	v Switzerland	Arsenal	6–0
13 May 1949	v Sweden	Stockholm	1–3

1952–53

8 June 1953	v USA	New York	6–3

1956–57

14 Nov 1956	v Wales	Wembley	3–1
28 Nov 1956	v Yugoslavia	Wembley	3–0
5 Dec 1956	v Denmark (WCQ)	Wolverhampton	5–2

DIXON, KERRY M. *Born:* 24.7.61 (Luton) *Club:* Chelsea *Caps:* 8 *Goals:* 4

1984–85

9 June 1985	*v* Mexico (sub)	Mexico City	0–1
12 June 1985	*v* West Germany	Mexico City	3–0 (2 goals)
16 June 1985	*v* USA	Los Angeles	5–0 (2 goals)

1985–86

13 Nov 1985	*v* Northern Ireland (WCQ)	Wembley	0–0
26 Feb 1986	*v* Israel	Tel Aviv	2–1
17 May 1986	*v* Mexico (sub)	Los Angeles	3–0
11 June 1986	*v* Poland (sub) (WC)	Monterrey	3–0

1986–87

10 Sept 1986	*v* Sweden	Stockholm	0–1

DIXON, LEE M. *Born:* 17.3.64 (Manchester) *Club:* Arsenal *Caps:* 20 *Goals:* 1

1989–90

25 April 1990	*v* Czechoslovakia	Wembley	4–2

1990–91

12 Sept 1990	*v* Hungary	Wembley	1–0
17 Oct 1990	*v* Poland (ECQ)	Wembley	2–0
14 Nov 1990	*v* Eire (ECQ)	Dublin	1–1
6 Feb 1991	*v* Cameroon	Wembley	2–0
27 March 1991	*v* Eire (ECQ)	Wembley	1–1 (1 goal)
1 May 1991	*v* Turkey (ECQ)	Izmir	1–0
25 May 1991	*v* Argentina	Wembley	2–2

1991–92

11 Sept 1991	*v* Germany	Wembley	0–1
16 Oct 1991	*v* Turkey (ECQ)	Wembley	1–0
13 Nov 1991	*v* Poland (ECQ)	Poznan	1–1
25 March 1992	*v* Czechoslovakia (sub)	Prague	2–2

1992–93

9 Sept 1992	*v* Spain	Santander	0–1
14 Oct 1992	*v* Norway (WCQ)	Wembley	1–1
18 Nov 1992	*v* Turkey (WCQ)	Wembley	4–0
17 Feb 1993	*v* San Marino (WCQ)	Wembley	6–0
31 March 1993	*v* Turkey (WCQ)	Izmir	2–0
28 April 1993	*v* Holland (WCQ)	Wembley	2–2
2 June 1993	*v* Norway (WCQ)	Oslo	0–2
9 June 1993	*v* USA (USC)	Boston	0–2

DOBSON, MARTIN J. *Born:* 14.2.48 (Blackburn) *Clubs:* Burnley, Everton *Caps:* 5

1973–74 (with Burnley)

3 April 1974	*v* Portugal	Lisbon	0–0
29 May 1974	*v* East Germany	Leipzig	1–1
1 June 1974	*v* Bulgaria	Sofia	1–0
5 June 1974	*v* Yugoslavia	Belgrade	2–2

1974–75 (with Everton)

| 30 Oct 1974 | *v* Czechoslovakia (ECQ) | Wembley | 3–0 |

DORIGO, ANTHONY R. *Born:* 31.12.65 (Melbourne) *Clubs:* Chelsea, Leeds United
Caps: 14

1989–90 (with Chelsea)

13 Dec 1989	*v* Yugoslavia (sub)	Wembley	2–1
25 April 1990	*v* Czechoslovakia (sub)	Wembley	4–2
15 May 1990	*v* Denmark (sub)	Wembley	1–0
7 July 1990	*v* Italy (WC)	Bari	1–2

1990–91

| 12 Sept 1990 | *v* Hungary (sub) | Wembley | 1–0 |
| 21 May 1991 | *v* USSR | Wembley | 3–1 |

1991–92 (with Leeds United)

11 Sept 1991	*v* Germany	Wembley	0–1
25 March 1992	*v* Czechoslovakia (sub)	Prague	2–2
12 May 1992	*v* Hungary	Budapest	1–0
17 May 1992	*v* Brazil	Wembley	1–1

1992–93

17 Feb 1993	*v* San Marino (WCQ)	Wembley	6–0
29 May 1993	*v* Poland (WCQ)	Chorzow	1–1
9 June 1993	*v* USA (USC)	Boston	0–2
13 June 1993	*v* Brazil (USC)	Washington	1–1

DOUGLAS, BRYAN *Born:* 27.5.34 (Blackburn) *Club:* Blackburn Rovers *Caps:* 36
Goals: 11

1957–58

19 Oct 1957	*v* Wales	Cardiff	4–0
6 Nov 1957	*v* Northern Ireland	Wembley	2–3
27 Nov 1957	*v* France	Wembley	4–0
19 April 1958	*v* Scotland	Glasgow	4–0 (1 goal)
7 May 1958	*v* Portugal	Wembley	2–1
11 May 1958	*v* Yugoslavia	Belgrade	0–5
18 May 1958	*v* USSR	Moscow	1–1
8 June 1958	*v* USSR (WC)	Gothenburg	2–2
11 June 1958	*v* Brazil (WC)	Gothenburg	0–0
15 June 1958	*v* Austria (WC)	Boras	2–2

1958–59

| 22 Oct 1958 | *v* USSR | Wembley | 5–0 |
| 11 April 1959 | *v* Scotland | Wembley | 1–0 |

1959–60

| 11 May 1960 | *v* Yugoslavia | Wembley | 3–3 (1 goal) |
| 22 May 1960 | *v* Hungary | Budapest | 0–2 |

1960–61

8 Oct 1960	*v* Northern Ireland	Belfast	5–2 (1 goal)
19 Oct 1960	*v* Luxembourg (WCQ)	Luxembourg	9–0
26 Oct 1960	*v* Spain	Wembley	4–2 (1 goal)

23 Nov 1960	v Wales	Wembley	5–1
15 April 1961	v Scotland	Wembley	9–3 (1 goal)
10 May 1961	v Mexico	Wembley	8–0 (2 goals)
21 May 1961	v Portugal (WCQ)	Lisbon	1–1
24 May 1961	v Italy	Rome	3–2
27 May 1961	v Austria	Vienna	1–3

1961–62

28 Sept 1961	v Luxembourg (WCQ)	Arsenal	4–1
14 Oct 1961	v Wales	Cardiff	1–1 (1 goal)
25 Oct 1961	v Portugal (WCQ)	Wembley	2–0
22 Nov 1961	v Northern Ireland	Wembley	1–1
14 April 1962	v Scotland	Glasgow	0–2
20 May 1962	v Peru	Lima	4–0
31 May 1962	v Hungary (WC)	Rancagua	1–2
2 June 1962	v Argentina (WC)	Rancagua	3–1
7 June 1962	v Bulgaria (WC)	Rancagua	0–0
10 June 1962	v Brazil (WC)	Vina del Mar	1–3

1962–63

6 April 1963	v Scotland	Wembley	1–2 (1 goal)
8 May 1963	v Brazil	Wembley	1–1 (1 goal)
5 June 1963	v Switzerland	Basle	8–1 (1 goal)

DOYLE, MIKE *Born:* 25.11.46 (Manchester) *Club:* Manchester City *Caps:* 5

1975–76

24 March 1976	v Wales (FAWC)	Wrexham	2–1
15 May 1976	v Scotland (sub)	Glasgow	1–2
23 May 1976	v Brazil (USABT)	Los Angeles	0–1
28 May 1976	v Italy (USABT)	New York	3–2

1976–77

9 Feb 1977	v Holland	Wembley	0–2

DUXBURY, MIKE *Born:* 1.9.59 (Accrington) *Club:* Manchester United *Caps:* 10

1983–84

16 Nov 1983	v Luxembourg (ECQ)	Luxembourg	4–0
29 Feb 1984	v France	Paris	0–2
2 May 1984	v Wales	Wrexham	0–1
26 May 1984	v Scotland	Glasgow	1–1
2 June 1984	v USSR	Wembley	0–2
10 June 1984	v Brazil	Rio de Janeiro	2–0
13 June 1984	v Uruguay	Montevideo	0–2
17 June 1984	v Chile	Santiago	0–0

1984–85

12 Sept 1984	v East Germany	Wembley	1–0
17 Oct 1984	v Finland (WCQ)	Wembley	5–0

EASTHAM, GEORGE E. *Born:* 23.9.36 (Blackpool) *Club:* Arsenal *Caps:* 19 *Goals:* 2

1962–63
8 May 1963	v Brazil	Wembley	1–1
20 May 1963	v Czechoslovakia	Bratislava	4–2
2 June 1963	v East Germany	Leipzig	2–1

1963–64
12 Oct 1963	v Wales	Cardiff	4–0
23 Oct 1963	v Rest of the World	Wembley	2–1
20 Nov 1963	v Northern Ireland	Wembley	8–3
11 April 1964	v Scotland	Glasgow	0–1
6 May 1964	v Uruguay	Wembley	2–1
17 May 1964	v Portugal	Lisbon	4–3
24 May 1964	v Eire	Dublin	3–1 (1 goal)
27 May 1964	v USA	New York	10–0
30 May 1964	v Brazil (BJT)	Rio de Janeiro	1–5
6 June 1964	v Argentina (BJT)	Rio de Janeiro	0–1

1964–65
5 May 1965	v Hungary	Wembley	1–0
12 May 1965	v West Germany	Nuremberg	1–0
16 May 1965	v Sweden	Gothenburg	2–1

1965–66
8 Dec 1965	v Spain	Madrid	2–0
5 Jan 1966	v Poland	Everton	1–1
3 July 1966	v Denmark	Copenhagen	2–0 (1 goal)

ECKERSLEY, WILLIAM *Born:* 16.7.26 (Southport) *Club:* Blackburn Rovers *Caps:* 17

1949–50
2 July 1950	v Spain (WC)	Rio de Janeiro	0–1

1950–51
22 Nov 1950	v Yugoslavia	Arsenal	2–2
14 April 1951	v Scotland	Wembley	2–3
9 May 1951	v Argentina	Wembley	2–1
19 May 1951	v Portugal	Everton	5–2

1951–52
28 Nov 1951	v Austria	Wembley	2–2
25 May 1952	v Austria	Vienna	3–2
28 May 1952	v Switzerland	Zurich	3–0

1952–53
4 Oct 1952	v Northern Ireland	Belfast	2–2
17 May 1953	v Argentina	Buenos Aires	0–0†
24 May 1953	v Chile	Santiago	2–1
31 May 1953	v Uruguay	Montevideo	1–2
8 June 1953	v USA	New York	6–3

1953–54
10 Oct 1953	v Wales (WCQ)	Cardiff	4–1
21 Oct 1953	v FIFA (Rest of Europe)	Wembley	4–4

| 11 Nov 1953 | *v* Northern Ireland (WCQ) | Everton | 3–1 |
| 25 Nov 1953 | *v* Hungary | Wembley | 3–6 |

EDWARDS, DUNCAN *Born:* 1.10.36 (Dudley) *Club:* Manchester United *Caps:* 18 *Goals:* 5

1954–55

2 April 1955	*v* Scotland	Wembley	7–2
15 May 1955	*v* France	Paris	0–1
18 May 1955	*v* Spain	Madrid	1–1
22 May 1955	*v* Portugal	Oporto	1–3

1955–56

14 April 1956	*v* Scotland	Glasgow	1–1
9 May 1956	*v* Brazil	Wembley	4–2
16 May 1956	*v* Sweden	Stockholm	0–0
20 May 1956	*v* Finland	Helsinki	5–1
26 May 1956	*v* West Germany	Berlin	3–1 (1 goal)

1956–57

6 Oct 1956	*v* Northern Ireland	Belfast	1–1
5 Dec 1956	*v* Denmark (WCQ)	Wolverhampton	5–2 (2 goals)
6 April 1957	*v* Scotland	Wembley	2–1 (1 goal)
8 May 1957	*v* Eire (WCQ)	Wembley	5–1
15 May 1957	*v* Denmark (WCQ)	Copenhagen	4–1
19 May 1957	*v* Eire (WCQ)	Dublin	1–1

1957–58

19 Oct 1957	*v* Wales	Cardiff	4–0
6 Nov 1957	*v* Northern Ireland	Wembley	2–3 (1 goal)
27 Nov 1957	*v* France	Wembley	4–0

ELLERINGTON, WILLIAM *Born:* 30.6.23 (Southampton) *Club:* Southampton *Caps:* 2

1948–49

| 18 May 1949 | *v* Norway | Oslo | 4–1 |
| 22 May 1949 | *v* France | Paris | 3–1 |

ELLIOTT, WILLIAM H. *Born:* 20.3.25 (Bradford) *Club:* Burnley *Caps:* 5 *Goals:* 3

1951–52

| 18 May 1952 | *v* Italy | Florence | 1–1 |
| 25 May 1952 | *v* Austria | Vienna | 3–2 |

1952–53

4 Oct 1952	*v* Northern Ireland	Belfast	2–2 (1 goal)
12 Nov 1952	*v* Wales	Wembley	5–2
26 Nov 1952	*v* Belgium	Wembley	5–0 (2 goals)

FANTHAM, JOHN *Born:* 6.2.39 (Sheffield) *Club:* Sheffield Wednesday *Caps:* 1

1961–62

| 28 Sept 1961 | *v* Luxembourg (WCQ) | Arsenal | 4–1 |

FASHANU, JOHN *Born:* 18.9.62 (Kensington) *Club:* Wimbledon *Caps:* 2

1988–89

| 23 May 1989 | *v* Chile (RC) | Wembley | 0–0 |
| 27 May 1989 | *v* Scotland (RC) | Glasgow | 2–0 |

FENWICK, TERRY *Born:* 17.11.59 (Durham) *Clubs:* Queens Park Rangers, Tottenham Hotspur *Caps:* 20

1983–84 (with Queens Park Rangers)

2 May 1984	*v* Wales (sub)	Wrexham	0–1
26 May 1984	*v* Scotland	Glasgow	1–1
2 June 1984	*v* USSR	Wembley	0–2
10 June 1984	*v* Brazil	Rio de Janeiro	2–0
13 June 1984	*v* Uruguay	Montevideo	0–2
17 June 1984	*v* Chile	Santiago	0–0

1984–85

22 May 1985	*v* Finland (WCQ)	Helsinki	1–1
25 May 1985	*v* Scotland (RC)	Glasgow	0–1
9 June 1985	*v* Mexico	Mexico City	0–1
16 June 1985	*v* USA	Los Angeles	5–0

1985–86

11 Sept 1985	*v* Romania (WCQ)	Wembley	1–1
16 Oct 1985	*v* Turkey (WCQ)	Wembley	5–0
13 Nov 1985	*v* Northern Ireland (WCQ)	Wembley	0–0
29 Jan 1986	*v* Egypt	Cairo	4–0
17 May 1986	*v* Mexico	Los Angeles	3–0
3 June 1986	*v* Portugal (WC)	Monterrey	0–1
6 June 1986	*v* Morocco (WC)	Monterrey	0–0
11 June 1986	*v* Poland (WC)	Monterrey	3–0
22 June 1986	*v* Argentina (WC)	Mexico City	1–2

1987–88 (with Tottenham Hotspur)

| 17 Feb 1988 | *v* Israel (sub) | Tel Aviv | 0–0 |

FERDINAND, LES *Born:* 18.12.66 (London) *Club:* Queens Park Rangers *Caps:* 4 *Goals:* 1

1992–93

17 Feb 1993	*v* San Marino (WCQ)	Wembley	6–0 (1 goal)
28 April 1993	*v* Holland (WCQ)	Wembley	2–2
2 June 1993	*v* Norway (WCQ)	Oslo	0–2
9 June 1993	*v* USA (USC)	Boston	0–2

FINNEY, TOM *Born:* 5.4.22 (Preston) *Club:* Preston North End *Caps:* 76 *Goals:* 30

1946–47

28 Sept 1946	*v* Northern Ireland	Belfast	7–2 (1 goal)
30 Sept 1946	*v* Eire	Dublin	1–0 (1 goal)
19 Oct 1946	*v* Wales	Manchester City	3–0
27 Nov 1946	*v* Holland	Huddersfield	8–2 (1 goal)
3 May 1947	*v* France	Arsenal	3–0 (1 goal)

27 May 1947	*v* Portugal	Lisbon	10–0 (1 goal)
1947–48			
21 Sept 1947	*v* Belgium	Brussels	5–2 (2 goals)
18 Oct 1947	*v* Wales	Cardiff	3–0 (1 goal)
5 Nov 1947	*v* Northern Ireland	Everton	2–2
19 Nov 1947	*v* Sweden	Arsenal	4–2
10 April 1948	*v* Scotland	Glasgow	2–0 (1 goal)
16 May 1948	*v* Italy	Turin	4–0 (2 goals)
1948–49			
9 Oct 1948	*v* Northern Ireland	Belfast	6–2
10 Nov 1948	*v* Wales	Aston Villa	1–0 (1 goal)
9 April 1949	*v* Scotland	Wembley	1–3
13 May 1949	*v* Sweden	Stockholm	1–3 (1 goal)
18 May 1949	*v* Norway	Oslo	4–1 (1 goal)
22 May 1949	*v* France	Paris	3–1
1949–50			
21 Sept 1949	*v* Eire	Everton	0–2
15 Oct 1949	*v* Wales (WCQ)	Cardiff	4–1
16 Nov 1949	*v* Northern Ireland (WCQ)	Manchester City	9–2
30 Nov 1949	*v* Italy	Tottenham	2–0
15 April 1950	*v* Scotland (WCQ)	Glasgow	1–0
14 May 1950	*v* Portugal	Lisbon	5–3 (4 goals)
18 May 1950	*v* Belgium	Brussels	4–1
25 June 1950	*v* Chile (WC)	Rio de Janeiro	2–0
29 June 1950	*v* USA (WC)	Belo Horizonte	0–1
2 July 1950	*v* Spain (WC)	Rio de Janeiro	0–1
1950–51			
15 Nov 1950	*v* Wales	Sunderland	4–2
14 April 1951	*v* Scotland	Wembley	2–3 (1 goal)
9 May 1951	*v* Argentina	Wembley	2–1
19 May 1951	*v* Portugal	Everton	5–2 (1 goal)
1951–52			
3 Oct 1951	*v* France	Arsenal	2–2
20 Oct 1951	*v* Wales	Cardiff	1–1
14 Nov 1951	*v* Northern Ireland	Aston Villa	2–0
5 April 1952	*v* Scotland	Glasgow	2–1
18 May 1952	*v* Italy	Florence	1–1
25 May 1952	*v* Austria	Vienna	3–2
28 May 1952	*v* Switzerland	Zurich	3–0
1952–53			
4 Oct 1952	*v* Northern Ireland	Belfast	2–2
12 Nov 1952	*v* Wales	Wembley	5–2 (1 goal)
26 Nov 1952	*v* Belgium	Wembley	5–0
18 April 1953	*v* Scotland	Wembley	2–2
17 May 1953	*v* Argentina	Buenos Aires	0–0†
24 May 1953	*v* Chile	Santiago	2–1
31 May 1953	*v* Uruguay	Montevideo	1–2
8 June 1953	*v* USA	New York	6–3 (2 goals)

1953–54

10 Oct 1953	*v* Wales (WCQ)	Cardiff	4–1
3 April 1954	*v* Scotland (WCQ)	Glasgow	4–2
16 May 1954	*v* Yugoslavia	Belgrade	0–1
23 May 1954	*v* Hungary	Budapest	1–7
17 June 1954	*v* Belgium (WC)	Basle	4–4
20 June 1954	*v* Switzerland (WC)	Berne	2–0
26 June 1954	*v* Uruguay (WC)	Basle	2–4 (1 goal)

1954–55

1 Dec 1954	*v* West Germany	Wembley	3–1

1955–56

2 Oct 1955	*v* Denmark	Copenhagen	5–1
22 Oct 1955	*v* Wales	Cardiff	1–2
2 Nov 1955	*v* Northern Ireland	Wembley	3–0 (1 goal)
30 Nov 1955	*v* Spain	Wembley	4–1 (1 goal)
14 April 1956	*v* Scotland	Glasgow	1–1

1956–57

14 Nov 1956	*v* Wales	Wembley	3–1 (1 goal)
28 Nov 1956	*v* Yugoslavia	Wembley	3–0
5 Dec 1956	*v* Denmark (WCQ)	Wolverhampton	5–2
6 April 1957	*v* Scotland	Wembley	2–1
8 May 1957	*v* Eire (WCQ)	Wembley	5–1
15 May 1957	*v* Denmark (WCQ)	Copenhagen	4–1
19 May 1957	*v* Eire (WCQ)	Dublin	1–1

1957–58

19 Oct 1957	*v* Wales	Cardiff	4–0 (1 goal)
27 Nov 1957	*v* France	Wembley	4–0
19 April 1958	*v* Scotland	Glasgow	4–0
7 May 1958	*v* Portugal	Wembley	2–1
11 May 1958	*v* Yugoslavia	Belgrade	0–5
18 May 1958	*v* USSR	Moscow	1–1
8 June 1958	*v* USSR (WC)	Gothenburg	2–2 (1 goal)

1958–59

4 Oct 1958	*v* Northern Ireland	Belfast	3–3 (1 goal)
22 Oct 1958	*v* USSR	Wembley	5–0

FLOWERS, RON *Born:* 28.7.34 (Edlington) *Club:* Wolverhampton Wanderers *Caps:* 49
Goals: 10

1954–55

15 May 1955	*v* France	Paris	0–1

1958–59

26 Nov 1958	*v* Wales	Aston Villa	2–2
11 April 1959	*v* Scotland	Wembley	1–0
6 May 1959	*v* Italy	Wembley	2–2
13 May 1959	*v* Brazil	Rio de Janeiro	0–2
17 May 1959	*v* Peru	Lima	1–4
24 May 1959	*v* Mexico (sub)	Mexico City	1–2
28 May 1959	*v* USA	Los Angeles	8–1 (2 goals)

1959–60

17 Oct 1959	*v* Wales	Cardiff	1–1
28 Oct 1959	*v* Sweden	Wembley	2–3
18 Nov 1959	*v* Northern Ireland	Wembley	2–1
9 April 1960	*v* Scotland	Glasgow	1–1
11 May 1960	*v* Yugoslavia	Wembley	3–3
15 May 1960	*v* Spain	Madrid	0–3
22 May 1960	*v* Hungary	Budapest	0–2

1960–61

8 Oct 1960	*v* Northern Ireland	Belfast	5–2
19 Oct 1960	*v* Luxembourg (WCQ)	Luxembourg	9–0
26 Oct 1960	*v* Spain	Wembley	4–2
23 Nov 1960	*v* Wales	Wembley	5–1
15 April 1961	*v* Scotland	Wembley	9–3
10 May 1961	*v* Mexico	Wembley	8–0 (1 goal)
21 May 1961	*v* Portugal (WCQ)	Lisbon	1–1 (1 goal)
24 May 1961	*v* Italy	Rome	3–2
27 May 1961	*v* Austria	Vienna	1–3

1961–62

28 Sept 1961	*v* Luxembourg (WCQ)	Arsenal	4–1
14 Oct 1961	*v* Wales	Cardiff	1–1
25 Oct 1961	*v* Portugal (WCQ)	Wembley	2–0
22 Nov 1961	*v* Northern Ireland	Wembley	1–1
4 April 1962	*v* Austria	Wembley	3–1 (1 goal)
14 April 1962	*v* Scotland	Glasgow	0–2
9 May 1962	*v* Switzerland	Wembley	3–1 (1 goal)
20 May 1962	*v* Peru	Lima	4–0 (1 goal)
23 May 1962	*v* Hungary (WC)	Rancagua	1–2 (1 goal)
2 June 1962	*v* Argentina (WC)	Rancagua	3–1 (1 goal)
7 June 1962	*v* Bulgaria (WC)	Rancagua	0–0
10 June 1962	*v* Brazil (WC)	Vina del Mar	1–3

1962–63

3 Oct 1962	*v* France (ECQ)	Sheffield Wednesday	1–1 (1 goal)
20 Oct 1962	*v* Northern Ireland	Belfast	3–1
21 Nov 1962	*v* Wales	Wembley	4–0
27 Feb 1963	*v* France (ECQ)	Paris	2–5
6 April 1963	*v* Scotland	Wembley	1–2
5 June 1963	*v* Switzerland	Basle	8–1

1963–64

24 May 1964	*v* Eire	Dublin	3–1
27 May 1964	*v* USA*	New York	10–0
4 June 1964	*v* Portugal (BJT)	Sao Paulo	1–1

1964–65

18 Nov 1964	*v* Wales*	Wembley	2–1
9 Dec 1964	*v* Holland*	Amsterdam	1–1
12 May 1965	*v* West Germany	Nuremberg	1–0

1965–66

29 June 1966	*v* Norway	Oslo	6–1

FLOWERS, TIM *Born:* 3.2.67 (Kenilworth) *Club:* Southampton *Caps:* 1

1992–93

13 June 1993	*v* Brazil (USC)	Washington	1–1

FOSTER, STEVE B. *Born:* 24.9.57 (Portsmouth) *Club:* Brighton & Hove Albion *Caps:* 3

1981–82

23 Feb 1982	*v* Northern Ireland	Wembley	4–0
25 May 1982	*v* Holland	Wembley	2–0
25 June, 1982	*v* Kuwait (WC)	Bilbao	1–0

FOULKES, WILLIAM A. *Born:* 5.1.32 (St Helens) *Club:* Manchester United *Caps:* 1

1954–55

2 Oct 1954	*v* Northern Ireland	Belfast	2–0

FRANCIS, GERRY C. J. *Born:* 6.12.51 (Chiswick) *Club:* Queens Park Rangers *Caps:* 12 *Goals:* 3

1974–75

30 Oct 1974	*v* Czechoslovakia (ECQ)	Wembley	3–0
20 Nov 1974	*v* Portugal (ECQ)	Wembley	0–0
21 May 1975	*v* Wales	Wembley	2–2
24 May 1975	*v* Scotland	Wembley	5–1 (2 goals)

1975–76

3 Sept 1975	*v* Switzerland*	Basle	2–1
30 Oct 1975	*v* Czechoslovakia* (ECQ)	Bratislava	1–2
19 Nov 1975	*v* Portugal* (ECQ)	Lisbon	1–1
8 May 1976	*v* Wales*	Cardiff	1–0
11 May 1976	*v* Northern Ireland*	Wembley	4–0 (1 goal)
15 May 1976	*v* Scotland*	Glasgow	1–2
23 May 1976	*v* Brazil* (USABT)	Los Angeles	0–1
13 June 1976	*v* Finland* (WCQ)	Helsinki	4–1

FRANCIS, TREVOR J. *Born:* 19.4.54 (Plymouth) *Clubs:* Birmingham City, Nottingham Forest, Manchester City, Sampdoria *Caps:* 52 *Goals:* 12

1976–77 (with Birmingham City)

9 Feb 1977	*v* Holland	Wembley	0–2
30 March 1977	*v* Luxembourg (WCQ)	Wembley	5–0 (1 goal)
4 June 1977	*v* Scotland	Wembley	1–2
8 June 1977	*v* Brazil	Rio de Janeiro	0–0

1977–78

7 Sept 1977	*v* Switzerland	Wembley	0–0
12 Oct 1977	*v* Luxembourg (WCQ)	Luxembourg	2–0
16 Nov 1977	*v* Italy (sub) (WCQ)	Wembley	2–0
22 Feb 1978	*v* West Germany (sub)	Munich	1–2
19 April 1978	*v* Brazil	Wembley	1–1
13 May 1978	*v* Wales	Cardiff	3–1
20 May 1978	*v* Scotland	Glasgow	1–0

24 May 1978	v Hungary	Wembley	4–1 (1 goal)

1978–79 (with Nottingham Forest)

6 June 1979	v Bulgaria (sub) (ECQ)	Sofia	3–0
10 June 1979	v Sweden	Stockholm	0–0
13 June 1979	v Austria (sub)	Vienna	3–4

1979–80

17 Oct 1979	v Northern Ireland (ECQ)	Belfast	5–1 (2 goals)
22 Nov 1979	v Bulgaria (ECQ)	Wembley	2–0
26 March 1980	v Spain	Barcelona	2–0 (1 goal)

1980–81

25 March 1981	v Spain	Wembley	1–2
29 April 1981	v Romania (WCQ)	Wembley	0–0
23 May 1981	v Scotland (sub)	Wembley	0–1
30 May 1981	v Switzerland (WCQ)	Basle	1–2

1981–82 (with Manchester City)

9 Sept 1981	v Norway (WCQ)	Oslo	1–2
23 Feb 1982	v Northern Ireland	Wembley	4–0
27 April 1982	v Wales	Cardiff	1–0 (1 goal)
29 May 1982	v Scotland (sub)	Glasgow	1–0
3 June 1982	v Finland (sub)	Helsinki	4–1
16 June 1982	v France (WC)	Bilbao	3–1
20 June 1982	v Czechoslovakia (WC)	Bilbao	2–0 (1 goal)
25 June 1982	v Kuwait (WC)	Bilbao	1–0 (1 goal)
29 June 1982	v West Germany (WC)	Madrid	0–0
5 July 1982	v Spain (WC)	Madrid	0–0

1982–83 (with Sampdoria)

22 Sept 1982	v Denmark (ECQ)	Copenhagen	2–2 (2 goals)
30 March 1983	v Greece (ECQ)	Wembley	0–0
27 April 1983	v Hungary (ECQ)	Wembley	2–0 (1 goal)
28 May 1983	v Northern Ireland	Belfast	0–0
1 June 1983	v Scotland	Wembley	2–0
12 June 1983	v Australia	Sydney	0–0
15 June 1983	v Australia	Brisbane	1–0
19 June 1983	v Australia	Melbourne	1–1 (1 goal)

1983–84

21 Sept 1983	v Denmark (ECQ)	Wembley	0–1
4 April 1984	v Northern Ireland	Wembley	1–0
2 June 1984	v USSR	Wembley	0–2

1984–85

12 Sept 1984	v East Germany (sub)	Wembley	1–0
14 Nov 1984	v Turkey (sub) (WCQ)	Istanbul	8–0
27 Feb 1985	v N. Ireland (sub) (WCQ)	Belfast	1–0
1 May 1985	v Romania (WCQ)	Bucharest	0–0
22 May 1985	v Finland (WCQ)	Helsinki	1–1
25 May 1985	v Scotland (RC)	Glasgow	0–1
6 June 1985	v Italy	Mexico City	1–2
9 June 1985	v Mexico	Mexico City	0–1

1985–86
23 April 1986   *v* Scotland   Wembley   2–1

FRANKLIN, NEIL C. *Born:* 24.1.22 (Stoke) *Club:* Stoke City *Caps:* 27

1946–47
28 Sept 1946   *v* Northern Ireland   Belfast   7–2
30 Sept 1946   *v* Eire   Dublin   1–0
19 Oct 1946   *v* Wales   Manchester City   3–0
27 Nov 1946   *v* Holland   Huddersfield   8–2
12 April 1947   *v* Scotland   Wembley   1–1
3 May 1947   *v* France   Arsenal   3–0
18 May 1947   *v* Switzerland   Zurich   0–1
27 May 1947   *v* Portugal   Lisbon   10–0

1947–48
21 Sept 1947   *v* Belgium   Brussels   5–2
18 Oct 1947   *v* Wales   Cardiff   3–0
5 Nov 1947   *v* Northern Ireland   Everton   2–2
19 Nov 1947   *v* Sweden   Arsenal   4–2
10 April 1948   *v* Scotland   Glasgow   2–0
16 May 1948   *v* Italy   Turin   4–0

1948–49
26 Sept 1948   *v* Denmark   Copenhagen   0–0
9 Oct 1948   *v* Northern Ireland   Belfast   6–2
10 Nov 1948   *v* Wales   Aston Villa   1–0
1 Dec 1948   *v* Switzerland   Arsenal   6–0
9 April 1949   *v* Scotland   Wembley   1–3
13 May 1949   *v* Sweden   Stockholm   1–3
18 May 1949   *v* Norway   Oslo   4–1
22 May 1949   *v* France   Paris   3–1

1949–50
21 Sept 1949   *v* Eire   Everton   0–2
15 Oct 1949   *v* Wales (WCQ)   Cardiff   4–1
16 Nov 1949   *v* Northern Ireland (WCQ)   Manchester City   9–2
30 Nov 1949   *v* Italy   Tottenham   2–0
15 April 1950   *v* Scotland (WCQ)   Glasgow   1–0

FROGGATT, JACK *Born:* 17.11.22 (Sheffield) *Club:* Portsmouth *Caps:* 13 *Goals:* 2

1949–50
16 Nov 1949   *v* Northern Ireland (WCQ)   Manchester City   9–2 (1 goal)
30 Nov 1949   *v* Italy   Tottenham   2–0
1950–51
14 April 1951   *v* Scotland   Wembley   2–3
1951–52
28 Nov 1951   *v* Austria   Wembley   2–2
5 April 1952   *v* Scotland   Glasgow   2–1
18 May 1952   *v* Italy   Florence   1–1
25 May 1952   *v* Austria   Vienna   3–2

28 May 1952	v Switzerland	Zurich	3–0

1952–53

4 Oct 1952	v Northern Ireland	Belfast	2–2
12 Nov 1952	v Wales	Wembley	5–2 (1 goal)
26 Nov 1952	v Belgium	Wembley	5–0
18 April 1953	v Scotland	Wembley	2–2
8 June 1953	v USA	New York	6–3

FROGGATT, REDFERN *Born:* 23.8.24 (Sheffield) *Club:* Sheffield Wednesday *Caps:* 4 *Goals:* 2

1952–53

12 Nov 1952	v Wales	Wembley	5–2
26 Nov 1952	v Belgium	Wembley	5–0 (1 goal)
18 April 1953	v Scotland	Wembley	2–2
8 June 1953	v USA	New York	6–3 (1 goal)

GARRETT, TOM *Born:* 28.2.27 (Durham) *Club:* Blackpool *Caps:* 3

1951–52

5 April 1952	v Scotland	Glasgow	2–1
18 May 1952	v Italy	Florence	1–1

1953–54

10 Oct 1953	v Wales (WCQ)	Cardiff	4–1

GASCOIGNE, PAUL J. *Born:* 26.5.67 (Gateshead) *Clubs:* Tottenham Hotspur, Lazio *Caps:* 27 *Goals:* 5

1988–89 (with Tottenham Hotspur)

14 Sept 1988	v Denmark (sub)	Wembley	1–0
16 Nov 1988	v Saudi Arabia (sub)	Riyadh	1–1
26 April 1989	v Albania (sub) (WCQ)	Wembley	5–0 (1 goal)
23 May 1989	v Chile (RC)	Wembley	0–0
27 May 1989	v Scotland (sub) (RC)	Glasgow	2–0

1989–90

6 Sept 1989	v Sweden (sub) (WCQ)	Stockholm	0–0
28 March 1990	v Brazil (sub)	Wembley	1–0
25 April 1990	v Czechoslovakia	Wembley	4–2 (1 goal)
15 May 1990	v Denmark	Wembley	1–0
22 May 1990	v Uruguay	Wembley	1–2
2 June 1990	v Tunisia	Tunis	1–1
11 June 1990	v Eire (WC)	Cagliari	1–1
16 June 1990	v Holland (WC)	Cagliari	0–0
21 June 1990	v Egypt (WC)	Cagliari	1–0
26 June 1990	v Belgium (WC)	Bologna	1–0 (aet)
1 July 1990	v Cameroon (WC)	Naples	3–2 (aet)
4 July 1990	v West Germany (WC)	Turin	1–1 (aet)

1990–91

12 Sept 1990	v Hungary	Wembley	1–0
17 Oct 1990	v Poland (ECQ)	Wembley	2–0

6 Feb 1991	*v* Cameroon	Wembley	2–0

1992–93 (with Lazio)

14 Oct 1992	*v* Norway (WCQ)	Wembley	1–1
18 Nov 1992	*v* Turkey (WCQ)	Wembley	4–0 (2 goals)
17 Feb 1993	*v* San Marino (WCQ)	Wembley	6–0
31 March 1993	*v* Turkey (WCQ)	Izmir	2–0 (1 goal)
28 April 1993	*v* Holland (WCQ)	Wembley	2–2
29 May 1993	*v* Poland (WCQ)	Chorzow	1–1
2 June 1993	*v* Norway (WCQ)	Oslo	0–2

GATES, ERIC L. *Born:* 28.6.55 (Ferryhill) *Club:* Ipswich Town *Caps:* 2

1980–81

10 Sept 1980	*v* Norway (WCQ)	Wembley	4–0
15 Oct 1980	*v* Romania (WCQ)	Bucharest	1–2

GEORGE, CHARLIE F. *Born:* 10.10.50 (Islington) *Club:* Derby County *Caps:* 1

1976–77

8 Sept 1976	*v* Eire	Wembley	1–1

GIDMAN, JOHN *Born:* 10.1.54 (Liverpool) *Club:* Aston Villa *Caps:* 1

1976–77

30 March 1977	*v* Luxembourg (WCQ)	Wembley	5–0

GILLARD, IAN T. *Born:* 9.10.50 (Hammersmith) *Club:* Queens Park Rangers *Caps:* 3

1974–75

12 March 1975	*v* West Germany	Wembley	2–0
21 May 1975	*v* Wales	Wembley	2–2

1975–76

30 Oct 1975	*v* Czechoslovakia (ECQ)	Bratislava	1–2

GODDARD, PAUL *Born:* 12.10.59 (Harlington) *Club:* West Ham United *Caps:* 1
Goals: 1

1981–82

2 June 1982	*v* Iceland (sub)	Reykjavik	1–1 (1 goal)

GRAINGER, COLIN *Born:* 10.6.33 (Wakefield) *Clubs:* Sheffield United, Sunderland
Caps: 7 *Goals:* 3

1955–56 (with Sheffield United)

9 May 1956	*v* Brazil	Wembley	4–2 (2 goals)
16 May 1956	*v* Sweden	Stockholm	0–0
20 May 1956	*v* Finland	Helsinki	5–1
26 May 1956	*v* West Germany	Berlin	3–1 (1 goal)

1956–57

6 Oct 1956	*v* Northern Ireland	Belfast	1–1
14 Nov 1956	*v* Wales	Wembley	3–1

(with Sunderland)

| 6 April 1957 | *v* Scotland | Wembley | 2–1 |

GRAY, ANDY *Born:* 22.2.64 (Lambeth) *Club:* Crystal Palace *Caps:* 1

1991–92

| 13 Nov 1991 | *v* Poland (ECQ) | Poznan | 1–1 |

GREAVES, JIMMY *Born:* 20.2.40 (East Ham) *Clubs:* Chelsea, Tottenham Hotspur
Caps: 57 *Goals:* 44

1958–59 (with Chelsea)

17 May 1959	*v* Peru	Lima	1–4 (1 goal)
24 May 1959	*v* Mexico	Mexico City	1–2
28 May 1959	*v* USA	Los Angeles	8–1

1959–60

17 Oct 1959	*v* Wales	Cardiff	1–1 (1 goal)
28 Oct 1959	*v* Sweden	Wembley	2–3
11 May 1960	*v* Yugoslavia	Wembley	3–3 (1 goal)
15 May 1960	*v* Spain	Madrid	0–3

1960–61

8 Oct 1960	*v* Northern Ireland	Belfast	5–2 (2 goals)
19 Oct 1960	*v* Luxembourg (WCQ)	Luxembourg	9–0 (3 goals)
26 Oct 1960	*v* Spain	Wembley	4–2 (1 goal)
23 Nov 1960	*v* Wales	Wembley	5–1 (2 goals)
15 April 1961	*v* Scotland	Wembley	9–3 (3 goals)
21 May 1961	*v* Portugal (WCQ)	Lisbon	1–1
24 May 1961	*v* Italy	Rome	3–2 (1 goal)
27 May 1961	*v* Austria	Vienna	1–3 (1 goal)

1961–62 (with Tottenham Hotspur)

14 April 1962	*v* Scotland	Glasgow	0–2
9 May 1962	*v* Switzerland	Wembley	3–1
20 May 1962	*v* Peru	Lima	4–0 (3 goals)
31 May 1962	*v* Hungary (WC)	Rancagua	1–2
2 June 1962	*v* Argentina (WC)	Rancagua	3–1 (1 goal)
7 June 1962	*v* Bulgaria (WC)	Rancagua	0–0
10 June 1962	*v* Brazil (WC)	Vina del Mar	1–3

1962–63

3 Oct 1962	*v* France (ECQ)	Sheffield Wednesday	1–1
20 Oct 1962	*v* Northern Ireland	Belfast	3–1 (1 goal)
21 Nov 1962	*v* Wales	Wembley	4–0 (1 goal)
27 Feb 1963	*v* France (ECQ)	Paris	2–5
6 April 1963	*v* Scotland	Wembley	1–2
8 May 1963	*v* Brazil	Wembley	1–1
29 May 1963	*v* Czechoslovakia	Bratislava	4–2 (2 goals)
5 June 1963	*v* Switzerland	Basle	8–1

1963–64

| 12 Oct 1963 | *v* Wales | Cardiff | 4–0 (1 goal) |
| 23 Oct 1963 | *v* Rest of the World | Wembley | 2–1 (1 goal) |

20 Nov 1963	v Northern Ireland	Wembley	8–3 (4 goals)
6 May 1964	v Uruguay	Wembley	2–1
17 May 1964	v Portugal	Lisbon	4–3
24 May 1964	v Eire	Dublin	3–1 (1 goal)
30 May 1964	v Brazil (BJT)	Rio de Janeiro	1–5 (1 goal)
4 June 1964	v Portugal (BJT)	Sao Paulo	1–1
6 June 1964	v Argentina (BJT)	Rio de Janeiro	0–1

1964–65

3 Oct 1964	v Northern Ireland	Belfast	4–3 (3 goals)
21 Oct 1964	v Belgium	Wembley	2–2
9 Dec 1964	v Holland	Amsterdam	1–1 (1 goal)
10 April 1965	v Scotland	Wembley	2–2 (1 goal)
5 May 1965	v Hungary	Wembley	1–0 (1 goal)
9 May 1965	v Yugoslavia	Belgrade	1–1

1965–66

2 Oct 1965	v Wales	Cardiff	0–0
20 Oct 1965	v Austria	Wembley	2–3
4 May 1966	v Yugoslavia	Wembley	2–0 (1 goal)
29 June 1966	v Norway	Oslo	6–1 (4 goals)
3 July 1966	v Denmark	Copenhagen	2–0
5 July 1966	v Poland	Chorzow	1–0
11 July 1966	v Uruguay (WC)	Wembley	0–0
16 July 1966	v Mexico (WC)	Wembley	2–0
20 July 1966	v France (WC)	Wembley	2–0

1966–67

15 April 1967	v Scotland (ECQ)	Wembley	2–3
24 May 1967	v Spain	Wembley	2–0 (1 goal)
27 May 1967	v Austria	Vienna	1–0

GREENHOFF, BRIAN *Born:* 28.4.53 (Barnsley) *Clubs:* Manchester United, Leeds United *Caps:* 18

1975–76 (with Manchester United)

8 May 1976	v Wales	Cardiff	1–0
11 May 1976	v Northern Ireland	Wembley	4–0

1976–77

8 Sept 1976	v Eire	Wembley	1–1
13 Oct 1976	v Finland (WCQ)	Wembley	2–1
17 Nov 1976	v Italy (WCQ)	Rome	0–2
9 Feb 1977	v Holland	Wembley	0–2
28 May 1977	v Northern Ireland	Belfast	2–1
31 May 1977	v Wales	Wembley	0–1
4 June 1977	v Scotland	Wembley	1–2
8 June 1977	v Brazil	Rio de Janeiro	0–0
12 June 1977	v Argentina	Buenos Aires	1–1
15 June 1977	v Uruguay	Montevideo	0–0

1977–78

19 April 1978	v Brazil	Wembley	1–1
13 May 1978	v Wales	Cardiff	3–1

16 May 1978	*v* Northern Ireland	Wembley	1–0
20 May 1978	*v* Scotland (sub)	Glasgow	1–0
24 May 1978	*v* Hungary (sub)	Wembley	4–1

1979–80 (with Leeds United)

31 May 1980	*v* Australia (sub)	Sydney	2–1

GREGORY, JOHN C. *Born:* 11.5.54 (Scunthorpe) *Club:* Queens Park Rangers *Caps:* 6

1982–83

12 June 1983	*v* Australia	Sydney	0–0
15 June 1983	*v* Australia	Brisbane	1–0
19 June 1983	*v* Australia	Melbourne	1–1

1983–84

21 Sept 1983	*v* Denmark (ECQ)	Wembley	0–1
12 Oct 1983	*v* Hungary (ECQ)	Budapest	3–0
2 May 1984	*v* Wales	Wrexham	0–1

HAGAN, JIMMY *Born:* 21.1.18 (Unsworth) *Club:* Sheffield United *Caps:* 1

1948–49

26 Sept 1948	*v* Denmark	Copenhagen	0–0

HAINES, JOHN T.W. *Born:* 24.4.20 (Wickhamford) *Club:* West Bromwich Albion *Caps:* 1
Goals: 2

1948–49

1 Dec 1948	*v* Switzerland	Arsenal	6–0 (2 goals)

HALL, JEFF J. *Born:* 7.9.29 (Scunthorpe) *Club:* Birmingham City *Caps:* 17

1955–56

2 Oct 1955	*v* Denmark	Copenhagen	5–1
22 Oct 1955	*v* Wales	Cardiff	1–2
2 Nov 1955	*v* Northern Ireland	Wembley	3–0
30 Nov 1955	*v* Spain	Wembley	4–1
14 April 1956	*v* Scotland	Glasgow	1–1
9 May 1956	*v* Brazil	Wembley	4–2
16 May 1956	*v* Sweden	Stockholm	0–0
20 May 1956	*v* Finland	Helsinki	5–1
26 May 1956	*v* West Germany	Berlin	3–1

1956–57

6 Oct 1956	*v* Northern Ireland	Belfast	1–1
14 Nov 1956	*v* Wales	Wembley	3–1
28 Nov 1956	*v* Yugoslavia	Wembley	3–0
5 Dec 1956	*v* Denmark (WCQ)	Wolverhampton	5–2
6 April 1957	*v* Scotland	Wembley	2–1
8 May 1957	*v* Eire (WCQ)	Wembley	5–1
15 May 1957	*v* Denmark (WCQ)	Copenhagen	4–1
19 May 1957	*v* Eire (WCQ)	Dublin	1–1

HANCOCKS, JOHNNY *Born:* 30.4.19 (Oakengates) *Club:* Wolverhampton Wanderers
Caps: 3 *Goals:* 2

1948–49
2 Dec 1948	*v* Switzerland	Arsenal	6–0 (2 goals)

1949–50
15 Oct 1949	*v* Wales (WCQ)	Cardiff	4–1

1950–51
22 Nov 1950	*v* Yugoslavia	Arsenal	2–2

HARDWICK, GEORGE F. M. *Born:* 2.2.20 (Saltburn) *Club:* Middlesbrough *Caps:* 13

1946–47
28 Sept 1946	*v* Northern Ireland*	Belfast	7–2
30 Sept 1946	*v* Eire*	Dublin	1–0
19 Oct 1946	*v* Wales*	Manchester City	3–0
27 Nov 1946	*v* Holland*	Huddersfield	8–2
12 April 1947	*v* Scotland*	Wembley	1–1
3 May 1947	*v* France*	Arsenal	3–0
18 May 1947	*v* Switzerland*	Zurich	0–1
27 May 1947	*v* Portugal*	Lisbon	10–0

1947–48
21 Sept 1947	*v* Belgium*	Brussels	5–2
18 Oct 1947	*v* Wales*	Cardiff	3–0
5 Nov 1947	*v* Northern Ireland*	Everton	2–2
19 Nov 1947	*v* Sweden*	Arsenal	4–2
10 April 1948	*v* Scotland*	Glasgow	2–0

HARFORD, MICK G. *Born:* 12.2.59 (Sunderland) *Club:* Luton Town *Caps:* 2

1987–88
17 Feb 1988	*v* Israel (sub)	Tel Aviv	0–0

1988–89
14 Sept 1988	*v* Denmark	Wembley	1–0

HARRIS, GORDON *Born:* 2.6.40 (Worksop) *Club:* Burnley *Caps:* 1

1965–66
5 Jan 1966	*v* Poland	Everton	1–1

HARRIS, PETER P. *Born:* 19.12.25 (Portsmouth) *Club:* Portsmouth *Caps:* 2

1949–50
21 Sept 1949	*v* Eire	Everton	0–2

1953–54
23 May 1954	*v* Hungary	Budapest	1–7

HARVEY, COLIN J. *Born:* 16.11.44 (Liverpool) *Club:* Everton *Caps:* 1

1970–71
3 Feb 1971	*v* Malta (ECQ)	Valletta	1–0

HASSALL, HAROLD W. *Born:* 4.3.29 (Astley) *Clubs:* Huddersfield Town, Bolton Wanderers *Caps:* 5 *Goals:* 4

1950–51 (with Huddersfield Town)
14 April 1951	*v* Scotland	Wembley	2–3 (1 goal)
9 May 1951	*v* Argentina	Wembley	2–1
19 May 1951	*v* Portugal	Everton	5–2 (1 goal)

1951–52
3 Oct 1951	*v* France	Arsenal	2–2

1953–54 (with Bolton Wanderers)
11 Nov 1953	*v* Northern Ireland (WCQ)	Everton	3–1 (2 goals)

HATELEY, MARK W. *Born:* 7.11.61 (Derby) *Clubs:* Portsmouth, AC Milan, Monaco, Rangers *Caps:* 32 *Goals:* 9

1983–84 (with Portsmouth)
2 June 1984	*v* USSR (sub)	Wembley	0–2
10 June 1984	*v* Brazil	Rio de Janeiro	2–0 (1 goal)
13 June 1984	*v* Uruguay	Montevideo	0–2
17 June 1984	*v* Chile	Santiago	0–0

1984–85 (with AC Milan)
12 Sept 1984	*v* East Germany (sub)	Wembley	1–0
17 Oct 1984	*v* Finland (WCQ)	Wembley	5–0 (2 goals)
27 Feb 1985	*v* Northern Ireland (WCQ)	Belfast	1–0 (1 goal)
26 March 1985	*v* Eire	Wembley	2–1
22 May 1985	*v* Finland (WCQ)	Helsinki	1–1 (1 goal)
25 May 1985	*v* Scotland (RC)	Glasgow	0–1
6 June 1985	*v* Italy	Mexico City	1–2 (1 goal)
9 June 1985	*v* Mexico	Mexico City	0–1

1985–86
11 Sept 1985	*v* Romania (WCQ)	Wembley	1–1
16 Oct 1985	*v* Turkey (WCQ)	Wembley	5–0
29 Jan 1986	*v* Egypt	Cairo	4–0
23 April 1986	*v* Scotland (RC)	Wembley	2–1
17 May 1986	*v* Mexico	Los Angeles	3–0 (2 goals)
24 May 1986	*v* Canada	Vancouver	1–0 (1 goal)
3 June 1986	*v* Portugal (WC)	Monterrey	0–1
6 June 1986	*v* Morocco (WC)	Monterrey	0–0
18 June 1986	*v* Paraguay (sub) (WC)	Mexico City	3–0

1986–87
29 April 1987	*v* Turkey (sub) (ECQ)	Izmir	0–0
19 May 1987	*v* Brazil (sub) (RC)	Wembley	1–1
23 May 1987	*v* Scotland (RC)	Glasgow	0–0

1987–88 (with Monaco)
9 Sept 1987	*v* West Germany (sub)	Düsseldorf	1–3
23 March 1988	*v* Holland (sub)	Wembley	2–2
27 April 1988	*v* Hungary (sub)	Budapest	0–0
24 May 1988	*v* Colombia (sub) (RC)	Wembley	1–1
12 June 1988	*v* Eire (sub) (EC)	Stuttgart	0–1

| 15 June 1988 | *v* Holland (sub) (EC) | Düsseldorf | 1–3 |
| 18 June 1988 | *v* USSR (sub) (EC) | Frankfurt | 1–3 |

1991–92 (with Rangers)

| 25 March 1992 | *v* Czechoslovakia | Prague | 2–2 |

HAYNES, JOHNNY N. *Born:* 17.10.34 (Edmonton) *Club:* Fulham *Caps:* 56 *Goals:* 18

1954–55

| 2 Oct 1954 | *v* Northern Ireland | Belfast | 2–0 (1 goal) |

1955–56

2 Nov 1955	*v* Northern Ireland	Wembley	3–0
30 Nov 1955	*v* Spain	Wembley	4–1
14 April 1956	*v* Scotland	Glasgow	1–1 (1 goal)
9 May 1956	*v* Brazil	Wembley	4–2
16 May 1956	*v* Sweden	Stockholm	0–0
20 May 1956	*v* Finland	Helsinki	5–1 (1 goal)
26 May 1956	*v* West Germany	Berlin	3–1 (1 goal)

1956–57

14 Nov 1956	*v* Wales	Wembley	3–1 (1 goal)
28 Nov 1956	*v* Yugoslavia	Wembley	3–0
8 May 1957	*v* Eire (WCQ)	Wembley	5–1
15 May 1957	*v* Denmark (WCQ)	Copenhagen	4–1 (1 goal)
19 May 1957	*v* Eire (WCQ)	Dublin	1–1

1957–58

19 Oct 1957	*v* Wales	Cardiff	4–0 (2 goals)
6 Nov 1957	*v* Northern Ireland	Wembley	2–3
27 Nov 1957	*v* France	Wembley	4–0
19 April 1958	*v* Scotland	Glasgow	4–0
7 May 1958	*v* Portugal	Wembley	2–1
11 May 1958	*v* Yugoslavia	Belgrade	0–5
18 May 1958	*v* USSR	Moscow	1–1
8 June 1958	*v* USSR (WC)	Gothenburg	2–2
11 June 1958	*v* Brazil (WC)	Gothenburg	0–0
15 June 1958	*v* Austria (WC)	Boras	2–2 (1 goal)
17 June 1958	*v* USSR (WC)	Gothenburg	0–1

1958–59

4 Oct 1958	*v* Northern Ireland	Belfast	3–3
22 Oct 1958	*v* USSR	Wembley	5–0 (3 goals)
11 April 1959	*v* Scotland	Wembley	1–0
6 May 1959	*v* Italy	Wembley	2–2
13 May 1959	*v* Brazil	Rio de Janeiro	0–2
17 May 1959	*v* Peru	Lima	1–4
24 May 1959	*v* Mexico	Mexico City	1–2
28 May 1959	*v* USA	Los Angeles	8–1 (1 goal)

1959–60

18 Nov 1959	*v* Northern Ireland	Wembley	2–1
11 May 1960	*v* Yugoslavia	Wembley	3–3 (1 goal)
15 May 1960	*v* Spain*	Madrid	0–3
22 May 1960	*v* Hungary*	Budapest	0–2

1960–61

8 Oct 1960	v Northern Ireland*	Belfast	5–2
19 Oct 1960	v Luxembourg* (WCQ)	Luxembourg	9–0 (1 goal)
26 Oct 1960	v Spain*	Wembley	4–2
23 Nov 1960	v Wales*	Wembley	5–1 (1 goal)
15 April 1961	v Scotland*	Wembley	9–3 (2 goals)
10 May 1961	v Mexico*	Wembley	8–0
21 May 1961	v Portugal* (WCQ)	Lisbon	1–1
24 May 1961	v Italy*	Rome	3–2
27 May 1961	v Austria*	Vienna	1–3

1961–62

14 Oct 1961	v Wales*	Cardiff	1–1
25 Oct 1961	v Portugal* (WCQ)	Wembley	2–0
22 Nov 1961	v Northern Ireland*	Wembley	1–1
4 April 1962	v Austria*	Wembley	3–1
14 April 1962	v Scotland*	Glasgow	0–2
9 May 1962	v Switzerland*	Wembley	3–1
20 May 1962	v Peru*	Lima	4–0
31 May 1962	v Hungary* (WC)	Rancagua	1–2
2 June 1962	v Argentina* (WC)	Rancagua	3–1
7 June 1962	v Bulgaria* (WC)	Rancagua	0–0
10 June 1962	v Brazil* (WC)	Vina del Mar	1–3

HECTOR, KEVIN J. *Born:* 2.11.44 (Leeds) *Club:* Derby County *Caps:* 2

1973–74

17 Oct 1973	v Poland (sub) (WCQ)	Wembley	1–1
14 Nov 1973	v Italy (sub)	Wembley	0–1

HELLAWELL, MIKE S. *Born:* 30.6.38 (Keighley) *Club:* Birmingham City *Caps:* 2

1962–63

3 Oct 1962	v France (ECQ)	Sheffield Wednesday	1–1
20 Oct 1962	v Northern Ireland	Belfast	3–1

HENRY, RON P. *Born:* 17.8.34 (Shoreditch) *Club:* Tottenham Hotspur *Caps:* 1

1962–63

27 Feb 1963	v France (ECQ)	Paris	2–5

HILL, FRED *Born:* 17.1.40 (Sheffield) *Club:* Bolton Wanderers *Caps:* 2

1962–63

20 Oct 1962	v Northern Ireland	Belfast	3–1
21 Nov 1962	v Wales	Wembley	4–0

HILL, GORDON A. *Born:* 1.4.54 (Sunbury) *Club:* Manchester United *Caps:* 6

1975–76

28 May 1976	v Italy (USABT)	New York	3–2

1976–77

8 Sept 1976	v Eire (sub)	Wembley	1–1

13 Oct 1976	*v* Finland (sub) (WCQ)	Wembley	2–1
30 March 1977	*v* Luxembourg (WCQ)	Wembley	5–0

1977–78

7 Sept 1977	*v* Switzerland (sub)	Wembley	0–0
12 Oct 1977	*v* Luxembourg (WCQ)	Luxembourg	2–0

HILL, RICKY A. *Born:* 5.3.59 (London) *Club:* Luton Town *Caps:* 3

1982–83

22 Sept 1982	*v* Denmark (sub) (ECQ)	Copenhagen	2–2
13 Oct 1982	*v* West Germany	Wembley	1–2

1985–86

29 Jan 1986	*v* Egypt (sub)	Cairo	4–0

HINTON, ALAN T. *Born:* 6.10.42 (Wednesbury) *Clubs:* Wolverhampton Wanderers, Nottingham Forest *Caps:* 3 *Goals:* 1

1962–63 (with Wolverhampton Wanderers)

3 Oct 1962	*v* France (ECQ)	Sheffield Wednesday	1–1

1964–65 (with Nottingham Forest)

21 Oct 1964	*v* Belgium	Wembley	2–2 (1 goal)
18 Nov 1964	*v* Wales	Wembley	2–1

HIRST, DAVID E. *Born:* 7.12.67 (Barnsley) *Club:* Sheffield Wednesday *Caps:* 3 *Goals:* 1

1990–91

1 June 1991	*v* Australia	Sydney	1–0
8 June 1991	*v* New Zealand (sub)	Wellington	2–0 (1 goal)

1991–92

19 Feb 1992	*v* France	Wembley	2–0

HITCHENS, GERRY A. *Born:* 8.10.34 (Rawnsley) *Clubs:* Aston Villa, Inter Milan *Caps:* 7 *Goals:* 5

1960–61 (with Aston Villa)

10 May 1961	*v* Mexico	Wembley	8–0 (1 goal)
24 May 1961	*v* Italy	Rome	3–2 (2 goals)
27 May 1961	*v* Austria	Vienna	1–3

1961–62 (with Inter Milan)

9 May 1962	*v* Switzerland	Wembley	3–1 (1 goal)
20 May 1962	*v* Peru	Lima	4–0
31 May 1962	*v* Hungary (WC)	Rancagua	1–2
10 June 1962	*v* Brazil (WC)	Vine del Mar	1–3 (1 goal)

HODDLE, GLENN *Born:* 27.10.57 (Hayes) *Clubs:* Tottenham Hotspur, Monaco *Caps:* 53 *Goals:* 8

1979–80 (with Tottenham Hotspur)

22 Nov 1979	*v* Bulgaria (ECQ)	Wembley	2–0 (1 goal)
17 May 1980	*v* Wales	Wrexham	1–4
31 May 1980	*v* Australia	Sydney	2–1 (1 goal)

18 June 1980	*v* Spain (EC)	Naples	2–1
1980–81			
25 March 1981	*v* Spain	Wembley	1–2 (1 goal)
20 May 1981	*v* Wales	Wembley	0–0
23 May 1981	*v* Scotland	Wembley	0–1
1981–82			
9 Sept 1981	*v* Norway (WCQ)	Oslo	1–2
23 Feb 1982	*v* Northern Ireland	Wembley	4–0 (1 goal)
27 April 1982	*v* Wales	Cardiff	1–0
2 June 1982	*v* Iceland	Reykjavik	1–1
20 June 1982	*v* Czechoslovakia (sub)(WC)	Bilbao	2–0
25 June 1982	*v* Kuwait (WC)	Bilbao	1–0
1982–83			
15 Dec 1982	*v* Luxembourg (sub) (ECQ)	Wembley	9–0 (1 goal)
28 May 1983	*v* Northern Ireland	Belfast	0–0
1 June 1983	*v* Scotland	Wembley	2–0
1983–84			
12 Oct 1983	*v* Hungary (ECQ)	Budapest	3–0 (1 goal)
16 Nov 1983	*v* Luxembourg (ECQ)	Luxembourg	4–0
29 Feb 1984	*v* France	Paris	0–2
1984–85			
26 March 1985	*v* Eire (sub)	Wembley	2–1
25 May 1985	*v* Scotland (RC)	Glasgow	0–1
6 June 1985	*v* Italy (sub)	Mexico City	1–2
9 June 1985	*v* Mexico	Mexico City	0–1
12 June 1985	*v* West Germany	Mexico City	3–0
16 June 1985	*v* USA	Los Angeles	5–0
1985–86			
11 Sept 1985	*v* Romania (WCQ)	Wembley	1–1 (1 goal)
16 Oct 1985	*v* Turkey (WCQ)	Wembley	5–0
13 Nov 1985	*v* Northern Ireland (WCQ)	Wembley	0–0
26 Feb 1986	*v* Israel	Tel Aviv	2–1
26 March 1986	*v* USSR	Tbilisi	1–0
23 April 1986	*v* Scotland (RC)	Wembley	2–1 (1 goal)
17 May 1986	*v* Mexico	Los Angeles	3–0
24 May 1986	*v* Canada	Vancouver	1–0
3 June 1986	*v* Portugal (WC)	Monterrey	0–1
6 June 1986	*v* Morocco (WC)	Monterrey	0–0
11 June 1986	*v* Poland (WC)	Monterrey	3–0
18 June 1986	*v* Paraguay (WC)	Mexico City	3–0
22 June 1986	*v* Argentina (WC)	Mexico City	1–2
1986–87			
10 Sep 1986	*v* Sweden	Stockholm	0–1
15 Oct 1986	*v* Northern Ireland (ECQ)	Wembley	3–0
12 Nov 1986	*v* Yugoslavia (ECQ)	Wembley	2–0
18 Feb 1987	*v* Spain	Madrid	4–2
29 April 1987	*v* Turkey (ECQ)	Izmir	0–0
23 May 1987	*v* Scotland (RC)	Glasgow	0–0

1987–88 (with Monaco)

9 Sept 1987	*v* West Germany	Düsseldorf	1–3
14 Oct 1987	*v* Turkey (sub) (ECQ)	Wembley	8–0
11 Nov 1987	*v* Yugoslavia (sub) (ECQ)	Belgrade	4–1
23 March 1988	*v* Holland (sub)	Wembley	2–2
27 April 1988	*v* Hungary (sub)	Budapest	0–0
24 May 1988	*v* Colombia (sub) (RC)	Wembley	1–1
12 June 1988	*v* Eire (sub) (EC)	Stuttgart	0–1
15 June 1988	*v* Holland (EC)	Düsseldorf	1–3
18 June 1988	*v* USSR (EC)	Frankfurt	1–3

HODGE, STEVE B. *Born:* 25.10.62 (Nottingham) *Clubs:* Aston Villa, Tottenham Hotspur, Nottingham Forest *Caps:* 24

1985–86 (with Aston Villa)

26 March 1986	*v* USSR (sub)	Tbilisi	1–0
23 April 1986	*v* Scotland (RC)	Wembley	2–1
24 May 1986	*v* Canada	Vancouver	1–0
3 June 1986	*v* Portugal (sub) (WC)	Monterrey	0–1
6 June 1986	*v* Morocco (sub) (WC)	Monterrey	0–0
11 June 1986	*v* Poland (WC)	Monterrey	3–0
18 June 1986	*v* Paraguay (WC)	Mexico City	3–0
22 June 1986	*v* Argentina (WC)	Mexico City	1–2

1986–87

10 Sept 1986	*v* Sweden	Stockholm	0–1
15 Oct 1986	*v* Northern Ireland (ECQ)	Wembley	3–0
12 Nov 1986	*v* Yugoslavia (ECQ)	Wembley	2–0
(with Tottenham Hotspur)			
18 Feb 1987	*v* Spain	Madrid	4–2
1 April 1987	*v* Northern Ireland (ECQ)	Belfast	2–0
29 April 1987	*v* Turkey (ECQ)	Izmir	0–0
23 May 1987	*v* Scotland (RC)	Glasgow	0–0

1988–89

14 Sept 1988	*v* Denmark	Wembley	1–0

1989–90 (with Nottingham Forest)

15 Nov 1989	*v* Italy (sub)	Wembley	0–0
13 Dec 1989	*v* Yugoslavia (sub)	Wembley	2–1
25 April 1990	*v* Czechoslovakia	Wembley	4–2
15 May 1990	*v* Denmark	Wembley	1–0
22 May 1990	*v* Uruguay	Wembley	1–2
2 June 1990	*v* Tunisia	Tunis	1–1

1990–91

6 Feb 1991	*v* Cameroon (sub)	Wembley	2–0
1 May 1991	*v* Turkey (sub) (ECQ)	Izmir	1–0

HODGKINSON, ALAN *Born:* 16.8.36 (Sheffield) *Club:* Sheffield United *Caps:* 5

1956–57

6 April 1957	*v* Scotland	Wembley	2–1
8 May 1957	*v* Eire (WCQ)	Wembley	5–1

15 May 1957	*v* Denmark (WCQ)	Copenhagen	4–1
19 May 1957	*v* Eire (WCQ)	Dublin	1–1

1960–61

23 Nov 1960	*v* Wales	Wembley	5–1

HOLDEN, DOUG A. *Born:* 28.9.30 (Manchester) *Club:* Bolton Wanderers *Caps:* 5

1958–59

11 April 1959	*v* Scotland	Wembley	1–0
6 May 1959	*v* Italy	Wembley	2–2
13 May 1959	*v* Brazil	Rio de Janeiro	0–2
17 May 1959	*v* Peru	Lima	1–4
24 May 1959	*v* Mexico	Mexico City	1–2

HOLLIDAY, EDWIN *Born:* 7.6.39 (Barnsley) *Club:* Middlesbrough *Caps:* 3

1959–60

17 Oct 1959	*v* Wales	Cardiff	1–1
28 Oct 1959	*v* Sweden	Wembley	2–3
18 Nov 1959	*v* Northern Ireland	Wembley	2–1

HOLLINS, JOHN W. *Born:* 16.7.46 (Guildford) *Club:* Chelsea *Caps:* 1

1966–67

24 May 1967	*v* Spain	Wembley	2–0

HOPKINSON, EDDIE *Born:* 29.10.35 (Royston) *Club:* Bolton Wanderers *Caps:* 14

1957–58

19 Oct 1957	*v* Wales	Cardiff	4–0
6 Nov 1957	*v* Northern Ireland	Wembley	2–3
27 Nov 1957	*v* France	Wembley	4–0
19 April 1958	*v* Scotland	Glasgow	4–0
7 May 1958	*v* Portugal	Wembley	2–1
11 May 1958	*v* Yugoslavia	Belgrade	0–5

1958–59

11 April 1959	*v* Scotland	Wembley	1–0
6 May 1959	*v* Italy	Wembley	2–2
13 May 1959	*v* Brazil	Rio de Janeiro	0–2
17 May 1959	*v* Peru	Lima	1–4
24 May 1959	*v* Mexico	Mexico City	1–2
28 May 1959	*v* USA	Los Angeles	8–1

1959–60

17 Oct 1959	*v* Wales	Cardiff	1–1
28 Oct 1959	*v* Sweden	Wembley	2–3

HOWE, DON *Born:* 12.10.35 (Wolverhampton) *Club:* West Bromwich Albion *Caps:* 23

1957–58

19 Oct 1957	*v* Wales	Cardiff	4–0
6 Nov 1957	*v* Northern Ireland	Wembley	2–3

27 Nov 1957	*v* France	Wembley	4–0
19 April 1958	*v* Scotland	Glasgow	4–0
7 May 1958	*v* Portugal	Wembley	2–1
11 May 1958	*v* Yugoslavia	Belgrade	0–5
18 May 1958	*v* USSR	Moscow	1–1
8 June 1958	*v* USSR (WC)	Gothenburg	2–2
11 June 1958	*v* Brazil (WC)	Gothenburg	0–0
15 June 1958	*v* Austria (WC)	Boras	2–2
17 June 1958	*v* USSR (WC)	Gothenburg	0–1

1958–59

4 Oct 1958	*v* Northern Ireland	Belfast	3–3
22 Oct 1958	*v* USSR	Wembley	5–0
26 Nov 1958	*v* Wales	Aston Villa	2–2
11 April 1959	*v* Scotland	Wembley	1–0
6 May 1959	*v* Italy	Wembley	2–2
13 May 1959	*v* Brazil	Rio de Janeiro	0–2
17 May 1959	*v* Peru	Lima	1–4
24 May 1959	*v* Mexico	Mexico City	1–2
28 May 1959	*v* USA	Los Angeles	8–1

1959–60

17 Oct 1959	*v* Wales	Cardiff	1–1
28 Oct 1959	*v* Sweden	Wembley	2–3
18 Nov 1959	*v* Northern Ireland	Wembley	2–1

HOWE, JACK R. *Born:* 7.10.15 (West Hartlepool) *Club:* Derby County *Caps:* 3

1947–48

16 May 1948	*v* Italy	Turin	4–0

1948–49

9 Oct 1948	*v* Northern Ireland	Belfast	6–2
9 April 1949	*v* Scotland	Wembley	1–3

HUDSON, ALAN A. *Born:* 21.6.51 (London) *Club:* Stoke City *Caps:* 2

1974–75

12 March 1975	*v* West Germany	Wembley	2–0
16 April 1975	*v* Cyprus (ECQ)	Wembley	5–0

HUGHES, EMLYN W. *Born:* 28.8.47 (Barrow) *Club:* Liverpool, Wolverhampton Wanderers *Caps:* 62 *Goals:* 1

1969–70 (with Liverpool)

5 Nov 1969	*v* Holland	Amsterdam	1–0
10 Dec 1969	*v* Portugal	Wembley	1–0
25 Feb 1970	*v* Belgium	Brussels	3–1
18 April 1970	*v* Wales	Cardiff	1–1
21 April 1970	*v* Northern Ireland	Wembley	3–1
25 April 1970	*v* Scotland	Glasgow	0–0

1970–71

25 Nov 1970	*v* East Germany	Wembley	3–1

3 Feb 1971	v Malta (ECQ)	Valletta	1–0
21 April 1971	v Greece (ECQ)	Wembley	3–0
12 May 1971	v Malta (ECQ)	Wembley	5–0
19 May 1971	v Wales	Wembley	0–0
1971–72			
10 Nov 1971	v Switzerland (ECQ)	Wembley	1–1
1 Dec 1971	v Greece (ECQ)	Athens	2–0
29 April 1972	v West Germany (ECQ)	Wembley	1–3
13 May 1972	v West Germany (ECQ)	Berlin	0–0
20 May 1972	v Wales	Cardiff	3–0 (1 goal)
23 May 1972	v Northern Ireland	Wembley	0–1
27 May 1972	v Scotland	Glasgow	1–0
1972–73			
15 Nov 1972	v Wales (WCQ)	Cardiff	1–0
24 Jan 1973	v Wales (WCQ)	Wembley	1–1
14 Feb 1973	v Scotland (SFAC)	Glasgow	5–0
15 May 1973	v Wales	Wembley	3–0
19 May 1973	v Scotland	Wembley	1–0
6 June 1973	v Poland (WCQ)	Chorzow	0–2
10 June 1973	v USSR	Moscow	2–1
14 June 1973	v Italy	Turin	0–2
1973–74			
26 Sept 1973	v Austria	Wembley	7–0
17 Oct 1973	v Poland (WCQ)	Wembley	1–1
14 Nov 1973	v Italy	Wembley	0–1
11 May 1974	v Wales*	Cardiff	2–0
15 May 1974	v Northern Ireland*	Wembley	1–0
18 May 1974	v Scotland*	Glasgow	0–2
22 May 1974	v Argentina*	Wembley	2–2
29 May 1974	v East Germany*	Leipzig	1–1
1 June 1974	v Bulgaria*	Sofia	1–0
5 June 1974	v Yugoslavia*	Belgrade	2–2
1974–75			
30 Oct 1974	v Czechoslovakia* (ECQ)	Wembley	3–0
20 Nov 1974	v Portugal* (ECQ)	Wembley	0–0
11 May 1975	v Cyprus (sub) (ECQ)	Limassol	1–0
17 May 1975	v Northern Ireland	Belfast	0–0
1976–77			
17 Nov 1976	v Italy (WCQ)	Rome	0–2
30 March 1977	v Luxembourg (WCQ)	Wembley	5–0
31 May 1977	v Wales	Wembley	0–1
4 June 1977	v Scotland*	Wembley	1–2
8 June 1977	v Brazil	Rio de Janeiro	0–0
12 June 1977	v Argentina	Buenos Aires	1–1
15 June 1977	v Uruguay	Montevideo	0–0
1977–78			
7 Sept 1977	v Switzerland*	Wembley	0–0
12 Oct 1977	v Luxembourg* (WCQ)	Luxembourg	2–0

16 Nov 1977	v Italy* (WCQ)	Wembley	2–0
22 Feb 1978	v West Germany*	Munich	1–2
16 May 1978	v Northern Ireland*	Wembley	1–0
20 May 1978	v Scotland*	Glasgow	1–0
24 May 1978	v Hungary*	Wembley	4–1

1978–79

20 Sept 1978	v Denmark* (ECQ)	Copenhagen	4–3
25 Oct 1978	v Eire* (ECQ)	Dublin	1–1
7 Feb 1979	v Northern Ireland* (ECQ)	Wembley	4–0
23 May 1979	v Wales*	Wembley	0–0
10 June 1979	v Sweden*	Stockholm	0–0

1979–80 (with Wolverhampton Wanderers)

26 March 1980	v Spain (sub)	Barcelona	2–0
20 May 1980	v Northern Ireland*	Wembley	1–1
24 May 1980	v Scotland (sub)	Glasgow	2–0

HUGHES, LAURIE *Born:* 2.3.24 (Liverpool) *Club:* Liverpool *Caps:* 3

1949–50

25 June 1950	v Chile (WC)	Rio de Janeiro	2–0
29 June 1950	v USA (WC)	Belo Horizonte	0–1
2 July 1950	v Spain (WC)	Rio de Janeiro	0–1

HUNT, ROGER. *Born:* 20.7.38 (Golborne) *Club:* Liverpool *Caps:* 34 *Goals:* 18

1961–62

4 April 1962	v Austria	Wembley	3–1 (1 goal)

1962–63

2 June 1963	v East Germany	Leipzig	2–1 (1 goal)

1963–64

11 April 1964	v Scotland	Glasgow	0–1
27 May 1964	v USA	New York	10–0 (4 goals)
4 June 1964	v Portugal (BJT)	Sao Paulo	1–1 (1 goal)

1964–65

18 Nov 1964	v Wales	Wembley	2–1

1965–66

8 Dec 1965	v Spain	Madrid	2–0 (1 goal)
5 Jan 1966	v Poland	Everton	1–1
23 Feb 1966	v West Germany	Wembley	1–0
2 April 1966	v Scotland	Glasgow	4–3 (2 goals)
26 June 1966	v Finland	Helsinki	3–0 (1 goal)
29 June 1966	v Norway	Oslo	6–1
5 July 1966	v Poland	Chorzow	1–0 (1 goal)
11 July 1966	v Uruguay (WC)	Wembley	0–0
16 July 1966	v Mexico (WC)	Wembley	2–0 (1 goal)
20 July 1966	v France (WC)	Wembley	2–0 (2 goals)
23 July 1966	v Argentina (WC)	Wembley	1–0
26 July 1966	v Portugal (WC)	Wembley	2–1
30 July 1966	v West Germany (WCF)	Wembley	4–2 (aet)

1966–67

22 Oct 1966	*v* Northern Ireland (ECQ)	Belfast	2–0 (1 goal)
2 Nov 1966	*v* Czechoslovakia	Wembley	0–0
16 Nov 1966	*v* Wales (ECQ)	Wembley	5–1
24 May 1967	*v* Spain	Wembley	2–0 (1 goal)
27 May 1967	*v* Austria	Vienna	1–0

1967–68

21 Oct 1967	*v* Wales (ECQ)	Cardiff	3–0
22 Nov 1967	*v* Northern Ireland (ECQ)	Wembley	2–0
6 Dec 1967	*v* USSR	Wembley	2–2
3 April 1968	*v* Spain (ECQ)	Wembley	1–0
8 May 1968	*v* Spain (ECQ)	Madrid	2–1
22 May 1968	*v* Sweden	Wembley	3–1 (1 goal)
5 June 1968	*v* Yugoslavia (EC)	Florence	0–1
8 June 1968	*v* USSR (EC)	Rome	2–0

1968–69

6 Nov 1968	*v* Romania	Bucharest	0–0
15 Jan 1969	*v* Romania	Wembley	1–1

HUNT, STEVE *Born:* 4.8.56 (Birmingham) *Club:* West Bromwich Albion *Caps:* 2

1983–84

26 May 1984	*v* Scotland (sub)	Glasgow	1–1
2 June 1984	*v* USSR (sub)	Wembley	0–2

HUNTER, NORMAN *Born:* 29.10.43 (Middlesbrough) *Club:* Leeds United *Caps:* 28 *Goals:* 2

1965–66

8 Dec 1965	*v* Spain (sub)	Madrid	2–0
23 Feb 1966	*v* West Germany	Wembley	1–0
4 May 1966	*v* Yugoslavia	Wembley	2–0
26 June 1966	*v* Finland	Helsinki	3–0

1966–67

27 May 1967	*v* Austria	Vienna	1–0

1967–68

8 May 1968	*v* Spain (ECQ)	Madrid	2–1 (1 goal)
22 May 1968	*v* Sweden	Wembley	3–1
1 June 1968	*v* West Germany	Hanover	0–1
5 June 1968	*v* Yugoslavia (EC)	Florence	0–1
8 June 1968	*v* USSR (EC)	Rome	2–0

1968–69

15 Jan 1969	*v* Romania	Wembley	1–1
7 May 1969	*v* Wales	Wembley	2–1

1969–70

14 Jan 1970	*v* Holland	Wembley	0–0
14 June 1970	*v* West Germany (sub) (WC)	Leon	2–3 (aet)

1970–71

3 Feb 1971	*v* Malta (ECQ)	Valletta	1–0

1971–72

29 April 1972	*v* West Germany (ECQ)	Wembley	1–3
13 May 1972	*v* West Germany (ECQ)	Berlin	0–0
20 May 1972	*v* Wales	Cardiff	3–0
23 May 1972	*v* Northern Ireland	Wembley	0–1
27 May 1972	*v* Scotland	Glasgow	1–0

1972–73

15 Nov 1972	*v* Wales (WCQ)	Cardiff	1–0
24 Jan 1973	*v* Wales (WCQ)	Wembley	1–1 (1 goal)
10 June 1973	*v* USSR (sub)	Moscow	2–1

1973–74

26 Sept 1973	*v* Austria	Wembley	7–0
17 Oct 1973	*v* Poland (WCQ)	Wembley	1–1
15 May 1974	*v* Northern Ireland (sub)	Wembley	1–0
18 May 1974	*v* Scotland	Glasgow	0–2

1974–75

30 Oct 1974	*v* Czechoslovakia (ECQ)	Wembley	3–0

HURST, GEOFF C. *Born:* 8.12.41 (Ashton) *Club:* West Ham United *Caps:* 49 *Goals:* 24

1965–66

22 Feb 1966	*v* West Germany	Wembley	1–0
2 April 1966	*v* Scotland	Glasgow	4–3 (1 goal)
4 May 1966	*v* Yugoslavia	Wembley	2–0
26 June 1966	*v* Finland	Helsinki	3–0
3 July 1966	*v* Denmark	Copenhagen	2–0
23 July 1966	*v* Argentina (WC)	Wembley	1–0 (1 goal)
26 July 1966	*v* Portugal (WC)	Wembley	2–1
30 July 1966	*v* West Germany (WCF)	Wembley	4–2 (aet)
			(3 goals)

1966–67

22 Oct 1966	*v* Northern Ireland (ECQ)	Belfast	2–0
2 Nov 1966	*v* Czechoslovakia	Wembley	0–0
16 Nov 1966	*v* Wales (ECQ)	Wembley	5–1 (2 goals)
15 April 1967	*v* Scotland (ECQ)	Wembley	2–3 (1 goal)
24 May 1967	*v* Spain	Wembley	2–0
27 May 1967	*v* Austria	Vienna	1–0

1967–68

21 Oct 1967	*v* Wales (ECQ)	Cardiff	3–0
22 Nov 1967	*v* Northern Ireland (ECQ)	Wembley	2–0 (1 goal)
6 Dec 1967	*v* USSR	Wembley	2–2
24 Feb 1968	*v* Scotland (ECQ)	Glasgow	1–1
22 May 1968	*v* Sweden (sub)	Wembley	3–1
1 June 1968	*v* West Germany	Hanover	0–1
8 June 1968	*v* USSR (EC)	Rome	2–0 (1 goal)

1968–69

6 Nov 1968	*v* Romania	Bucharest	0–0
11 Dec 1968	*v* Bulgaria	Wembley	1–1 (1 goal)
15 Jan 1969	*v* Romania	Wembley	1–1

12 March 1969	*v* France	Wembley	5–0 (3 goals)
3 May 1969	*v* Northern Ireland	Belfast	3–1 (1 goal)
10 May 1969	*v* Scotland	Wembley	4–1 (2 goals)
1 June 1969	*v* Mexico	Mexico City	0–0
8 June 1969	*v* Uruguay	Montevideo	2–1 (1 goal)
12 June 1969	*v* Brazil	Rio de Janeiro	1–2

1969–70

5 Nov 1969	*v* Holland	Amsterdam	1–0
14 Jan 1970	*v* Holland (sub)	Wembley	0–0
20 Feb 1970	*v* Belgium	Brussels	3–1 (1 goal)
18 April 1970	*v* Wales	Cardiff	1–1
21 April 1970	*v* Northern Ireland	Wembley	3–1 (1 goal)
25 April 1970	*v* Scotland	Glasgow	0–0
20 May 1970	*v* Colombia	Bogota	4–0
24 May 1970	*v* Ecuador	Quito	2–0
2 June 1970	*v* Romania (WC)	Guadalajara	1–0 (1 goal)
7 June 1970	*v* Brazil (WC)	Gudalajara	0–1
14 June 1970	*v* West Germany (WC)	Leon	2–3 (aet)

1970–71

25 Nov 1970	*v* East Germany	Wembley	3–1
21 April 1971	*v* Greece (ECQ)	Wembley	3–0 (1 goal)
19 May 1971	*v* Wales	Wembley	0–0
22 May 1971	*v* Scotland	Wembley	3–1

1971–72

13 Oct 1971	*v* Switzerland (ECQ)	Basle	3–2 (1 goal)
10 Nov 1971	*v* Switzerland (ECQ)	Wembley	1–1
1 Dec 1971	*v* Greece (ECQ)	Athens	2–0 (1 goal)
29 April 1972	*v* West Germany (ECQ)	Wembley	1–3

INCE, PAUL *Born:* 21.10.67 (Ilford) *Club:* Manchester United *Caps:* 9

1992–93

9 Sept 1992	*v* Spain	Santander	0–1
14 Oct 1992	*v* Norway (WCQ)	Wembley	1–1
18 Nov 1992	*v* Turkey (WCQ)	Wembley	4–0
31 March 1993	*v* Turkey (WCQ)	Izmir	2–0
28 April 1993	*v* Holland (WCQ)	Wembley	2–2
29 May 1993	*v* Poland (WCQ)	Chorzow	1–1
9 June 1993	*v* USA* (USC)	Boston	0–2
13 June 1993	*v* Brazil* (USC)	Washington	1–1
19 June 1993	*v* Germany (USC)	Detroit	1–2

JEZZARD, BEDFORD A.G. *Born:* 19.10.27 (Clerkenwell) *Club:* Fulham *Caps:* 2

1953–54

23 May 1954	*v* Hungary	Budapest	1–7

1955–56

2 Nov 1955	*v* Northern Ireland	Wembley	3–0

JOHNSON, DAVID E. *Born:* 23.10.51 (Liverpool) *Clubs:* Ipswich Town, Liverpool
Caps: 8 *Goals:* 6

1974–75 (with Ipswich Town)
21 May 1975	*v* Wales	Wembley	2–2 (2 goals)
24 May 1975	*v* Scotland	Wembley	5–1 (1 goal)

1975–76
3 Sept 1975	*v* Switzerland	Basle	2–1

1979–80 (with Liverpool)
6 Feb 1980	*v* Eire (ECQ)	Wembley	2–0
13 May 1980	*v* Argentina	Wembley	3–1 (2 goals)
20 May 1980	*v* Northern Ireland	Wembley	1–1 (1 goal)
24 May 1980	*v* Scotland	Glasgow	2–0
12 June 1980	*v* Belgium (EC)	Turin	1–1

JOHNSTON, HARRY *Born:* 26.9.19 (Manchester) *Club:* Blackpool *Caps:* 10

1946–47
27 Nov 1946	*v* Holland	Huddersfield	8–2
12 April 1947	*v* Scotland	Wembley	1–1

1950–51
14 April 1951	*v* Scotland	Wembley	2–3

1952–53
17 May 1953	*v* Argentina	Buenos Aires	0–0†
24 May 1953	*v* Chile	Santiago	2–1
31 May 1953	*v* Uruguay	Montevideo	1–2
8 June 1953	*v* USA	New York	6–3

1953–54
10 Oct 1953	*v* Wales (WCQ)	Cardiff	4–1
11 Nov 1953	*v* Northern Ireland (WCQ)	Everton	3–1
25 Nov 1953	*v* Hungary	Wembley	3–6

JONES, MICK D. *Born:* 24.4.45 (Worksop) *Clubs:* Sheffield United, Leeds United *Caps:* 3

1964–65 (with Sheffield United)
12 May 1965	*v* West Germany	Nuremberg	1–0
16 May 1965	*v* Sweden	Gothenburg	2–1

1969–70 (with Leeds United)
14 Jan 1970	*v* Holland	Wembley	0–0

JONES, ROB *Born:* 5.11.71 (Wrexham) *Club:* Liverpool *Caps:* 1

1991–92
19 Feb 1992	*v* France	Wembley	2–0

JONES, WILLIAM H. *Born:* 13.5.21 (Whalley) *Club:* Liverpool *Caps:* 2

1949–50
14 May 1950	*v* Portugal	Lisbon	5–3
18 May 1950	*v* Belgium	Brussels	4–1

KAY, ANTHONY H. *Born:* 13.5.37 (Sheffield) *Club:* Everton *Caps:* 1 *Goals:* 1

1962–63
5 June 1963	*v* Switzerland	Basle	8–1 (1 goal)

KEEGAN, J. KEVIN *Born:* 14.2.51 (Doncaster) *Clubs:* Liverpool, SV Hamburg, Southampton *Caps:* 63 *Goals:* 21

1972–73 (with Liverpool)
15 Nov 1972	*v* Wales (WCQ)	Cardiff	1–0
24 Jan 1973	*v* Wales (WCQ)	Wembley	1–1

1973–74
11 May 1974	*v* Wales	Cardiff	2–0 (1 goal)
15 May 1974	*v* Northern Ireland	Wembley	1–0
22 May 1974	*v* Argentina	Wembley	2–2
29 May 1974	*v* East Germany	Leipzig	1–1
1 June 1974	*v* Bulgaria	Sofia	1–0
5 June 1974	*v* Yugoslavia	Belgrade	2–2 (1 goal)

1974–75
30 Oct 1974	*v* Czechoslovakia (ECQ)	Wembley	3–0
12 March 1975	*v* West Germany	Wembley	2–0
16 April 1975	*v* Cyprus (ECQ)	Wembley	5–0
11 May 1975	*v* Cyprus (ECQ)	Limassol	1–0 (1 goal)
17 May 1975	*v* Northern Ireland	Belfast	0–0
24 May 1975	*v* Scotland	Wembley	5–1

1975–76
3 Sept 1975	*v* Switzerland	Basle	2–1 (1 goal)
30 Oct 1975	*v* Czechoslovakia (ECQ)	Bratislava	1–2
19 Nov 1975	*v* Portugal (ECQ)	Lisbon	1–1
24 March 1976	*v* Wales* (FAWC)	Wrexham	2–1
8 May 1976	*v* Wales	Cardiff	1–0
11 May 1976	*v* Northern Ireland	Wembley	4–0
15 May 1976	*v* Scotland	Glasgow	1–2
23 May 1976	*v* Brazil (USABT)	Los Angeles	0–1
13 June 1976	*v* Finland (WCQ)	Helsinki	4–1 (2 goals)

1976–77
8 Sept 1976	*v* Eire*	Wembley	1–1
13 Oct 1976	*v* Finland* (WCQ)	Wembley	2–1
17 Nov 1976	*v* Italy* (WCQ)	Rome	0–2
9 Feb 1977	*v* Holland*	Wembley	0–2
30 March 1977	*v* Luxembourg* (WCQ)	Wembley	5–0 (1 goal)
(with SV Hamburg)			
31 May 1977	*v* Wales*	Wembley	0–1
8 June 1977	*v* Brazil*	Rio de Janeiro	0–0
12 June 1977	*v* Argentina*	Buenos Aires	1–1
15 June 1977	*v* Uruguay*	Montevideo	0–0

1977–78
7 Sept 1977	*v* Switzerland	Wembley	0–0
16 Nov 1977	*v* Italy (WCQ)	Wembley	2–0 (1 goal)

22 Feb 1978	v West Germany	Munich	1–2
19 April 1978	v Brazil*	Wembley	1–1 (1 goal)
24 May 1978	v Hungary	Wembley	4–1

1978–79

28 Sept 1978	v Denmark (ECQ)	Copenhagen	4–3 (2 goals)
25 Oct 1978	v Eire (ECQ)	Dublin	1–1
29 Nov 1978	v Czechoslovakia*	Wembley	1–0
7 Feb 1979	v Northern Ireland (ECQ)	Wembley	4–0 (1 goal)
23 May 1979	v Wales	Wembley	0–0
26 May 1979	v Scotland*	Wembley	3–1 (1 goal)
6 June 1979	v Bulgaria* (ECQ)	Sofia	3–0 (1 goal)
10 June 1979	v Sweden	Stockholm	0–0
13 June 1979	v Austria*	Vienna	3–4 (1 goal)

1979–80

9 Sept 1979	v Denmark* (ECQ)	Wembley	1–0 (1 goal)
17 Oct 1979	v Northern Ireland* (ECQ)	Belfast	5–1
6 Feb 1980	v Eire* (ECQ)	Wembley	2–0 (2 goals)
26 March 1980	v Spain*	Barcelona	2–0
13 May 1980	v Argentina*	Wembley	3–1 (1 goal)
12 June 1980	v Belgium* (EC)	Turin	1–1
15 June 1980	v Italy* (EC)	Turin	0–1
18 June 1980	v Spain* (EC)	Naples	2–1

1980–81 (with Southampton)

25 March 1981	v Spain*	Wembley	1–2
30 May 1981	v Switzerland* (WCQ)	Basle	1–2
6 June 1981	v Hungary* (WCQ)	Budapest	3–1 (1 goal)

1981–82

9 Sept 1981	v Norway* (WCQ)	Oslo	1–2
18 Nov 1981	v Hungary* (WCQ)	Wembley	1–0
23 Feb 1982	v Northern Ireland*	Wembley	4–0 (1 goal)
29 May 1982	v Scotland*	Glasgow	1–0
3 June 1982	v Finland*	Helsinki	4–1
5 July 1982	v Spain (sub) (WC)	Madrid	0–0

KENNEDY, ALAN P. *Born:* 31.8.54 (Sunderland) *Club:* Liverpool *Caps:* 2

1983–84

4 April 1984	v Northern Ireland	Wembley	1–0
2 May 1984	v Wales	Wrexham	0–1

KENNEDY, RAY *Born:* 28.7 .51 (Seaton Delaval) *Club:* Liverpool *Caps:* 17 *Goals:* 3

1975–76

24 March 1976	v Wales (FAWC)	Wrexham	2–1 (1 goal)
8 May 1976	v Wales	Cardiff	1–0
11 May 1976	v Northern Ireland	Wembley	4–0
15 May 1976	v Scotland	Glasgow	1–2

1976–77

30 March 1977	v Luxembourg (WCQ)	Wembley	5–0 (1 goal)

31 May 1977	v Wales	Wembley	0–1
4 June 1977	v Scotland	Wembley	1–2
8 June 1977	v Brazil (sub)	Rio de Janeiro	0–0
12 June 1977	v Argentina (sub)	Buenos Aires	1–1

1977–78

7 Sept 1977	v Switzerland	Wembley	0–0
12 Oct 1977	v Luxembourg (WCQ)	Luxembourg	2–0 (1 goal)

1979–80

22 Nov 1979	v Bulgaria (ECQ)	Wembley	2–0
26 March 1980	v Spain	Barcelona	2–0
13 May 1980	v Argentina	Wembley	3–1
17 May 1980	v Wales	Wrexham	1–4
12 June 1980	v Belgium (sub) (EC)	Turin	1–1
15 June 1980	v Italy (EC)	Turin	0–1

KEOWN, MARTIN R. *Born:* 24.7.66 (Oxford) *Clubs:* Everton, Arsenal *Caps:* 11 *Goals:* 1

1991–92 (with Everton)

19 Feb 1992	v France	Wembley	2–0
25 March 1992	v Czechoslovakia	Prague	2–2 (1 goal)
29 April 1992	v CIS	Moscow	2–2
12 May 1992	v Hungary	Budapest	1–0
17 May 1992	v Brazil	Wembley	1–1
3 June 1992	v Finland	Helsinki	2–1
11 June 1992	v Denmark (EC)	Malmo	0–0
14 June 1992	v France (EC)	Malmo	0–0
17 June 1992	v Sweden (EC)	Stockholm	1–2

1992–93 (with Arsenal)

28 April 1993	v Holland (WCQ)	Wembley	2–2
19 June 1993	v Germany (sub) (USC)	Detroit	1–2

KEVAN, DEREK T. *Born:* 6.3.35 (Ripon) *Club:* West Bromwich Albion *Caps:* 14 *Goals:* 8

1956–57

6 April 1957	v Scotland	Wembley	2–1 (1 goal)

1957–58

19 Oct 1957	v Wales	Cardiff	4–0
6 Nov 1957	v Northern Ireland	Wembley	2–3
19 April 1958	v Scotland	Glasgow	4–0 (2 goals)
7 May 1958	v Portugal	Wembley	2–1
11 May 1958	v Yugoslavia	Belgrade	0–5
18 May 1958	v USSR	Moscow	1–1 (1 goal)
8 June 1958	v USSR (WC)	Gothenburg	2–2 (1 goal)
11 June 1958	v Brazil (WC)	Gothenburg	0–0
15 June 1958	v Austria (WC)	Boras	2–2 (1 goal)
17 June 1958	v USSR (WC)	Gothenburg	0–1

1958–59

24 May 1959	v Mexico	Mexico City	1–2 (1 goal)
28 May 1959	v USA	Los Angeles	8–1 (1 goal)

1960–61

10 May 1961	v Mexico	Wembley	8–0

KIDD, BRIAN *Born:* 29.5.49 (Manchester) *Club:* Manchester United *Caps:* 2 *Goals:* 1

1969–70

21 April 1970	v Northern Ireland	Wembley	3–1
24 May 1970	v Ecuador (sub)	Quito	2–0 (1 goal)

KNOWLES, CYRIL *Born:* 13.7.44 (Pontefract) *Club:* Tottenham Hotspur *Caps:* 4

1967–68

6 Dec 1967	v USSR	Wembley	2–2
3 April 1968	v Spain (ECQ)	Wembley	1–0
22 May 1968	v Sweden	Wembley	3–1
1 June 1968	v West Germany	Hanover	0–1

LABONE, BRIAN L. *Born:* 23.1.40 (Liverpool) *Club:* Everton *Caps:* 26

1962–63

20 Oct 1962	v Northern Ireland	Belfast	3–1
21 Nov 1962	v Wales	Wembley	4–0
27 Feb 1963	v France (ECQ)	Paris	2–5

1966–67

24 May 1967	v Spain	Wembley	2–0
27 May 1967	v Austria	Vienna	1–0

1967–68

24 Feb 1968	v Scotland (ECQ)	Glasgow	1–1
8 May 1968	v Spain (ECQ)	Madrid	2–1
22 May 1968	v Sweden	Wembley	3–1
1 June 1968	v West Germany	Hanover	0–1
5 June 1968	v Yugoslavia (EC)	Florence	0–1
8 June 1968	v USSR (EC)	Rome	2–0

1968–69

6 Nov 1968	v Romania	Bucharest	0–0
11 Dec 1968	v Bulgaria	Wembley	1–1
3 May 1969	v Northern Ireland	Belfast	3–1
10 May 1969	v Scotland	Wembley	4–1
1 June 1969	v Mexico	Mexico City	0–0
8 June 1969	v Uruguay	Montevideo	2–1
12 June 1969	v Brazil	Rio de Janeiro	1–2

1969–70

25 Feb 1970	v Belgium	Brussels	3–1
18 April 1970	v Wales	Cardiff	1–1
25 April 1970	v Scotland	Glasgow	0–0
20 May 1970	v Colombia	Bogota	4–0
24 May 1970	v Ecuador	Quito	2–0

2 June 1970	*v* Romania (WC)	Guadalajara	1–0
7 June 1970	*v* Brazil (WC)	Guadalajara	0–1
14 June 1970	*v* West Germany (WC)	Leon	2–3 (aet)

LAMPARD, FRANK R.G. *Born:* 20.9.48 (West Ham) *Club:* West Ham United *Caps:* 2

1972–73
11 Oct 1972	*v* Yugoslavia	Wembley	1–1

1979–80
31 May 1980	*v* Australia	Sydney	2–1

LANGLEY, JIM E. *Born:* 7.2.29 (Kilburn) *Club:* Fulham *Caps:* 3

1957–58
19 April 1958	*v* Scotland	Glasgow	4–0
7 May 1958	*v* Portugal	Wembley	2–1
11 May 1958	*v* Yugoslavia	Belgrade	0–5

LANGTON, ROBERT *Born:* 8.9.18 (Burscough) *Clubs:* Blackburn Rovers, Preston North End, Bolton Wanderers *Caps:* 11 *Goals:* 1

1946–47 (with Blackburn Rovers)
28 Sept 1946	*v* Northern Ireland	Belfast	7–2 (1 goal)
30 Sept 1946	*v* Eire	Dublin	1–0
13 Nov 1946	*v* Wales	Manchester City	3–0
27 Nov 1946	*v* Holland	Huddersfield	8–2
3 May 1947	*v* France	Arsenal	3–0
18 May 1947	*v* Switzerland	Zurich	0–1

1947–48
19 Nov 1947	*v* Sweden	Arsenal	4–2

1948–49 (with Preston North End)
26 Sept 1948	*v* Denmark	Copenhagen	0–0
13 May 1949	*v* Sweden	Stockholm	1–3

1949–1950 (with Bolton Wanderers)
15 April 1950	*v* Scotland (WCQ)	Glasgow	1–0

1950–51
7 Oct 1950	*v* Northern Ireland	Belfast	4–1

LATCHFORD, ROBERT D. *Born:* 18.1.51 (Birmingham) *Club:* Everton *Caps:* 12 *Goals:* 5

1977–78
16 Nov 1977	*v* Italy (WCQ)	Wembley	2–0
19 April 1978	*v* Brazil	Wembley	1–1
13 May 1978	*v* Wales	Cardiff	3–1 (1 goal)

1978–79
20 Sept 1978	*v* Denmark (ECQ)	Copenhagen	4–3 (1 goal)
25 Oct 1978	*v* Eire (ECQ)	Dublin	1–1 (1 goal)
29 Nov 1978	*v* Czechoslovakia (sub)	Wembley	1–0
7 Feb 1979	*v* Northern Ireland (ECQ)	Wembley	4–0 (2 goals)
19 May 1979	*v* Northern Ireland	Belfast	2–0

23 May 1979	v Wales	Wembley	0–0
26 May 1979	v Scotland	Wembley	3–1
6 June 1979	v Bulgaria (ECQ)	Sofia	3–0
13 June 1979	v Austria	Vienna	3–4

LAWLER, CHRIS *Born:* 20.10.43 (Liverpool) *Club:* Liverpool *Caps:* 4 *Goals:* 1

1970–71

12 May 1971	v Malta (ECQ)	Wembley	5–0 (1 goal)
19 May 1971	v Wales	Wembley	0–0
22 May 1971	v Scotland	Wembley	3–1

1971–72

13 Oct 1971	v Switzerland (ECQ)	Basle	3–2

LAWTON, TOMMY *Born:* 6.10.19 (Bolton) *Clubs:* Chelsea, Notts County *Caps:* 23 (includes 8 pre-war) *Goals:* 16

1946–47 (with Chelsea)

28 Sept 1946	v Northern Ireland	Belfast	7–2 (1 goal)
30 Sept 1946	v Eire	Dublin	1–0
13 Nov 1946	v Wales	Manchester City	3–0 (1 goal)
27 Nov 1946	v Holland	Huddersfield	8–2 (4 goals)
12 April 1947	v Scotland	Wembley	1–1
3 May 1947	v France	Arsenal	3–0
18 May 1947	v Switzerland	Zurich	0–1
27 May 1947	v Portugal	Lisbon	10–0 (4 goals)

1947–48

21 Sept 1947	v Belgium	Brussels	5–2 (2 goals)
18 Oct 1947	v Wales	Cardiff	3–0 (1 goal)
5 Nov 1947	v Northern Ireland	Everton	2–2 (1 goal)
(with Notts County)			
19 Nov 1947	v Sweden	Arsenal	4–2 (1 goal)
10 April 1948	v Scotland	Glasgow	2–0
16 May 1948	v Italy	Turin	4–0 (1 goal)

1948–49

26 Sept 1948	v Denmark	Copenhagen	0–0

LEE, FRANCIS H. *Born:* 29.4 .44 (West Houghton) *Club:* Manchester City *Caps:* 27 *Goals:* 10

1968–69

11 Dec 1968	v Bulgaria	Wembley	1–1
12 March 1969	v France	Wembley	5–0 (1 goal)
3 May 1969	v Northern Ireland	Belfast	3–1 (1 goal)
7 May 1969	v Wales	Wembley	2–1 (1 goal)
10 May 1969	v Scotland	Wembley	4–1
1 June 1969	v Mexico	Mexico City	0–0
8 June 1969	v Uruguay	Montevideo	2–1 (1 goal)

1969–70

5 Nov 1969	v Holland	Amsterdam	1–0

10 Dec 1969	*v* Portugal	Wembley	1–0
14 Jan 1970	*v* Holland	Wembley	0–0
20 Feb 1970	*v* Belgium	Brussels	3–1
18 April 1970	*v* Wales	Cardiff	1–1 (1 goal)
20 May 1970	*v* Colombia	Bogota	4–0
24 May 1970	*v* Ecuador	Quito	2–0 (1 goal)
2 June 1970	*v* Romania (WC)	Guadalajara	1–0
7 June 1970	*v* Brazil (WC)	Guadalajara	0–1
14 June 1970	*v* West Germany (WC)	Leon	2–3 (aet)

1970–71

25 Nov 1970	*v* East Germany	Wembley	3–1 (1 goal)
21 April 1971	*v* Greece (ECQ)	Wembley	3–0 (1 goal)
12 May 1971	*v* Malta (ECQ)	Wembley	5–0 (1 goal)
15 May 1971	*v* Northern Ireland	Belfast	1–0
19 May 1971	*v* Wales	Wembley	0–0
22 May 1971	*v* Scotland	Wembley	3–1

1971–72

13 Oct 1971	*v* Switzerland (ECQ)	Basle	3–2
10 Nov 1971	*v* Switzerland (ECQ)	Wembley	1–1
1 Dec 1971	*v* Greece (ECQ)	Athens	2–0
29 April 1972	*v* West Germany (ECQ)	Wembley	1–3 (1 goal)

LEE, JACKIE *Born:* 4.11.20 (Sileby) *Club:* Derby County *Caps:* 1 *Goals:* 1

1950–51

7 Oct 1950	*v* Northern Ireland	Belfast	4–1 (1 goal)

LEE, SAMMY *Born:* 7.2.59 (Liverpool) *Club:* Liverpool *Caps:* 14 *Goals:* 2

1982–83

17 Nov 1982	*v* Greece (ECQ)	Salonika	3–0 (1 goal)
15 Dec 1982	*v* Luxembourg (ECQ)	Wembley	9–0
23 Feb 1983	*v* Wales	Wembley	2–1
30 March 1983	*v* Greece (ECQ)	Wembley	0–0
27 April 1983	*v* Hungary (ECQ)	Wembley	2–0
1 June 1983	*v* Scotland	Wembley	2–0
19 June 1983	*v* Australia	Melbourne	1–1

1983–84

21 Sept 1983	*v* Denmark (ECQ)	Wembley	0–1
12 Oct 1983	*v* Hungary (ECQ)	Budapest	3–0 (1 goal)
16 Nov 1983	*v* Luxembourg (ECQ)	Luxembourg	4–0
29 Feb 1984	*v* France	Paris	0–2
4 April 1984	*v* Northern Ireland	Wembley	1–0
2 May 1984	*v* Wales	Wrexham	0–1
17 June 1984	*v* Chile (sub)	Santiago	0–0

LINDSAY, ALEC *Born:* 27.2.48 (Bury) *Club:* Liverpool *Caps:* 4

1973–74

22 May 1974	*v* Argentina	Wembley	2–2

29 May 1974	*v* East Germany	Leipzig	1–1
1 June 1974	*v* Bulgaria	Sofia	1–0
5 June 1974	*v* Yugoslavia	Belgrade	2–2

LINEKER, GARY *Born:* 30.11.60 (Leicester) *Clubs:* Leicester City, Everton, Barcelona, Tottenham Hotspur *Caps:* 80 *Goals:* 48

1983–84 (with Leicester City)

26 May 1984	*v* Scotland (sub)	Glasgow	1–1

1984–85

26 March 1985	*v* Eire	Wembley	2–1 (1 goal)
1 May 1985	*v* Romania (sub) (WCQ)	Bucharest	0–0
25 May 1985	*v* Scotland (sub) (RC)	Glasgow	0–1
6 June 1985	*v* Italy (sub)	Mexico City	1–2
12 June 1985	*v* West Germany	Mexico City	3–0
16 June 1985	*v* USA	Los Angeles	5–0 (2 goals)

1985–86 (with Everton)

11 Sept 1985	*v* Romania (WCQ)	Wembley	1–1
16 Oct 1985	*v* Turkey (WCQ)	Wembley	5–0 (3 goals)
13 Nov 1985	*v* Northern Ireland (WCQ)	Wembley	0–0
29 Jan 1986	*v* Egypt	Cairo	4–0
26 March 1986	*v* USSR	Tbilisi	1–0
24 May 1986	*v* Canada	Vancouver	1–0
3 June 1986	*v* Portugal (WC)	Monterrey	0–1
6 June 1986	*v* Morocco (WC)	Monterrey	0–0
11 June 1986	*v* Poland (WC)	Monterrey	3–0 (3 goals)
18 June 1986	*v* Paraguay (WC)	Mexico City	3–0 (2 goals)
22 June 1986	*v* Argentina (WC)	Mexico City	1–2 (1 goal)

1986–87 (with Barcelona)

15 Oct 1986	*v* Northern Ireland (ECQ)	Wembley	3–0 (2 goals)
12 Nov 1986	*v* Yugoslavia (ECQ)	Wembley	2–0
18 Feb 1987	*v* Spain	Madrid	4–2 (4 goals)
1 April 1987	*v* Northern Ireland (ECQ)	Belfast	2–0
29 April 1987	*v* Turkey (ECQ)	Izmir	0–0
19 May 1987	*v* Brazil (RC)	Wembley	1–1 (1 goal)

1987–88

9 Sept 1987	*v* West Germany	Düsseldorf	1–3 (1 goal)
14 Oct 1987	*v* Turkey (ECQ)	Wembley	8–0 (3 goals)
11 Nov 1987	*v* Yugoslavia (ECQ)	Belgrade	4–1
23 March 1988	*v* Holland	Wembley	2–2 (1 goal)
27 April 1988	*v* Hungary	Budapest	0–0
21 May 1988	*v* Scotland (RC)	Wembley	1–0
24 May 1988	*v* Colombia (RC)	Wembley	1–1 (1 goal)
28 May 1988	*v* Switzerland	Lausanne	1–0 (1 goal)
12 June 1988	*v* Eire (EC)	Stuttgart	0–1
15 June 1988	*v* Holland (EC)	Düsseldorf	1–3
18 June 1988	*v* USSR (EC)	Frankfurt	1–3

1988–89

19 Oct 1988	*v* Sweden (WCQ)	Wembley	0–0

16 Nov 1988	*v* Saudi Arabia	Riyadh	1–1
8 Feb 1989	*v* Greece	Athens	2–1
8 March 1989	*v* Albania (WCQ)	Tirana	2–0
26 April 1989	*v* Albania (WCQ)	Wembley	5–0 (1 goal)
3 June 1989	*v* Poland (WCQ)	Wembley	3–0 (1 goal)
7 June 1989	*v* Denmark	Copenhagen	1–1 (1 goal)

1989–90 (with Tottenham Hotspur)

6 Sept 1989	*v* Sweden (WCQ)	Stockholm	0–0
11 Oct 1989	*v* Poland (WCQ)	Katowice	0–0
15 Nov 1989	*v* Italy	Wembley	0–0
13 Dec 1989	*v* Yugoslavia	Wembley	2–1
28 March 1990	*v* Brazil	Wembley	1–0 (1 goal)
25 April 1990	*v* Czechoslovakia	Wembley	4–2
15 May 1990	*v* Denmark	Wembley	1–0 (1 goal)
22 May 1990	*v* Uruguay	Wembley	1–2
2 June 1990	*v* Tunisia	Tunis	1–1
11 June 1990	*v* Eire (WC)	Cagliari	1–1 (1 goal)
16 June 1990	*v* Holland (WC)	Cagliari	0–0
21 June 1990	*v* Egypt (WC)	Cagliari	1–0
26 June 1990	*v* Belgium (WC)	Bologna	1–0 (aet)
1 July 1990	*v* Cameroon (WC)	Naples	3–2 (aet) (2 goals)
4 July 1990	*v* West Germany (WC)	Turin	1–1 (aet) (1 goal)
7 July 1990	*v* Italy (WC)	Bari	1–2

1990–91

12 Sept 1990	*v* Hungary*	Wembley	1–0 (1 goal)
17 Oct 1990	*v* Poland* (ECQ)	Wembley	2–0 (1 goal)
14 Nov 1990	*v* Eire*(ECQ)	Dublin	1–1
6 Feb 1991	*v* Cameroon	Wembley	2–0 (2 goals)
27 March 1991	*v* Eire (ECQ)	Wembley	1–1
1 May 1991	*v* Turkey* (ECQ)	Izmir	1–0
25 May 1991	*v* Argentina*	Wembley	2–2 (1 goal)
1 June 1991	*v* Australia*	Sydney	1–0
3 June 1991	*v* New Zealand*	Auckland	1–0 (1 goal)
12 June 1991	*v* Malaysia*	Kuala Lumpur	4–2 (4 goals)

1991–92

11 Sept 1991	*v* Germany*	Wembley	0–1
16 Oct 1991	*v* Turkey* (ECQ)	Wembley	1–0
13 Nov 1991	*v* Poland* (ECQ)	Poznan	1–1 (1 goal)
19 Feb 1992	*v* France (sub)	Wembley	2–0 (1 goal)
25 March 1992	*v* Czechoslovakia (sub)	Prague	2–2
29 April 1992	*v* CIS*	Moscow	2–2 (1 goal)
12 May 1992	*v* Hungary*	Budapest	1–0
17 May 1992	*v* Brazil*	Wembley	1–1
3 June 1992	*v* Finland*	Helsinki	2–1
11 June 1992	*v* Denmark* (EC)	Malmo	0–0
14 June 1992	*v* France* (EC)	Malmo	0–0
17 June 1992	*v* Sweden* (EC)	Stockholm	1–2

LITTLE, BRIAN *Born:* 25.11.53 (Durham) *Club:* Aston Villa *Caps:* 1

1974–75

21 May 1975	*v* Wales (sub)	Wembley	2–2

LLOYD, LARRY V. *Born:* 6.10.48 (Bristol) *Clubs:* Liverpool, Nottingham Forest *Caps:* 4

1970–71 (with Liverpool)

19 May 1971	*v* Wales	Wembley	0–0

1971–72

10 Nov 1971	*v* Switzerland (ECQ)	Wembley	1–1
23 May 1972	*v* Northern Ireland	Wembley	0–1

1979–80 (with Nottingham Forest)

17 May 1980	*v* Wales	Wrexham	1–4

LOFTHOUSE, NAT *Born:* 27.8.25 (Bolton) *Club:* Bolton Wanderers *Caps:* 33 *Goals:* 30

1950–51

22 Nov 1950	*v* Yugoslavia	Arsenal	2–2 (2 goals)

1951–52

20 Oct 1951	*v* Wales	Cardiff	1–1
14 Nov 1951	*v* Northern Ireland	Aston Villa	2–0 (2 goals)
28 Nov 1951	*v* Austria	Wembley	2–2 (1 goal)
15 April 1952	*v* Scotland	Glasgow	2–1
18 May 1952	*v* Italy	Florence	1–1
25 May 1952	*v* Austria	Vienna	3–2 (2 goals)
28 May 1952	*v* Switzerland	Zurich	3–0 (2 goals)

1952–53

4 Oct 1952	*v* Northern Ireland	Belfast	2–2 (1 goal)
12 Nov 1952	*v* Wales	Wembley	5–2 (2 goals)
26 Nov 1952	*v* Belgium	Wembley	5–0 (2 goals)
18 April 1953	*v* Scotland	Wembley	2–2
17 May 1953	*v* Argentina	Buenos Aires	0–0†
24 May 1953	*v* Chile	Santiago	2–1 (1 goal)
31 May 1953	*v* Uruguay	Montevideo	1–2
8 June 1953	*v* USA	New York	6–3 (2 goals)

1953–54

10 Oct 1953	*v* Wales (WCQ)	Cardiff	4–1 (2 goals)
21 Oct 1953	*v* FIFA (Rest of Europe)	Wembley	4–4
11 Nov 1953	*v* Northern Ireland (WCQ)	Everton	3–1 (1 goal)
17 June 1954	*v* Belgium (WC)	Basle	4–4 (2 goals)
26 June 1954	*v* Uruguay (WC)	Basle	2–4 (1 goal)

1954–55

2 Oct 1954	*v* Northern Ireland	Belfast	2–0
2 April 1955	*v* Scotland	Wembley	7–2 (2 goals)
15 May 1955	*v* France	Paris	0–1
18 May 1955	*v* Spain	Madrid	1–1
22 May 1955	*v* Portugal	Oporto	1–3

1955–56

2 Oct 1955	*v* Denmark	Copenhagen	5–1 (2 goals)
22 Oct 1955	*v* Wales	Cardiff	1–2
30 Nov 1955	*v* Spain	Wembley	4–1
14 April 1956	*v* Scotland	Glasgow	1–1
20 May 1956	*v* Finland (sub)	Helsinki	5–1 (2 goals)

1958–59

22 Oct 1958	*v* USSR	Wembley	5–0 (1 goal)
26 Nov 1958	*v* Wales	Aston Villa	2–2

LOWE, EDDIE *Born:* 11.7.25 (Halesowen) *Club:* Aston Villa *Caps:* 3

1946–47

3 May 1947	*v* France	Arsenal	3–0
18 May 1947	*v* Switzerland	Zurich	0–1
27 May 1947	*v* Portugal	Lisbon	10–0

MABBUTT, GARY V. *Born:* 23.8.61 (Bristol) *Club:* Tottenham Hotspur *Caps:* 16 *Goals:* 1

1982–83

13 Oct 1982	*v* West Germany	Wembley	1–2
17 Nov 1982	*v* Greece (ECQ)	Salonika	3–0
15 Dec 1982	*v* Luxembourg (ECQ)	Wembley	9–0
23 Feb 1983	*v* Wales	Wembley	2–1
30 March 1983	*v* Greece (ECQ)	Wembley	0–0
27 April 1983	*v* Hungary (ECQ)	Wembley	2–0
28 May 1983	*v* Northern Ireland	Belfast	0–0
1 June 1983	*v* Scotland (sub)	Wembley	2–0

1983–84

12 Oct 1983	*v* Hungary (ECQ)	Budapest	3–0

1986–87

12 Nov 1986	*v* Yugoslavia (ECQ)	Wembley	2–0 (1 goal)
1 April 1987	*v* Northern Ireland (ECQ)	Belfast	2–0
29 April 1987	*v* Turkey (ECQ)	Izmir	0–0

1987–88

9 Sept 1987	*v* West Germany	Düsseldorf	1–3

1991–92

16 Oct 1991	*v* Turkey (ECQ)	Wembley	1–0
13 Nov 1991	*v* Poland (ECQ)	Poznan	1–1
25 March 1992	*v* Czechoslovakia	Prague	2–2

MACDONALD, MALCOLM *Born:* 7.1.50 (Fulham) *Club:* Newcastle United *Caps:* 14 *Goals:* 6

1971–72

20 May 1972	*v* Wales	Cardiff	3–0
23 May 1972	*v* Northern Ireland	Wembley	0–1
27 May 1972	*v* Scotland (sub)	Glasgow	1–0

1972–73

10 June 1973	*v* USSR (sub)	Moscow	2–1

1973–74

3 April 1974	*v* Portugal	Lisbon	0–0
18 May 1974	*v* Scotland (sub)	Glasgow	0–2
5 June 1974	*v* Yugoslavia (sub)	Belgrade	2–2

1974–75

12 March 1975	*v* West Germany	Wembley	2–0 (1 goal)
16 April 1975	*v* Cyprus (ECQ)	Wembley	5–0 (5 goals)
11 May 1975	*v* Cyprus (ECQ)	Limassol	1–0
17 May 1975	*v* Northern Ireland	Belfast	0–0

1975–76

3 Sept 1975	*v* Switzerland (sub)	Basle	2–1
30 Oct 1975	*v* Czechoslovakia (ECQ)	Bratislava	1–2
19 Nov 1975	*v* Portugal (ECQ)	Lisbon	1–1

MADELEY, PAUL E. *Born:* 20.9.44 (Leeds) *Club:* Leeds United *Caps:* 24

1970–71

15 May 1971	*v* Northern Ireland	Belfast	1–0

1971–72

13 Oct 1971	*v* Switzerland (ECQ)	Basle	3–2
10 Nov 1971	*v* Switzerland (ECQ)	Wembley	1–1
1 Dec 1971	*v* Greece (ECQ)	Athens	2–0
29 April 1972	*v* West Germany (ECQ)	Wembley	1–3
13 May 1972	*v* West Germany (ECQ)	Berlin	0–0
20 May 1972	*v* Wales	Cardiff	3–0
27 May 1972	*v* Scotland	Glasgow	1–0

1972–73

14 Feb 1973	*v* Scotland (SFAC)	Glasgow	5–0
27 May 1973	*v* Czechoslovakia	Prague	1–1
6 June 1973	*v* Poland (WCQ)	Chorzow	0–2
10 June 1973	*v* USSR	Moscow	2–1
14 June 1973	*v* Italy	Turin	0–2

1973–74

26 Sept 1973	*v* Austria	Wembley	7–0
17 Oct 1973	*v* Poland (WCQ)	Wembley	1–1
14 Nov 1973	*v* Italy	Wembley	0–1

1974–75

30 Oct 1974	*v* Czechoslovakia (ECQ)	Wembley	3–0
20 Nov 1974	*v* Portugal (ECQ)	Wembley	0–0
16 April 1975	*v* Cyprus (ECQ)	Wembley	5–0

1975–76

30 Oct 1975	*v* Czechoslovakia (ECQ)	Bratislava	1–2
19 Nov 1975	*v* Portugal (ECQ)	Lisbon	1–1
13 June 1976	*v* Finland (WCQ)	Helsinki	4–1

1976–77

8 Sept 1976	*v* Eire	Wembley	1–1
9 Feb 1977	*v* Holland	Wembley	0–2

MANNION, WILF J. *Born:* 16.5.18 (South Bank) *Club:* Middlesbrough *Caps:* 26
Goals: 11

1946–47
28 Sept 1946	*v* Northern Ireland	Belfast	7–2 (3 goals)
30 Sept 1946	*v* Eire	Dublin	1–0
19 Oct 1946	*v* Wales	Manchester City	3–0 (2 goals)
27 Nov 1946	*v* Holland	Huddersfield	8–2 (1 goal)
12 April 1947	*v* Scotland	Wembley	1–1
3 May 1947	*v* France	Arsenal	3–0 (1 goal)
18 May 1947	*v* Switzerland	Zurich	0–1
27 May 1947	*v* Portugal	Lisbon	10–0

1947–48
21 Sept 1947	*v* Belgium	Brussels	5–2
18 Oct 1947	*v* Wales	Cardiff	3–0
5 Nov 1947	*v* Northern Ireland	Everton	2–2 (1 goal)
19 Nov 1947	*v* Sweden	Arsenal	4–2
16 May 1948	*v* Italy	Turin	4–0

1948–49
18 May 1949	*v* Norway	Oslo	4–1
22 May 1949	*v* France	Paris	3–1

1949–50
21 Sept 1949	*v* Eire	Everton	0–2
15 April 1950	*v* Scotland (WCQ)	Glasgow	1–0
14 May 1950	*v* Portugal	Lisbon	5–3
18 May 1950	*v* Belgium	Brussels	4–1 (1 goal)
25 June 1950	*v* Chile (WC)	Rio de Janeiro	2–0 (1 goal)
29 June 1950	*v* USA (WC)	Belo Horizonte	0–1

1950–51
7 Oct 1950	*v* Northern Ireland	Belfast	4–1
15 Nov 1950	*v* Wales	Sunderland	4–2 (1 goal)
22 Nov 1950	*v* Yugoslavia	Arsenal	2–2
14 April 1951	*v* Scotland	Wembley	2–3

1951–52
3 Oct 1951	*v* France	Arsenal	2–2

MARINER, PAUL *Born:* 22.5.53 (Bolton) *Clubs:* Ipswich Town, Arsenal *Caps:* 35
Goals: 13

1976–77 (with Ipswich Town)
30 March 1977	*v* Luxembourg (sub) (WCQ)	Wembley	5–0
28 May 1977	*v* Northern Ireland	Belfast	2–1

1977–78
12 Oct 1977	*v* Luxembourg (WCQ)	Luxembourg	2–0 (1 goal)
13 May 1978	*v* Wales (sub)	Cardiff	3–1
20 May 1978	*v* Scotland	Glasgow	1–0

1979–80
17 May 1980	*v* Wales	Wrexham	1–4 (1 goal)

20 May 1980	*v* Northern Ireland (sub)	Wembley	1–1
24 May 1980	*v* Scotland	Glasgow	2–0
31 May 1980	*v* Australia	Sydney	2–1 (1 goal)
15 June 1980	*v* Italy (sub) (EC)	Turin	0–1
18 June 1980	*v* Spain (sub) (EC)	Naples	2–1

1980–81

10 Sept 1980	*v* Norway (WCQ)	Wembley	4–0 (1 goal)
19 Nov 1980	*v* Switzerland (WCQ)	Wembley	2–1 (1 goal)
25 March 1981	*v* Spain	Wembley	1–2
30 May 1981	*v* Switzerland (WCQ)	Basle	1–2
6 June 1981	*v* Hungary (WCQ)	Budapest	3–1

1981–82

9 Sept 1981	*v* Norway (WCQ)	Oslo	1–2
18 Nov 1981	*v* Hungary (WCQ)	Wembley	1–0 (1 goal)
25 May 1982	*v* Holland	Wembley	2–0 (1 goal)
29 May 1982	*v* Scotland	Glasgow	1–0 (1 goal)
3 June 1982	*v* Finland	Helsinki	4–1 (2 goals)
16 June 1982	*v* France (WC)	Bilbao	3–1 (1 goal)
20 June 1982	*v* Czechoslovakia (WC)	Bilbao	2–0
25 June 1982	*v* Kuwait (WC)	Bilbao	1–0
29 June 1982	*v* West Germany (WC)	Madrid	0–0
5 July 1982	*v* Spain (WC)	Madrid	0–0

1982–83

22 Sept 1982	*v* Denmark (ECQ)	Copenhagen	2–2
13 Oct 1982	*v* West Germany	Wembley	1–2
17 Nov 1982	*v* Greece (ECQ)	Salonika	3–0
23 Feb 1983	*v* Wales	Wembley	2–1

1983–84

21 Sept 1983	*v* Denmark (ECQ)	Wembley	0–1
12 Oct 1983	*v* Hungary (ECQ)	Budapest	3–0 (1 goal)
16 Nov 1983	*v* Luxembourg (ECQ)	Luxembourg	4–0 (1 goal)

1984–85 (with Arsenal)

12 Sept 1984	*v* East Germany	Wembley	1–0
1 May 1985	*v* Romania (WCQ)	Bucharest	0–0

MARSH, RODNEY W. *Born:* 11.10.34 (Hatfield) *Clubs:* Queens Park Rangers, Manchester City *Caps:* 9 *Goals:* 1

1971–72 (with Queens Park Rangers)

10 Nov 1971	*v* Switzerland (sub) (ECQ)	Wembley	1–1

(with Manchester City)

29 April 1972	*v* West Germany (sub) (ECQ)	Wembley	1–3
13 May 1972	*v* West Germany (ECQ)	Berlin	0–0
20 May 1972	*v* Wales	Cardiff	3–0 (1 goal)
23 May 1972	*v* Northern Ireland	Wembley	0–1
27 May 1972	*v* Scotland	Glasgow	1–0

1972–73

11 Oct 1972	*v* Yugoslavia	Wembley	1–1
15 Nov 1972	*v* Wales (WCQ)	Cardiff	1–0

24 Jan 1973	*v* Wales (WCQ)	Wembley	1–1

MARTIN, ALVIN E. *Born:* 29.7.58 (Bootle) *Club:* West Ham United *Caps:* 17

1980–81
12 May 1981	*v* Brazil	Wembley	0–1
23 May 1981	*v* Scotland (sub)	Wembley	0–1

1981–82
18 Nov 1981	*v* Hungary (WCQ)	Wembley	1–0
3 June 1982	*v* Finland	Helsinki	4–1

1982–83
17 Nov 1982	*v* Greece (ECQ)	Salonika	3–0
15 Dec 1982	*v* Luxembourg (ECQ)	Wembley	9–0
23 Feb 1983	*v* Wales	Wembley	2–1
30 March 1983	*v* Greece (ECQ)	Wembley	0–0
27 April 1983	*v* Hungary (ECQ)	Wembley	2–0

1983–84
12 Oct 1983	*v* Hungary (ECQ)	Budapest	3–0
16 Nov 1983	*v* Luxembourg (ECQ)	Luxembourg	4–0
4 April 1984	*v* Northern Ireland	Wembley	1–0
2 May 1984	*v* Wales	Wrexham	0–1

1985–86
26 Feb 1986	*v* Israel	Tel Aviv	2–1
24 May 1986	*v* Canada	Vancouver	1–0
18 June 1986	*v* Paraguay (WC)	Mexico City	3–0

1986–87
10 Sept 1986	*v* Sweden	Stockholm	0–1

MARTYN, NIGEL A. *Born:* 11.8.66 (St Austell) *Club:* Crystal Palace *Caps:* 3

1991–92
29 April 1992	*v* CIS (sub)	Moscow	2–2
12 May 1992	*v* Hungary	Budapest	1–0

1992–93
19 June 1993	*v* Germany (USC)	Detroit	1–2

MARWOOD, BRIAN *Born:* 5.2.60 (Seaham Harbour) *Club:* Arsenal *Caps:* 1

1988–89
16 Nov 1988	*v* Saudi Arabia (sub)	Riyadh	1–1

MATTHEWS, REG D. *Born:* 20.12.33 (Coventry) *Club:* Coventry City *Caps:* 5

1955–56
14 April 1956	*v* Scotland	Glasgow	1–1
9 May 1956	*v* Brazil	Wembley	4–2
16 May 1956	*v* Sweden	Stockholm	0–0
26 May 1956	*v* West Germany	Berlin	3–1

1956–57
6 Oct 1956	*v* Northern Ireland	Belfast	1–1

MATTHEWS, STANLEY *Born:* 1.2.15 (Hanley) *Clubs:* Stoke City, Blackpool *Caps:* 54 (including 17 pre-war) *Goals: 3*

1946–47 (with Stoke City)

12 April 1947	*v* Scotland	Wembley	1–1
(with Blackpool)			
18 May 1947	*v* Switzerland	Zurich	0–1
27 May 1947	*v* Portugal	Lisbon	10–0 (1 goal)

1947–48

21 Sept 1947	*v* Belgium	Brussels	5–2
18 Oct 1947	*v* Wales	Cardiff	3–0
5 Nov 1947	*v* Northern Ireland	Everton	2–2
10 April 1948	*v* Scotland	Glasgow	2–0
16 May 1948	*v* Italy	Turin	4–0

1948–49

26 Sept 1948	*v* Denmark	Copenhagen	0–0
9 Oct 1948	*v* Northern Ireland	Belfast	6–2 (1 goal)
10 Nov 1948	*v* Wales	Aston Villa	1–0
1 Dec 1948	*v* Switzerland	Arsenal	6–0
9 April 1949	*v* Scotland	Wembley	1–3

1949–50

2 July 1950	*v* Spain (WC)	Rio de Janeiro	0–1

1950–51

7 Oct 1950	*v* Northern Ireland	Belfast	4–1
14 April 1951	*v* Scotland	Wembley	2–3

1953–54

21 Oct 1953	*v* FIFA (Rest of Europe)	Wembley	4–4
11 Nov 1953	*v* Northern Ireland (WCQ)	Everton	3–1
25 Nov 1953	*v* Hungary	Wembley	3–6
17 June 1954	*v* Belgium (WC)	Basle	4–4
26 June 1954	*v* Uruguay (WC)	Basle	2–4

1954–55

2 Oct 1954	*v* Northern Ireland	Belfast	2–0
10 Nov 1954	*v* Wales	Wembley	3–2
1 Dec 1954	*v* West Germany	Wembley	3–1
2 April 1955	*v* Scotland	Wembley	7–2
15 May 1955	*v* France	Paris	0–1
18 May 1955	*v* Spain	Madrid	1–1
22 May 1955	*v* Portugal	Oporto	1–3

1955–56

22 Oct 1955	*v* Wales	Cardiff	1–2
9 May 1956	*v* Brazil	Wembley	4–2

1956–57

6 Oct 1956	*v* Northern Ireland	Belfast	1–1 (1 goal)
14 Nov 1956	*v* Wales	Wembley	3–1
28 Nov 1956	*v* Yugoslavia	Wembley	3–0
5 Dec 1956	*v* Denmark (WCQ)	Wolverhampton	5–2
6 April 1957	*v* Scotland	Wembley	2–1

8 May 1957	*v* Eire (WCQ)	Wembley	5–1
15 May 1957	*v* Denmark (WCQ)	Copenhagen	4–1

McDERMOTT, TERRY *Born:* 8.12.51 (Kirkby) *Club:* Liverpool *Caps:* 25 *Goals:* 3

1977–78

7 Sept 1977	*v* Switzerland	Wembley	0–0
12 Oct 1977	*v* Luxembourg (WCQ)	Luxembourg	2–0

1978–79

19 May 1979	*v* Northern Ireland	Belfast	2–0
23 May 1979	*v* Wales	Wembley	0–0
10 June 1979	*v* Sweden	Stockholm	0–0

1979–80

12 Sept 1979	*v* Denmark (ECQ)	Wembley	1–0
17 Oct 1979	*v* Northern Ireland (sub)(ECQ)	Belfast	5–1
6 Feb 1980	*v* Eire (ECQ)	Wembley	2–0
20 May 1980	*v* Northern Ireland	Wembley	1–1
24 May 1980	*v* Scotland	Glasgow	2–0
12 June 1980	*v* Belgium (sub) (EC)	Turin	1–1
18 June 1980	*v* Spain (EC)	Naples	2–1

1980–81

10 Sept 1980	*v* Norway (WCQ)	Wembley	4–0 (2 goals)
15 Oct 1980	*v* Romania (WCQ)	Bucharest	1–2
19 Nov 1980	*v* Switzerland (WCQ)	Wembley	2–1
29 April 1981	*v* Romania (sub) (WCQ)	Wembley	0–0
12 May 1981	*v* Brazil	Wembley	0–1
30 May 1981	*v* Switzerland (sub) (WCQ)	Basle	1–2 (1 goal)
6 June 1981	*v* Hungary (WCQ)	Budapest	3–1

1981–82

9 Sept 1981	*v* Norway (WCQ)	Oslo	1–2
18 Nov 1981	*v* Hungary (WCQ)	Wembley	1–0
27 April 1982	*v* Wales (sub)	Cardiff	1–0
25 May 1982	*v* Holland	Wembley	2–0
29 May 1982	*v* Scotland (sub)	Glasgow	1–0
2 June 1982	*v* Iceland	Reykjavik	1–1

McDONALD, COLIN A. *Born:* 15.10.30 (Tottington) *Club:* Burnley *Caps:* 8

1957–58

18 May 1958	*v* USSR	Moscow	1–1
8 June 1958	*v* USSR (WC)	Gothenburg	2–2
11 June 1958	*v* Brazil (WC)	Gothenburg	0–0
15 June 1958	*v* Austria (WC)	Boras	2–2
17 June 1958	*v* USSR (WC)	Gothenburg	0–1

1958–59

4 Oct 1958	*v* Northern Ireland	Belfast	3–3
22 Oct 1958	*v* USSR	Wembley	5–0
26 Nov 1958	*v* Wales	Aston Villa	2–2

McFARLAND, ROY L. *Born:* 5.4.48 (Liverpool) *Club:* Derby County *Caps:* 28

1970–71
3 Feb 1971	*v* Malta (ECQ)	Valletta	1–0
21 April 1971	*v* Greece (ECQ)	Wembley	3–0
12 May 1971	*v* Malta (ECQ)	Wembley	5–0
15 May 1971	*v* Northern Ireland	Belfast	1–0
22 May 1971	*v* Scotland	Wembley	3–1

1971–72
13 Oct 1971	*v* Switzerland (ECQ)	Basle	3–2
1 Dec 1971	*v* Greece (ECQ)	Athens	2–0
13 May 1972	*v* West Germany (ECQ)	Berlin	0–0
20 May 1972	*v* Wales	Cardiff	3–0
27 May 1972	*v* Scotland	Glasgow	1–0

1972–73
15 Nov 1972	*v* Wales (WCQ)	Cardiff	1–0
24 Jan 1973	*v* Wales (WCQ)	Wembley	1–1
12 May 1973	*v* Northern Ireland	Everton	2–1
15 May 1973	*v* Wales	Wembley	3–0
19 May 1973	*v* Scotland	Wembley	1–0
27 May 1973	*v* Czechoslovakia	Prague	1–1
6 June 1973	*v* Poland (WCQ)	Chorzow	0–2
10 June 1973	*v* USSR	Moscow	2–1
14 June 1973	*v* Italy	Turin	0–2

1973–74
26 Sept 1973	*v* Austria	Wembley	7–0
17 Oct 1973	*v* Poland (WCQ)	Wembley	1–1
14 Nov 1973	*v* Italy	Wembley	0–1
11 May 1974	*v* Wales	Cardiff	2–0
15 May 1974	*v* Northern Ireland	Wembley	1–0

1975–76
30 Oct 1975	*v* Czechoslovakia (ECQ)	Bratislava	1–2
15 May 1976	*v* Scotland	Glasgow	1–2

1976–77
8 Sept 1976	*v* Eire	Wembley	1–1
17 Nov 1976	*v* Italy (WCQ)	Rome	0–2

McGARRY, WILLIAM H. *Born:* 10.6.27 (Stoke) *Club:* Huddersfield Town *Caps:* 4

1953–54
20 June 1954	*v* Switzerland (WC)	Berne	2–0
26 June 1954	*v* Uruguay (WC)	Basle	2–4

1955–56
2 Oct 1955	*v* Denmark	Copenhagen	5–1
22 Oct 1955	*v* Wales	Cardiff	1–2

McGUINNESS, WILF *Born:* 25.10.37 (Manchester) *Club:* Manchester United *Caps:* 2

1958–59

4 Oct 1958	*v* Northern Ireland	Belfast	3–3
24 May 1959	*v* Mexico	Mexico City	1–2

McMAHON, STEVE *Born:* 20.8.61 (Liverpool) *Club:* Liverpool *Caps:* 17

1987–88

17 Feb 1988	*v* Israel	Tel Aviv	0–0
27 April 1988	*v* Hungary	Budapest	0–0
24 May 1988	*v* Colombia (RC)	Wembley	1–1
18 June 1988	*v* USSR (EC)	Frankfurt	1–3

1988–89

7 June 1989	*v* Denmark (sub)	Copenhagen	1–1

1989–90

6 Sept 1989	*v* Sweden (WCQ)	Stockholm	0–0
11 Oct 1989	*v* Poland (WCQ)	Katowice	0–0
15 Nov 1989	*v* Italy	Wembley	0–0
13 Dec 1989	*v* Yugoslavia (sub)	Wembley	2–1
28 March 1990	*v* Brazil	Wembley	1–0
25 April 1990	*v* Czechoslovakia (sub)	Wembley	4–2
15 May 1990	*v* Denmark	Wembley	1–0
11 June 1990	*v* Eire (sub) (WC)	Cagliari	1–1
21 June 1990	*v* Egypt (WC)	Cagliari	1–0
26 June 1990	*v* Belgium (WC)	Bologna	1–0 (aet)
7 July 1990	*v* Italy (WC)	Bari	1–2

1990–91

14 Nov 1990	*v* Eire (ECQ)	Dublin	1–1

McNAB, ROBERT *Born:* 20.7.43 (Huddersfield) *Club:* Arsenal *Caps:* 4

1968–69

6 Nov 1968	*v* Romania (sub)	Bucharest	0–0
11 Dec 1968	*v* Bulgaria	Wembley	1–1
15 Jan 1969	*v* Romania	Wembley	1–1
3 May 1969	*v* Northern Ireland	Belfast	3–1

McNEIL, MICK *Born:* 7.2.40 (Middlesbrough) *Club:* Middlesbrough *Caps:* 9

1960–61

8 Oct 1960	*v* Northern Ireland	Belfast	5–2
19 Oct 1960	*v* Luxembourg (WCQ)	Luxembourg	9–0
26 Oct 1960	*v* Spain	Wembley	4–2
23 Nov 1960	*v* Wales	Wembley	5–1
15 April 1961	*v* Scotland	Wembley	9–3
10 May 1961	*v* Mexico	Wembley	8–0
21 May 1961	*v* Portugal (WCQ)	Lisbon	1–1
24 May 1961	*v* Italy	Rome	3–2

1961–62

28 Sept 1961	*v* Luxembourg (WCQ)	Arsenal	4–1

MEADOWS, JAMES *Born:* 21.7 .31 (Bolton) *Club:* Manchester City *Caps:* 1

1954–55

2 April 1955	*v* Scotland	Wembley	7–2

MEDLEY, LES D. *Born:* 3.9.20 (Edmonton) *Club:* Tottenham Hotspur *Caps:* 6 *Goals:* 1

1950–51

15 Nov 1950	*v* Wales	Sunderland	4–2
22 Nov 1950	*v* Yugoslavia	Arsenal	2–2

1951–52

3 Oct 1951	*v* France	Arsenal	2–2 (1 goal)
20 Oct 1951	*v* Wales	Cardiff	1–1
14 Nov 1951	*v* Northern Ireland	Aston Villa	2–0
28 Nov 1951	*v* Austria	Wembley	2–2

MELIA, JIMMY *Born:* 1.11.37 (Liverpool) *Club:* Liverpool *Caps:* 2 *Goals:* 1

1962–62

6 April 1963	*v* Scotland	Wembley	1–2
5 June 1963	*v* Switzerland	Basle	8–1 (1 goal)

MERRICK, GIL H. *Born:* 26.1.22 (Birmingham) *Club:* Birmingham City *Caps:* 23

1951–52

14 Nov 1951	*v* Northern Ireland	Aston Villa	2–0
28 Nov 1951	*v* Austria	Wembley	2–2
5 April 1952	*v* Scotland	Glasgow	2–1
18 May 1952	*v* Italy	Florence	1–1
25 May 1952	*v* Austria	Vienna	3–2
28 May 1952	*v* Switzerland	Zurich	3–0

1952–53

4 Oct 1952	*v* Northern Ireland	Belfast	2–2
12 Nov 1952	*v* Wales	Wembley	5–2
25 Nov 1952	*v* Belgium	Wembley	5–0
18 April 1953	*v* Scotland	Wembley	2–2
17 May 1953	*v* Argentina	Buenos Aires	0–0†
24 May 1953	*v* Chile	Santiago	2–1
31 May 1953	*v* Uruguay	Montevideo	1–2

1953–54

10 Oct 1953	*v* Wales (WCQ)	Cardiff	4–1
21 Oct 1953	*v* FIFA (Rest of Europe)	Wembley	4–4
11 Nov 1953	*v* Northern Ireland (WCQ)	Everton	3–1
25 Nov 1953	*v* Hungary	Wembley	3–6
3 April 1954	*v* Scotland (WCQ)	Glasgow	4–2
16 May 1954	*v* Yugoslavia	Belgrade	0–1
23 May 1954	*v* Hungary	Budapest	1–7
17 June 1954	*v* Belgium (WC)	Basle	4–4

| 20 June 1954 | v Switzerland (WC) | Berne | 2–0 |
| 26 June 1954 | v Uruguay (WC) | Basle | 2–4 |

MERSON, PAUL C. *Born:* 20.3.68 (London) *Club:* Arsenal *Caps:* 12 *Goals:* 1

1991–92

11 Sept 1991	v Germany (sub)	Wembley	0–1
25 March 1992	v Czechoslovakia	Prague	2–2 (1 goal)
12 May 1992	v Hungary	Budapest	1–0
17 May 1992	v Brazil (sub)	Wembley	1–1
3 June 1992	v Finland (sub)	Helsinki	2–1
11 June 1992	v Denmark (EC)	Malmo	0–0
17 June 1992	v Sweden (sub) (EC)	Stockholm	1–2

1992–93

9 Sept 1992	v Spain (sub)	Santander	0–1
14 Oct 1992	v Norway (sub) (WCQ)	Wembley	1–1
28 April 1993	v Holland (sub) (WCQ)	Wembley	2–2
13 June 1993	v Brazil (sub) (USC)	Washington	1–1
19 June 1993	v Germany (USC)	Detroit	1–2

METCALFE, VIC *Born:* 3.2.22 (Barrow) *Club:* Huddersfield Town *Caps:* 2

1950–51

| 9 May 1951 | v Argentina | Wembley | 2–1 |
| 19 May 1951 | v Portugal | Everton | 5–2 |

MILBURN, JOHN E.T. (JACKIE) *Born:* 11.5.24 (Ashington) *Club:* Newcastle United
Caps: 13 *Goals:* 10

1948–49

9 Oct 1948	v Northern Ireland	Belfast	6–2 (1 goal)
10 Nov 1948	v Wales	Aston Villa	1–0
1 Dec 1948	v Switzerland	Arsenal	6–0 (1 goal)
9 April 1949	v Scotland	Wembley	1–3 (1 goal)

1949–50

15 Oct 1949	v Wales (WCQ)	Cardiff	4–1 (3 goals)
14 May 1950	v Portugal	Lisbon	5–3
18 May 1950	v Belgium	Brussels	4–1
2 July 1950	v Spain (WC)	Rio de Janeiro	0–1
15 Nov 1950	v Wales	Sunderland	4–2 (1 goal)

1950–51

| 9 May 1951 | v Argentina | Wembley | 2–1 (1 goal) |
| 19 May 1951 | v Portugal | Everton | 5–2 (2 goals) |

1951–52

| 3 Oct 1951 | v France | Arsenal | 2–2 |

1955–56

| 2 Oct 1955 | v Denmark | Copenhagen | 5–1 |

MILLER, BRIAN G.   *Born:* 19.1.37 (Burnley)   *Club:* Burnley   *Caps:* 1

1960–61

27 May 1961	*v* Austria	Vienna	1–3

MILLS, MICK D.   *Born:* 4.1.49 (Godalming)   *Club:* Ipswich Town   *Caps:* 42

1972–73

11 Oct 1972	*v* Yugoslavia	Wembley	1–1

1975–76

24 March 1976	*v* Wales	Wrexham	2–1
8 May 1976	*v* Wales (FAWC)	Cardiff	1–0
11 May 1976	*v* Northern Ireland	Wembley	4–0
15 May 1976	*v* Scotland	Glasgow	1–2
23 May 1976	*v* Brazil (USABT)	Los Angeles	0–1
28 May 1976	*v* Italy (sub) (USABT)	New York	3–2
13 June 1976	*v* Finland (WCQ)	Helsinki	4–1

1976–77

13 Oct 1976	*v* Finland (sub) (WCQ)	Wembley	2–1
17 Nov 1976	*v* Italy (WCQ)	Rome	0–2
28 May 1977	*v* Northern Ireland	Belfast	2–1
31 May 1977	*v* Wales	Wembley	0–1
4 June 1977	*v* Scotland	Wembley	1–2

1977–78

22 Feb 1978	*v* West Germany	Munich	1–2
19 April 1978	*v* Brazil	Wembley	1–1
13 May 1978	*v* Wales*	Cardiff	3–1
16 May 1978	*v* Northern Ireland	Wembley	1–0
20 May 1978	*v* Scotland	Glasgow	1–0
24 May 1978	*v* Hungary	Wembley	4–1

1978–79

20 Sept 1978	*v* Denmark (ECQ)	Copenhagen	4–3
25 Oct 1978	*v* Eire (ECQ)	Dublin	1–1
7 Feb 1979	*v* Northern Ireland (ECQ)	Wembley	4–0
19 May 1979	*v* Northern Ireland*	Belfast	2–0
26 May 1979	*v* Scotland	Wembley	3–1
6 June 1979	*v* Bulgaria (ECQ)	Sofia	3–0
13 June 1979	*v* Austria	Vienna	3–4

1979–80

12 Sept 1979	*v* Denmark (ECQ)	Wembley	1–0
17 Oct 1979	*v* Northern Ireland (ECQ)	Belfast	5–1
26 March 1980	*v* Spain	Barcelona	2–0
18 June 1980	*v* Spain (EC)	Naples	2–1

1980–81

19 Nov 1980	*v* Switzerland* (WCQ)	Wembley	2–1
30 May 1981	*v* Switzerland (WCQ)	Basle	1–2
6 June 1981	*v* Hungary (WCQ)	Budapest	3–1

1981–82

9 Sept 1981	*v* Norway (WCQ)	Oslo	1–2
18 Nov 1981	*v* Hungary (WCQ)	Wembley	1–0
29 May 1982	*v* Scotland	Glasgow	1–0
3 June 1982	*v* Finland	Helsinki	4–1
16 June 1982	*v* France* (WC)	Bilbao	3–1
20 June 1982	*v* Czechoslovakia* (WC)	Bilbao	2–0
25 June 1982	*v* Kuwait* (WC)	Bilbao	1–0
29 June 1982	*v* West Germany* (WC)	Madrid	0–0
5 July 1982	*v* Spain* (WC)	Madrid	0–0

MILNE, GORDON *Born:* 29.3.37 (Preston) *Club:* Liverpool *Caps:* 14

1962–63

8 May 1963	*v* Brazil	Wembley	1–1
20 May 1963	*v* Czechoslovakia	Bratislava	4–2
2 June 1963	*v* East Germany	Leipzig	2–1

1963–64

12 Oct 1963	*v* Wales	Cardiff	4–0
23 Oct 1963	*v* Rest of the World	Wembley	2–1
20 Nov 1963	*v* Northern Ireland	Wembley	8–3
11 April 1964	*v* Scotland	Glasgow	0–1
6 May 1964	*v* Uruguay	Wembley	2–1
17 May 1964	*v* Portugal	Lisbon	4–3
24 May 1964	*v* Eire	Dublin	3–1
30 May 1964	*v* Brazil (BJT)	Rio de Janeiro	1–5
6 June 1964	*v* Argentina (BJT)	Rio de Janeiro	0–1

1964–65

3 Oct 1964	*v* Northern Ireland	Belfast	4–3
21 Oct 1964	*v* Belgium	Wembley	2–2

MILTON, ARTHUR C. *Born:* 10.3.28 (Bristol) *Club:* Arsenal *Caps:* 1

1951–52

28 Nov 1951	*v* Austria	Wembley	2–2

MOORE, ROBERT F. (BOBBY) *Born:* 12.4 .41 (Barking) *Club:* West Ham United *Caps:* 108 *Goals:* 2

1961–62

20 May 1962	*v* Peru	Lima	4–0
31 May 1962	*v* Hungary (WC)	Rancagua	1–2
2 June 1962	*v* Argentina (WC)	Rancagua	3–1
7 June 1962	*v* Bulgaria (WC)	Rancagua	0–0
10 June 1962	*v* Brazil (WC)	Vina del Mar	1–3

1962–63

3 Oct 1962	*v* France (ECQ)	Sheffield Wednesday	1–1
20 Oct 1962	*v* Northern Ireland	Belfast	3–1
21 Nov 1962	*v* Wales	Wembley	4–0
27 Feb 1963	*v* France (ECQ)	Paris	2–5

6 April 1963	v Scotland	Wembley	1–2
8 May 1963	v Brazil	Wembley	1–1
20 May 1963	v Czechoslovakia*	Bratislava	4–2
2 June 1963	v East Germany	Leipzig	2–1
5 June 1963	v Switzerland	Basle	8–1

1963–64

12 Oct 1963	v Wales	Cardiff	4–0
23 Oct 1963	v Rest of the World	Wembley	2–1
20 Nov 1963	v Northern Ireland	Wembley	8–3
11 April 1964	v Scotland	Glasgow	0–1
6 May 1964	v Uruguay*	Wembley	2–1
17 May 1964	v Portugal*	Lisbon	4–3
24 May 1964	v Eire*	Dublin	3–1
30 May 1964	v Brazil* (BJT)	Rio de Janeiro	1–5
4 June 1964	v Portugal* (BJT)	Sao Paulo	1–1
6 June 1964	v Argentina* (BJT)	Rio de Janeiro	0–1

1964–65

3 Oct 1964	v Northern Ireland*	Belfast	4–3
21 Oct 1964	v Belgium*	Wembley	2–2
10 April 1965	v Scotland*	Wembley	2–2
5 May 1965	v Hungary*	Wembley	1–0
9 May 1965	v Yugoslavia*	Belgrade	1–1
12 May 1965	v West Germany*	Nuremberg	1–0
16 May 1965	v Sweden*	Gothenburg	2–1

1965–66

2 Oct 1965	v Wales*	Cardiff	0–0
20 Oct 1965	v Austria*	Wembley	2–3
10 Nov 1965	v Northern Ireland*	Wembley	2–1
8 Dec 1965	v Spain*	Madrid	2–0
5 Jan 1966	v Poland*	Everton	1–1 (1 goal)
23 Feb 1966	v West Germany*	Wembley	1–0
2 April 1966	v Scotland*	Glasgow	4–3
29 June 1966	v Norway*	Oslo	6–1 (1 goal)
3 July 1966	v Denmark*·	Copenhagen	2–0
5 July 1966	v Poland*	Chorzow	1–0
11 July 1966	v Uruguay* (WC)	Wembley	0–0
16 July 1966	v Mexico* (WC)	Wembley	2–0
20 July 1966	v France* (WC)	Wembley	2–0
23 July 1966	v Argentina* (WC)	Wembley	1–0
26 July 1966	v Portugal* (WC)	Wembley	2–1
30 July 1966	v West Germany* (WCF)	Wembley	4–2 (aet)

1966–67

22 Oct 1966	v Northern Ireland* (ECQ)	Belfast	2–0
2 Nov 1966	v Czechoslovakia*	Wembley	0–0
16 Nov 1966	v Wales* (ECQ)	Wembley	5–1
15 April 1967	v Scotland* (ECQ)	Wembley	2–3
24 May 1967	v Spain*	Wembley	2–0
27 May 1967	v Austria*	Vienna	1–0

1967–68

21 Oct 1967	v Wales* (ECQ)	Cardiff	3–0
22 Nov 1967	v Northern Ireland* (ECQ)	Wembley	2–0
6 Dec 1967	v USSR*	Wembley	2–2
24 Feb 1968	v Scotland* (ECQ)	Glasgow	1–1
3 April 1968	v Spain* (ECQ)	Wembley	1–0
8 May 1968	v Spain* (ECQ)	Madrid	2–1
22 May 1968	v Sweden*	Wembley	3–1
1 June 1968	v West Germany*	Hanover	0–1
5 June 1968	v Yugoslavia* (EC)	Florence	0–1
8 June 1968	v USSR* (EC)	Rome	2–0

1968–69

6 Nov 1968	v Romania*	Bucharest	0–0
11 Dec 1968	v Bulgaria*	Wembley	1–1
12 March 1969	v France*	Wembley	5–0
3 May 1969	v Northern Ireland*	Belfast	3–1
7 May 1969	v Wales*	Wembley	2–1
10 May 1969	v Scotland*	Wembley	4–1
1 June 1969	v Mexico*	Mexico City	0–0
8 June 1969	v Uruguay*	Montevideo	2–1
12 June 1969	v Brazil*	Rio de Janeiro	1–2

1969–70

5 Nov 1969	v Holland*	Amsterdam	1–0
10 Dec 1969	v Portugal*	Wembley	1–0
25 Feb 1970	v Belgium*	Brussels	3–1
18 April 1970	v Wales*	Cardiff	1–1
21 April 1970	v Northern Ireland*	Wembley	3–1
25 April 1970	v Scotland*	Glasgow	0–0
25 May 1970	v Colombia*	Bogota	4–0
24 May 1970	v Ecuador*	Quito	2–0
2 June 1970	v Romania* (WC)	Guadalajara	1–0
7 June 1970	v Brazil* (WC)	Guadalajara	0–1
11 June 1970	v Czechoslovakia* (WC)	Guadalajara	1–0
14 June 1970	v West Germany* (WC)	Leon	2–3 (aet)

1970–71

25 Nov 1970	v East Germany*	Wembley	3–1
21 April 1971	v Greece* (ECQ)	Wembley	3–0
12 May 1971	v Malta* (ECQ)	Wembley	5–0
15 May 1971	v Northern Ireland*	Belfast	1–0
22 May 1971	v Scotland*	Wembley	3–1

1971–72

13 Oct 1971	v Switzerland* (ECQ)	Basle	3–2
10 Nov 1971	v Switzerland* (ECQ)	Wembley	1–1
1 Dec 1971	v Greece* (ECQ)	Athens	2–0
29 April 1972	v West Germany* (ECQ)	Wembley	1–3
13 May 1972	v West Germany* (ECQ)	Berlin	0–0
20 May 1972	v Wales*	Cardiff	3–0
27 May 1972	v Scotland*	Glasgow	1–0

1972–73

11 Oct 1972	v Yugoslavia*	Wembley	1–1
15 Nov 1972	v Wales* (WCQ)	Cardiff	1–0
24 Jan 1973	v Wales* (WCQ)	Wembley	1–1
14 Feb 1973	v Scotland* (SFAC)	Glasgow	5–0
12 May 1973	v Northern Ireland*	Everton	2–1
15 May 1973	v Wales*	Wembley	3–0
19 May 1973	v Scotland*	Wembley	1–0
27 May 1973	v Czechoslovakia*	Prague	1–1
6 June 1973	v Poland* (WCQ)	Chorzow	0–2
10 June 1973	v USSR*	Moscow	2–1
14 June 1973	v Italy*	Turin	0–2

1973–74

14 Nov 1973	v Italy*	Wembley	0–1

MORLEY, ANTONY W. *Born:* 26.8.54 (Ormskirk) *Club:* Aston Villa *Caps:* 6

1981–82

18 Nov 1981	v Hungary (sub) (WCQ)	Wembley	1–0
23 Feb 1982	v Northern Ireland	Wembley	4–0
27 April 1982	v Wales	Cardiff	1–0
2 June 1982	v Iceland	Reykjavik	1–1

1982–83

22 Sept 1982	v Denmark (ECQ)	Copenhagen	2–2
17 Nov 1982	v Greece (ECQ)	Salonika	3–0

MORRIS, JOHN *Born:* 27.9.24 (Radcliffe) *Club:* Derby County *Caps:* 3 *Goals:* 3

1948–49

18 May 1949	v Norway	Oslo	4–1 (1 goal)
22 May 1949	v France	Paris	3–1 (2 goals)

1949–50

21 Sept 1949	v Eire	Everton	0–2

MORTENSEN, STANLEY H. *Born:* 26.5.21 (South Shields) *Club:* Blackpool *Caps:* 25 *Goals:* 23

1946–47

27 May 1947	v Portugal	Lisbon	10–0 (4 goals)

1947–48

21 Sept 1947	v Belgium	Brussels	5–2 (1 goal)
18 Oct 1947	v Wales	Cardiff	3–0 (1 goal)
5 Nov 1947	v Northern Ireland	Everton	2–2
19 Nov 1947	v Sweden	Arsenal	4–2 (3 goals)
10 April 1948	v Scotland	Glasgow	2–0 (1 goal)
16 May 1948	v Italy	Turin	4–0 (1 goal)

1948–49

9 Oct 1948	v Northern Ireland	Belfast	6–2 (3 goals)
10 Nov 1948	v Wales	Aston Villa	1–0
9 April 1949	v Scotland	Wembley	1–3

13 May 1949	*v* Sweden	Stockholm	1–3
18 May 1949	*v* Norway	Oslo	4–1

1949–50

15 Oct 1949	*v* Wales (WCQ)	Cardiff	4–1 (1 goal)
16 Nov 1949	*v* Northern Ireland (WCQ)	Manchester City	9–2 (2 goals)
30 Nov 1949	*v* Italy	Tottenham	2–0
15 April 1950	*v* Scotland (WCQ)	Glasgow	1–0
14 May 1950	*v* Portugal	Lisbon	5–3 (1 goal)
18 May 1950	*v* Belgium	Brussels	4–1 (1 goal)
25 June 1950	*v* Chile (WC)	Rio de Janeiro	2–0 (1 goal)
29 June 1950	*v* USA (WC)	Belo Horizonte	0–1
2 July 1950	*v* Spain (WC)	Rio de Janeiro	0–1

1950–51

14 April 1951	*v* Scotland	Wembley	2–3
9 May 1951	*v* Argentina	Wembley	2–1 (1 goal)

1953–54

21 Oct 1953	*v* FIFA (Rest of Europe)	Wembley	4–4 (1 goal)
25 Nov 1953	*v* Hungary	Wembley	3–6 (1 goal)

MOZLEY, BERT *Born:* 23.9.23 (Derby) *Club:* Derby County *Caps:* 3

1949–50

21 Sept 1949	*v* Eire	Everton	0–2
15 Oct 1949	*v* Wales (WCQ)	Cardiff	4–1
16 Nov 1949	*v* Northern Ireland (WCQ)	Manchester City	9–2

MULLEN, JAMES *Born:* 6.1.23 (Newcastle) *Club:* Wolverhampton Wanderers *Caps:* 12
Goals: 6

1946–47

12 April 1947	*v* Scotland	Wembley	1–1

1948–49

18 May 1949	*v* Norway	Oslo	4–1 (1 goal)
22 May 1949	*v* France	Paris	3–1

1949–50

18 May 1950	*v* Belgium (sub)	Brussels	4–1 (1 goal)
25 June 1950	*v* Chile (WC)	Rio de Janeiro	2–0
29 June 1950	*v* USA (WC)	Belo Horinzonte	0–1

1953–54

10 Oct 1953	*v* Wales (WCQ)	Cardiff	4–1
21 Oct 1953	*v* FIFA (Rest of Europe)	Wembley	4–4 (2 goals)
11 Nov 1953	*v* Northern Ireland (WCQ)	Everton	3–1
3 April 1954	*v* Scotland	Glasgow	4–2 (1 goal)
16 May 1954	*v* Yugoslavia	Belgrade	0–1
20 June 1954	*v* Switzerland (WC)	Berne	2–0 (1 goal)

MULLERY, ALAN P. *Born:* 23.11.41 (Notting Hill) *Club:* Tottenham Hotspur *Caps:* 35 *Goals:* 1

1964–65

| 9 Dec 1964 | *v* Holland | Amsterdam | 1–1 |

1966–67

| 24 May 1967 | *v* Spain | Wembley | 2–0 |
| 27 May 1967 | *v* Austria | Vienna | 1–0 |

1967–68

21 Oct 1967	*v* Wales (ECQ)	Cardiff	3–0
22 Nov 1967	*v* Northern Ireland (ECQ)	Wembley	2–0
6 Dec 1967	*v* USSR	Wembley	2–2
24 Feb 1968	*v* Scotland (ECQ)	Glasgow	1–1
3 April 1968	*v* Spain (ECQ)	Wembley	1–0
8 May 1968	*v* Spain (ECQ)	Madrid	2–1
22 May 1968	*v* Sweden	Wembley	3–1
5 June 1968	*v* Yugoslavia (EC)	Florence	0–1

1968–69

6 Nov 1968	*v* Romania	Bucharest	0–0
11 Dec 1968	*v* Bulgaria	Wembley	1–1
12 March 1969	*v* France	Wembley	5–0
3 May 1969	*v* Northern Ireland	Belfast	3–1
10 May 1969	*v* Scotland	Wembley	4–1
1 June 1969	*v* Mexico	Mexico City	0–0
8 June 1969	*v* Uruguay	Montevideo	2–1
12 June 1969	*v* Brazil	Rio de Janeiro	1–2

1969–70

5 Nov 1969	*v* Holland	Amsterdam	1–0
10 Dec 1969	*v* Portugal	Wembley	1–0
14 Jan 1970	*v* Holland (sub)	Wembley	0–0
18 April 1970	*v* Wales	Cardiff	1–1
21 April 1970	*v* Northern Ireland	Wembley	3–1
25 April 1970	*v* Scotland (sub)	Glasgow	0–0
20 May 1970	*v* Colombia	Bogota	4–0
24 May 1970	*v* Ecuador	Quito	2–0
2 June 1970	*v* Romania (WC)	Guadalajara	1–0
7 June 1970	*v* Brazil (WC)	Guadalajara	0–1
11 June 1970	*v* Czechoslovakia (WC)	Guadalajara	1–0
14 June 1970	*v* West Germany (WC)	Leon	2–3 (aet) (1 goal)

1970–71

25 Nov 1970	*v* East Germany	Wembley	3–1
3 Feb 1971	*v* Malta* (ECQ)	Valletta	1–0
21 April 1971	*v* Greece (ECQ)	Wembley	3–0

1971–72

| 13 Oct 1971 | *v* Switzerland (ECQ) | Basle | 3–2 |

NEAL, PHILIP G. *Born:* 22.2.51 (Irchester) *Club:* Liverpool *Caps:* 50 *Goals:* 5

1975-76

24 March 1976	*v* Wales (FAWC)	Wrexham	2–1
28 May 1976	*v* Italy (USABT)	New York	3–2

1976–77

31 May 1977	*v* Wales	Wembley	0–1
4 June 1977	*v* Scotland	Wembley	1–2
8 June 1977	*v* Brazil	Rio de Janeiro	0–0
12 June 1977	*v* Argentina	Buenos Aires	1–1
15 June 1977	*v* Uruguay	Montevideo	0–0

1977–78

7 Sept 1977	*v* Switzerland	Wembley	0–0
16 Nov 1977	*v* Italy (WCQ)	Wembley	2–0
22 Feb 1978	*v* West Germany	Munich	1–2
16 May 1978	*v* Northern Ireland	Wembley	1–0 (1 goal)
20 May 1978	*v* Scotland	Glasgow	1–0
24 May 1978	*v* Hungary	Wembley	4–1 (1 goal)

1978–79

20 Sept 1978	*v* Denmark (ECQ)	Copenhagen	4–3 (1 goal)
25 Oct 1978	*v* Eire (ECQ)	Dublin	1–1
7 Feb 1979	*v* Northern Ireland (ECQ)	Wembley	4–0
19 May 1979	*v* Northern Ireland	Belfast	2–0
26 May 1979	*v* Scotland	Wembley	3–1
6 June 1979	*v* Bulgaria (ECQ)	Sofia	3–0
13 June 1979	*v* Austria	Vienna	3–4

1979–80

12 Sept 1979	*v* Denmark (ECQ)	Wembley	1–0
17 Oct 1979	*v* Northern Ireland (ECQ)	Belfast	5–1
26 March 1980	*v* Spain	Barcelona	2–0
13 May 1980	*v* Argentina	Wembley	3–1
17 May 1980	*v* Wales	Wrexham	1–4
12 June 1980	*v* Belgium (EC)	Turin	1–1
15 June 1980	*v* Italy (EC)	Turin	0–1

1980–81

15 Oct 1980	*v* Romania (WCQ)	Bucharest	1–2
19 Nov 1980	*v* Switzerland (WCQ)	Wembley	2–1
25 March 1981	*v* Spain	Wembley	1–2
12 May 1981	*v* Brazil	Wembley	0–1
6 June 1981	*v* Hungary (WCQ)	Budapest	3–1

1981–82

9 Sept 1981	*v* Norway (WCQ)	Oslo	1–2
18 Nov 1981	*v* Hungary (WCQ)	Wembley	1–0
27 April 1982	*v* Wales	Cardiff	1–0
25 May 1982	*v* Holland	Wembley	2–0
2 June 1982	*v* Iceland*	Reykjavik	1–1
16 June 1982	*v* France (sub) (WC)	Bilbao	3–1
25 June 1982	*v* Kuwait (WC)	Bilbao	1–0

1982–83

22 Sept 1982	v Denmark (ECQ)	Copenhagen	2–2
17 Nov 1982	v Greece (ECQ)	Salonika	3–0
15 Dec 1982	v Luxembourg (ECQ)	Wembley	9–0 (1 goal)
23 Feb 1983	v Wales	Wembley	2–1 (1 goal)
30 March 1983	v Greece (ECQ)	Wembley	0–0
27 April 1983	v Hungary (ECQ)	Wembley	2–0
28 May 1983	v Northern Ireland	Belfast	0–0
1 June 1983	v Scotland	Wembley	2–0
15 June 1983	v Australia	Brisbane	1–0
19 June 1983	v Australia	Melbourne	1–1

1983–84

21 Sept 1983	v Denmark (ECQ)	Wembley	0–1

NEWTON, KEITH R. *Born:* 23.6.41 (Manchester) *Clubs:* Blackburn Rovers, Everton
Caps: 27

1965–66 (with Blackburn Rovers)

23 Feb 1966	v West Germany	Wembley	1–0
2 April 1966	v Scotland	Glasgow	4–3

1966–67

24 May 1967	v Spain	Wembley	2–0
27 May 1967	v Austria	Vienna	1–0

1967–68

21 Oct 1967	v Wales (ECQ)	Cardiff	3–0
24 Feb 1968	v Scotland (ECQ)	Glasgow	1–1
8 May 1968	v Spain (ECQ)	Madrid	2–1
22 May 1968	v Sweden	Wembley	3–1
1 June 1968	v West Germany	Hanover	0–1
5 June 1968	v Yugoslavia (EC)	Florence	0–1

1968–69

6 Nov 1968	v Romania	Bucharest	0–0
11 Dec 1968	v Bulgaria	Wembley	1–1
12 March 1969	v France	Wembley	5–0
3 May 1969	v Northern Ireland	Belfast	3–1
7 May 1969	v Wales	Wembley	2–1
10 May 1969	v Scotland	Wembley	4–1
1 June 1969	v Mexico	Mexico City	0–0
8 June 1969	v Uruguay	Montevideo	2–1
12 June 1969	v Brazil	Rio de Janeiro	1–2

1969–70 (with Everton)

14 Jan 1970	v Holland	Wembley	0–0
21 April 1970	v Northern Ireland	Wembley	3–1
25 April 1970	v Scotland	Glasgow	0–0
20 May 1970	v Colombia	Bogota	4–0
24 May 1970	v Ecuador	Quito	2–0
2 June 1970	v Romania (WC)	Guadalajara	1–0
11 June 1970	v Czechoslovakia (WC)	Guadalajara	1–0
14 June 1970	v West Germany (WC)	Leon	2–3 (aet)

NICHOLLS, JOHNNY *Born:* 3.4.31 (Wolverhampton) *Club:* West Bromwich Albion
Caps: 2 *Goals:* 1

1953–54
3 April 1954	*v* Scotland (WCQ)	Glasgow	4–2 (1 goal)
16 May 1954	*v* Yugoslavia	Belgrade	0–1

NICHOLSON, WILLIAM E. *Born:* 26.1.19 (Scarborough) *Club:* Tottenham Hotspur
Caps: 1 *Goals:* 1

1950–51
19 May 1951	*v* Portugal	Everton	5–2 (1 goal)

NISH, DAVID J. *Born:* 26.9.47 (Burton) *Club:* Derby County *Caps:* 5

1972–73
12 May 1973	*v* Northern Ireland	Everton	2–1

1973–74
3 April 1974	*v* Portugal	Lisbon	0–0
11 May 1974	*v* Wales	Cardiff	2–0
15 May 1974	*v* Northern Ireland	Wembley	1–0
18 May 1974	*v* Scotland	Glasgow	0–2

NORMAN, MAURICE *Born:* 8.5.34 (Mulbarton) *Club:* Tottenham Hotspur *Caps:* 23

1961–62
20 May 1962	*v* Peru	Lima	4–0
31 May 1962	*v* Hungary (WC)	Rancagua	1–2
2 June 1962	*v* Argentina (WC)	Rancagua	3–1
7 June 1962	*v* Bulgaria (WC)	Rancagua	0–0
10 June 1962	*v* Brazil (WC)	Vina del Mar	1–3

1962–63
3 Oct 1962	*v* France (ECQ)	Sheffield Wednesday	1–1
6 April 1963	*v* Scotland	Wembley	1–2
8 May 1963	*v* Brazil	Wembley	1–1
20 May 1963	*v* Czechoslovakia	Bratislava	4–2
2 June 1963	*v* East Germany	Leipzig	2–1

1963–64
12 Oct 1963	*v* Wales	Cardiff	4–0
23 Oct 1963	*v* Rest of the World	Wembley	2–1
20 Nov 1963	*v* Northern Ireland	Wembley	8–3
11 April 1964	*v* Scotland	Glasgow	0–1
6 May 1964	*v* Uruguay	Wembley	2–1
17 May 1964	*v* Portugal	Lisbon	4–3
27 May 1964	*v* USA	New York	10–0
30 May 1964	*v* Brazil (BJT)	Rio de Janeiro	1–5
4 June 1964	*v* Portugal (BJT)	Sao Paulo	1–1
6 June 1964	*v* Argentina (BJT)	Rio de Janeiro	0–1

1964–65
3 Oct 1964	*v* Northern Ireland	Belfast	4–3

| 21 Oct 1964 | *v* Belgium | Wembley | 2–2 |
| 9 Dec 1964 | *v* Holland | Amsterdam | 1–1 |

O'GRADY, MIKE *Born:* 11.10.42 (Leeds) *Clubs:* Huddersfield Town, Leeds United
Caps: 2 *Goals:* 3

1962–63 (with Huddersfield Town)
| 20 Oct 1962 | *v* Northern Ireland | Belfast | 3–1 (2 goals) |

1968–69 (with Leeds United)
| 12 March 1969 | *v* France | Wembley | 5–0 (1 goal) |

OSGOOD, PETER L. *Born:* 20.2.47 (Windsor) *Club:* Chelsea *Caps:* 4

1969–70
25 Feb 1970	*v* Belgium	Brussels	3–1
2 June 1970	*v* Romania (sub) (WC)	Guadalajara	1–0
11 June 1970	*v* Czechoslovakia (sub)(WC)	Guadalajara	1–0

1973–74
| 14 Nov 1973 | *v* Italy | Wembley | 0–1 |

OSMAN, RUSSELL C. *Born:* 14.2.59 (Ilkeston) *Club:* Ipswich Town *Caps:* 11

1979–80
| 31 May 1980 | *v* Australia | Sydney | 2–1 |

1980–81
25 March 1981	*v* Spain	Wembley	1–2
29 April 1981	*v* Romania (WCQ)	Wembley	0–0
30 May 1981	*v* Switzerland (WCQ)	Basle	1–2

1981–82
| 9 Sept 1981 | *v* Norway (WCQ) | Oslo | 1–2 |
| 2 June 1982 | *v* Iceland | Reykjavik | 1–1 |

1982–83
22 Sept 1982	*v* Denmark (ECQ)	Copenhagen	2–2
12 June 1983	*v* Australia	Sydney	0–0
15 June 1983	*v* Australia	Brisbane	1–0
19 June 1983	*v* Australia	Melbourne	1–1

1983–84
| 21 Sept 1983 | *v* Denmark (ECQ) | Wembley | 0–1 |

OWEN, SID W. *Born:* 29.9.22 (Birmingham) *Club:* Luton Town *Caps:* 3

1953–54
16 May 1954	*v* Yugoslavia	Belgrade	0–1
23 May 1954	*v* Hungary	Budapest	1–7
17 June 1954	*v* Belgium (WC)	Basle	4–4

PAINE, TERRY L. *Born:* 23.3.39 (Winchester) *Club:* Southampton *Caps:* 19 *Goals:* 7

1962–63
| 20 May 1963 | *v* Czechoslovakia | Bratislava | 4–2 |

2 June 1963	*v* East Germany	Leipzig	2–1

1963–64

12 Oct 1963	*v* Wales	Cardiff	4–0
23 Oct 1963	*v* Rest of the World	Wembley	2–1 (1 goal)
20 Nov 1963	*v* Northern Ireland	Wembley	8–3 (3 goals)
11 April 1964	*v* Scotland	Glasgow	0–1
6 May 1964	*v* Uruguay	Wembley	2–1
27 May 1964	*v* USA	New York	10–0 (2 goals)
4 June 1964	*v* Portugal (BJT)	Sao Paulo	1–1

1964–65

3 Oct 1964	*v* Northern Ireland	Belfast	4–3
5 May 1965	*v* Hungary	Wembley	1–0
9 May 1965	*v* Yugoslavia	Belgrade	1–1
12 May 1965	*v* West Germany	Nuremberg	1–0 (1 goal)
16 May 1965	*v* Sweden	Gothenburg	2–1

1965–66

2 Oct 1965	*v* Wales	Cardiff	0–0
20 Oct 1965	*v* Austria	Wembley	2–3
4 May 1966	*v* Yugoslavia	Wembley	2–0
29 June 1966	*v* Norway	Oslo	6–1
16 July 1966	*v* Mexico (WC)	Wembley	2–0

PALLISTER, GARY A. *Born:* 30.6.65 (Ramsgate) *Clubs:* Middlesbrough, Manchester United *Caps:* 9

1987–88 (with Middlesbrough)

27 April 1988	*v* Hungary	Budapest	0–0

1988–89

16 Nov 1988	*v* Saudi Arabia	Riyadh	1–1

1990–91 (with Manchester United)

6 Feb 1991	*v* Cameroon (sub)	Wembley	2–0
1 May 1991	*v* Turkey (ECQ)	Izmir	1–0

1991–92

11 Sept 1991	*v* Germany	Wembley	0–1

1992–93

2 June 1993	*v* Norway (WCQ)	Oslo	0–2
9 June 1993	*v* USA (USC)	Boston	0–2
13 June 1993	*v* Brazil (USC)	Washington	1–1
19 June 1993	*v* Germany (USC)	Detroit	1–2

PALMER, CARLTON L. *Born:* 5.12.65 (West Bromwich) *Club:* Sheffield Wednesday *Caps:* 17 *Goals:* 1

1991–92

29 April 1992	*v* CIS	Moscow	2–2
12 May 1992	*v* Hungary	Budapest	1–0
17 May 1992	*v* Brazil	Wembley	1–1
3 June 1992	*v* Finland (sub)	Helsinki	2–1
11 June 1992	*v* Denmark (EC)	Malmo	0–0

14 June 1992	v France (EC)	Malmo	0–0
17 June 1992	v Sweden (EC)	Stockholm	1–2

1992–93

9 Sept 1992	v Spain (sub)	Santander	0–1
14 Oct 1992	v Norway (sub) (WCQ)	Wembley	1–1
18 Nov 1992	v Turkey (WCQ)	Wembley	4–0
17 Feb 1993	v San Marino (WCQ)	Wembley	6–0 (1 goal)
31 March 1993	v Turkey (WCQ)	Izmir	2–0
28 April 1993	v Holland (WCQ)	Wembley	2–2
29 May 1993	v Poland (WCQ)	Chorzow	1–1
2 June 1993	v Norway (WCQ)	Oslo	0–2
9 June 1993	v USA (USC)	Boston	0–2
13 June 1993	v Brazil (sub) (USC)	Washington	1–1

PARKER, PAUL A. *Born:* 4 .4.64 (Essex) *Clubs:* Queens Park Rangers, Manchester United *Caps:* 17

1988–89 (with Queens Park Rangers)

26 April 1989	v Albania (sub) (WCQ)	Wembley	5–0
23 May 1989	v Chile (RC)	Wembley	0–0
7 June 1989	v Denmark	Copenhagen	1–1

1989–1990

13 Dec 1989	v Yugoslavia	Wembley	2–1
22 May 1990	v Uruguay	Wembley	1–2
16 June 1990	v Holland (WC)	Cagliari	0–0
21 June 1990	v Egypt (WC)	Cagliari	1–0
26 June 1990	v Belgium (WC)	Bologna	1–0 (aet)
1 July 1990	v Cameroon (WC)	Naples	3–2 (aet)
4 July 1990	v West Germany (WC)	Turin	1–1 (aet)
7 July 1990	v Italy (WC)	Bari	1–2

1990–91

12 Sept 1990	v Hungary	Wembley	1–0
17 Oct 1990	v Poland (ECQ)	Wembley	2–0
21 May 1991	v USSR	Wembley	3–1
1 June 1991	v Australia	Sydney	1–0
3 June 1991	v New Zealand	Auckland	1–0

1991–92 (with Manchester United)

11 Sept 1991	v Germany	Wembley	0–1

PARKES, PHILIP B. *Born:* 8.8.50 (Sedgley) *Club:* Queens Park Rangers *Caps:* 1

1973–74

3 April 1974	v Portugal	Lisbon	0–0

PARRY, RAY A. *Born:* 19.1.36 (Derby) *Club:* Bolton Wanderers *Caps:* 2 *Goals:* 1

1959–60

18 Nov 1959	v Northern Ireland	Wembley	2–1 (1 goal)
19 April 1960	v Scotland	Glasgow	1–1

PEACOCK, ALAN *Born:* 29.10.37 (Middlesbrough) *Clubs:* Middlesbrough, Leeds United
Caps: 6 *Goals:* 3

1961–62 (with Middlesbrough)

2 June 1962	*v* Argentina (WC)	Rancagua	3–1
7 June 1962	*v* Bulgaria (WC)	Rancagua	0–0

1962–63

20 Oct 1962	*v* Northern Ireland	Belfast	3–1
21 Nov 1962	*v* Wales	Wembley	4–0 (2 goals)

1965–66 (with Leeds United)

2 Oct 1965	*v* Wales	Cardiff	0–0
10 Nov 1965	*v* Northern Ireland	Wembley	2–1 (1 goal)

PEARCE, STUART *Born:* 24.4.62 (Shepherds Bush) *Club:* Nottingham Forest *Caps:* 53
Goals: 3

1986–87

19 May 1987	*v* Brazil (RC)	Wembley	1–1
23 May 1987	*v* Scotland (RC)	Glasgow	0–0

1987–88

9 Sept 1987	*v* West Germany (sub)	Düsseldorf	1–3
17 Feb 1988	*v* Israel	Tel Aviv	0–0
27 April 1988	*v* Hungary	Budapest	0–0

1988–89

14 Sept 1988	*v* Denmark	Wembley	1–0
19 Oct 1988	*v* Sweden (WCQ)	Wembley	0–0
16 Nov 1988	*v* Saudi Arabia	Riyadh	1–1
8 Feb 1989	*v* Greece	Athens	2–1
8 March 1989	*v* Albania (WCQ)	Tirana	2–0
26 April 1989	*v* Albania (WCQ)	Wembley	5–0
23 May 1989	*v* Chile (RC)	Wembley	0–0
27 May 1989	*v* Scotland (RC)	Glasgow	2–0
3 June 1989	*v* Poland (WCQ)	Wembley	3–0
7 June 1989	*v* Denmark	Copenhagen	1–1

1989–90

6 Sept 1989	*v* Sweden (WCQ)	Stockholm	0–0
11 Oct 1989	*v* Poland (WCQ)	Katowice	0–0
15 Nov 1989	*v* Italy	Wembley	0–0
13 Dec 1989	*v* Yugoslavia	Wembley	2–1
28 March 1990	*v* Brazil	Wembley	1–0
25 April 1990	*v* Czechoslovakia	Wembley	4–2 (1 goal)
15 May 1990	*v* Denmark	Wembley	1–0
22 May 1990	*v* Uruguay	Wembley	1–2
2 June 1990	*v* Tunisia	Tunis	1–1
11 June 1990	*v* Eire (WC)	Cagliari	1–1
16 June 1990	*v* Holland (WC)	Cagliari	0–0
21 June 1990	*v* Egypt (WC)	Cagliari	1–0
26 June 1990	*v* Belgium (WC)	Bologna	1–0 (aet)
1 July 1990	*v* Cameroon (WC)	Naples	3–2 (aet)

4 July 1990	*v* West Germany (WC)	Turin	1–1 (aet)

1990–91

12 Sept 1990	*v* Hungary	Wembley	1–0
17 Oct 1990	*v* Poland (ECQ)	Wembley	2–0
14 Nov 1990	*v* Eire (ECQ)	Dublin	1–1
6 Feb 1991	*v* Cameroon	Wembley	2–0
27 March 1991	*v* Eire (ECQ)	Wembley	1–1
1 May 1991	*v* Turkey (ECQ)	Izmir	1–0
25 May 1991	*v* Argentina	Wembley	2–2
1 June 1991	*v* Australia	Sydney	1–0
3 June 1991	*v* New Zealand	Auckland	1–0
8 June 1991	*v* New Zealand*	Wellington	2–0 (1 goal)
12 June 1991	*v* Malaysia	Kuala Lumpur	4–2

1991–92

16 Oct 1991	*v* Turkey (ECQ)	Wembley	1–0
13 Nov 1991	*v* Poland (ECQ)	Poznan	1–1
19 Feb 1992	*v* France*	Wembley	2–0
25 March 1992	*v* Czechoslovakia*	Prague	2–2
17 May 1992	*v* Brazil	Wembley	1–1
3 June 1992	*v* Finland	Helsinki	2–1
11 June 1992	*v* Denmark (EC)	Malmo	0–0
14 June 1992	*v* France (EC)	Malmo	0–0
17 June 1992	*v* Sweden (EC)	Stockholm	1–2

1992–93

9 Sept 1992	*v* Spain*	Santander	0–1
14 Nov 1992	*v* Norway* (WCQ)	Wembley	1–1
18 Nov 1992	*v* Turkey* (WCQ)	Wembley	4–0 (1 goal)

PEARSON, STUART J. *Born:* 21.6.49 (Hull) *Club:* Manchester United *Caps:* 15 *Goals:* 5

1975–76

8 May 1976	*v* Wales	Cardiff	1–0
11 May 1976	*v* Northern Ireland	Wembley	4–0 (1 goal)
15 May 1976	*v* Scotland	Glasgow	1–2
23 May 1976	*v* Brazil (USABT)	Los Angeles	0–1
13 June 1976	*v* Finland (WCQ)	Helsinki	4–1 (1 goal)

1976–77

8 Sept 1976	*v* Eire	Wembley	1–1 (1 goal)
9 Feb 1977	*v* Holland (sub)	Wembley	0–2
31 May 1977	*v* Wales	Wembley	0–1
4 June 1977	*v* Scotland	Wembley	1–2
8 June 1977	*v* Brazil	Rio de Janeiro	0–0
12 June 1977	*v* Argentina	Buenos Aires	1–1 (1 goal)
15 June 1977	*v* Uruguay	Montevideo	0–0

1977–78

16 Nov 1977	*v* Italy (sub) (WCQ)	Wembley	2–0
22 Feb 1978	*v* West Germany	Munich	1–2 (1 goal)
16 May 1978	*v* Northern Ireland	Wembley	1–0

PEARSON, STAN C. *Born:* 11.1.19 (Salford) *Club:* Manchester United *Caps:* 8 *Goals:* 5

1947–48
10 April 1948	*v* Scotland	Glasgow	2–0

1948–49
9 Oct 1948	*v* Northern Ireland	Belfast	6–2 (1 goal)
9 April 1949	*v* Scotland	Wembley	1–3

1949–50
16 Nov 1949	*v* Northern Ireland (WCQ)	Manchester City	9–2 (2 goals)
30 Nov 1949	*v* Italy	Tottenham	2–0

1950–51
19 May 1951	*v* Portugal	Everton	5–2

1951–52
5 April 1952	*v* Scotland	Glasgow	2–1 (2 goals)
18 May 1952	*v* Italy	Florence	1–1

PEGG, DAVID *Born:* 20.9.35 (Doncaster) *Club:* Manchester United *Caps:* 1

1956–57
19 May 1957	*v* Eire (WCQ)	Dublin	1–1

PEJIC, MIKE *Born:* 25.1.50 (Chesterton) *Club:* Stoke City *Caps:* 4

1973–74
3 April 1974	*v* Portugal	Lisbon	0–0
11 May 1974	*v* Wales	Cardiff	2–0
15 May 1974	*v* Northern Ireland	Wembley	1–0
18 May 1974	*v* Scotland	Glasgow	0–2

PERRY, WILLIAM *Born:* 10.9.30 (South Africa) *Club:* Blackpool *Caps:* 3 *Goals:* 2

1955–56
2 Nov 1955	*v* Northern Ireland	Wembley	3–0
30 Nov 1955	*v* Spain	Wembley	4–1 (2 goals)
14 April 1956	*v* Scotland	Glasgow	1–1

PERRYMAN, STEVE J. *Born:* 21.12.51 (Ealing) *Club:* Tottenham Hotspur *Caps:* 1

1981–82
2 June 1982	*v* Iceland (sub)	Reykjavik	1–1

PETERS, MARTIN S. *Born:* 8.11.43 (Plaistow) *Clubs:* West Ham United, Tottenham Hotspur *Caps:* 67 *Goals:* 20

1965–66 (with West Ham United)
4 May 1966	*v* Yugoslavia	Wembley	2–0
26 June 1966	*v* Finland	Helsinki	3–0 (1 goal)
5 July 1966	*v* Poland	Chorzow	1–0
16 July 1966	*v* Mexico (WC)	Wembley	2–0
20 July 1966	*v* France (WC)	Wembley	2–0
23 July 1966	*v* Argentina (WC)	Wembley	1–0

26 July 1966	*v* Portugal (WC)	Wembley	2–1
30 July 1966	*v* West Germany (WCF)	Wembley	4–2 (aet)
			(1 goal)

1966–67

22 Oct 1966	*v* Northern Ireland (ECQ)	Belfast	2–0 (1 goal)
2 Nov 1966	*v* Czechoslovakia	Wembley	0–0
16 Nov 1966	*v* Wales (ECQ)	Wembley	5–1
15 April 1967	*v* Scotland (ECQ)	Wembley	2–3

1967–68

21 Oct 1967	*v* Wales (ECQ)	Cardiff	3–0 (1 goal)
22 Nov 1967	*v* Northern Ireland (ECQ)	Wembley	2–0
6 Dec 1967	*v* USSR	Wembley	2–2 (1 goal)
24 Feb 1968	*v* Scotland (ECQ)	Glasgow	1–1 (1 goal)
3 April 1968	*v* Spain (ECQ)	Wembley	1–0
8 May 1968	*v* Spain (ECQ)	Madrid	2–1 (1 goal)
22 May 1968	*v* Sweden	Wembley	3–1 (1 goal)
5 June 1968	*v* Yugoslavia (EC)	Florence	0–1
8 June 1968	*v* USSR (EC)	Rome	2–0

1968–69

6 Nov 1968	*v* Romania	Bucharest	0–0
11 Dec 1968	*v* Bulgaria	Wembley	1–1
12 March 1969	*v* France	Wembley	5–0
3 May 1969	*v* Northern Ireland	Belfast	3–1 (1 goal)
10 May 1969	*v* Scotland	Wembley	4–1 (2 goals)
1 June 1969	*v* Mexico	Mexico City	0–0
8 June 1969	*v* Uruguay	Montevideo	2–1
12 June 1969	*v* Brazil	Rio de Janeiro	1–2

1969–70

5 Nov 1969	*v* Holland	Amsterdam	1–0
10 Dec 1969	*v* Portugal (sub)	Wembley	1–0
14 Jan 1970	*v* Holland	Wembley	0–0
25 Feb 1970	*v* Belgium	Brussels	3–1
18 April 1970	*v* Wales	Cardiff	1–1

(with Tottenham Hotspur)

21 April 1970	*v* Northern Ireland	Wembley	3–1 (1 goal)
25 April 1970	*v* Scotland	Glasgow	0–0
20 May 1970	*v* Colombia	Bogota	4–0 (2 goals)
24 May 1970	*v* Ecuador	Quito	2–0
2 June 1970	*v* Romania (WC)	Guadalajara	1–0
7 June 1970	*v* Brazil (WC)	Guadalajara	0–1
11 June 1970	*v* Czechoslovakia (WC)	Guadalajara	1–0
14 June 1970	*v* West Germany (WC)	Leon	2–3 (aet)
			(1 goal)

1970–71

25 Nov 1970	*v* East Germany	Wembley	3–1 (1 goal)
3 Feb 1971	*v* Malta (ECQ)	Valletta	1–0 (1 goal)
21 April 1971	*v* Greece (ECQ)	Wembley	3–0
12 May 1971	*v* Malta (ECQ)	Wembley	5–0

15 May 1971	*v* Northern Ireland	Belfast	1–0
19 May 1971	*v* Wales*	Wembley	0–0
22 May 1971	*v* Scotland	Wembley	3–1 (1 goal)

1971–72

13 Oct 1971	*v* Switzerland (ECQ)	Basle	3–2
1 Dec 1971	*v* Greece (ECQ)	Athens	2–0
29 April 1972	*v* West Germany (ECQ)	Wembley	1–3
13 May 1972	*v* West Germany (sub)(ECQ)	Berlin	0–0
23 May 1972	*v* Northern Ireland (sub)	Wembley	0–1

1972–73

14 Feb 1973	*v* Scotland (SFAC)	Glasgow	5–0
12 May 1973	*v* Northern Ireland	Everton	2–1
15 May 1973	*v* Wales	Wembley	3–0 (1 goal)
19 May 1973	*v* Scotland	Wembley	1–0 (1 goal)
27 May 1973	*v* Czechoslovakia	Prague	1–1
6 June 1973	*v* Poland (WCQ)	Chorzow	0–2
10 June 1973	*v* USSR	Moscow	2–1
14 June 1973	*v* Italy	Turin	0–2

1973–74

26 Sept 1973	*v* Austria*	Wembley	7–0
17 Oct 1973	*v* Poland (WCQ)*	Wembley	1–1
14 Nov 1973	*v* Italy	Wembley	0–1
3 April 1974	*v* Portugal*	Lisbon	0–0
18 May 1974	*v* Scotland	Glasgow	0–2

PHELAN, MIKE C. *Born:* 24.9.62 (Nelson) *Club:* Manchester United *Caps:* 1

1989–90

15 Nov 1989	*v* Italy (sub)	Wembley	0–0

PHILLIPS, LEN H. *Born:* 11.9.22 (Hackney) *Club:* Portsmouth *Caps:* 3

1951–52

14 Nov 1951	*v* Northern Ireland	Aston Villa	2–0

1954–55

10 Nov 1954	*v* Wales	Wembley	3–2
1 Dec 1954	*v* West Germany	Wembley	3–1

PICKERING, FRED *Born:* 19.1.41 (Blackburn) *Club:* Everton *Caps:* 3 *Goals:* 5

1963–64

27 May 1964	*v* USA	New York	10–0 (3 goals)

1964–65

3 Oct 1964	*v* Northern Ireland	Belfast	4–3 (1 goal)
21 Oct 1964	*v* Belgium	Wembley	2–2 (1 goal)

PICKERING, NICK *Born:* 4.8.63 (Newcastle) *Club:* Sunderland *Caps:* 1

1982–83

19 June 1983	*v* Australia	Melbourne	1–1

PILKINGTON, BRIAN *Born:* 12.2.33 (Leyland) *Club:* Burnley *Caps:* 1

1954–55

2 Oct 1954	*v* Northern Ireland	Belfast	2–0

PLATT, DAVID *Born:* 10.6.66 (Chadderton) *Clubs:* Aston Villa, Bari, Juventus *Caps:* 42
Goals: 20

1989–90 (with Aston Villa)

15 Nov 1989	*v* Italy (sub)	Wembley	0–0
13 Dec 1989	*v* Yugoslavia (sub)	Wembley	2–1
28 March 1990	*v* Brazil	Wembley	1–0
15 May 1990	*v* Denmark (sub)	Wembley	1–0
2 June 1990	*v* Tunisia (sub)	Tunis	1–1
16 June 1990	*v* Holland (sub) (WC)	Cagliari	0–0
21 June 1990	*v* Egypt (sub) (WC)	Cagliari	0–0
26 June 1990	*v* Belgium (sub) (WC)	Bologna	1–0 (aet) (1 goal)
1 July 1990	*v* Cameroon (WC)	Naples	3–2 (aet) (1 goal)
4 July 1990	*v* West Germany (WC)	Turin	1–1 (aet)
7 July 1990	*v* Italy (WC)	Bari	1–2 (1 goal)

1990–91

12 Sept 1990	*v* Hungary	Wembley	1–0
17 Oct 1990	*v* Poland (ECQ)	Wembley	2–0
14 Nov 1990	*v* Eire (ECQ)	Dublin	1–1 (1 goal)
27 March 1991	*v* Eire (ECQ)	Wembley	1–1
1 May 1991	*v* Turkey (ECQ)	Izmir	1–0
21 May 1991	*v* USSR	Wembley	3–1 (2 goals)
25 May 1991	*v* Argentina	Wembley	2–2 (1 goal)
1 June 1991	*v* Australia	Sydney	1–0
3 June 1991	*v* New Zealand	Auckland	1–0
8 June 1991	*v* New Zealand	Wellington	2–0
12 June 1991	*v* Malaysia	Kuala Lumpur	4–2

1991–92 (with Bari)

11 Sept 1991	*v* Germany	Wembley	0–1
16 Oct 1991	*v* Turkey (ECQ)	Wembley	1–0
11 Nov 1991	*v* Poland (ECQ)	Poznan	1–1
25 March 1992	*v* Czechoslovakia	Prague	2–2
29 April 1992	*v* CIS	Moscow	2–2
17 May 1992	*v* Brazil	Wembley	1–1 (1 goal)
3 June 1992	*v* Finland	Helsinki	2–1 (2 goals)
11 June 1992	*v* Denmark (EC)	Malmo	0–0
14 June 1992	*v* France (EC)	Malmo	0–0
17 June 1992	*v* Sweden (EC)	Stockholm	1–2 (1 goal)

1992–93 (with Juventus)

9 Sept 1992	*v* Spain	Santander	0–1
14 Oct 1992	*v* Norway (WCQ)	Wembley	1–1 (1 goal)
18 Nov 1992	*v* Turkey (WCQ)	Wembley	4–0
17 Feb 1993	*v* San Marino* (WCQ)	Wembley	6–0 (4 goals)

31 March 1993	v Turkey* (WCQ)	Izmir	2–0 (1 goal)
28 April 1993	v Holland* (WCQ)	Wembley	2–2 (1 goal)
29 May 1993	v Poland* (WCQ)	Chorzow	1–1
2 June 1993	v Norway* (WCQ)	Oslo	0–2
13 June 1993	v Brazil (sub) (USC)	Washington	1–1 (1 goal)
19 June 1993	v Germany* (USC)	Detroit	1–2 (1 goal)

POINTER, RAY *Born:* 10.10.36 (Cramlington) *Club:* Burnley *Caps:* 3 *Goals:* 2

1961–62

28 Sept 1961	v Luxembourg (WCQ)	Arsenal	4–1 (1 goal)
14 Oct 1961	v Wales	Cardiff	1–1
25 Oct 1961	v Portugal (WCQ)	Wembley	2–0 (1 goal)

PYE, JESSE *Born:* 22.12.19 (Rotherham) *Club:* Wolverhampton Wanderers *Caps:* 1

1949–50

21 Sept 1949	v Eire	Everton	0–2

QUIXALL, ALBERT *Born:* 9.8.33 (Sheffield) *Club:* Sheffield Wednesday *Caps:* 5

1953–54

10 Oct 1953	v Wales (WCQ)	Cardiff	4–1
21 Oct 1953	v FIFA (Rest of Europe)	Wembley	4–4
11 Nov 1953	v Northern Ireland (WCQ)	Everton	3–1

1954–55

18 May 1955	v Spain	Madrid	1–1
22 May 1955	v Portugal (sub)	Oporto	1–3

RADFORD, JOHN *Born:* 22.2.47 (Pontefract) *Club:* Arsenal *Caps:* 2

1968–69

15 Jan 1969	v Romania	Wembley	1–1

1971–72

13 Oct 1971	v Switzerland (sub) (ECQ)	Basle	3–2

RAMSEY, ALF E. *Born:* 22.1.20 (Dagenham) *Clubs:* Southampton, Tottenham Hotspur *Caps:* 32 *Goals:* 3

1948–49 (with Southampton)

2 Dec 1948	v Switzerland	Arsenal	6–0

1949–50 (with Tottenham Hotspur)

30 Nov 1949	v Italy	Tottenham	2–0
15 April 1950	v Scotland (WCQ)	Glasgow	1–0
14 May 1950	v Portugal	Lisbon	5–3
18 May 1950	v Belgium	Brussels	4–1
25 June 1950	v Chile (WC)	Rio de Janeiro	2–0
29 June 1950	v USA (WC)	Belo Horizonte	0–1
2 July 1950	v Spain (WC)	Rio de Janeiro	0–1

1950–51

7 Oct 1950	v Northern Ireland	Belfast	4–1

15 Nov 1950	*v* Wales*	Sunderland	4–2
22 Nov 1950	*v* Yugoslavia*	Arsenal	2–2
14 April 1951	*v* Scotland	Wembley	2–3
9 May 1951	*v* Argentina	Wembley	2–1
19 May 1951	*v* Portugal*	Everton	5–2

1951–52

3 Oct 1951	*v* France	Arsenal	2–2
20 Oct 1951	*v* Wales	Cardiff	1–1
14 Nov 1951	*v* Northern Ireland	Aston Villa	2–0
28 Nov 1951	*v* Austria	Wembley	2–2 (1 goal)
5 April 1952	*v* Scotland	Glasgow	2–1
18 May 1952	*v* Italy	Florence	1–1
25 May 1952	*v* Austria	Vienna	3–2
28 May 1952	*v* Switzerland	Zurich	3–0

1952–53

4 Oct 1952	*v* Northern Ireland	Belfast	2–2
12 Nov 1952	*v* Wales	Wembley	5–2
26 Nov 1952	*v* Belgium	Wembley	5–0
18 April 1953	*v* Scotland	Wembley	2–2
17 May 1953	*v* Argentina	Buenos Aires	0–0†
24 May 1953	*v* Chile	Santiago	2–1
31 May 1953	*v* Uruguay	Montevideo	1–2
8 June 1953	*v* USA	New York	6–3

1953–54

| 21 Oct 1953 | *v* FIFA (Rest of Europe) | Wembley | 4–4 (1 goal) |
| 25 Nov 1953 | *v* Hungary | Wembley | 3–6 (1 goal) |

REANEY, PAUL *Born:* 22.10.44 (London) *Club:* Leeds United *Caps:* 3

1968–69
| 11 Dec 1968 | *v* Bulgaria (sub) | Wembley | 1–1 |

1969–70
| 10 Dec 1969 | *v* Portugal | Wembley | 1–0 |

1970–71
| 3 Feb 1971 | *v* Malta (ECQ) | Valletta | 1–0 |

REEVES, KEVIN P. *Born:* 20.10.57 (Burley) *Clubs:* Norwich City, Manchester City *Caps:* 2

1979–80 (with Norwich City)
| 22 Nov 1979 | *v* Bulgaria (ECQ) | Wembley | 2–0 |

(with Manchester City)
| 20 May 1980 | *v* Northern Ireland | Wembley | 1–1 |

REGIS, CYRILLE *Born:* 9.2.58 (French Guyana) *Clubs:* West Bromwich Albion, Coventry City *Caps:* 5

1981–82 (with West Bromwich Albion)
| 23 Feb 1982 | *v* Northern Ireland (sub) | Wembley | 4–0 |
| 27 April 1982 | *v* Wales (sub) | Cardiff | 1–0 |

2 June 1982	*v* Iceland	Reykjavik	1–1

1982–83

13 Oct 1982	*v* West Germany	Wembley	1–2

1987–88 (with Coventry City)

14 Oct 1987	*v* Turkey (sub) (ECQ)	Wembley	8–0

REID, PETER *Born:* 20.6.56 (Huyton) *Club:* Everton *Caps:* 13

1984–85

9 June 1985	*v* Mexico (sub)	Mexico City	0–1
12 June 1985	*v* West Germany	Mexico City	3–0
16 June 1985	*v* USA (sub)	Los Angeles	5–0

1985–86

11 Sept 1985	*v* Romania (WCQ)	Wembley	1–1
23 April 1986	*v* Scotland (sub) (RC)	Wembley	2–1
24 May 1986	*v* Canada (sub)	Vancouver	1–0
11 June 1986	*v* Poland (WC)	Monterrey	3–0
18 June 1986	*v* Paraguay (WC)	Mexico City	3–0
22 June 1986	*v* Argentina (WC)	Mexico City	1–2

1986–87

19 May 1987	*v* Brazil (RC)	Wembley	1–1

1987–88

9 Sept 1987	*v* West Germany	Düsseldorf	1–3
11 Nov 1987	*v* Yugoslavia (sub) (ECQ)	Belgrade	4–1
28 May 1988	*v* Switzerland (sub)	Lausanne	1–0

REVIE, DON G. *Born:* 10.7.27 (Middlesbrough) *Club:* Manchester City *Caps:* 6 *Goals:* 4

1954–55

2 Oct 1954	*v* Northern Ireland	Belfast	2–0 (1 goal)
2 April 1955	*v* Scotland	Wembley	7–2 (1 goal)
15 May 1955	*v* France	Paris	0–1

1955–56

2 Oct 1955	*v* Denmark	Copenhagen	5–1 (2 goals)
22 Oct 1955	*v* Wales	Cardiff	1–2

1956–57

6 Oct 1956	*v* Northern Ireland	Belfast	1–1

RICHARDS, JOHN P. *Born:* 9.11.50 (Warrington) *Club:* Wolverhampton Wanderers *Caps:* 1

1972–73

12 May 1973	*v* Northern Ireland	Everton	2–1

RICKABY, STAN *Born:* 12.3.24 (Stockton) *Club:* West Bromwich Albion *Caps:* 1

1953–54

11 Nov 1953	*v* Northern Ireland (WC)	Everton	3–1

RIMMER, JIMMY J. *Born:* 10.2.48 (Southport) *Club:* Arsenal *Caps:* 1

1975–76
28 May 1976	*v* Italy (USABT)	New York	3–2

RIX, GRAHAM *Born:* 23.10.57 (Doncaster) *Club:* Arsenal *Caps:* 17

1980–81
10 Sept 1980	*v* Norway (WCQ)	Wembley	4–0
15 Oct 1980	*v* Romania (WCQ)	Bucharest	1–2
19 Nov 1980	*v* Switzerland (sub) (WCQ)	Wembley	2–1
12 May 1981	*v* Brazil	Wembley	0–1
20 May 1981	*v* Wales	Wembley	0–0
23 May 1981	*v* Scotland	Wembley	0–1

1981–82
25 May 1982	*v* Holland (sub)	Wembley	2–0
3 June 1982	*v* Finland (sub)	Helsinki	4–1
16 June 1982	*v* France (WC)	Bilbao	3–1
20 June 1982	*v* Czechoslovakia (WC)	Bilbao	2–0
25 June 1982	*v* Kuwait (WC)	Bilbao	1–0
29 June 1982	*v* West Germany (WC)	Madrid	0–0
5 July 1982	*v* Spain (WC)	Madrid	0–0

1982–83
22 Sept 1982	*v* Denmark (ECQ)	Copenhagen	2–2
13 Oct 1982	*v* West Germany (sub)	Wembley	1–2
30 March 1983	*v* Greece (sub) (ECQ)	Wembley	0–0

1983–84
4 April 1984	*v* Northern Ireland	Wembley	1–0

ROBB, GEORGE *Born:* 1.6.26 (Finchley) *Club:* Tottenham Hotspur *Caps:* 1

1953–54
25 Nov 1953	*v* Hungary	Wembley	3–6

ROBERTS, GRAHAM P. *Born:* 3.7.59 (Southampton) *Club:* Tottenham Hotspur *Caps:* 6

1982–83
28 May 1983	*v* Northern Ireland	Belfast	0–0
1 June 1983	*v* Scotland	Wembley	2–0

1983–84
29 Feb 1984	*v* France	Paris	0–2
4 April 1984	*v* Northern Ireland	Wembley	1–0
26 May 1984	*v* Scotland	Glasgow	1–1
2 June 1984	*v* USSR	Wembley	0–2

ROBSON, BRYAN *Born:* 11.1.57 (Chester-Le-Street) *Clubs:* West Bromwich Albion, Manchester United *Caps:* 90 *Goals:* 26

1979–80 (with West Bromwich Albion)
6 Feb 1980	*v* Eire (ECQ)	Wembley	2–0
31 May 1980	*v* Australia	Sydney	2-1

1980–81

10 Sept 1980	*v* Norway (WCQ)	Wembley	4–0
15 Oct 1980	*v* Romania (WCQ)	Bucharest	1–2
19 Nov 1980	*v* Switzerland (WCQ)	Wembley	2–1
25 March 1981	*v* Spain	Wembley	1–2
29 April 1981	*v* Romania (WCQ)	Wembley	0–0
12 May 1981	*v* Brazil	Wembley	0–1
20 May 1981	*v* Wales	Wembley	0–0
23 May 1981	*v* Scotland	Wembley	0–1
30 May 1981	*v* Switzerland (WCQ)	Basle	1–2
6 June 1981	*v* Hungary (WCQ)	Budapest	3–1

1981–82 (with Manchester United)

9 Sept 1981	*v* Norway (WCQ)	Oslo	1–2 (1 goal)
18 Nov 1981	*v* Hungary (WCQ)	Wembley	1–0
23 Feb 1982	*v* Northern Ireland	Wembley	4–0 (1 goal)
27 April 1982	*v* Wales	Cardiff	1–0
25 May 1982	*v* Holland	Wembley	2–0
29 May 1982	*v* Scotland	Glasgow	1–0
3 June 1982	*v* Finland	Helsinki	4–1 (2 goals)
16 June, 1982	*v* France (WC)	Bilbao	3–1 (2 goals)
20 June 1982	*v* Czechoslovakia (WC)	Bilbao	2–0
29 June 1982	*v* West Germany (WC)	Madrid	0–0
5 July 1982	*v* Spain (WC)	Madrid	0–0

1982–83

22 Sept 1982	*v* Denmark (ECQ)	Copenhagen	2–2
17 Nov 1982	*v* Greece* (ECQ)	Salonika	3–0
15 Dec 1982	*v* Luxembourg * (ECQ)	Wembley	9–0
1 June 1983	*v* Scotland*	Wembley	2–0 (1 goal)

1983–84

12 Oct 1983	*v* Hungary* (ECQ)	Budapest	3–0
16 Nov 1983	*v* Luxembourg* (ECQ)	Luxembourg	1–0 (2 goals)
29 Feb 1984	*v* France*	Paris	0–2
4 April 1984	*v* Northern Ireland*	Wembley	1–0
26 May 1984	*v* Scotland*	Glasgow	1–1
2 June 1984	*v* USSR*	Wembley	0–2
10 June 1984	*v* Brazil*	Rio de Janeiro	2–0
13 June 1984	*v* Uruguay*	Montevideo	0–2
17 June 1984	*v* Chile*	Santiago	0–0

1984–85

12 Sept 1984	*v* East Germany*	Wembley	1–0 (1 goal)
17 Oct 1984	*v* Finland* (WCQ)	Wembley	5–0 (1 goal)
14 Nov 1984	*v* Turkey* (WCQ)	Istanbul	8–0 (3 goals)
26 March 1985	*v* Eire*	Wembley	2–1
1 May 1985	*v* Romania* (WCQ)	Bucharest	0–0
22 May 1985	*v* Finland* (WCQ)	Helsinki	1–1
25 May 1985	*v* Scotland* (RC)	Glasgow	0–1
6 June 1985	*v* Italy*	Mexico City	1–2
9 June 1985	*v* Mexico*	Mexico City	0–1
12 June 1985	*v* West Germany*	Mexico City	3–0 (1 goal)

16 June 1985	*v* USA*	Los Angeles	5–0

1985–86

11 Sept 1985	*v* Romania* (WCQ)	Wembley	1–1
16 Oct 1985	*v* Turkey* (WCQ)	Wembley	5–0 (1 goal)
26 Feb 1986	*v* Israel*	Tel Aviv	2–1 (2 goals)
17 May 1986	*v* Mexico*	Los Angeles	3–0
3 June 1986	*v* Portugal* (WC)	Monterrey	0–1
6 June 1986	*v* Morocco* (WC)	Monterrey	0–0

1986–87

15 Oct 1986	*v* Northern Ireland* (ECQ)	Wembley	3–0
18 Feb 1987	*v* Spain*	Madrid	4–2
1 April 1987	*v* Northern Ireland* (ECQ)	Belfast	2–0 (1 goal)
29 April 1987	*v* Turkey* (ECQ)	Izmir	0–0
19 May 1987	*v* Brazil* (RC)	Wembley	1–1
23 May 1987	*v* Scotland* (RC)	Glasgow	0–0

1987–88

14 Oct 1987	*v* Turkey* (ECQ)	Wembley	8-0 (1 goal)
11 Nov 1987	*v* Yugoslavia* (ECQ)	Belgrade	4–1 (1 goal)
23 March 1988	*v* Holland*	Wembley	2–2
27 April 1988	*v* Hungary*	Budapest	0–0
21 May 1988	*v* Scotland* (RC)	Wembley	1–0
24 May 1988	*v* Colombia* (RC)	Wembley	1–1
28 May 1988	*v* Switzerland*	Lausanne	1–0
12 June 1988	*v* Eire* (EC)	Stuttgart	0–1
15 June 1988	*v* Holland* (EC)	Düsseldorf	1–3 (1 goal)
18 June 1988	*v* USSR* (EC)	Frankfurt	1–3

1988–89

14 Sept 1988	*v* Denmark*	Wembley	1–0
19 Oct 1988	*v* Sweden* (WCQ)	Wembley	0–0
16 Nov 1988	*v* Saudi Arabia*	Riyadh	1–1
8 Feb 1989	*v* Greece*	Athens	2–1 (1 goal)
8 March 1989	*v* Albania* (WCQ)	Tirana	2–0 (1 goal)
26 April 1989	*v* Albania* (WCQ)	Wembley	5–0
23 May 1989	*v* Chile* (RC)	Wembley	0–0
27 May 1989	*v* Scotland* (RC)	Glasgow	2–0
3 June 1989	*v* Poland* (WCQ)	Wembley	3–0
7 June 1989	*v* Denmark*	Copenhagen	1–1

1989–90

11 Oct 1989	*v* Poland* (WCQ)	Katowice	0–0
15 Nov 1989	*v* Italy*	Wembley	0–0
13 Dec 1989	*v* Yugoslavia*	Wembley	2–1 (2 goals)
25 April 1990	*v* Czechoslovakia*	Wembley	4–2
22 May 1990	*v* Uruguay*	Wembley	1–2
2 June 1990	*v* Tunisia*	Tunis	1–1
11 June 1990	*v* Eire*(WC)	Cagliari	1–1
16 June 1990	*v* Holland* (WC)	Cagliari	0–0

1990–91

6 Feb 1991	*v* Cameroon*	Wembley	2–0

27 March 1991	v Eire* (ECQ)	Wembley	1–1

1991–92

16 Oct 1991	v Turkey (ECQ)	Wembley	1–0

ROBSON, ROBERT W. (BOBBY) *Born:* 18.2.33 (Langley Park) *Club:* West Bromwich Albion
Caps: 20 *Goals:* 4

1957–58

27 Nov 1957	v France	Wembley	4–0 (2 goals)
18 May 1958	v USSR	Moscow	1–1
8 June 1958	v USSR (WC)	Gothenburg	2–2
11 June 1958	v Brazil (WC)	Gothenburg	0–0
15 June 1958	v Austria (WC)	Boras	2–2

1959–60

15 May 1960	v Spain	Madrid	0–3
22 May 1960	v Hungary	Budapest	0–2

1960–61

8 Oct 1960	v Northern Ireland	Belfast	5–2
19 Oct 1960	v Luxembourg (WCQ)	Luxembourg	9–0
26 Oct 1960	v Spain	Wembley	4–2
23 Nov 1960	v Wales	Wembley	5–1
15 April 1961	v Scotland	Wembley	9–3 (1 goal)
10 May 1961	v Mexico	Wembley	8–0 (1 goal)
21 May 1961	v Portugal (WCQ)	Lisbon	1–1
24 May 1961	v Italy	Rome	3–2

1961–62

28 Sept 1961	v Luxembourg (WCQ)	Arsenal	4–1
14 Oct 1961	v Wales	Cardiff	1–1
25 Oct 1961	v Portugal (WCQ)	Wembley	2–0
22 Nov 1961	v Northern Ireland	Wembley	1–1
9 May 1962	v Switzerland	Wembley	3–1

ROCASTLE, DAVID *Born:* 2.5.67 (Lewisham) *Club:* Arsenal *Caps:* 14

1988–89

14 Sept 1988	v Denmark	Wembley	1–0
16 Nov 1988	v Saudi Arabia	Riyadh	1–1
8 Feb 1989	v Greece	Athens	2–1
8 March 1989	v Albania (WCQ)	Tirana	2–0
26 April 1989	v Albania (WCQ)	Wembley	5–0
3 June 1989	v Poland (sub) (WCQ)	Wembley	3–0
7 June 1989	v Denmark	Copenhagen	1–1

1989–90

6 Sept 1989	v Sweden (sub) (WCQ)	Stockholm	0–0
11 Oct 1989	v Poland (WCQ)	Katowice	0–0
13 Dec 1989	v Yugoslavia	Wembley	2–1
15 May 1990	v Denmark (sub)	Wembley	1–0

1991–92

13 Nov 1991	v Poland (ECQ)	Poznan	1–1

25 March 1992	*v* Czechoslovakia	Prague	2–2
17 May 1992	*v* Brazil (sub)	Wembley	1–1

ROWLEY, JOHN F. *Born:* 7.10.20 (Wolverhampton) *Club:* Manchester United *Caps:* 6
Goals: 6

1948–49

2 Dec 1948	*v* Switzerland	Arsenal	6–0 (1 goal)
13 May 1949	*v* Sweden	Stockholm	1–3
22 May 1949	*v* France	Paris	3–1

1949–50

16 Nov 1949	*v* Northern Ireland (WCQ)	Manchester City	9–2 (4 goals)
30 Nov 1949	*v* Italy	Tottenham	2–0 (1 goal)

1951–52

5 April 1952	*v* Scotland	Glasgow	2–1

ROYLE, JOE *Born:* 8.4.49 (Liverpool) *Clubs:* Everton, Manchester City *Caps:* 6 *Goals:* 2

1970–71 (with Everton)

3 Feb 1971	*v* Malta (ECQ)	Valletta	1–0

1972–73

11 Oct 1972	*v* Yugoslavia	Wembley	1–1 (1 goal)

1975–76 (with Manchester City)

11 May 1976	*v* Northern Ireland (sub)	Wembley	4–0
28 May 1976	*v* Italy (USABT)	New York	3–2

1976–77

13 Oct 1976	*v* Finland (WCQ)	Wembley	2–1 (1 goal)
30 March 1977	*v* Luxembourg (WCQ)	Wembley	5–0

SADLER, DAVID *Born:* 5.2.46 (Yalding) *Club:* Manchester United *Caps:* 4

1967–68

22 Nov 1967	*v* Northern Ireland (ECQ)	Wembley	2–0
6 Dec 1967	*v* USSR	Wembley	2–2

1969–70

24 May 1970	*v* Ecuador (sub)	Quito	2–0

1970–71

25 Nov 1970	*v* East Germany	Wembley	3–1

SALAKO, JOHN A. *Born:* 11.2.69 (Nigeria) *Club:* Crystal Palace *Caps:* 5

1990–91

1 June 1991	*v* Australia (sub)	Sydney	1–0
3 June 1991	*v* New Zealand (sub)	Auckland	1–0
8 June 1991	*v* New Zealand	Wellington	2–0
12 June 1991	*v* Malaysia	Kuala Lumpur	4–2

1991–92

11 Sept 1991	*v* Germany	Wembley	0–1

SANSOM, KENNY G. *Born:* 26.9.58 (Camberwell) *Clubs:* Crystal Palace, Arsenal
Caps: 86 *Goals:* 1

1978–79 (with Crystal Palace)

23 May 1979	v Wales	Wembley	0–0

1979–80

22 Nov 1979	v Bulgaria (ECQ)	Wembley	2–0
6 Feb 1980	v Eire (ECQ)	Wembley	2–0
13 May 1980	v Argentina	Wembley	3–1
17 May 1980	v Wales (sub)	Wrexham	1–4
20 May 1980	v Northern Ireland	Wembley	1–1
24 May 1980	v Scotland	Glasgow	2–0
12 June 1980	v Belgium (EC)	Turin	1–1
15 June 1980	v Italy (EC)	Turin	0–1

1980–81 (with Arsenal)

10 Sept 1980	v Norway (WCQ)	Wembley	4–0
15 Oct 1980	v Romania (WCQ)	Bucharest	1–2
19 Nov 1980	v Switzerland (WCQ)	Wembley	2–1
25 March 1981	v Spain	Wembley	1–2
29 April 1981	v Romania (WCQ)	Wembley	0–0
12 May 1981	v Brazil	Wembley	0–1
20 May 1981	v Wales	Wembley	0–0
23 May 1981	v Scotland	Wembley	0–1
30 May 1981	v Switzerland (WCQ)	Basle	1–2

1981–82

23 Feb 1982	v Northern Ireland	Wembley	4–0
27 April 1982	v Wales	Cardiff	1–0
25 May 1982	v Holland	Wembley	2–0
29 May 1982	v Scotland	Glasgow	1–0
3 June 1982	v Finland	Helsinki	4–1
16 June 1982	v France (WC)	Bilbao	3–1
20 June 1982	v Czechoslovakia (WC)	Bilbao	2–0
29 June 1982	v West Germany (WC)	Madrid	0–0
5 July 1982	v Spain (WC)	Madrid	0–0

1982–83

22 Sept 1982	v Denmark (ECQ)	Copenhagen	2–2
13 Oct 1982	v West Germany	Wembley	1–2
17 Nov 1982	v Greece (ECQ)	Salonika	3–0
15 Dec 1982	v Luxembourg (ECQ)	Wembley	9–0
30 March 1983	v Greece (ECQ)	Wembley	0–0
27 April 1983	v Hungary (ECQ)	Wembley	2–0
28 May 1983	v Northern Ireland	Belfast	0–0
1 June 1983	v Scotland	Wembley	2–0

1983–84

21 Sept 1983	v Denmark (ECQ)	Wembley	0–1
12 Oct 1983	v Hungary (ECQ)	Budapest	3–0
16 Nov 1983	v Luxembourg (ECQ)	Luxembourg	4–0
29 Feb 1984	v France	Paris	0–2
26 May 1984	v Scotland	Glasgow	1–1

2 June 1984	v USSR	Wembley	0–2
10 June 1984	v Brazil	Rio de Janeiro	2–0
13 June 1984	v Uruguay	Montevideo	0–2
17 June 1984	v Chile	Santiago	0–0

1984–85

12 Sept 1984	v East Germany	Wembley	1–0
17 Oct 1984	v Finland (WCQ)	Wembley	5–0 (1 goal)
14 Nov 1984	v Turkey (WCQ)	Istanbul	8–0
27 Feb 1985	v Northern Ireland (WCQ)	Belfast	1–0
26 March 1985	v Eire	Wembley	2–1
1 May 1985	v Romania (WCQ)	Bucharest	0–0
22 May 1985	v Finland (WCQ)	Helsinki	1–1
25 May 1985	v Scotland (RC)	Glasgow	0–1
6 June 1985	v Italy	Mexico City	1–2
9 June 1985	v Mexico	Mexico City	0–1
12 June 1985	v West Germany	Mexico City	3–0
16 June 1985	v USA	Los Angeles	5–0

1985–86

11 Sept 1985	v Romania (WCQ)	Wembley	1–1
16 Oct 1985	v Turkey (WCQ)	Wembley	5–0
13 Nov 1985	v Northern Ireland (WCQ)	Wembley	0–0
29 Jan 1986	v Egypt	Cairo	4–0
26 Feb 1986	v Israel	Tel Aviv	2–1
26 March 1986	v USSR	Tbilisi	1–0
23 April 1986	v Scotland (RC)	Wembley	2–1
17 May 1986	v Mexico	Los Angeles	3–0
24 May 1986	v Canada	Vancouver	1–0
3 June 1986	v Portugal (WC)	Monterrey	0–1
6 June 1986	v Morocco (WC)	Monterrey	0–0
11 June 1986	v Poland (WC)	Monterrey	3–0
18 June 1986	v Paraguay (WC)	Mexico City	3–0
22 June 1986	v Argentina (WC)	Mexico City	1–2

1986–87

10 Sept 1986	v Sweden	Stockholm	0–1
15 Oct 1986	v Northern Ireland (ECQ)	Wembley	3–0
12 Nov 1986	v Yugoslavia (ECQ)	Wembley	2–0
18 Feb 1987	v Spain	Madrid	4–2
1 April 1987	v Northern Ireland (ECQ)	Belfast	2–0
29 April 1987	v Turkey (ECQ)	Izmir	0–0

1987–88

9 Sept 1987	v West Germany	Düsseldorf	1–3
14 Oct 1987	v Turkey (ECQ)	Wembley	8–0
11 Nov 1987	v Yugoslavia (ECQ)	Belgrade	4–1
23 March 1988	v Holland	Wembley	2–2
21 May 1988	v Scotland (RC)	Wembley	1–0
24 May 1988	v Colombia (RC)	Wembley	1–1
28 May 1988	v Switzerland	Lausanne	1–0
12 June 1988	v Eire (EC)	Stuttgart	0–1
15 June 1988	v Holland (EC)	Düsseldorf	1–3

| 18 June 1988 | *v* USSR (EC) | Frankfurt | 1–3 |

SCOTT, LAURIE *Born:* 23.4.17 (Sheffield) *Club:* Arsenal *Caps:* 17

1946–47

28 Sept 1946	*v* Northern Ireland	Belfast	7–2
30 Sept 1946	*v* Eire	Dublin	1–0
13 Nov 1946	*v* Wales	Manchester City	3–0
27 Nov 1946	*v* Holland	Huddersfield	8–2
12 April 1947	*v* Scotland	Wembley	1–1
3 May 1947	*v* France	Arsenal	3–0
18 May 1947	*v* Switzerland	Zurich	0–1
27 May 1947	*v* Portugal	Lisbon	10–0

1947–48

21 Sept 1947	*v* Belgium	Brussels	5–2
18 Oct 1947	*v* Wales	Cardiff	3–0
5 Nov 1947	*v* Northern Ireland	Everton	2–2
19 Nov 1947	*v* Sweden	Arsenal	4–2
10 April 1948	*v* Scotland	Glasgow	2–0
16 May 1948	*v* Italy	Turin	4–0

1948–49

26 Sept 1948	*v* Denmark	Copenhagen	0–0
9 Oct 1948	*v* Northern Ireland	Belfast	6–2
10 Nov 1948	*v* Wales	Aston Villa	1–0

SEAMAN, DAVID A. *Born:* 19.9.63 (Rotherham) *Clubs:* Queens Park Rangers, Arsenal *Caps:* 9

1988–89 (with Queens Park Rangers)

| 16 Nov 1988 | *v* Saudi Arabia | Riyadh | 1–1 |
| 7 June 1989 | *v* Denmark (sub) | Copenhagen | 1–1 |

1989–90

| 25 April 1990 | *v* Czechoslovakia (sub) | Wembley | 4–2 |

1990–91 (with Arsenal)

6 Feb 1991	*v* Cameroon	Wembley	2–0
27 March 1991	*v* Eire (ECQ)	Wembley	1–1
1 May 1991	*v* Turkey (ECQ)	Izmir	1–0
25 May 1991	*v* Argentina	Wembley	2–2

1991–92

| 25 March 1992 | *v* Czechoslovakia | Prague | 2–2 |
| 12 May 1992 | *v* Hungary (sub) | Budapest | 1–0 |

SEWELL, JOHN *Born:* 24.1.27 (Whitehaven) *Club:* Sheffield Wednesday *Caps:* 6 *Goals:* 3

1951–52

14 Nov 1951	*v* Northern Ireland	Aston Villa	2–0
25 May 1952	*v* Austria	Vienna	3–2 (1 goal)
28 May 1952	*v* Switzerland	Zurich	3–0 (1 goal)

1952–53

4 Oct 1952	*v* Northern Ireland	Belfast	2–2

1953–54

25 Nov 1953	*v* Hungary	Wembley	3–6 (1 goal)
23 May 1954	*v* Hungary	Budapest	1–7

SHACKLETON, LEN F. *Born:* 3.5.22 (Bradford) *Club:* Sunderland *Caps:* 5 *Goals:* 1

1948–49

26 Sept 1948	*v* Denmark	Copenhagen	0–0
10 Nov 1948	*v* Wales	Aston Villa	1–0

1949–50

15 Oct 1949	*v* Wales (WCQ)	Cardiff	4–1

1954–55

10 Nov 1954	*v* Wales	Wembley	3–2
1 Dec 1954	*v* West Germany	Wembley	3–1 (1 goal)

SHARPE, LEE S. *Born:* 25.7.71 (Halesowen) *Club:* Manchester United *Caps:* 6

1990–91

27 March 1991	*v* Eire (sub) (ECQ)	Wembley	1–1

1992–93

31 March 1993	*v* Turkey (sub) (WCQ)	Izmir	2–0
2 June 1993	*v* Norway (WCQ)	Oslo	0–2
9 June 1993	*v* USA (USC)	Boston	0–2
13 June 1993	*v* Brazil (USC)	Washington	1–1
19 June 1993	*v* Germany (USC)	Detroit	1–2

SHAW, GRAHAM L. *Born:* 9.7.34 (Sheffield) *Club:* Sheffield United *Caps:* 5

1958–59

22 Oct 1958	*v* USSR	Wembley	5–0
26 Nov 1958	*v* Wales	Aston Villa	2–2
11 April 1959	*v* Scotland	Wembley	1–0
6 May 1959	*v* Italy	Wembley	2–2

1962–63

21 Nov 1962	*v* Wales	Wembley	4–0

SHEARER, ALAN *Born:* 13.8.70 (Newcastle) *Clubs:* Southampton, Blackburn Rovers *Caps:* 6 *Goals:* 2

1991–92

19 Feb 1992	*v* France	Wembley	2–0 (1 goal)
29 April 1992	*v* CIS	Moscow	2–2
14 June 1992	*v* France (EC)	Malmo	0–0

1992–93

9 Sept 1992	*v* Spain	Santander	0–1
14 Oct 1992	*v* Norway (WCQ)	Wembley	1–1
18 Nov 1992	*v* Turkey (WCQ)	Wembley	4–0 (1 goal)

SHELLITO, KEN J. *Born:* 18.4.40 (East Ham) *Club:* Chelsea *Caps:* 1

1962–63

| 29 May 1963 | *v* Czechoslovakia | Bratislava | 4–2 |

SHERINGHAM, TEDDY *Born:* 2.4.66 (Highams Park) *Club:* Tottenham Hotspur *Caps:* 2

1992–93

| 29 May 1993 | *v* Poland (WCQ) | Chorzow | 1–1 |
| 2 June 1993 | *v* Norway (WCQ) | Oslo | 0–2 |

SHILTON, PETER L. *Born:* 18.9.49 (Leicester) *Clubs:* Leicester City, Stoke City, Nottingham Forest, Southampton, Derby County *Caps:* 125

1970–71 (with Leicester City)

| 25 Nov 1970 | *v* East Germany | Wembley | 3–1 |
| 19 May 1971 | *v* Wales | Wembley | 0–0 |

1971–72

| 10 Nov 1971 | *v* Switzerland (ECQ) | Wembley | 1–1 |
| 23 May 1972 | *v* Northern Ireland | Wembley | 0–1 |

1972–73

11 Oct 1972	*v* Yugoslavia	Wembley	1–1
14 Feb 1973	*v* Scotland (SFAC)	Glasgow	5–0
12 May 1973	*v* Northern Ireland	Everton	2–1
15 May 1973	*v* Wales	Wembley	3–0
19 May 1973	*v* Scotland	Wembley	1–0
27 May 1973	*v* Czechoslovakia	Prague	1–1
6 June 1973	*v* Poland (WCQ)	Chorzow	0–2
10 June 1973	*v* USSR	Moscow	2–1
14 June 1973	*v* Italy	Turin	0–2

1973–74

26 Sept 1973	*v* Austria	Wembley	7–0
17 Oct 1973	*v* Poland (WCQ)	Wembley	1–1
14 Nov 1973	*v* Italy	Wembley	0–1
11 May 1974	*v* Wales	Cardiff	2–0
12 May 1974	*v* Northern Ireland	Wembley	1–0
18 May 1974	*v* Scotland	Glasgow	0–2
22 May 1974	*v* Argentina	Wembley	2–2

1974–75 (with Stoke City)

| 16 April 1975 | *v* Cyprus (ECQ) | Wembley | 5–0 |

1976–77

| 28 May 1977 | *v* Northern Ireland | Belfast | 2–1 |
| 31 May 1977 | *v* Wales | Wembley | 0–1 |

1977–78 (with Nottingham Forest)

| 13 May 1978 | *v* Wales | Cardiff | 3–1 |
| 24 May 1978 | *v* Hungary | Wembley | 4–1 |

1978–79

| 29 Nov 1978 | *v* Czechoslovakia | Wembley | 1–0 |
| 10 June 1979 | *v* Sweden | Stockholm | 0–0 |

13 June 1979	*v* Austria	Vienna	3–4

1979–80

17 Oct 1979	*v* Northern Ireland (ECQ)	Belfast	5–1
26 March 1980	*v* Spain	Barcelona	2–0
15 June 1980	*v* Italy (EC)	Turin	0–1

1980–81

10 Sept 1980	*v* Norway (WCQ)	Wembley	4–0
19 Nov 1980	*v* Switzerland (WCQ)	Wembley	2–1
29 April 1981	*v* Romania (WCQ)	Wembley	0–0

1981–82

18 Nov 1981	*v* Hungary (WCQ)	Wembley	1–0
25 May 1982	*v* Holland*	Wembley	2–0
29 May 1982	*v* Scotland	Glasgow	1–0
16 June 1982	*v* France (WC)	Bilbao	3–1
20 June 1982	*v* Czechoslovakia (WC)	Bilbao	2–0
25 June 1982	*v* Kuwait (WC)	Bilbao	1–0
29 June 1982	*v* West Germany (WC)	Madrid	0–0
5 July 1982	*v* Spain (WC)	Madrid	0–0

1982–83 (with Southampton)

22 Sept 1982	*v* Denmark (ECQ)	Copenhagen	2–2
13 Oct 1982	*v* West Germany	Wembley	1–2
17 Nov 1982	*v* Greece (ECQ)	Salonika	3–0
23 Feb 1983	*v* Wales*	Cardiff	2–1
30 March 1983	*v* Greece* (ECQ)	Wembley	0–0
27 April 1983	*v* Hungary* (ECQ)	Wembley	2–0
28 May 1983	*v* Northern Ireland*	Belfast	0–0
1 June 1983	*v* Scotland	Wembley	2–0
12 June 1983	*v* Australia*	Sydney	0–0
15 June 1983	*v* Australia*	Brisbane	1–0
19 June 1983	*v* Australia*	Melbourne	1–1

1983–84

21 Sept 1983	*v* Denmark (ECQ)	Wembley	0–1
12 Oct 1983	*v* Hungary (ECQ)	Budapest	3–0
29 Feb 1984	*v* France	Paris	0–2
4 April 1984	*v* Northern Ireland	Wembley	1–0
2 May 1984	*v* Wales	Wrexham	0–1
26 May 1984	*v* Scotland	Glasgow	1–1
2 June 1984	*v* USSR	Wembley	0–2
10 June 1984	*v* Brazil	Rio de Janeiro	2–0
13 June 1984	*v* Uruguay	Montevideo	0–2
17 June 1984	*v* Chile	Santiago	0–0

1984–85

12 Sept 1984	*v* East Germany	Wembley	1–0
17 Oct 1984	*v* Finland (WCQ)	Wembley	5–0
14 Nov 1984	*v* Turkey (WCQ)	Istanbul	8–0
26 Feb 1985	*v* Northern Ireland (WCQ)	Belfast	1–0
1 May 1985	*v* Romania (WCQ)	Bucharest	0–0
22 May 1985	*v* Finland (WCQ)	Helsinki	1–1

25 May 1985	*v* Scotland (RC)	Glasgow	0–1
6 June 1985	*v* Italy	Mexico City	1–2
12 June 1985	*v* West Germany	Mexico City	3–0

1985–86

11 Sept 1985	*v* Romania (WCQ)	Wembley	1–1
16 Oct 1985	*v* Turkey (WCQ)	Wembley	5–0
13 Nov 1985	*v* Northern Ireland (WCQ)	Wembley	0–0
29 Jan 1986	*v* Egypt	Cairo	4–0
26 Feb 1986	*v* Israel	Tel Aviv	2–1
26 March 1986	*v* USSR	Tbilisi	1–0
23 April 1986	*v* Scotland (RC)	Wembley	2–1
17 May 1986	*v* Mexico	Los Angeles	3–0
24 May 1986	*v* Canada	Vancouver	1–0
3 June 1986	*v* Portugal (WC)	Monterrey	0–1
6 June 1986	*v* Morocco (WC)	Monterrey	0–0
11 June 1986	*v* Poland* (WC)	Monterrey	3–0
18 June 1986	*v* Paraguay* (WC)	Mexico City	3–0
22 June 1986	*v* Argentina* (WC)	Mexico City	1–2

1986–87

10 Sept 1986	*v* Sweden*	Stockholm	0–1
15 Oct 1986	*v* Northern Ireland (ECQ)	Wembley	3–0
18 Feb 1987	*v* Spain	Madrid	4–2
1 Apr 1987	*v* Northern Ireland (ECQ)	Belfast	2–0
19 May 1987	*v* Brazil (RC)	Wembley	1–1

1987–88 (with Derby County)

9 Sept 1987	*v* West Germany*	Düsseldorf	1–3
14 Oct 1987	*v* Turkey (ECQ)	Wembley	8–0
11 Nov 1987	*v* Yugoslavia (ECQ)	Belgrade	4–1
23 March 1988	*v* Holland	Wembley	2–2
21 May 1988	*v* Scotland (RC)	Wembley	1–0
24 May 1988	*v* Colombia (RC)	Wembley	1–1
28 May 1988	*v* Switzerland	Lausanne	1–0
12 June 1988	*v* Eire (EC)	Stuttgart	0–1
15 June 1988	*v* Holland (EC)	Düsseldorf	1–3

1988–89

14 Sept 1988	*v* Denmark	Wembley	1–0
19 Oct 1988	*v* Sweden (WCQ)	Wembley	0–0
8 Feb 1989	*v* Greece	Athens	2–1
8 Mar 1989	*v* Albania (WCQ)	Tirana	2–0
26 April 1989	*v* Albania (WCQ)	Wembley	5–0
23 May 1989	*v* Chile (RC)	Wembley	0–0
27 May 1989	*v* Scotland (RC)	Glasgow	2–0
3 June 1989	*v* Poland (WCQ)	Wembley	3–0
7 June 1989	*v* Denmark	Copenhagen	1–1

1989–90

6 Sept 1989	*v* Sweden (WCQ)	Stockholm	0–0
11 Oct 1989	*v* Poland (WCQ)	Katowice	0–0
15 Nov 1989	*v* Italy	Wembley	0–0

13 Dec 1989	*v* Yugoslavia	Wembley	2–1
28 March 1990	*v* Brazil	Wembley	1–0
25 April 1990	*v* Czechoslovakia	Wembley	4–2
15 May 1990	*v* Denmark	Wembley	1–0
22 May 1990	*v* Uruguay	Wembley	1–2
2 June 1990	*v* Tunisia	Tunis	1–1
11 June 1990	*v* Eire (WC)	Cagliari	1–1
16 June 1990	*v* Holland (WC)	Cagliari	0–0
21 June 1990	*v* Egypt* (WC)	Cagliari	1–0
26 June 1990	*v* Belgium (WC)	Bologna	1–0 (aet)
1 July 1990	*v* Cameroon (WC)	Naples	3–2 (aet)
4 July 1990	*v* West Germany (WC)	Turin	1–1 (aet)
7 July 1990	*v* Italy* (WC)	Bari	1–2

SHIMWELL, EDDIE *Born:* 27.2.20 (Matlock) *Club:* Blackpool *Caps:* 1

1948–49

13 May 1949	*v* Sweden	Stockholm	1–3

SILLETT, PETER R. *Born:* 1.2.33 (Southampton) *Club:* Chelsea *Caps:* 3

1954–55

15 May 1955	*v* France	Paris	0–1
18 May 1955	*v* Spain	Madrid	1–1
22 May 1955	*v* Portugal	Oporto	1–3

SINTON, ANDY *Born:* 19.3.66 (Newcastle) *Club:* Queens Park Rangers *Caps:* 10

1991–92

13 Nov 1991	*v* Poland (ECQ)	Poznan	1–1
29 April 1992	*v* CIS	Moscow	2–2
12 May 1992	*v* Hungary (sub)	Budapest	1–0
17 May 1992	*v* Brazil	Wembley	1–1
14 June 1992	*v* France (EC)	Malmo	0–0
17 June 1992	*v* Sweden (EC)	Stockholm	1–2

1992–93

9 Sept 1992	*v* Spain	Santander	0–1
31 March 1993	*v* Turkey (WCQ)	Izmir	2–0
13 June 1993	*v* Brazil (USC)	Washington	1–1
19 June 1993	*v* Germany (USC)	Detroit	1–2

SLATER, WILLIAM J. *Born:* 29.4.27 (Clitheroe) *Club:* Wolverhampton Wanderers *Caps:* 12

1954–55

10 Nov 1954	*v* Wales	Wembley	3–2
1 Dec 1954	*v* West Germany	Wembley	3–1

1957–58

19 April 1958	*v* Scotland	Glasgow	4–0
7 May 1958	*v* Portugal	Wembley	2–1
11 May 1958	*v* Yugoslavia	Belgrade	0–5

18 May 1958	*v* USSR	Moscow	1–1
8 June 1958	*v* USSR (WC)	Gothenburg	2–2
11 June 1958	*v* Brazil (WC)	Gothenburg	0–0
15 June 1958	*v* Austria (WC)	Boras	2–2
17 June 1958	*v* USSR (WC)	Gothenburg	0–1

1958–59

22 Oct 1958	*v* USSR	Wembley	5–0

1959–60

19 April 1960	*v* Scotland	Glasgow	1–1

SMITH, ALAN M. *Born:* 21.11.62 (Birmingham) *Club:* Arsenal *Caps:* 13 *Goals:* 2

1988–89

16 Nov 1988	*v* Saudi Arabia (sub)	Riyadh	1–1
8 Feb 1989	*v* Greece	Athens	2–1
8 March 1989	*v* Albania (sub)(WCQ)	Tirana	2–0
3 June 1989	*v* Poland (sub)(WCQ)	Wembley	3–0

1990–91

1 May 1991	*v* Turkey (ECQ)	Izmir	1–0
21 May 1991	*v* USSR	Wembley	3–1 (1 goal)
25 May 1991	*v* Argentina	Wembley	2–2

1991–92

11 Sept 1991	*v* Germany	Wembley	0–1
16 Oct 1991	*v* Turkey (ECQ)	Wembley	1–0 (1 goal)
13 Nov 1991	*v* Poland (sub)(ECQ)	Poznan	1–1
12 May 1992	*v* Hungary (sub)	Budapest	1–0
11 June 1992	*v* Denmark (EC)	Malmo	0–0
17 June 1992	*v* Sweden (sub) (EC)	Gothenburg	1–2

SMITH, LIONEL *Born:* 23.8.20 (Mexborough) *Club:* Arsenal *Caps:* 6

1950–51

15 Nov 1950	*v* Wales	Sunderland	4–2

1951–52

20 Oct 1951	*v* Wales	Cardiff	1–1
14 Nov 1951	*v* Northern Ireland	Aston Villa	2–0

1952–53

12 Nov 1952	*v* Wales	Wembley	5–2
26 Nov 1952	*v* Belgium	Wembley	5–0
18 April 1953	*v* Scotland	Wembley	2–2

SMITH, ROBERT A. *Born:* 22.2.33 (Langdale) *Club:* Tottenham Hotspur *Caps:* 15 *Goals:* 13

1960–61

8 Oct 1960	*v* Northern Ireland	Belfast	5–2 (1 goal)
19 Oct 1960	*v* Luxembourg (WCQ)	Luxembourg	9–0 (2 goals)
26 Oct 1960	*v* Spain	Wembley	4–2 (2 goals)
23 Nov 1960	*v* Wales	Wembley	5–1 (1 goal)
15 April 1961	*v* Scotland	Wembley	9–3 (2 goals)

21 May 1961	*v* Portugal (WCQ)	Lisbon	1–1

1961–62

14 April 1962	*v* Scotland	Glasgow	0–2

1962–63

27 Feb 1963	*v* France (ECQ)	Paris	2–5 (1 goal)
6 April 1963	*v* Scotland	Wembley	1–2
8 May 1963	*v* Brazil	Wembley	1–1
29 May 1963	*v* Czechoslovakia	Bratislava	4–2 (1 goal)
2 June 1963	*v* East Germany	Leipzig	2–1

1963–64

12 Oct 1963	*v* Wales	Cardiff	4–0 (2 goals)
23 Oct 1963	*v* Rest of the World	Wembley	2–1
20 Nov 1963	*v* Northern Ireland	Wembley	8–3 (1 goal)

SMITH, TREVOR *Born:* 13.4.36 (Brierley Hill) *Club:* Birmingham City *Caps:* 2

1959–60

17 Oct 1959	*v* Wales	Cardiff	1–1
28 Oct 1959	*v* Sweden	Wembley	2–3

SMITH, TOMMY *Born:* 5.4.45 (Liverpool) *Club:* Liverpool *Caps:* 1

1970–71

19 May 1971	*v* Wales	Wembley	0–0

SPINK, NIGEL P. *Born:* 8.8.58 (Chelmsford) *Club:* Aston Villa *Caps:* 1

1982–83

19 June 1983	*v* Australia (sub)	Melbourne	1–1

SPRINGETT, RON D. G. *Born:* 22.7.35 (Fulham) *Club:* Sheffield Wednesday *Caps:* 33

1959–60

18 Nov 1959	*v* Northern Ireland	Wembley	2–1
9 April 1960	*v* Scotland	Glasgow	1–1
11 May 1960	*v* Yugoslavia	Wembley	3–3
15 May 1960	*v* Spain	Madrid	0–3
22 May 1960	*v* Hungary	Budapest	0–2

1960–61

8 Oct 1960	*v* Northern Ireland	Belfast	5–2
19 Oct 1960	*v* Luxembourg (WCQ)	Luxembourg	9–0
26 Oct 1960	*v* Spain	Wembley	4–2
15 April 1961	*v* Scotland	Wembley	9–3
10 May 1961	*v* Mexico	Wembley	8–0
21 May 1961	*v* Portugal (WCQ)	Lisbon	1–1
24 May 1961	*v* Italy	Rome	3–2
27 May 1961	*v* Austria	Vienna	1–3

1961–62

28 Sept 1961	*v* Luxembourg (WCQ)	Arsenal	4–1
14 Oct 1961	*v* Wales	Cardiff	1–1

25 Oct 1961	*v* Portugal (WCQ)	Wembley	2–0
22 Nov 1961	*v* Northern Ireland	Wembley	1–1
4 April 1962	*v* Austria	Wembley	3–1
14 April 1962	*v* Scotland	Glasgow	0–2
9 May 1962	*v* Switzerland	Wembley	3–1
20 May 1962	*v* Peru	Lima	4–0
31 May 1962	*v* Hungary (WC)	Rancagua	1–2
2 June 1962	*v* Argentina (WC)	Rancagua	3–1
7 June 1962	*v* Bulgaria (WC)	Rancagua	0–0
10 June 1962	*v* Brazil (WC)	Vina del Mar	1–3
1962–63			
3 Oct 1962	*v* France (ECQ)	Sheffield Wednesday	1–1
20 Oct 1962	*v* Northern Ireland	Belfast	3–1
21 Nov 1962	*v* Wales	Wembley	4–0
27 Feb 1963	*v* France (ECQ)	Paris	2–5
5 June 1963	*v* Switzerland	Basle	8–1
1965–66			
2 Oct 1965	*v* Wales	Cardiff	0–0
20 Oct 1965	*v* Austria	Wembley	2–3
29 June 1966	*v* Norway	Oslo	6–1

STANIFORTH, RON *Born:* 13.4.24 (Manchester) *Club:* Huddersfield Town *Caps:* 8

1953–54			
3 April 1954	*v* Scotland (WCQ)	Glasgow	4–2
16 May 1954	*v* Yugoslavia	Belgrade	0–1
23 May 1954	*v* Hungary	Budapest	1–7
17 June 1954	*v* Belgium (WC)	Basle	4–4
20 June 1954	*v* Switzerland (WC)	Berne	2–0
26 June 1954	*v* Uruguay (WC)	Basle	2–4
1954–55			
10 Nov 1954	*v* Wales	Wembley	3–2
1 Dec 1954	*v* West Germany	Wembley	3–1

STATHAM, DEREK *Born:* 24.3.59 (Wolverhampton) *Club:* West Bromwich Albion *Caps:* 3

1982–83			
23 Feb 1983	*v* Wales	Wembley	2–1
12 June 1983	*v* Australia	Sydney	0–0
15 June 1983	*v* Australia	Brisbane	1–0

STEIN, BRIAN *Born:* 19.10.57 (South Africa) *Club:* Luton Town *Caps:* 1

1983–84			
29 Feb 1984	*v* France	Paris	0–2

STEPNEY, ALEX C. *Born:* 18.9.44 (Mitcham) *Club:* Manchester United *Caps:* 1

1967–68			
22 May 1968	*v* Sweden	Wembley	3–1

STERLAND, MEL *Born:* 1.10.61 (Sheffield) *Club:* Sheffield Wednesday *Caps:* 1

1988–89

16 Nov 1988	*v* Saudi Arabia	Riyadh	1–1

STEVEN, TREVOR M. *Born:* 21.9.63 (Berwick) *Clubs:* Everton, Rangers, Marseille
Caps: 36 *Goals:* 4

1984–85 (with Everton)

27 Feb 1985	*v* Northern Ireland (WCQ)	Belfast	1–0
26 March 1985	*v* Eire	Wembley	2–1 (1 goal)
1 May 1985	*v* Romania (WCQ)	Bucharest	0–0
22 May 1985	*v* Finland (WCQ)	Helsinki	1–1
6 June 1985	*v* Italy	Mexico City	1–2
16 June 1985	*v* USA (sub)	Los Angeles	5–0 (1 goal)

1985–86

16 Oct 1985	*v* Turkey (sub) (WCQ)	Wembley	5–0
29 Jan 1986	*v* Egypt	Cairo	4–0 (1 goal)
26 March 1986	*v* USSR (sub)	Tbilisi	1–0
17 May 1986	*v* Mexico (sub)	Los Angeles	3–0
11 June 1986	*v* Poland (WC)	Monterrey	3–0
18 June 1986	*v* Paraguay (WC)	Mexico City	3–0
22 June 1986	*v* Argentina (WC)	Mexico City	1–2

1986–87

10 Sept 1986	*v* Sweden	Stockholm	0–1
12 Nov 1986	*v* Yugoslavia (sub) (ECQ)	Wembley	2–0
18 Feb 1987	*v* Spain (sub)	Madrid	4–2

1987–88

14 Oct 1987	*v* Turkey (ECQ)	Wembley	8–0
11 Nov 1987	*v* Yugoslavia (ECQ)	Belgrade	4–1
23 March 1988	*v* Holland	Wembley	2–2
27 April 1988	*v* Hungary	Budapest	0–0
21 May 1988	*v* Scotland (RC)	Wembley	1–0
28 May 1988	*v* Switzerland	Lausanne	1–0
15 June 1988	*v* Holland (EC)	Düsseldorf	1–3
18 June 1988	*v* USSR (EC)	Frankfurt	1–3

1988–89

27 May 1989	*v* Scotland (RC)	Glasgow	2–0

1989–90 (with Rangers)

25 April 1990	*v* Czechoslovakia	Wembley	4–2
1 July 1990	*v* Cameroon (sub) (WC)	Naples	3–2 (aet)
4 July 1990	*v* West Germany (sub) (WC)	Turin	1–1 (aet)
7 July 1990	*v* Italy (WC)	Bari	1–2

1990–91

6 Feb 1991	*v* Cameroon	Wembley	2–0

1991–92 (with Marseille)

11 Sept 1991	*v* Germany	Wembley	0–1
29 April 1992	*v* CIS	Moscow	2–2 (1 goal)
17 May 1992	*v* Brazil	Wembley	1–1

3 June 1992	*v* Finland	Helsinki	2–1
11 June 1992	*v* Denmark (EC)	Malmo	0–0
14 June 1992	*v* France (EC)	Malmo	0–0

STEVENS, GARY A. *Born:* 30.3.62 (Hillingdon) *Club:* Tottenham Hotspur *Caps:* 7

1984–85

17 Oct 1984	*v* Finland (sub) (WCQ)	Wembley	5–0
14 Nov 1984	*v* Turkey (sub) (WCQ)	Istanbul	8–0
27 Feb 1985	*v* Northern Ireland (WCQ)	Belfast	1–0

1985–86

23 April 1986	*v* Scotland (sub) (RC)	Wembley	2–1
17 May 1986	*v* Mexico (sub)	Los Angeles	3–0
6 June 1986	*v* Morocco (sub) (WC)	Monterrey	0–0
18 June 1986	*v* Paraguay (sub) (WC)	Mexico City	3–0

STEVENS, M. GARY *Born:* 27.3.63 (Barrow) *Clubs:* Everton, Rangers *Caps:* 46

1984–85 (with Everton)

6 June 1985	*v* Italy	Mexico City	1–2
12 June 1985	*v* West Germany	Mexico City	3–0

1985–86

11 Sept 1985	*v* Romania (WCQ)	Wembley	1–1
16 Oct 1985	*v* Turkey (WCQ)	Wembley	5–0
13 Nov 1985	*v* Northern Ireland (WCQ)	Wembley	0–0
29 Jan 1986	*v* Egypt	Cairo	4–0
26 Feb 1986	*v* Israel	Tel Aviv	2–1
23 April 1986	*v* Scotland (RC)	Wembley	2–1
24 May 1986	*v* Canada	Vancouver	1–0
3 June 1986	*v* Portugal (WC)	Monterrey	0–1
6 June 1986	*v* Morocco (WC)	Monterrey	0–0
11 June 1986	*v* Poland (WC)	Monterrey	3–0
18 June 1986	*v* Paraguay (WC)	Mexico City	3–0
22 June 1986	*v* Argentina (WC)	Mexico City	1–2

1986–87

19 May 1987	*v* Brazil (RC)	Wembley	1–1
23 May 1987	*v* Scotland (RC)	Glasgow	0–0

1987–88

14 Oct 1987	*v* Turkey (ECQ)	Wembley	8–0
11 Nov 1987	*v* Yugoslavia (ECQ)	Belgrade	4–1
17 Feb 1988	*v* Israel	Tel Aviv	0–0
23 March 1988	*v* Holland	Wembley	2–2
27 April 1988	*v* Hungary (sub)	Budapest	0–0
21 May 1988	*v* Scotland (RC)	Wembley	1–0
28 May 1988	*v* Switzerland	Lausanne	1–0
12 June 1988	*v* Eire (EC)	Stuttgart	0–1
15 June 1988	*v* Holland (EC)	Düsseldorf	1–3
18 June 1988	*v* USSR (EC)	Frankfurt	1–3

1988–89 (with Rangers)

14 Sept 1988	v Denmark	Wembley	1–0
19 Oct 1988	v Sweden (WCQ)	Wembley	0–0
8 Feb 1989	v Greece	Athens	2–1
8 March 1989	v Albania (WCQ)	Tirana	2–0
26 April 1989	v Albania (WCQ)	Wembley	5–0
27 May 1989	v Scotland (RC)	Glasgow	2–0
3 June 1989	v Poland (WCQ)	Wembley	3–0

1989–90

6 Sept 1989	v Sweden (WCQ)	Stockholm	0–0
11 Oct 1989	v Poland (WCQ)	Katowice	0–0
15 Nov 1989	v Italy	Wembley	0–0
28 March 1990	v Brazil	Wembley	1–0
15 May 1990	v Denmark	Wembley	1–0
2 June 1990	v Tunisia	Tunis	1–1
11 June 1990	v Eire (WC)	Cagliari	1–1
7 July 1990	v Italy (WC)	Bari	1–2

1990–91

21 May 1991	v USSR	Wembley	3–1

1991–92

29 April 1992	v CIS	Moscow	2–2
12 May 1992	v Hungary	Budapest	1–0
17 May 1992	v Brazil	Wembley	1–1
3 June 1992	v Finland	Helsinki	2–1

STEWART, PAUL A. *Born:* 7.10.64 (Manchester) *Club:* Tottenham Hotspur *Caps:* 3

1991–92

11 Sept 1991	v Germany (sub)	Wembley	0–1
25 March 1992	v Czechoslovakia (sub)	Prague	2–2
29 April 1992	v CIS (sub)	Moscow	2–2

STILES, NORBERT P. (NOBBY) *Born:* 18.5.42 (Manchester) *Club:* Manchester United *Caps:* 28 *Goals:* 1

1964–65

10 April 1965	v Scotland	Wembley	2–2
5 May 1965	v Hungary	Wembley	1–0
9 May 1965	v Yugoslavia	Belgrade	1–1
16 May 1965	v Sweden	Gothenburg	2–1

1965–66

2 Oct 1965	v Wales	Cardiff	0–0
20 Oct 1965	v Austria	Wembley	2–3
10 Nov 1965	v Northern Ireland	Wembley	2–1
8 Dec 1965	v Spain	Madrid	2–0
5 Jan 1966	v Poland	Everton	1–1
23 Feb 1966	v West Germany	Wembley	1–0 (1 goal)
2 April 1966	v Scotland	Glasgow	4–3
29 June 1966	v Norway	Oslo	6–1
3 July 1966	v Denmark	Copenhagen	2–0

5 July 1966	*v* Poland	Chorzow	1–0
11 July 1966	*v* Uruguay (WC)	Wembley	0–0
16 July 1966	*v* Mexico (WC)	Wembley	2–0
20 July 1966	*v* France (WC)	Wembley	2–0
23 July 1966	*v* Argentina (WC)	Wembley	1–0
26 July 1966	*v* Portugal (WC)	Wembley	2–1
30 July 1966	*v* West Germany (WCF)	Wembley	4–2 (aet)

1966–67

22 Oct 1966	*v* Northern Ireland (ECQ)	Belfast	2–0
2 Nov 1966	*v* Czechoslovakia	Wembley	0–0
16 Nov 1966	*v* Wales (ECQ)	Wembley	5–1
15 April 1967	*v* Scotland (ECQ)	Wembley	2–3

1967–68

8 June 1968	*v* USSR (EC)	Rome	2–0

1968–69

15 Jan 1969	*v* Romania	Wembley	1–1

1969–70

21 April 1970	*v* Northern Ireland	Wembley	3–1
25 April 1970	*v* Scotland	Glasgow	0–0

STOREY, PETER E. *Born:* 7.9.45 (Farnham) *Club:* Arsenal *Caps:* 19

1970–71

21 April 1971	*v* Greece (ECQ)	Wembley	3–0
15 May 1971	*v* Northern Ireland	Belfast	1–0
22 May 1971	*v* Scotland	Wembley	3–1

1971–72

10 Nov 1971	*v* Switzerland (ECQ)	Wembley	1–1
13 May 1972	*v* West Germany (ECQ)	Berlin	0–0
20 May 1972	*v* Wales	Cardiff	3–0
23 May 1972	*v* Northern Ireland	Wembley	0–1
27 May 1972	*v* Scotland	Glasgow	1–0

1972–73

11 Oct 1972	*v* Yugoslavia	Wembley	1–1
15 Nov 1972	*v* Wales (WCQ)	Cardiff	1–0
24 Jan 1973	*v* Wales (WCQ)	Wembley	1–1
14 Feb 1973	*v* Scotland (SFAC)	Glasgow	5–0
12 May 1973	*v* Northern Ireland	Everton	2–1
15 May 1973	*v* Wales	Wembley	3–0
19 May 1973	*v* Scotland	Wembley	1–0
27 May 1973	*v* Czechoslovakia	Prague	1–1
6 June 1973	*v* Poland (WCQ)	Chorzow	0–2
10 June 1973	*v* USSR	Moscow	2–1
14 June 1973	*v* Italy	Turin	0–2

STOREY-MOORE, IAN *Born:* 17.1.45 (Ipswich) *Club:* Nottingham Forest *Caps:* 1

1969–70

14 Jan 1970	*v* Holland	Wembley	0–0

STRETEN, BERNARD *Born:* 14.1.21 (Gillingham) *Club:* Luton Town *Caps:* 1

1949–50

| 16 Nov 1949 | *v* Northern Ireland (WCQ) | Manchester City | 9–2 |

SUMMERBEE, MIKE G. *Born:* 15.12.42 (Cheltenham) *Club:* Manchester City *Caps:* 8
Goals: 1

1967–68

24 Feb 1968	*v* Scotland (ECQ)	Glasgow	1–1
3 April 1968	*v* Spain (ECQ)	Wembley	1–0
1 June 1968	*v* West Germany	Hanover	0–1

1971–72

10 Nov 1971	*v* Switzerland (ECQ)	Wembley	1–1 (1 goal)
13 May 1972	*v* West Germany (sub) (ECQ)	Berlin	0–0
20 May 1972	*v* Wales	Cardiff	3–0
23 May 1972	*v* Northern Ireland	Wembley	0–1

1972–73

| 10 June 1973 | *v* USSR (sub) | Moscow | 2–1 |

SUNDERLAND, ALAN *Born:* 1.7.53 (Mexborough) *Club:* Arsenal *Caps:* 1

1979–80

| 31 May 1980 | *v* Australia | Sydney | 2–1 |

SWAN, PETER *Born:* 8.10.36 (South Elmsall) *Club:* Sheffield Wednesday *Caps:* 19

1959–60

11 May 1960	*v* Yugoslavia	Wembley	3–3
15 May 1960	*v* Spain	Madrid	0–3
22 May 1960	*v* Hungary	Budapest	0–2

1960–61

8 Oct 1960	*v* Northern Ireland	Belfast	5–2
19 Oct 1960	*v* Luxembourg (WCQ)	Luxembourg	9–0
26 Oct 1960	*v* Spain	Wembley	4–2
23 Nov 1960	*v* Wales	Wembley	5–1
15 April 1961	*v* Scotland	Wembley	9–3
10 May 1961	*v* Mexico	Wembley	8–0
21 May 1961	*v* Portugal (WCQ)	Lisbon	1–1
24 May 1961	*v* Italy	Rome	3–2
27 May 1961	*v* Austria	Vienna	1–3

1961–62

28 Sept 1961	*v* Luxembourg (WCQ)	Arsenal	4–1
14 Oct 1961	*v* Wales	Cardiff	1–1
25 Oct 1961	*v* Portugal (WCQ)	Wembley	2–0
22 Nov 1961	*v* Northern Ireland	Wembley	1–1
4 April 1962	*v* Austria	Wembley	3–1
14 April 1962	*v* Scotland	Glasgow	0–2
9 May 1962	*v* Switzerland	Wembley	3–1

SWIFT, FRANK V. *Born:* 26.12.13 (Blackpool) *Club:* Manchester City *Caps:* 19

1946–47

28 Sept 1946	*v* Northern Ireland	Belfast	7–2
30 Sept 1946	*v* Eire	Dublin	1–0
13 Nov 1946	*v* Wales	Manchester City	3–0
27 Nov 1946	*v* Holland	Huddersfield	8–2
12 April 1947	*v* Scotland	Wembley	1–1
3 May 1947	*v* France	Arsenal	3–0
18 May 1947	*v* Switzerland	Zurich	0–1
27 May 1947	*v* Portugal	Lisbon	10–0

1947–48

21 Sept 1947	*v* Belgium	Brussels	5–2
18 Oct 1947	*v* Wales	Cardiff	3–0
5 Nov 1947	*v* Northern Ireland	Everton	2–2
19 Nov 1947	*v* Sweden	Arsenal	4–2
10 April 1948	*v* Scotland	Glasgow	2–0
16 May 1948	*v* Italy*	Turin	4–0

1948–49

26 Sept 1948	*v* Denmark*	Copenhagen	0–0
9 Oct 1948	*v* Northern Ireland	Belfast	6–2
10 Nov 1948	*v* Wales	Aston Villa	1–0
9 April 1949	*v* Scotland	Wembley	1–3
18 May 1949	*v* Norway	Oslo	4–1

TALBOT, BRIAN E. *Born:* 21.7.53 (Ipswich) *Clubs:* Ipswich Town, Arsenal *Caps:* 6

1976–77 (with Ipswich)

28 May 1977	*v* Northern Ireland (sub)	Belfast	2–1
4 June 1977	*v* Scotland	Wembley	1–2
8 June 1977	*v* Brazil	Rio de Janeiro	0–0
12 June 1977	*v* Argentina	Buenos Aires	1–1
15 June 1977	*v* Uruguay	Montevideo	0–0

1979–80 (with Arsenal)

31 May 1980	*v* Australia	Sydney	2–1

TAMBLING, ROBERT V. *Born:* 18.9.41 (Storrington) *Club:* Chelsea *Caps:* 3 *Goals:* 1

1962–63

21 Nov 1962	*v* Wales	Cardiff	4–0
27 Feb 1963	*v* France (ECQ)	Paris	2–5 (1 goal)

1965–66

4 May 1966	*v* Yugoslavia	Wembley	2–0

TAYLOR, ERNIE *Born:* 2.9.25 (Sunderland) *Club:* Blackpool *Caps:* 1

1953–54

25 Nov 1953	*v* Hungary	Wembley	3–6

TAYLOR, JAMES G. *Born:* 5.11.17 (Hillingdon) *Club:* Fulham *Caps:* 2

1950–51

9 May 1951	*v* Argentina	Wembley	2–1
19 May 1951	*v* Portugal	Everton	5–2

TAYLOR, PETER J. *Born:* 3.1.53 (Southend) *Club:* Crystal Palace *Caps:* 4 *Goals:* 2

1975–76

24 March 1976	*v* Wales (sub) (FAWC)	Wrexham	2–1 (1 goal)
8 May 1976	*v* Wales	Cardiff	1–0 (1 goal)
11 May 1976	*v* Northern Ireland	Wembley	4–0
15 May 1976	*v* Scotland	Glasgow	1–2

TAYLOR, PHILIP. H. *Born:* 18.9.17 (Bristol) *Club:* Liverpool *Caps:* 3

1947–48

18 Oct 1947	*v* Wales	Cardiff	3–0
5 Nov 1947	*v* Northern Ireland	Everton	2–2
19 Nov 1947	*v* Sweden	Arsenal	4–2

TAYLOR, THOMAS *Born:* 29.1.32 (Barnsley) *Club:* Manchester United *Caps:* 19 *Goals:* 16

1952–53

17 May 1953	*v* Argentina	Buenos Aires	0–0†
24 May 1953	*v* Chile	Santiago	2–1 (1 goal)
31 May 1953	*v* Uruguay	Montevideo	1–2 (1 goal)

1953–54

17 June 1954	*v* Belgium (WC)	Basle	4–4
20 June 1954	*v* Switzerland (WC)	Berne	2–0

1955–56

14 April 1956	*v* Scotland	Glasgow	1–1
9 May 1956	*v* Brazil	Wembley	4–2 (2 goals)
16 May 1956	*v* Sweden	Stockholm	0–0
20 May 1956	*v* Finland	Helsinki	5–1
26 May 1956	*v* West Germany	Berlin	3–1

1956–57

6 Oct 1956	*v* Northern Ireland	Belfast	1–1
28 Nov 1956	*v* Yugoslavia (sub)	Wembley	3–0 (2 goals)
5 Dec 1956	*v* Denmark (WCQ)	Wolverhampton	5–2 (3 goals)
8 May 1957	*v* Eire (WCQ)	Wembley	5–1 (3 goals)
15 May 1957	*v* Denmark (WCQ)	Copenhagen	4–1 (2 goals)
19 May 1957	*v* Eire (WCQ)	Dublin	1–1

1957–58

19 Oct 1957	*v* Wales	Cardiff	4–0
6 Nov 1957	*v* Northern Ireland	Wembley	2–3
27 Nov 1957	*v* France	Wembley	4–0 (2 goals)

TEMPLE, DEREK W. *Born:* 13.11.38 (Liverpool) *Club:* Everton *Caps:* 1

1964–65

12 May 1965	*v* West Germany	Nuremberg	1–0

THOMAS, DANNY J. *Born:* 12.11.61 (Worksop) *Club:* Coventry City *Caps:* 2

1982–83

12 June 1983	*v* Australia	Sydney	0–0
19 June 1983	*v* Australia (sub)	Melbourne	1–1

THOMAS, DAVID *Born:* 5.10.50 (Kirkby) *Club:* Queens Park Rangers *Caps:* 8

1974–75

30 Oct 1974	*v* Czechoslovakia (sub)(ECQ)	Wembley	3–0
20 Nov 1974	*v* Portugal (ECQ)	Wembley	0–0
16 April 1975	*v* Cyprus (sub) (ECQ)	Wembley	5–0
11 May 1975	*v* Cyprus (ECQ)	Limassol	1–0
21 May 1975	*v* Wales	Wembley	2–2
24 May 1975	*v* Scotland (sub)	Wembley	5–1

1975–76

30 Oct 1975	*v* Czechoslovakia (sub)(ECQ)	Bratislava	1–2
19 Nov 1975	*v* Portugal (sub) (ECQ)	Lisbon	1–1

THOMAS, GEOFF R. *Born:* 5.8.64 (Manchester) *Club:* Crystal Palace *Caps:* 9

1990–91

1 May 1991	*v* Turkey (ECQ)	Izmir	1–0
21 May 1991	*v* USSR	Wembley	3–1
25 May 1991	*v* Argentina	Wembley	2–2
1 June 1991	*v* Australia	Sydney	1–0
3 June 1991	*v* New Zealand	Auckland	1–0
8 June 1991	*v* New Zealand	Wellington	2–0
12 June 1991	*v* Malaysia	Kuala Lumpur	4–2

1991–92

13 Nov 1991	*v* Poland (ECQ)	Poznan	1–1
19 Feb 1992	*v* France	Wembley	2–0

THOMAS, MICHAEL L. *Born:* 24.8.67 (Lambeth) *Club:* Arsenal *Caps:* 2

1988–89

16 Nov 1988	*v* Saudi Arabia	Riyadh	1–1

1989–90

13 Dec 1989	*v* Yugoslavia	Wembley	2–1

THOMPSON, PETER *Born:* 27.11.42 (Carlisle) *Club:* Liverpool *Caps:* 16

1963–64

17 May 1964	*v* Portugal	Lisbon	4–3
24 May 1964	*v* Eire	Dublin	3–1
27 May 1964	*v* USA	New York	10–0

30 May 1964	v Brazil (BJT)	Rio de Janeiro	1–5
4 June 1964	v Portugal (BJT)	Sao Paulo	1–1
6 June 1964	v Argentina (BJT)	Rio de Janeiro	0–1

1964–65

3 Oct 1964	v Northern Ireland	Belfast	4–3
21 Oct 1964	v Belgium	Wembley	2–2
18 Nov 1964	v Wales	Wembley	2–1
9 Dec 1964	v Holland	Amsterdam	1–1
10 April 1965	v Scotland	Wembley	2–2

1965–66

10 Nov 1965	v Northern Ireland	Wembley	2–1

1967–68

22 Nov 1967	v Northern Ireland (ECQ)	Wembley	2–0
1 June 1968	v West Germany	Hanover	0–1

1969–70

5 Nov 1969	v Holland (sub)	Amsterdam	1–0
25 April 1970	v Scotland	Glasgow	0–0

THOMPSON, PHILIP B. *Born:* 21.1.54 (Liverpool) *Club:* Liverpool *Caps:* 42 *Goals:* 1

1975–76

24 March 1976	v Wales (FAWC)	Wrexham	2–1
8 May 1976	v Wales	Cardiff	1–0
11 May 1976	v Northern Ireland	Wembley	4–0
15 May 1976	v Scotland	Glasgow	1–2
23 May 1976	v Brazil (USABT)	Los Angeles	0–1
28 May 1976	v Italy (USABT)	New York	3–2 (1 goal)
13 June 1976	v Finland (WCQ)	Helsinki	4–1

1976–77

13 Oct 1976	v Finland (WCQ)	Wembley	2–1

1978–79

25 Oct 1978	v Eire (ECQ)	Dublin	1–1
29 Nov 1978	v Czechoslovakia	Wembley	1–0
19 May 1979	v Northern Ireland	Belfast	2–0
26 May 1979	v Scotland	Wembley	3–1
6 June 1979	v Bulgaria (ECQ)	Sofia	3–0
13 June 1979	v Austria	Vienna	3–4

1979–80

12 Sept 1979	v Denmark (ECQ)	Wembley	1–0
17 Oct 1979	v Northern Ireland (ECQ)	Belfast	5–1
22 Nov 1979	v Bulgaria* (ECQ)	Wembley	2–0
6 Feb 1980	v Eire (ECQ)	Wembley	2–0
26 March 1980	v Spain	Barcelona	2–0
13 May 1980	v Argentina	Wembley	3–1
17 May 1980	v Wales*	Wrexham	1–4
24 May 1980	v Scotland*	Wembley	2–0
12 June 1980	v Belgium (EC)	Turin	1–1
15 June 1980	v Italy (EC)	Turin	0–1

18 June 1980	v Spain (EC)	Naples	2–1

1980–81

10 Sept 1980	v Norway* (WCQ)	Wembley	4–0
15 Oct 1980	v Romania* (WCQ)	Bucharest	1–2
6 June 1981	v Hungary (WCQ)	Budapest	3–1

1981–82

9 Sept 1981	v Norway (WCQ)	Oslo	1–2
18 Nov 1981	v Hungary (WCQ)	Wembley	1–0
27 April 1982	v Wales*	Cardiff	1–0
25 May 1982	v Holland	Wembley	2–0
29 May 1982	v Scotland	Glasgow	1–0
3 June 1982	v Finland	Helsinki	4–1
16 June 1982	v France (WC)	Bilbao	3–1
20 June 1982	v Czechoslovakia (WC)	Bilbao	2–0
25 June 1982	v Kuwait (WC)	Bilbao	1–0
29 June 1982	v West Germany (WC)	Madrid	0–0
5 July 1982	v Spain (WC)	Madrid	0–0

1982–83

13 Oct 1982	v West Germany	Wembley	1–2
17 Nov 1982	v Greece (ECQ)	Salonika	3–0

THOMPSON, THOMAS *Born:* 10.11.28 (Fencehouses) *Clubs:* Aston Villa, Preston North End *Caps:* 2

1951–52 (with Aston Villa)

20 Oct 1951	v Wales	Cardiff	1–1

1956–57 (with Preston North End)

6 April 1957	v Scotland	Wembley	2–1

THOMSON, ROBERT A. *Born:* 5.12.43 (Smethwick) *Club:* Wolverhampton Wanderers *Caps:* 8

1963–64

20 Nov 1963	v Northern Ireland	Wembley	8–3
27 May 1964	v USA	New York	10–0
4 June 1964	v Portugal (BJT)	Sao Paulo	1–1
6 June 1964	v Argentina (BJT)	Rio de Janeiro	0–1

1964–65

3 Oct 1964	v Northern Ireland	Belfast	4–3
21 Oct 1964	v Belgium	Wembley	2–2
18 Nov 1964	v Wales	Wembley	2–1
9 Dec 1964	v Holland	Amsterdam	1–1

TODD, COLIN *Born:* 12.12.48 (Chester-le-Street) *Club:* Derby County *Caps:* 27

1971–72

23 May 1972	v Northern Ireland	Wembley	0–1

1973–74

3 April 1974	v Portugal	Lisbon	0–0
11 May 1974	v Wales	Cardiff	2–0

15 May 1974	*v* Northern Ireland	Wembley	1–0
18 May 1974	*v* Scotland	Glasgow	0–2
22 May 1974	*v* Argentina	Wembley	2–2
29 May 1974	*v* East Germany	Leipzig	1–1
1 June 1974	*v* Bulgaria	Sofia	1–0
5 June 1974	*v* Yugoslavia	Belgrade	2–2

1974–75

20 Nov 1974	*v* Portugal (sub) (ECQ)	Wembley	0–0
12 March 1975	*v* West Germany	Wembley	2–0
16 April 1975	*v* Cyprus (ECQ)	Wembley	5–0
11 May 1975	*v* Cyprus (ECQ)	Limassol	1–0
17 May 1975	*v* Northern Ireland	Belfast	0–0
21 May 1975	*v* Wales	Wembley	2–2
24 May 1975	*v* Scotland	Wembley	5–1

1975–76

3 Sept 1975	*v* Switzerland	Basle	2–1
30 Oct 1975	*v* Czechoslovakia (ECQ)	Bratislava	1–2
19 Nov 1975	*v* Portugal (ECQ)	Lisbon	1–1
11 May 1976	*v* Northern Ireland	Wembley	4–0
15 May 1976	*v* Scotland	Glasgow	1–2
23 May 1976	*v* Brazil (USABT)	Los Angeles	0–1
13 June 1976	*v* Finland (WCQ)	Helsinki	4–1

1976–77

8 Sept 1976	*v* Eire	Wembley	1–1
13 Oct 1976	*v* Finland (WCQ)	Wembley	2–1
9 Feb 1977	*v* Holland (sub)	Wembley	0–2
28 May 1977	*v* Northern Ireland	Belfast	2–1

TOWERS, ANTHONY M. *Born:* 13.4.52 (Manchester) *Club:* Sunderland *Caps:* 3

1975–76

8 May 1976	*v* Wales	Cardiff	1–0
11 May 1976	*v* Northern Ireland (sub)	Wembley	4–0
28 May 1976	*v* Italy (USABT)	New York	3–2

TUEART, DENNIS *Born:* 27.11.49 (Newcastle) *Club:* Manchester City *Caps:* 6 *Goals:* 2

1974–75

11 May 1975	*v* Cyprus (sub) (ECQ)	Limassol	1–0
17 May 1975	*v* Northern Ireland	Belfast	0–0

1976–77

13 Oct 1976	*v* Finland (WCQ)	Wembley	2–1 (1 goal)
28 May 1977	*v* Northern Ireland	Belfast	2–1 (1 goal)
31 May 1977	*v* Wales (sub)	Wembley	0–1
4 June 1977	*v* Scotland (sub)	Wembley	1–2

UFTON, DEREK G. *Born:* 31.5.28 (Bexleyheath) *Club:* Charlton Athletic *Caps:* 1

1953–54

21 Oct 1953	*v* FIFA (Rest of Europe)	Wembley	4–4

VENABLES, TERRY F. *Born:* 6.1.43 (Bethnal Green) *Club:* Chelsea *Caps:* 2

1964–65

21 Oct 1964	*v* Belgium	Wembley	2–2
9 Dec 1964	*v* Holland	Amsterdam	1–1

VILJOEN, COLIN *Born:* 20.6.48 (South Africa) *Club:* Ipswich Town *Caps:* 2

1974–75

17 May 1975	*v* Northern Ireland	Belfast	0–0
21 May 1975	*v* Wales	Wembley	2–2

VIOLLET, DENNIS S. *Born:* 20.9.33 (Manchester) *Club:* Manchester United *Caps:* 2 *Goals:* 1

1959–60

22 May 1960	*v* Hungary	Budapest	0–2

1961–62

28 Sept 1961	*v* Luxembourg (WCQ)	Arsenal	4–1 (1 goal)

WADDLE, CHRIS R. *Born:* 14.12.60 (Gateshead) *Clubs:* Newcastle United, Tottenham Hotspur, Marseille *Caps:* 62 *Goals:* 6

1984–85 (with Newcastle United)

26 March 1985	*v* Eire	Wembley	2–1
1 May 1985	*v* Romania (sub) (WCQ)	Bucharest	0–0
22 May 1985	*v* Finland (sub) (WCQ)	Helsinki	1–1
25 May 1985	*v* Scotland (sub) (RC)	Glasgow	0–1
6 June 1985	*v* Italy	Mexico City	1–2
9 June 1985	*v* Mexico (sub)	Mexico City	0–1
12 June 1985	*v* West Germany	Mexico City	3–0
16 June 1985	*v* USA	Los Angeles	5–0

1985–86 (with Tottenham Hotspur)

11 Sept 1985	*v* Romania (WCQ)	Wembley	1–1
16 Oct 1985	*v* Turkey (WCQ)	Wembley	5–0 (1 goal)
13 Nov 1985	*v* Northern Ireland (WCQ)	Wembley	0–0
26 Feb 1986	*v* Israel	Tel Aviv	2–1
26 March 1986	*v* USSR	Tbilisi	1–0 (1 goal)
23 April 1986	*v* Scotland (RC)	Wembley	2–1
17 May 1986	*v* Mexico	Los Angeles	3–0
24 May 1986	*v* Canada	Vancouver	1–0
3 June 1986	*v* Portugal (WC)	Monterrey	0–1
6 June 1986	*v* Morocco (WC)	Monterrey	0–0
11 June 1986	*v* Poland (sub) (WC)	Monterrey	3–0
22 June 1986	*v* Argentina (sub) (WC)	Mexico City	1–2

1986–87

10 Sept 1986	*v* Sweden (sub)	Stockholm	0–1
15 Oct 1986	*v* Northern Ireland (ECQ)	Wembley	3–0 (1 goal)
12 Nov 1986	*v* Yugoslavia (ECQ)	Wembley	2–0
18 Feb 1987	*v* Spain	Madrid	4–2

1 April 1987	v Northern Ireland (ECQ)	Belfast	2–0 (1 goal)
29 April 1987	v Turkey (ECQ)	Izmir	0–0
19 May 1987	v Brazil (RC)	Wembley	1–1
23 May 1987	v Scotland (RC)	Glasgow	0–0

1987–88

9 Sept 1987	v West Germany	Düsseldorf	1–3
17 Feb 1988	v Israel	Tel Aviv	0–0
27 April 1988	v Hungary	Budapest	0–0
21 May 1988	v Scotland (sub) (RC)	Wembley	1–0
24 May 1988	v Colombia (RC)	Wembley	1–1
28 May 1988	v Switzerland (sub)	Lausanne	1–0
12 June 1988	v Eire (EC)	Stuttgart	0–1
15 June 1988	v Holland (sub) (EC)	Düsseldorf	1–3

1988–89

19 Oct 1988	v Sweden (WCQ)	Wembley	0–0
16 Nov 1988	v Saudi Arabia	Riyadh	1–1
8 March 1989	v Albania (WCQ)	Tirana	2–0
26 April 1989	v Albania (WCQ)	Wembley	5–0 (1 goal)
23 May 1989	v Chile (RC)	Wembley	0–0
27 May 1989	v Scotland (RC)	Glasgow	2–0 (1 goal)
3 June 1989	v Poland (WCQ)	Wembley	3–0
7 June 1989	v Denmark (sub)	Copenhagen	1–1

1989–90 (with Marseille)

6 Sept 1989	v Sweden (WCQ)	Stockholm	0–0
11 Oct 1989	v Poland (WCQ)	Katowice	0–0
15 Nov 1989	v Italy	Wembley	0–0
13 Dec 1989	v Yugoslavia	Wembley	3–1
28 March 1990	v Brazil	Wembley	1–0
15 May 1990	v Denmark	Wembley	1–0
22 May 1990	v Uruguay	Wembley	1–2
2 June 1990	v Tunisia	Tunis	1–1
11 June 1990	v Eire (WC)	Cagliari	1–1
16 June 1990	v Holland (WC)	Cagliari	0–0
21 June 1990	v Egypt (WC)	Cagliari	1–0
26 June 1990	v Belgium (WC)	Bologna	1–0 (aet)
1 July 1990	v Cameroon (WC)	Naples	3–2 (aet)
4 July 1990	v West Germany (WC)	Turin	1–1 (aet)
7 July 1990	v Italy (sub) (WC)	Bari	1–2

1990–91

12 Sept 1990	v Hungary (sub)	Wembley	1–0
17 Oct 1990	v Poland (sub) (ECQ)	Wembley	2–0

1991–92

16 Oct 1991	v Turkey (ECQ)	Wembley	1–0

WAITERS, ANTHONY K. *Born:* 1.2.37 (Southport) *Club:* Blackpool *Caps:* 5

1963–64

24 May 1964	v Eire	Dublin	3–1
30 May 1964	v Brazil (BJT)	Rio de Janeiro	1–5

1964–65

21 Oct 1964	*v* Belgium	Wembley	2–2
18 Nov 1964	*v* Wales	Wembley	2–1
9 Dec 1964	*v* Holland	Amsterdam	1–1

WALKER, DES S. *Born:* 26.11.65 (Hackney) *Clubs:* Nottingham Forest, Sampdoria
Caps: 58

1988–89 (with Nottingham Forest)

14 Sept 1988	*v* Denmark (sub)	Wembley	1–0
19 Oct 1988	*v* Sweden (sub) (WCQ)	Wembley	0–0
8 Feb 1989	*v* Greece	Athens	2–1
8 March 1989	*v* Albania (WCQ)	Tirana	2–0
26 April 1989	*v* Albania (WCQ)	Wembley	5–0
23 May 1989	*v* Chile (RC)	Wembley	0–0
27 May 1989	*v* Scotland (RC)	Glasgow	2–0
3 June 1989	*v* Poland (WCQ)	Wembley	3–0
7 June 1989	*v* Denmark	Copenhagen	1–1

1989–90

6 Sept 1989	*v* Sweden (WCQ)	Stockholm	0–0
11 Oct 1989	*v* Poland (WCQ)	Katowice	0–0
15 Nov 1989	*v* Italy	Wembley	0–0
13 Dec 1989	*v* Yugoslavia	Wembley	2–1
28 March 1990	*v* Brazil	Wembley	1–0
25 April 1990	*v* Czechoslovakia	Wembley	4–2
15 May 1990	*v* Denmark	Wembley	1–0
22 May 1990	*v* Uruguay	Wembley	1–2
2 June 1990	*v* Tunisia	Tunis	1–1
11 June 1990	*v* Eire (WC)	Cagliari	1–1
16 June 1990	*v* Holland (WC)	Cagliari	0–0
21 June 1990	*v* Egypt (WC)	Cagliari	1–0
26 June 1990	*v* Belgium (WC)	Bologna	1–0 (aet)
1 July 1990	*v* Cameroon (WC)	Naples	3–2 (aet)
4 July 1990	*v* West Germany (WC)	Turin	1–1 (aet)
7 July 1990	*v* Italy (WC)	Bari	1–2

1990–91

12 Sept 1990	*v* Hungary	Wembley	1–0
17 Oct 1990	*v* Poland (ECQ)	Wembley	2–0
14 Nov 1990	*v* Eire (ECQ)	Dublin	1–1
6 Feb 1991	*v* Cameroon	Wembley	2–0
27 March 1991	*v* Eire (ECQ)	Wembley	1–1
1 May 1991	*v* Turkey (ECQ)	Izmir	1–0
25 May 1991	*v* Argentina	Wembley	2–2
1 June 1991	*v* Australia	Sydney	1–0
3 June 1991	*v* New Zealand	Auckland	1–0
8 June 1991	*v* New Zealand	Wellington	2–0
12 June 1991	*v* Malaysia	Kuala Lumpur	4–2

1991–92

16 Oct 1991	*v* Turkey (ECQ)	Wembley	1–0

13 Nov 1991	*v* Poland (ECQ)	Poznan	1–1
19 Feb 1992	*v* France	Wembley	2–0
25 March 1992	*v* Czechoslovakia	Prague	2–2
29 April 1992	*v* CIS	Moscow	2–2
12 May 1992	*v* Hungary	Budapest	1–0
17 May 1992	*v* Brazil	Wembley	1–1
3 June 1992	*v* Finland	Helsinki	2–1
11 June 1992	*v* Denmark (EC)	Malmo	0–0
14 June 1992	*v* France (EC)	Malmo	0–0
17 June 1992	*v* Sweden (EC)	Stockholm	1–2

1992–1993 (with Sampdoria)

9 Sept 1992	*v* Spain	Santander	0–1
14 Oct 1992	*v* Norway (WCQ)	Wembley	1–1
18 Nov 1992	*v* Turkey (WCQ)	Wembley	4–0
17 Feb 1993	*v* San Marino (WCQ)	Wembley	6–0
31 March 1993	*v* Turkey (WCQ)	Izmir	2–0
28 April 1993	*v* Holland (WCQ)	Wembley	2–2
29 May 1993	*v* Poland (WCQ)	Chorzow	1–1
2 June 1993	*v* Norway (WCQ)	Oslo	0–2
9 June 1993	*v* USA (sub) (USC)	Boston	0–2
13 June 1993	*v* Brazil (USC)	Washington	1–1
19 June 1993	*v* Germany (USC)	Detroit	1–2

WALLACE, DANNY L. *Born:* 21.1.64 (London) *Club:* Southampton *Caps:* 1 *Goals:* 1

1985–86
29 Jan 1986	*v* Egypt	Cairo	4–0 (1 goal)

WALSH, PAUL A. *Born:* 1.10.62 (Plumstead) *Club:* Luton Town *Caps:* 5 *Goals:* 1

1982–83
12 June 1983	*v* Australia (sub)	Sydney	0–0
15 June 1983	*v* Australia	Brisbane	1–0 (1 goal)
19 June 1983	*v* Australia	Melbourne	1–1

1983–84
29 Feb 1984	*v* France	Paris	0–2
2 May 1984	*v* Wales	Wrexham	0–1

WALTERS, MARK K. *Born:* 12.1.61 (Birmingham) *Club:* Rangers *Caps:* 1

1990–91
3 June 1991	*v* New Zealand	Auckland	1–0

WARD, PETER *Born:* 27.7.55 (Derby) *Club:* Brighton & Hove Albion *Caps:* 1

1979–80
31 May 1980	*v* Australia (sub)	Sydney	2–1

WARD, TIM V. *Born:* 17.10.18 (Cheltenham) *Club:* Derby County *Caps:* 2

1947–48
21 Sept 1947	*v* Belgium	Brussels	5–2

1948–49

10 Nov 1948	*v* Wales	Aston Villa	1–0

WATSON, DAVE *Born:* 20.11.61 (Liverpool) *Clubs:* Norwich City, Everton *Caps:* 12

1983–84 (with Norwich City)

10 June 1984	*v* Brazil	Rio de Janeiro	2–0
13 June 1984	*v* Uruguay	Montevideo	0–2
17 June 1984	*v* Chile	Santiago	0–0

1984–85

9 June 1985	*v* Mexico	Mexico City	0–1
16 June 1985	*v* USA (sub)	Los Angeles	5–0

1985–86

23 April 1986	*v* Scotland (RC)	Wembley	2–1

1986–87 (with Everton)

15 Oct 1986	*v* Northern Ireland (ECQ)	Wembley	3–0

1987–88

17 Feb 1988	*v* Israel	Tel Aviv	0–0
23 March 1988	*v* Holland	Wembley	2–2
21 May 1988	*v* Scotland (RC)	Wembley	1–0
28 May 1988	*v* Switzerland (sub)	Lausanne	1–0
18 June 1988	*v* USSR (EC)	Frankfurt	1–3

WATSON, DAVE V. *Born:* 15.10.46 (Stapleford) *Clubs:* Sunderland, Manchester City, Werder Bremen, Southampton, Stoke City *Caps:* 65 *Goals:* 4

1973–74 (with Sunderland)

3 April 1974	*v* Portugal	Lisbon	0–0
18 May 1974	*v* Scotland (sub)	Glasgow	0–2
22 May 1974	*v* Argentina	Wembley	2–2
29 May 1974	*v* East Germany	Leipzig	1–1
1 June 1974	*v* Bulgaria	Sofia	1–0
5 June 1974	*v* Yugoslavia	Belgrade	2–2

1974–75

30 Oct 1974	*v* Czechoslovakia (ECQ)	Wembley	3–0
20 Nov 1974	*v* Portugal (ECQ)	Wembley	0–0
12 March 1975	*v* West Germany	Wembley	2–0
16 April 1975	*v* Cyprus (ECQ)	Wembley	5–0
11 May 1975	*v* Cyprus (ECQ)	Limassol	1–0
17 May 1975	*v* Northern Ireland	Belfast	0–0
21 May 1975	*v* Wales	Wembley	2–2
24 May 1975	*v* Scotland	Wembley	5–1

1975–76 (with Manchester City)

3 Sept 1975	*v* Switzerland	Basle	2–1
30 Oct 1975	*v* Czechoslovakia (sub)(ECQ)	Bratislava	1–2
19 Nov 1975	*v* Portugal (ECQ)	Lisbon	1–1

1976–77

9 Feb 1977	*v* Holland	Wembley	0–2
30 March 1977	*v* Luxembourg (WCQ)	Wembley	5–0

28 May 1977	*v* Northern Ireland	Belfast	2–1
31 May 1977	*v* Wales	Wembley	0–1
4 June 1977	*v* Scotland	Wembley	1–2
8 June 1977	*v* Brazil	Rio de Janeiro	0–0
12 June 1977	*v* Argentina	Buenos Aires	1–1
15 June 1977	*v* Uruguay	Montevideo	0–0

1977–78

7 Sept 1977	*v* Switzerland	Wembley	0–0
12 Oct 1977	*v* Luxembourg (WCQ)	Luxembourg	2–0
16 Nov 1977	*v* Italy (WCQ)	Wembley	2–0
22 Feb 1978	*v* West Germany	Munich	1–2
19 April 1978	*v* Brazil	Wembley	1–1
13 May 1978	*v* Wales	Cardiff	3–1
16 May 1978	*v* Northern Ireland	Wembley	1–0
20 May 1978	*v* Scotland	Glasgow	1–0
24 May 1978	*v* Hungary	Wembley	4–1

1978–79

20 Sept 1978	*v* Denmark (ECQ)	Copenhagen	4–3
25 Oct 1978	*v* Eire (ECQ)	Dublin	1–1
29 Nov 1978	*v* Czechoslovakia	Wembley	1–0
7 Feb 1979	*v* Northern Ireland (ECQ)	Wembley	4–0 (1 goal)
19 May 1979	*v* Northern Ireland	Belfast	2–0 (1 goal)
23 May 1979	*v* Wales	Wembley	0–0
26 May 1979	*v* Scotland	Wembley	3–1
6 June 1979	*v* Bulgaria (ECQ)	Sofia	3–0 (1 goal)
10 June 1979	*v* Sweden	Stockholm	0–0
13 June 1979	*v* Austria	Vienna	3–4

1979–80 (with Werder Bremen)

12 Sept 1979	*v* Denmark (ECQ)	Wembley	1–0

(with Southampton)

17 Oct 1979	*v* Northern Ireland (ECQ)	Belfast	5–1
22 Nov 1979	*v* Bulgaria (ECQ)	Wembley	2–0 (1 goal)
6 Feb 1980	*v* Eire (ECQ)	Wembley	2–0
26 March 1980	*v* Spain	Barcelona	2–0
13 May 1980	*v* Argentina	Wembley	3–1
20 May 1980	*v* Northern Ireland	Wembley	1–1
24 May 1980	*v* Scotland	Glasgow	2–0
12 June 1980	*v* Belgium (EC)	Turin	1–1
15 June 1980	*v* Italy (EC)	Turin	0–1
18 June 1980	*v* Spain (EC)	Naples	2–1

1980–81

10 Sept 1980	*v* Norway (WCQ)	Wembley	4–0
15 Oct 1980	*v* Romania (WCQ)	Bucharest	1–2
19 Nov 1980	*v* Switzerland (WCQ)	Wembley	2–1
29 April 1981	*v* Romania* (WCQ)	Wembley	0–0
20 May 1981	*v* Wales*	Wembley	0–0
23 May 1981	*v* Scotland*	Wembley	0–1
30 May 1981	*v* Switzerland (WCQ)	Basle	1–2
6 June 1981	*v* Hungary (WCQ)	Budapest	3–1

1981–82 (with Stoke City)

23 Feb 1982	*v* Northern Ireland	Wembley	4–0
2 June 1982	*v* Iceland	Reykjavik	1–1

WATSON, WILLIAM *Born:* 7.3.20 (Bolton-on-Dearne) *Club:* Sunderland *Caps:* 4

1949–50

16 Nov 1949	*v* Northern Ireland (WCQ)	Manchester City	9–2
30 Nov 1949	*v* Italy	Tottenham	2–0

1950–51

15 Nov 1950	*v* Wales	Sunderland	4–2
22 Nov 1950	*v* Yugoslavia	Arsenal	2–2

WEBB, NEIL J. *Born:* 30.7.63 (Reading) *Clubs:* Nottingham Forest, Manchester United *Caps:* 26 *Goals:* 4

1987–88 (with Nottingham Forest)

9 Sept 1987	*v* West Germany (sub)	Düsseldorf	1–3
14 Oct 1987	*v* Turkey (ECQ)	Wembley	8–0 (1 goal)
11 Nov 1987	*v* Yugoslavia (ECQ)	Belgrade	4–1
17 Feb 1988	*v* Israel	Tel Aviv	0–0
23 March 1988	*v* Holland	Wembley	2–2
21 May 1988	*v* Scotland (RC)	Wembley	1–0
28 May 1988	*v* Switzerland	Lausanne	1–0
12 June 1988	*v* Eire (EC)	Stuttgart	0–1
18 June 1988	*v* USSR (sub) (EC)	Frankfurt	1–3

1988–89

14 Sept 1988	*v* Denmark	Wembley	1–0 (1 goal)
19 Oct 1988	*v* Sweden (WCQ)	Wembley	0–0
8 Feb 1989	*v* Greece	Athens	2–1
8 March 1989	*v* Albania (WCQ)	Tirana	2–0
26 April 1989	*v* Albania (WCQ)	Wembley	5–0
23 May 1989	*v* Chile (RC)	Wembley	0–0
27 May 1989	*v* Scotland (RC)	Glasgow	2–0
3 June 1989	*v* Poland (WCQ)	Wembley	3–0 (1 goal)
7 June 1989	*v* Denmark	Copenhagen	1–1

1989–90 (with Manchester United)

6 Sept 1989	*v* Sweden (WCQ)	Stockholm	0–0
7 July 1990	*v* Italy (sub) (WC)	Bari	1–2

1991–92

19 Feb 1992	*v* France	Wembley	2–0
12 May 1992	*v* Hungary	Budapest	1–0 (1 goal)
17 May 1992	*v* Brazil (sub)	Wembley	1–1
3 June 1992	*v* Finland	Helsinki	2–1
11 June 1992	*v* Denmark (sub) (EC)	Malmo	0–0
17 June 1992	*v* Sweden (EC)	Stockholm	1–2

WELLER, KEITH *Born:* 11.6.46 (Islington) *Club:* Leicester City *Caps:* 4 *Goals:* 1

1973–74

11 May 1974	*v* Wales	Cardiff	2–0
15 May 1974	*v* Northern Ireland	Wembley	1–0 (1 goal)
18 May 1974	*v* Scotland	Glasgow	0–2
22 May 1974	*v* Argentina	Wembley	2–2

WEST, GORDON *Born:* 24.4.43 (Barnsley) *Club:* Everton *Caps:* 3

1968–69

11 Dec 1968	*v* Bulgaria	Wembley	1–1
7 May 1969	*v* Wales	Wembley	2–1
1 June 1969	*v* Mexico	Mexico City	0–0

WHEELER, JOHN E. *Born:* 26.7.28 (Liverpool) *Club:* Bolton Wanderers *Caps:* 1

1954–55

| 2 Oct 1954 | *v* Northern Ireland | Belfast | 2–0 |

WHITE, DAVID *Born:* 30.10.67 (Manchester) *Club:* Manchester City *Caps:* 1

1992–93

| 9 Sept 1992 | *v* Spain | Santander | 0–1 |

WHITWORTH, STEVE *Born:* 20.3.52 (Coalville) *Club:* Leicester City *Caps:* 7

1974–75

12 March 1975	*v* West Germany	Wembley	2–0
11 May 1975	*v* Cyprus (ECQ)	Limassol	1–0
17 May 1975	*v* Northern Ireland	Belfast	0–0
21 May 1975	*v* Wales	Wembley	2–2
24 May 1975	*v* Scotland	Wembley	5–1

1975–76

| 3 Sept 1975 | *v* Switzerland | Basle | 2–1 |
| 19 Nov 1975 | *v* Portugal (ECQ) | Lisbon | 1–1 |

WHYMARK, TREVOR J. *Born:* 4.5.50 (Burston) *Club:* Ipswich Town *Caps:* 1

1977–78

| 12 Oct 1977 | *v* Luxembourg (sub) | Luxembourg | 2–0 |

WIGNALL, FRANK *Born:* 21.8.39 (Chorley) *Club:* Nottingham Forest *Caps:* 2 *Goals:* 2

1964–65

| 18 Nov 1964 | *v* Wales | Wembley | 2–1 (2 goals) |
| 9 Dec 1964 | *v* Holland | Amsterdam | 1–1 |

WILKINS, RAY C. *Born:* 14.9.56 (Hillingdon) *Clubs:* Chelsea, Manchester United, AC Milan *Caps:* 84 *Goals:* 3

1975–76 (with Chelsea)

| 28 May 1976 | *v* Italy (USABT) | New York | 3–2 |

1976–77

8 Sept 1976	*v* Eire	Wembley	1–1
13 Oct 1976	*v* Finland (WCQ)	Wembley	2–1
28 May 1977	*v* Northern Ireland	Belfast	2–1
8 June 1977	*v* Brazil	Rio de Janeiro	0–0
12 June 1977	*v* Argentina	Buenos Aires	1–1
15 June 1977	*v* Uruguay	Montevideo	0–0

1977–78

7 Sept 1977	*v* Switzerland (sub)	Wembley	0–0
12 Oct 1977	*v* Luxembourg (WCQ)	Luxembourg	2–0
16 Nov 1977	*v* Italy (WCQ)	Wembley	2–0
22 Feb 1978	*v* West Germany	Munich	1–2
13 May 1978	*v* Wales	Cardiff	3–1
16 May 1978	*v* Northern Ireland	Wembley	1–0
20 May 1978	*v* Scotland	Glasgow	1–0
24 May 1978	*v* Hungary	Wembley	4–1

1978–79

20 Sept 1978	*v* Denmark (ECQ)	Copenhagen	4–3
25 Oct 1978	*v* Eire (ECQ)	Dublin	1–1
29 Nov 1978	*v* Czechoslovakia	Wembley	1–0
19 May 1979	*v* Northern Ireland	Belfast	2–0
23 May 1979	*v* Wales	Wembley	0–0
26 May 1979	*v* Scotland	Wembley	3–1
6 June 1979	*v* Bulgaria (ECQ)	Sofia	3–0
10 June 1979	*v* Sweden (sub)	Stockholm	0–0
13 June 1979	*v* Austria	Vienna	3–4 (1 goal)

1979–80 (with Manchester United)

12 Sept 1979	*v* Denmark (ECQ)	Wembley	1–0
17 Oct 1979	*v* Northern Ireland (ECQ)	Belfast	5–1
22 Nov 1979	*v* Bulgaria (ECQ)	Wembley	2–0
26 March 1980	*v* Spain	Barcelona	2–0
13 May 1980	*v* Argentina	Wembley	3–1
17 May 1980	*v* Wales (sub)	Wrexham	1–4
20 May 1980	*v* Northern Ireland	Wembley	1–1
24 May 1980	*v* Scotland	Glasgow	2–0
12 June 1980	*v* Belgium (EC)	Turin	1–1 (1 goal)
15 June 1980	*v* Italy (EC)	Turin	0–1
18 June 1980	*v* Spain (EC)	Naples	2–1

1980–81

25 March 1981	*v* Spain (sub)	Wembley	1–2
29 April 1981	*v* Romania (WCQ)	Wembley	0–0
12 May 1981	*v* Brazil	Wembley	0–1
20 May 1981	*v* Wales	Wembley	0–0
23 May 1981	*v* Scotland	Wembley	0–1
30 May 1981	*v* Switzerland (WCQ)	Basle	1–2
6 June 1981	*v* Hungary (WCQ)	Budapest	3–1

1981–82

23 Feb 1982	*v* Northern Ireland	Wembley	4–0 (1 goal)

27 April 1982	v Wales	Cardiff	1–0
25 May 1982	v Holland	Wembley	2–0
29 May 1982	v Scotland	Glasgow	1–0
3 June 1982	v Finland	Helsinki	4–1
16 June 1982	v France (WC)	Bilbao	3–1
20 June 1982	v Czechoslovakia (WC)	Bilbao	2–0
25 June 1982	v Kuwait (WC)	Bilbao	1–0
29 June 1982	v West Germany (WC)	Madrid	0–0
5 July 1982	v Spain (WC)	Madrid	0–0

1982–83

22 Sept 1982	v Denmark* (ECQ)	Copenhagen	2–2
13 Oct 1982	v West Germany*	Wembley	1–2

1983–84

21 Sept 1983	v Denmark* (ECQ)	Wembley	0–1
4 April 1984	v Northern Ireland	Wembley	1–0
2 May 1984	v Wales*	Wrexham	0–1
26 May 1984	v Scotland	Glasgow	1–1
2 June 1984	v USSR	Wembley	0–2
10 June 1984	v Brazil	Rio de Janeiro	2–0
13 June 1984	v Uruguay	Montevideo	0–2
17 June 1984	v Chile	Santiago	0–0

1984–85 (with AC Milan)

12 Sept 1984	v East Germany	Wembley	1–0
17 Oct 1984	v Finland (WCQ)	Wembley	5–0
14 Nov 1984	v Turkey (WCQ)	Istanbul	8–0
27 Feb 1985	v Northern Ireland* (WCQ)	Belfast	1–0
26 March 1985	v Eire	Wembley	2–1
1 May 1985	v Romania (WCQ)	Bucharest	0–0
22 May 1985	v Finland (WCQ)	Helsinki	1–1
25 May 1985	v Scotland (RC)	Glasgow	0–1
6 June 1985	v Italy	Mexico City	1–2
9 June 1985	v Mexico	Mexcio City	0–1

1985–86

16 Oct 1985	v Turkey (WCQ)	Wembley	5–0
13 Nov 1985	v Northern Ireland* (WCQ)	Wembley	0–0
29 Jan 1986	v Egypt*	Cairo	4–0
26 Feb 1986	v Israel	Tel Aviv	2–1
26 March 1986	v USSR*	Tbilisi	1–0
23 April 1986	v Scotland* (RC)	Wembley	2–1
17 May 1986	v Mexico	Los Angeles	3–0
24 May 1986	v Canada*	Vancouver	1–0
3 June 1986	v Portugal (WC)	Monterrey	0–1
6 June 1986	v Morocco (WC)	Monterrey	0–0

1986–87

10 Sept 1986	v Sweden	Stockholm	0–1
12 Nov 1986	v Yugoslavia (sub) (ECQ)	Wembley	2–0

WILLIAMS, BERT F. *Born:* 31.1.20 (Bilston) *Club:* Wolverhampton Wanderers *Caps:* 24

1948–49
22 May 1949	v France	Paris	3–1

1949–50
21 Sept 1949	v Eire	Everton	0–2
15 Oct 1949	v Wales (WCQ)	Cardiff	4–1
30 Nov 1949	v Italy	Tottenham	2–0
15 April 1950	v Scotland (WCQ)	Glasgow	1–0
14 May 1950	v Portugal	Lisbon	5–3
18 May 1950	v Belgium	Brussels	4–1
25 June 1950	v Chile (WC)	Rio de Janeiro	2–0
29 June 1950	v USA (WC)	Belo Horizonte	0–1
2 July 1950	v Spain (WC)	Rio de Janeiro	0–1

1950–51
7 Oct 1950	v Northern Ireland	Belfast	4–1
15 Nov 1950	v Wales	Sunderland	4–2
22 Nov 1950	v Yugoslavia	Arsenal	2–2
14 April 1951	v Scotland	Wembley	2–3
9 May 1951	v Argentina	Wembley	2–1
19 May 1951	v Portugal	Everton	5–2

1951–52
3 Oct 1951	v France	Arsenal	2–2
20 Oct 1951	v Wales	Cardiff	1–1

1954–55
1 Dec 1954	v West Germany	Wembley	3–1
2 April 1955	v Scotland	Wembley	7–2
15 May 1955	v France	Paris	0–1
18 May 1955	v Spain	Madrid	1–1
22 May 1955	v Portugal	Oporto	1–3

1955–56
22 Oct 1955	v Wales	Cardiff	1–2

WILLIAMS, STEVE C. *Born:* 12.7.58 (London) *Club:* Southampton *Caps:* 6

1982–83
12 June 1983	v Australia	Sydney	0–0
15 June 1983	v Australia (sub)	Brisbane	1–0

1983–84
29 Feb 1984	v France	Paris	0–2

1984–85
12 Sept 1984	v East Germany	Wembley	1–0
17 Oct 1984	v Finland (WCQ)	Wembley	5–0
14 Nov 1984	v Turkey (WCQ)	Istanbul	8–0

WILLIS, ARTHUR *Born:* 2.2.20 (Denby) *Club:* Tottenham Hotspur *Caps:* 1

1951–52
3 Oct 1951	v France	Arsenal	2–2

WILSHAW, DENNIS J. *Born:* 11.3.26 (Stoke) *Club:* Wolverhampton Wanderers *Caps:* 12 *Goals:* 10

1953–54

10 Oct 1953	*v* Wales (WCQ)	Cardiff	4–1 (2 goals)
20 June 1954	*v* Switzerland (WC)	Berne	2–0 (1 goal)
26 June 1954	*v* Uruguay (WC)	Basle	2–4

1954–55

2 April 1955	*v* Scotland	Wembley	7–2 (4 goals)
15 May 1955	*v* France	Paris	0–1
18 May 1955	*v* Spain	Madrid	1–1
22 May 1955	*v* Portugal	Oporto	1–3

1955–56

22 Oct 1955	*v* Wales	Cardiff	1–2
2 Nov 1955	*v* Northern Ireland	Wembley	3–0 (2 goals)
20 May 1956	*v* Finland	Helsinki	5–1 (1 goal)
26 May 1956	*v* West Germany	Berlin	3–1

1956–57

6 Oct 1956	*v* Northern Ireland	Belfast	1–1

WILSON, RAY *Born:* 17.12.34 (Shirebrook) *Clubs:* Huddersfield Town, Everton *Caps:* 63

1959–60 (with Huddersfield Town)

19 April 1960	*v* Scotland	Glasgow	1–1
11 May 1960	*v* Yugoslavia	Wembley	3–3
15 May 1960	*v* Spain	Madrid	0–3
22 May 1960	*v* Hungary	Budapest	0–2

1961–62

14 Oct 1961	*v* Wales	Cardiff	1–1
25 Oct 1961	*v* Portugal (WCQ)	Wembley	2–0
22 Nov 1961	*v* Northern Ireland	Wembley	1–1
4 April 1962	*v* Austria	Wembley	3–1
14 April 1962	*v* Scotland	Glasgow	0–2
9 May 1962	*v* Switzerland	Wembley	3–1
20 May 1962	*v* Peru	Lima	4–0
31 May 1962	*v* Hungary (WC)	Rancagua	1–2
2 June 1962	*v* Argentina (WC)	Rancagua	3–1
7 June 1962	*v* Bulgaria (WC)	Rancagua	0–0
10 June 1962	*v* Brazil (WC)	Vina del Mar	1–3

1962–63

3 Oct 1962	*v* France (ENC)	Sheffield Wednesday	1–1
20 Oct 1962	*v* Northern Ireland	Belfast	3–1
8 May 1963	*v* Brazil	Wembley	1–1
29 May 1963	*v* Czechoslovakia	Bratislava	4–2
2 June 1963	*v* East Germany	Leipzig	2–1
5 June 1963	*v* Switzerland	Basle	8–1

1963–64

12 Oct 1963	*v* Wales	Cardiff	4–0

23 Oct 1963	*v* Rest of the World	Wembley	2–1
11 April 1964	*v* Scotland	Glasgow	0–1
6 May 1964	*v* Uruguay	Wembley	2–1
17 May 1964	*v* Portugal	Lisbon	4–3
24 May 1964	*v* Eire	Dublin	3–1
30 May 1964	*v* Brazil (BJT)	Rio de Janeiro	1–5
4 June 1964	*v* Portugal (BJT)	Sao Paulo	1–1
6 June 1964	*v* Argentina (BJT)	Rio de Janeiro	0–1

1964–65 (with Everton)

10 April 1965	*v* Scotland	Wembley	2–2
5 May 1965	*v* Hungary	Wembley	1–0
9 May 1965	*v* Yugoslavia	Belgrade	1–1
12 May 1965	*v* West Germany	Nuremberg	1–0
16 May 1965	*v* Sweden	Gothenburg	2–1

1965–66

2 Oct 1965	*v* Wales	Cardiff	0–0
20 Oct 1965	*v* Austria	Wembley	2–3
10 Nov 1965	*v* Northern Ireland	Wembley	2–1
8 Dec 1965	*v* Spain	Madrid	2–0
5 Jan 1966	*v* Poland	Everton	1–1
23 Feb 1966	*v* West Germany (sub)	Wembley	1–0
4 May 1966	*v* Yugoslavia	Wembley	2–0
26 June 1966	*v* Finland	Helsinki	3–0
3 July 1966	*v* Denmark	Copenhagen	2–0
5 July 1966	*v* Poland	Chorzow	1–0
11 July 1966	*v* Uruguay (WC)	Wembley	0–0
16 July 1966	*v* Mexico (WC)	Wembley	2–0
20 July 1966	*v* France (WC)	Wembley	2–0
23 July 1966	*v* Argentina (WC)	Wembley	1–0
26 July 1966	*v* Portugal (WC)	Wembley	2–1
30 July 1966	*v* West Germany (WCF)	Wembley	4–2 (aet)

1966–67

22 Oct 1966	*v* Northern Ireland (ECQ)	Wembley	2–0
2 Nov 1966	*v* Czechoslovakia	Wembley	0–0
16 Nov 1966	*v* Wales (ECQ)	Wembley	5–1
15 April 1967	*v* Scotland (ECQ)	Wembley	2–3
27 May 1967	*v* Austria	Vienna	1–0

1967–68

22 Nov 1967	*v* Northern Ireland (ECQ)	Wembley	2–0
6 Dec 1967	*v* USSR	Wembley	2–2
24 Feb 1968	*v* Scotland (ECQ)	Glasgow	1–1
3 April 1968	*v* Spain (ECQ)	Wembley	1–0
8 May 1968	*v* Spain (ECQ)	Madrid	2–1
5 June 1968	*v* Yugoslavia (EC)	Florence	0–1
8 June 1968	*v* USSR (EC)	Rome	2–0

WINTERBURN, NIGEL *Born:* 11.12.63 (Nuneaton) *Club:* Arsenal *Caps:* 2

1989–90

15 Nov 1989	*v* Italy (sub)	Wembley	0–0

1992–93

19 June 1993	*v* Germany (sub) (USC)	Detroit	1–2

WISE, DENNIS F. *Born:* 15.12.66 (Kensington) *Club:* Chelsea *Caps:* 5 Goals: 1

1990–91

1 May 1991	*v* Turkey (ECQ)	Izmir	1–0 (1 goal)
21 May 1991	*v* USSR	Wembley	3–1
1 June 1991	*v* Australia (sub)	Sydney	1–0
3 June 1991	*v* New Zealand	Auckland	1–0
8 June 1991	*v* New Zealand	Wellington	2–0

WITHE, PETER *Born:* 30.8.51 (Liverpool) *Club:* Aston Villa *Caps:* 11 *Goals:* 1

1980–81

12 May 1981	*v* Brazil	Wembley	0–1
20 May 1981	*v* Wales	Wrexham	0–0
23 May 1981	*v* Scotland	Wembley	0–1

1981–82

9 Sept 1981	*v* Norway (sub) (WCQ)	Oslo	1–2
27 April 1982	*v* Wales	Cardiff	1–0
2 June 1982	*v* Iceland	Reykjavik	1–1

1982–83

27 April 1983	*v* Hungary (ECQ)	Wembley	2–0 (1 goal)
28 May 1983	*v* Northern Ireland	Belfast	0–0
1 June 1983	*v* Scotland	Wembley	2–0

1983–84

12 Oct 1983	*v* Hungary (sub) (ECQ)	Budapest	3–0

1984–85

14 Nov 1984	*v* Turkey (WCQ)	Istanbul	8–0

WOOD, RAY E. *Born:* 11.6.31 (Hebburn) *Club:* Manchester United *Caps:* 3

1954–55

2 Oct 1954	*v* Northern Ireland	Belfast	2–0
10 Nov 1954	*v* Wales	Wembley	3–2

1955–56

20 May 1956	*v* Finland	Helsinki	5–1

WOODCOCK, ANTHONY S. *Born:* 6.12.55 (Nottingham) *Clubs:* Nottingham Forest, Cologne, Arsenal *Caps:* 42 *Goals:* 16

1977–78 (with Nottingham Forest)

16 May 1978	*v* Northern Ireland	Wembley	1–0

1978–79

25 Oct 1978	*v* Eire (sub) (ECQ)	Dublin	1–1

29 Nov 1978	*v* Czechoslovakia	Wembley	1–0
6 June 1979	*v* Bulgaria (sub) (ECQ)	Sofia	3–0
10 June 1979	*v* Sweden	Stockholm	0–0

1979–80

17 Oct 1979	*v* Northern Ireland (ECQ)	Belfast	5–1 (2 goals)
(with Cologne)			
22 Nov 1979	*v* Bulgaria (ECQ)	Wembley	2–0
6 Feb 1980	*v* Eire (ECQ)	Wembley	2–0
26 March 1980	*v* Spain	Barcelona	2–0 (1 goal)
13 May 1980	*v* Argentina	Wembley	3–1
12 June 1980	*v* Belgium (EC)	Turin	1–1
15 June 1980	*v* Italy (EC)	Turin	0–1
18 June 1980	*v* Spain (EC)	Naples	2–1 (1 goal)

1980–81

10 Sept 1980	*v* Norway (WCQ)	Wembley	4–0 (1 goal)
15 Oct 1980	*v* Romania (WCQ)	Bucharest	1–2 (1 goal)
19 Nov 1980	*v* Switzerland (WCQ)	Wembley	2–1
29 April 1981	*v* Romania (WCQ)	Wembley	0–0
20 May 1981	*v* Wales (sub)	Wembley	0–0
23 May 1981	*v* Scotland	Glasgow	0–1

1981–82

23 Feb 1982	*v* Northern Ireland (sub)	Wembley	4–0
25 May 1982	*v* Holland	Wembley	2–0 (1 goal)
3 June 1982	*v* Finland (sub)	Helsinki	4–1
29 June 1982	*v* West Germany (sub) (WC)	Madrid	0–0
5 July 1982	*v* Spain (WC)	Madrid	0–0

1982–83 (with Arsenal)

13 Oct 1982	*v* West Germany (sub)	Wembley	1–2 (1 goal)
17 Nov 1982	*v* Greece (ECQ)	Salonika	3–0 (2 goals)
15 Dec 1982	*v* Luxembourg (ECQ)	Wembley	9–0 (1 goal)
30 March 1983	*v* Greece (ECQ)	Wembley	0–0

1983–84

16 Nov 1983	*v* Luxembourg (ECQ)	Luxembourg	4–0
29 Feb 1984	*v* France (sub)	Paris	0–2
4 April 1984	*v* Northern Ireland	Wembley	1–0 (1 goal)
2 May 1984	*v* Wales	Wrexham	0–1
26 May 1984	*v* Scotland	Glasgow	1–1 (1 goal)
10 June 1984	*v* Brazil	Rio de Janeiro	2–0
13 June 1984	*v* Uruguay (sub)	Montevideo	0–2

1984–85

12 Sept 1984	*v* East Germany	Wembley	1–0
17 Oct 1984	*v* Finland (WCQ)	Wembley	5–0 (1 goal)
14 Nov 1984	*v* Turkey (WCQ)	Istanbul	8–0 (2 goals)
27 Feb 1985	*v* Northern Ireland (WCQ)	Belfast	1–0

1985–86

11 Sept 1985	*v* Romania (sub) (WCQ)	Wembley	1–1
16 Oct 1985	*v* Turkey (sub) (WCQ)	Wembley	5–0
26 Feb 1986	*v* Israel (sub)	Tel Aviv	2–1

WOODS, CHRIS C. E. *Born:* 14.11.59 (Boston) *Clubs:* Norwich City, Rangers, Sheffield Wednesday *Caps:* 43

1984–85 (with Norwich City)

| 16 June 1985 | *v* USA | Los Angeles | 5–0 |

1985–86

29 Jan 1986	*v* Egypt (sub)	Cairo	4–0
26 Feb 1986	*v* Israel (sub)	Tel Aviv	2–1
24 May 1986	*v* Canada (sub)	Vancouver	1–0

1986–87 (with Rangers)

12 Nov 1986	*v* Yugoslavia (ECQ)	Wembley	2–0
18 Feb 1987	*v* Spain (sub)	Madrid	4–2
1 April 1987	*v* Northern Ireland (sub)(ECQ)	Belfast	2–0
29 April 1987	*v* Turkey (ECQ)	Izmir	0–0
23 May 1987	*v* Scotland (RC)	Glasgow	0–0

1987–88

17 Feb 1988	*v* Israel	Tel Aviv	0–0
27 April 1988	*v* Hungary	Budapest	0–0
28 May 1988	*v* Switzerland (sub)	Lausanne	1–0
18 June 1988	*v* USSR (EC)	Frankfurt	1–3

1988–89

| 14 Sept 1988 | *v* Denmark (sub) | Wembley | 1–0 |

1989–90

| 28 March 1990 | *v* Brazil (sub) | Wembley | 1–0 |
| 15 May 1990 | *v* Denmark (sub) | Wembley | 1–0 |

1990–91

12 Sept 1990	*v* Hungary	Wembley	1–0
17 Oct 1990	*v* Poland (ECQ)	Wembley	2–0
14 Nov 1990	*v* Eire (ECQ)	Dublin	1–1
21 May 1991	*v* USSR	Wembley	3–1
1 June 1991	*v* Australia	Sydney	1–0
3 June 1991	*v* New Zealand	Auckland	1–0
8 June 1991	*v* New Zealand	Wellington	2–0
12 June 1991	*v* Malaysia	Kuala Lumpur	4–2

1991–92 (with Sheffield Wednesday)

11 Sept 1991	*v* Germany	Wembley	0–1
16 Oct 1991	*v* Turkey (ECQ)	Wembley	1–0
13 Nov 1991	*v* Poland (ECQ)	Poznan	1–1
19 Feb 1992	*v* France	Wembley	2–0
29 April 1992	*v* CIS	Moscow	2–2
17 May 1992	*v* Brazil	Wembley	1–1
3 June 1992	*v* Finland	Helsinki	2–1
11 June 1992	*v* Denmark (EC)	Malmo	0–0
14 June 1992	*v* France (EC)	Malmo	0–0
17 June 1992	*v* Sweden (EC)	Stockholm	1–2

1992–93

| 9 Sept 1992 | *v* Spain | Santander | 0–1 |
| 14 Oct 1992 | *v* Norway (WCQ) | Wembley | 1–1 |

18 Nov 1992	*v* Turkey (WCQ)	Wembley	4–0
17 Feb 1993	*v* San Marino (WCQ)	Wembley	6–0
31 March 1993	*v* Turkey (WCQ)	Izmir	2–0
28 April 1993	*v* Holland (WCQ)	Wembley	2–2
29 May 1993	*v* Poland (WCQ)	Chorzow	1–1
2 June 1993	*v* Norway (WCQ)	Oslo	0–2
9 June 1993	*v* USA (USC)	Boston	0–2

WORTHINGTON, FRANK S. *Born:* 23.11.48 (Halifax) *Club:* Leicester City *Caps:* 8 *Goals:* 2

1973–74

15 May 1974	*v* Northern Ireland (sub)	Wembley	1–0
18 May 1974	*v* Scotland	Glasgow	0–2
22 May 1974	*v* Argentina	Wembley	2–2 (1 goal)
29 May 1974	*v* East Germany	Leipzig	1–1
1 June 1974	*v* Bulgaria	Sofia	1–0 (1 goal)
5 June 1974	*v* Yugoslavia	Belgrade	2–2

1974–75

30 Oct 1974	*v* Czechoslovakia (ECQ)	Wembley	3–0
20 Nov 1974	*v* Portugal (sub) (ECQ)	Wembley	0–0

WRIGHT, IAN E. *Born:* 3.11.63 (Woolwich) *Clubs:* Crystal Palace, Arsenal *Caps:* 13 *Goals:* 1

1990–91 (with Crystal Palace)

6 Feb 1991	*v* Cameroon	Wembley	2–0
27 March 1991	*v* Eire (sub) (ECQ)	Wembley	1–1
21 May 1991	*v* USSR	Wembley	3–1
8 June 1991	*v* New Zealand	Wellington	2–0

1991–92 (with Arsenal)

12 May 1992	*v* Hungary (sub)	Budapest	1–0

1992–93

14 Oct 1992	*v* Norway (WCQ)	Wembley	1–1
18 Nov 1992	*v* Turkey (WCQ)	Wembley	4–0
31 March 1993	*v* Turkey (WCQ)	Izmir	2–0
29 May 1993	*v* Poland (sub) (WCQ)	Chorzow	1–1 (1 goal)
2 June 1993	*v* Norway (sub) (WCQ)	Oslo	0–2
9 June 1993	*v* USA (sub) (USC)	Boston	0–2
13 June 1993	*v* Brazil (USC)	Washington	1–1
19 June 1993	*v* Germany (sub) (USC)	Detroit	1–2

WRIGHT, MARK *Born:* 1.8.63 (Dorchester) *Clubs:* Southampton, Derby County, Liverpool *Caps:* 43 *Goals:* 1

1983–84 (with Southampton)

2 May 1984	*v* Wales	Wrexham	0–1

1984–85

12 Sept 1984	*v* East Germany	Wembley	1–0
17 Oct 1984	*v* Finland (WCQ)	Wembley	5–0

14 Nov 1984	*v* Turkey (WCQ)	Istanbul	8–0
26 March 1985	*v* Eire	Wembley	2–1
1 May 1985	*v* Romania (WCQ)	Bucharest	0–0
6 June 1985	*v* Italy	Mexico City	1–2
12 June 1985	*v* West Germany	Mexico City	3–0

1985–86

11 Sept 1985	*v* Romania (WCQ)	Wembley	1–1
16 Oct 1985	*v* Turkey (WCQ)	Wembley	5–0
13 Nov 1985	*v* Northern Ireland (WCQ)	Wembley	0–0
29 Jan 1986	*v* Egypt	Cairo	4–0
26 March 1986	*v* USSR	Tbilisi	1–0

1986–87

12 Nov 1986	*v* Yugoslavia (ECQ)	Wembley	2–0
1 April 1987	*v* Northern Ireland (ECQ)	Belfast	2–0
23 May 1987	*v* Scotland (RC)	Glasgow	0–0

1987–88 (with Derby County)

17 Feb 1988	*v* Israel	Tel Aviv	0–0
23 March 1988	*v* Holland (sub)	Wembley	2–2
24 May 1988	*v* Colombia (RC)	Wembley	1–1
28 May 1988	*v* Switzerland	Lausanne	1–0
12 June 1988	*v* Eire (EC)	Stuttgart	0–1
15 June 1988	*v* Holland (EC)	Düsseldorf	1–3

1989–90

25 April 1990	*v* Czechoslovakia (sub)	Wembley	4–2
2 June 1990	*v* Tunisia (sub)	Tunis	1–1
16 June 1990	*v* Holland (WC)	Cagliari	0–0
21 June 1990	*v* Egypt (WC)	Cagliari	1–0 (1 goal)
26 June 1990	*v* Belgium (WC)	Bologna	1–0 (aet)
1 July 1990	*v* Cameroon (WC)	Naples	3–2 (aet)
4 July 1990	*v* West Germany (WC)	Turin	1–1 (aet)
7 July 1990	*v* Italy (WC)	Bari	1–2

1990–91

12 Sept 1990	*v* Hungary	Wembley	1–0
17 Oct 1990	*v* Poland (ECQ)	Wembley	2–0
14 Nov 1990	*v* Eire (ECQ)	Dublin	1–1
6 Feb 1991	*v* Cameroon	Wembley	2–0
27 March 1991	*v* Eire (ECQ)	Wembley	1–1
21 May 1991	*v* USSR*	Wembley	3–1
25 May 1991	*v* Argentina	Wembley	2–2
1 June 1991	*v* Australia	Sydney	1–0
8 June 1991	*v* New Zealand	Auckland	2–0
12 June 1991	*v* Malaysia	Kuala Lumpur	4–2

1991–92 (with Liverpool)

19 Feb 1992	*v* France	Wembley	2–0
3 June 1992	*v* Finland	Helsinki	2–1

1992–93

9 Sept 1992	*v* Spain	Santander	0–1

WRIGHT, THOMAS J. *Born:* 21.10.44 (Liverpool) *Club:* Everton *Caps:* 11

1967–68

| 8 June 1968 | *v* USSR (EC) | Rome | 2–0 |

1968–69

6 Nov 1968	*v* Romania	Bucharest	0–0
15 Jan 1969	*v* Romania	Wembley	1–1
1 June 1969	*v* Mexico (sub)	Mexico City	0–0
8 June 1969	*v* Uruguay	Montevideo	2–1
12 June 1969	*v* Brazil	Rio de Janeiro	1–2

1969–70

5 Nov 1969	*v* Holland	Amsterdam	1–0
25 Feb 1970	*v* Belgium	Brussels	3–1
18 April 1970	*v* Wales	Cardiff	1–1
2 June 1970	*v* Romania (sub) (WC)	Guadalajara	1–0
7 June 1970	*v* Brazil (WC)	Guadalajara	0–1

WRIGHT, WILLIAM A. *Born:* 6.2.24 (Ironbridge) *Club:* Wolverhampton Wanderers
Caps: 105 *Goals:* 3

1946–47

28 Sept 1946	*v* Northern Ireland	Belfast	7–2
30 Sept 1946	*v* Eire	Dublin	1–0
13 Nov 1946	*v* Wales	Manchester City	3–0
27 Nov 1946	*v* Holland	Huddersfield	8–2
12 April 1947	*v* Scotland	Wembley	1–1
3 May 1947	*v* France	Arsenal	3–0
18 May 1947	*v* Switzerland	Zurich	0–1
25 May 1947	*v* Portugal	Lisbon	10–0

1947–48

21 Sept 1947	*v* Belgium	Brussels	5–2
18 Oct 1947	*v* Wales	Cardiff	3–0
5 Nov 1947	*v* Northern Ireland	Everton	2–2
19 Nov 1947	*v* Sweden	Arsenal	4–2
10 April 1948	*v* Scotland	Glasgow	2–0
16 May 1948	*v* Italy	Turin	4–0

1948–49

26 Sept 1948	*v* Denmark	Copenhagen	0–0
9 Oct 1948	*v* Northern Ireland*	Belfast	6–2
10 Nov 1948	*v* Wales*	Aston Villa	1–0
2 Dec 1948	*v* Switzerland*	Arsenal	6–0
9 April 1949	*v* Scotland*	Wembley	1–3
13 May 1949	*v* Sweden*	Stockholm	1–3
18 May 1949	*v* Norway*	Oslo	4–1
22 May 1949	*v* France*	Paris	3–1 (1 goal)

1949–50

21 Sept 1949	*v* Eire*	Everton	0–2
15 Oct 1949	*v* Wales* (WCQ)	Cardiff	4–1
16 Nov 1949	*v* Northern Ireland* (WCQ)	Manchester City	9–2

30 Nov 1949	*v* Italy*	Tottenham	2–0 (1 goal)
15 April 1950	*v* Scotland* (WCQ)	Glasgow	1–0
14 May 1950	*v* Portugal*	Lisbon	5–3
18 May 1950	*v* Belgium*	Brussels	4–1
25 June 1950	*v* Chile* (WC)	Rio de Janeiro	2–0
29 June 1950	*v* USA* (WC)	Belo Horizonte	0–1
2 July 1950	*v* Spain* (WC)	Rio de Janeiro	0–1

1950–51

7 Oct 1950	*v* Northern Ireland*	Belfast	4–1 (1 goal)
14 April 1951	*v* Scotland*	Wembley	2–3
9 May 1951	*v* Argentina*	Wembley	2–1

1951–52

3 Oct 1951	*v* France*	Arsenal	2–2
20 Oct 1951	*v* Wales*	Cardiff	1–1
14 Nov 1951	*v* Northern Ireland*	Aston Villa	2–0
28 Nov 1951	*v* Austria*	Wembley	2–2
5 April 1952	*v* Scotland*	Glasgow	2–1
18 May 1952	*v* Italy*	Florence	1–1
25 May 1952	*v* Austria*	Vienna	3–2
28 May 1952	*v* Switzerland*	Zurich	3–0

1952–53

4 Oct 1952	*v* Northern Ireland*	Belfast	2–2
12 Nov 1952	*v* Wales*	Wembley	5–2
26 Nov 1952	*v* Belgium*	Wembley	5–0
18 April 1953	*v* Scotland*	Wembley	2–2
17 May 1953	*v* Argentina*	Buenos Aires	0–0†
24 May 1953	*v* Chile*	Santiago	2–1
31 May 1953	*v* Uruguay*	Montevideo	1–2
8 June 1953	*v* USA*	New York	6–3

1953–54

10 Oct 1953	*v* Wales* (WCQ)	Cardiff	4–1
21 Oct 1953	*v* FIFA (Rest of Europe)*	Wembley	4–4
11 Nov 1953	*v* Northern Ireland* (WCQ)	Everton	3–1
25 Nov 1953	*v* Hungary*	Wembley	3–6
3 April 1954	*v* Scotland* (WCQ)	Glasgow	4–2
16 May 1954	*v* Yugoslavia*	Belgrade	0–1
23 May 1954	*v* Hungary*	Budapest	1–7
17 June 1954	*v* Belgium* (WC)	Basle	4–4
20 June 1954	*v* Switzerland* (WC)	Berne	2–0
26 June 1954	*v* Uruguay* (WC)	Basle	2–4

1954–55

2 Oct 1954	*v* Northern Ireland*	Belfast	2–0
10 Nov 1954	*v* Wales*	Wembley	3–2
1 Dec 1954	*v* West Germany*	Wembley	3–1
2 April 1955	*v* Scotland*	Wembley	7–2
15 May 1955	*v* France*	Paris	0–1
18 May 1955	*v* Spain*	Madrid	1–1
22 May 1955	*v* Portugal*	Oporto	1–3

1955–56

2 Oct 1955	v Denmark*	Copenhagen	5–1
22 Oct 1955	v Wales*	Cardiff	1–2
2 Nov 1955	v Northern Ireland*	Wembley	3–0
30 Nov 1955	v Spain*	Wembley	4–1
14 April 1956	v Scotland*	Glasgow	1–1
9 May 1956	v Brazil*	Wembley	4–2
16 May 1956	v Sweden*	Stockholm	0–0
20 May 1956	v Finland*	Helsinki	5–1
26 May 1956	v West Germany*	Berlin	3–1

1956–57

6 Oct 1956	v Northern Ireland*	Belfast	1–1
14 Nov 1956	v Wales*	Wembley	3–1
28 Nov 1956	v Yugoslavia*	Wembley	3–0
5 Dec 1956	v Denmark* (WCQ)	Wolverhampton	5–2
6 April 1957	v Scotland*	Wembley	2–1
8 May 1957	v Eire (WCQ)	Wembley	5–1
15 May 1957	v Denmark* (WCQ)	Copenhagen	4–1
19 May 1957	v Eire* (WCQ)	Dublin	1–1

1957–58

19 Oct 1957	v Wales*	Cardiff	4–0
6 Nov 1957	v Northern Ireland*	Wembley	2–3
27 Nov 1957	v France*	Wembley	4–0
19 April 1958	v Scotland*	Glasgow	4–0
7 May 1958	v Portugal*	Wembley	2–1
11 May 1958	v Yugoslavia*	Belgrade	0–5
18 May 1958	v USSR*	Moscow	1–1
8 June 1958	v USSR* (WC)	Gothenburg	2–2
11 June 1958	v Brazil* (WC)	Gothenburg	0–0
15 June 1958	v Austria* (WC)	Boras	2–2
17 June 1958	v USSR* (WC)	Gothenburg	0–1

1958–59

4 Oct 1958	v Northern Ireland*	Belfast	3–3
22 Oct 1958	v USSR*	Wembley	5–0
26 Nov 1958	v Wales*	Aston Villa	2–2
11 April 1959	v Scotland*	Wembley	1–0
6 May 1959	v Italy*	Wembley	2–2
13 May 1959	v Brazil*	Rio de Janeiro	0–2
17 May 1959	v Peru*	Lima	1–4
24 May 1959	v Mexico*	Mexico City	1–2
28 May 1959	v USA*	Los Angeles	8–1

YOUNG, GERRY M. *Born:* 1.10.36 (South Shields) *Club:* Sheffield Wednesday *Caps:* 1

1964–65

18 Nov 1964	v Wales	Wembley	2–1

ENGLAND CAPTAINS 1945–1993

Moore, R. F.	91	Mills, M. D.	8	Charlton, R.	2
Wright, W. A.	90	Butcher, T.	7	Ince, P.	2
Robson, B.	65	Ball, A. J.	6	Swift, F. V.	2
Keegan, J. K.	31	Pearce, S.	6	Beardsley, P. A.	1
Hughes, E. W.	23	Platt, D.	6	Bell, C.	1
Haynes, J. N.	22	Thompson, P. B.	6	Cherry, T. J.	1
Lineker, G.	18	Clayton, R.	5	Clemence, R. N.	1
Armfield, J. C.	15	Peters, M.	4	Mullery, A. P.	1
Shilton, P. L.	15	Flowers, R.	3	Neal, P. G.	1
Hardwick, G. F. M.	13	Ramsey, A. E.	3	Wright, M.	1
Wilkins, R. G.	10	Watson, D. V.	3		
Francis, G. C. J.	8	Channon, M. R.	2		

ONE-CAP WONDERS

Angus, J.
Armstrong, K.
Barlow, R. J.
Blockley, J.
Boyer, P. J.
Bradford, G. R. W.
Brown, A.
Brown, K.
Charnley, R. O.
Clapton, D. R.
Clarke, H. A.
Crowe, C.
Davenport, P.
Fantham, J.
Flowers, T.
Foulkes, W. A.
George, C. F.
Gidman, J.
Goddard, P.
Gray, A.
Hagan, J.
Haines, J. T. W.

Harris, G.
Harvey, J. C.
Henry, R. P.
Hollins, J. W.
Kay, A. H.
Lee, J.
Little, B.
Marwood, B.
Meadows, J.
Miller, B. G.
Milton, A. C.
Nicholson, W. E.
Parkes, P. B.
Pegg, D.
Perryman, S. J.
Phelan, M. C.
Pickering, N.
Pilkington, B.
Pye, J.
Richards, J. P.
Rickaby, S.
Rimmer, J. J.

Robb, G.
Shellito, K. J.
Shimwell, E.
Smith, T.
Spink, N. P.
Stein, B.
Stepney, A. C.
Sterland, M.
Storey-Moore, I.
Streten, B.
Sunderland, A.
Taylor, E.
Temple, D. W.
Ufton, D. G.
Wallace, D. L.
Walters, K. M.
Ward, P.
Wheeler, J. E.
White, D.
Whymark, T. J.
Willis, A.
Young, G. M.

ENGLAND APPEARANCES BY CLUB

AC MILAN
Blissett, L.
Hateley, M. W.
Wilkins, R. G.

ARSENAL
Adams, T. A.
Anderson, V. A.
Baker, J. H.
Ball, A. J.
Blockley, J.
Clapton, D. R.
Compton, L. H.
Dixon, L. M.
Eastham, G. E.
Keown, M. R.
Mariner, P.
Marwood, B.
McNab, R.
Merson, P. C.
Milton, A. C.
Radford, J.
Rimmer, J.
Rix, G.
Rocastle, D.
Sansom, K. G.
Scott, L.
Seaman, D. A.
Smith, A. M.
Smith, L.
Storey, P. E.
Sunderland, A.
Talbot, B. E.
Thomas, M. L.
Winterburn, N.
Woodcock, A. S.
Wright, I. E.

ASTON VILLA
Barrett, E. D.
Cowans, G. S.
Daley, A. M.
Gidman, J.
Hitchens, G. A.
Hodge, S. B.
Little, B.
Lowe, E.

Morley, A. W.
Platt, D.
Spink, N. P.
Thompson, T.
Withe, P.

BARCELONA
Lineker, G.

BARI
Cowans, G. S.
Platt, D.

BIRMINGHAM CITY
Astall, G.
Francis, T. J.
Hall, J. J.
Hellawell, M. S.
Merrick, G. H.
Smith, T.

BLACKBURN ROVERS
Clayton, R.
Douglas, B.
Eckersley, W.
Langton, R.
Newton, K. R.
Shearer, A.

BLACKPOOL
Armfield, J.
Ball, A. J.
Charnley, R. O.
Garrett, T.
Johnston, H.
Matthews, S.
Mortensen, S. H.
Perry, W.
Shimwell, E.
Taylor, E.
Waiters, A. K.

BOLTON WANDERERS
Banks, T.
Barrass, M. W.
Hassall, H. W.
Hill, F.

Holden, D. A.
Hopkinson, E.
Langton, R.
Lofthouse, N.
Parry, R. A.
Wheeler, J. E.

BRIGHTON & HOVE ALBION
Foster, S. B.
Ward, P.

BRISTOL CITY
Atyeo, P. J.

BRISTOL ROVERS
Bradford, G. R. W.

BURNLEY
Angus, J.
Coates, R.
Connelly, J. M.
Dobson, J. M.
Elliott, W. H.
Harris, G.
McDonald, C. A.
Miller, B. G.
Pilkington, B.
Pointer, R.

CHARLTON ATHLETIC
Bailey, M. A.
Ufton, D. G.

CHELSEA
Armstrong, K.
Beasant, D. J.
Bentley, R. T. F.
Blunstone, F.
Bonetti, P. P.
Brabrook, P.
Bridges, B. J.
Dixon, K. M.
Dorigo, A. R.
Greaves, J.
Hollins, J. W.
Lawton, T.
Osgood, P. L.

Shellito, K. J.
Sillett, P. R.
Tambling, R. V.
Venables, T. F.
Wilkins, R. G.
Wise, D. F.

COLOGNE
Woodcock, A. S.

COVENTRY CITY
Matthews, R. D.
Regis, C.
Thomas, D. J.

CRYSTAL PALACE
Byrne, J. J.
Gray, A.A.
Martyn, A. N.
Salako, J. A.
Sansom, K. G.
Taylor, P. J.
Thomas, G. R.
Wright, I. E.

DERBY COUNTY
Carter, H. S.
George, C. F.
Hector, K. J.
Howe, J. R.
Lee, J.
McFarland, R. L.
Morris, J.
Mozley, B.
Nish, D. J.
Shilton, P. L.
Todd, C.
Ward, T. V.
Wright, M.

EVERTON
Ball, A. J.
Bracewell, P. W.
Cottee, T. R.
Dobson, J. M.
Harvey, J. C.
Kay, A. H.
Keown, M. R.
Labone, B. L.

Latchford, R. D.
Lineker, G.
Newton, K. R.
Pickering, F.
Reid, P.
Royle, J.
Steven, T. M.
Stevens, M. G.
Temple, D.
Watson, D.
West, G.
Wilson, R.
Wright, T. J.

FULHAM
Cohen, G. R.
Haynes, J. N.
Jezzard, B. A. G.
Langley, E. J.
Taylor, J. G.

HIBERNIAN
Baker, J. H.

HUDDERSFIELD TOWN
Hassall, H. W.
McGarry, W. H.
Metcalfe, V.
O'Grady, M.
Staniforth, R.
Wilson, R.

INTER MILAN
Hitchens, G. A.

IPSWICH TOWN
Beattie, T. K.
Butcher, T.
Crawford, R.
Gates, E. L.
Johnson, D. E.
Mariner, P.
Mills, M. D.
Osman, R. C.
Talbot, B. E.
Viljoen, C.
Whymark, T. J.

JUVENTUS
Platt, D.

LAZIO
Gascoigne, P. J.

LEEDS UNITED
Barnes, P. S.
Batty, D.
Charlton, J.
Cherry, T.
Clarke, A. J.
Cooper, T.
Currie, A. W.
Dorigo, A. R.
Greenhoff, B.
Hunter, N.
Jones, M. D.
Madeley, P. E.
O'Grady, M.
Peacock, A.
Reaney, P.

LEICESTER CITY
Banks, G.
Lineker, G.
Shilton, P. L.
Weller, K.
Whitworth, S.
Worthington, F. S.

LIVERPOOL
A'Court, A.
Barnes, J.
Beardsley, P. A.
Byrne, G.
Callaghan, I. R.
Clemence, R. N.
Hughes, E. W.
Hughes, L.
Hunt, R.
Johnson, D. E.
Jones, R.
Jones, W. H.
Keegan, J. K.
Kennedy, A. P.
Kennedy, R.
Lawler, C.
Lee, S.

Lindsay, A.
Lloyd, L. V.
McDermott, T.
McMahon, S.
Melia, J.
Milne, G.
Neal, P. G.
Smith, T.
Taylor, P. H.
Thompson, Peter
Thompson, Phil B.
Wright, M.

LUTON TOWN

Baynham, R. L.
Harford, M. G.
Hill, R. A.
Owen, S. W.
Stein, B.
Streten, B.
Walsh, P.A.

MANCHESTER CITY

Barnes, P. S.
Bell, C.
Broadis, I. A.
Channon, M. R.
Corrigan, J. T.
Curle, K.
Doyle, M.
Francis, T. J.
Lee, F. H.
Marsh, R. W.
Meadows, J.
Reeves, K. P.
Revie, D. G.
Royle, J.
Summerbee, M. G.
Swift, F. V.
Tueart, D.
Watson, D. V.
White, D.

MANCHESTER UNITED

Anderson, V. A.
Aston, J.
Bailey, G. R.
Berry, J. J.
Bradley, W.

Byrne, R. W.
Charlton, R.
Chilton, A. C.
Cockburn, H.
Connelly, J. M.
Coppell, S. J.
Duxbury, M.
Edwards, D.
Foulkes, W. A.
Greenhoff, B.
Hill, G. A.
Ince, P.
Kidd, B.
McGuinness, W.
Pallister, G. A.
Parker, P.A.
Pearson, J. Stuart,
Pearson, Stan C.
Pegg, D.
Phelan, M. C.
Robson, B.
Rowley, J. F.
Sadler, D.
Sharpe, L. S.
Stepney, A.C.
Stiles, N. P.
Taylor, T.
Viollet, D. S.
Webb, N. J.
Wilkins, R. G.
Wood, R. E.

MARSEILLE

Steven, T. M.
Waddle, C. R.

MIDDLESBROUGH

Armstrong, D.
Clough, B. H.
Hardwick, G. F. M.
Holliday, E.
Mannion, W. J.
McNeil, M.
Pallister, G. A.
Peacock, A.

MONACO

Hateley, M. W.
Hoddle, G.

NEWCASTLE UNITED

Beardsley, P. A.
Broadis, I. A.
Macdonald, M.
Milburn, J. E. T.
Waddle, C. R.

NORWICH CITY

Barham, M.
Boyer, P. J.
Reeves, K. P.
Watson, D.
Woods, C. E. C.

NOTTS COUNTY

Lawton, T.

NOTTINGHAM FOREST

Anderson, V. A.
Birtles, G.
Charles, G. A.
Clough, N. H.
Davenport, P.
Francis, T. J.
Hinton, A. T.
Hodge, S. B.
Lloyd, L. V.
Clough, N. H.
Pearce, S.
Shilton, P. L.
Storey-Moore, I.
Walker, D. S.
Webb, N. J.
Wignall, F.
Woodcock, A. S.

OLDHAM ATHLETIC

Barrett, E. D.

PORTSMOUTH

Dickinson, J. W.
Froggatt, J.
Harris, P. P.
Hateley, M. W.
Phillips, L. H.

PRESTON NORTH END

Finney, T.
Langton, R.

Thompson, T.

QUEENS PARK RANGERS
Allen, C. D.
Bardsley, D.
Bowles, S.
Clement, D. T.
Fenwick, T.
Ferdinand, L.
Francis, G. C. J.
Gillard, I. T.
Gregory, J. C.
Marsh, R. W.
Parker, P. A.
Parkes, P. B.
Seaman, D. A.
Sinton, A.
Thomas, D.

RANGERS
Butcher, T.
Hateley, M. W.
Steven, T. M.
Stevens, M. G.
Walters, K. M.
Woods, C. E. C.

REAL MADRID
Cunningham, L.

SAMPDORIA
Francis, T. J.
Walker, D. S.

SHEFFIELD UNITED
Currie, A. W.
Deane, B. C.
Grainger, C.
Hagan, J.
Hodgkinson, A.
Jones, M. D.
Shaw, G. L.

SHEFFIELD WEDNESDAY
Fantham, J.
Froggatt, R.
Hirst, D. E.
Palmer, C.
Quixall, A.

Sewell, J.
Springett, R. D. R.
Sterland, M.
Swan, P.
Woods, C. E. C.
Young, G. M.

SOUTHAMPTON
Armstrong, D.
Channon, M. R.
Ellerington, W.
Flowers, T.
Keegan, J. K.
Paine, T. L.
Ramsey, A. E.
Shearer, A.
Shilton, P. L.
Wallace, D. L.
Watson, D. V.
Williams, S. C.
Wright, M.

STOKE CITY
Allen, A.
Banks, G.
Chamberlain, M.
Franklin, C. N.
Hudson, A. A.
Matthews, S.
Pejic, M.
Shilton, P. L.
Watson, D. V.

SUNDERLAND
Anderson, S.
Grainger, C.
Pickering, N.
Shackleton, L. E.
Towers, A. M.
Watson, D. V.
Watson, W.

SV HAMBURG
Keegan, J. K.

TOTTENHAM HOTSPUR
Allen, C. D.
Baily, E. F.
Brooks, J.

Chivers, M.
Clarke, H. A.
Clemence, R. N.
Coates, R.
Ditchburn, E. G.
Fenwick, T.
Gascoigne, P. J.
Greaves, J.
Henry, R. P.
Hoddle, G.
Hodge, S. B.
Knowles, C.
Lineker, G.
Mabbutt, G. V.
Medley, L. D.
Mullery, A. P.
Nicholson, W. E.
Norman, M.
Perryman, S. J.
Peters, M. S.
Ramsey, A. E.
Robb, G.
Roberts, G. P.
Sheringham, E.
Smith, R. A.
Stevens, G. A.
Stewart, P. A.
Waddle, C. R.
Willis, A.

WATFORD
Barnes, J.
Blissett, L.

WERDER BREMEN
Watson, D. V.

WEST BROMWICH ALBION
Allen, R.
Astle, J.
Barlow, R. J.
Barnes, P. S.
Brown, A.
Cunningham, L.
Haines, J. T. W.
Howe, D.
Hunt, S.
Kevan, D. T.
Nicholls, J.

Regis, C.
Rickaby, S.
Robson, B.
Robson, R. W.
Statham, D.

WEST HAM UNITED

Brooking, T. D.
Brown, K.
Byrne, J. J.
Cottee, T. R.
Devonshire, A.
Goddard, P.
Hurst, G. C.

Lampard, F. R. G.
Martin, A. E.
Moore, R. F.
Peters, M. S.

WIMBLEDON

Fashanu, J.

WOLVERHAMPTON WANDERERS

Broadbent, P. F.
Bull, S. G.
Clamp, E.

Crowe, C.
Deeley, N. V.
Flowers, R.
Hancocks, J.
Hinton, A. T.
Hughes, E. W.
Mullen, J.
Pye, J.
Richards, J. P.
Slater, W. J.
Thomson, R. A.
Williams, B. F.
Wilshaw, D. J.
Wright, W. A.

ENGLAND'S FULL INTERNATIONAL TEAMS 1945–1993

(Up to and including 19 June, 1993)

versus	venue	result	1	2	3	4	5
1946–47							
N Ireland	A	7–2	Swift	Scott	Hardwick*	W Wright	Franklin
Rep of Ireland	A	1–0	Swift	Scott	Hardwick*	W Wright	Franklin
Wales	H	3–0	Swift	Scott	Hardwick*	W Wright	Franklin
Holland	H	8–2	Swift	Scott	Hardwick*	W Wright	Franklin
Scotland	H	1–1	Swift	Scott	Hardwick*	W Wright	Franklin
France	H	3–0	Swift	Scott	Hardwick*	W Wright	Franklin
Switzerland	A	0–1	Swift	Scott	Hardwick*	W Wright	Franklin
Portugal	A	10–0	Swift	Scott	Hardwick*	W Wright	Franklin
1947–48							
Belgium	A	5–2	Swift	Scott	Hardwick*	Ward	Franklin
Wales	A	3–0	Swift	Scott	Hardwick*	P Taylor	Franklin
N Ireland	H	2–2	Swift	Scott	Hardwick*	P Taylor	Franklin
Sweden	H	4–2	Swift	Scott	Hardwick*	P Taylor	Franklin
Scotland	A	2–0	Swift	Scott	Hardwick*	W Wright	Franklin
Italy	A	4–0	Swift*	Scott	J Howe	W Wright	Franklin
1948–49							
Denmark	A	0–0	Swift*	Scott	Aston	W Wright	Franklin
N Ireland	A	6–2	Swift	Scott	J Howe	W Wright*	Franklin
Wales	H	1–0	Swift	Scott	Aston	Ward	Franklin
Switzerland	H	6–0	Ditchburn	Ramsey	Aston	W Wright*	Franklin
Scotland	H	1–3	Swift	Aston	J Howe	W Wright*	Franklin
Sweden	A	1–3	Ditchburn	Shimwell	Aston	W Wright*	Franklin
Norway	A	4–1	Swift	Ellerington	Aston	W Wright*	Franklin
France	A	3–1	Williams	Ellerington	Aston	W Wright*[1]	Franklin
1949–50							
Rep of Ireland	H	0–2	Williams	Mozley	Aston	W Wright*	Franklin
Wales	A	4–1	Williams	Mozley	Aston	W Wright*	Franklin
N Ireland	H	9–2	Streten	Mozley	Aston	Watson	Franklin
Italy	H	2–0	Williams	Ramsey	Aston	Watson	Franklin
Scotland	A	1–0	Williams	Ramsey	Aston	W Wright*	Franklin
Portugal	A	5–3	Williams	Ramsey	Aston	W Wright*	WH Jones
Belgium	A	4–1	Williams	Ramsey	Aston	W Wright*	WH Jones
Chile	N	2–0	Williams	Ramsey	Aston	W Wright*	L Hughes
USA	N	0–1	Williams	Ramsey	Aston	W Wright*	L Hughes
Spain	N	0–1	Williams	Ramsey	Eckersley	W Wright*	L Hughes
1950–51							
N Ireland	A	4–1	Williams	Ramsey	Aston	W Wright*[1]	Chilton
Wales	H	4–2	Williams	Ramsey*	L Smith	Watson	L Compton
Yugoslavia	H	2–2	Williams	Ramsey*	Eckersley	Watson	L Compton
Scotland	H	2–3	Williams	Ramsey	Eckersley	Johnston	J Froggatt
Argentina	H	2–1	Williams	Ramsey	Eckersley	W Wright*	J Taylor
Portugal	H	5–2	Williams	Ramsey*	Eckersley	Nicholson[1]	J Taylor
1951–52							
France	H	2–2	Williams	Ramsey	Willis	W Wright*	Chilton
Wales	A	1–1	Williams	Ramsey	L Smith	W Wright*	Barrass
N Ireland	H	2–0	Merrick	Ramsey[1]	L Smith	W Wright*	Barrass
Austria	H	2–2	Merrick	Ramsey[1]	Eckersley	W Wright*	J Froggatt
Scotland	A	2–1	Merrick	Ramsey	Garrett	W Wright*	J Froggatt
Italy	A	1–1	Merrick	Ramsey	Garrett	W Wright*	J Froggatt
Austria	A	3–2	Merrick	Ramsey	Eckersley	W Wright*	J Froggatt

*captain   †own goal   Small numerals goals scored   Numbers after sub player replaced

	7	8	9	10	11	substitutes
ckburn	Finney[1]	Carter[1]	Lawton[1]	Mannion[3]	Langton[1]	
ckburn	Finney[1]	Carter	Lawton	Mannion	Langton	
ckburn	Finney	Carter	Lawton[1]	Mannion[2]	Langton	
nston	Finney	Carter[2]	Lawton[4]	Mannion[1]	Langton	
nston	S Matthews	Carter[1]	Lawton	Mannion	Mullen	
we	Finney[1]	Carter[1]	Lawton	Mannion[1]	Langton	
we	S Matthews[1]	Carter	Lawton	Mannion	Langton	
we	S Matthews[1]	Mortensen[4]	Lawton[4]	Mannion	Finney[1]	
Wright	S Matthews	Mortensen[1]	Lawton[2]	Mannion	Finney[2]	
Wright	S Matthews	Mortensen[1]	Lawton[1]	Mannion	Finney[1]	
Wright	S Matthews	Mortensen	Lawton[1]	Mannion[1]	Finney	
Wright	Finney	Mortensen[3]	Lawton[1]	Mannion	Langton	
ckburn	S Matthews	Mortensen[1]	Lawton	Pearson	Finney[1]	
ckburn	S Matthews	Mortensen[1]	Lawton[1]	Mannion	Finney[2]	
ckburn	S Matthews	Hagan	Lawton	Shackleton	Langton	
ckburn	S Matthews[1]	Mortensen[3]	Milburn[1]	Pearson[1]	Finney	
Wright*	S Matthews	Mortensen	Milburn	Shackleton	Finney[1]	
ckburn	S Matthews	J Rowley[1]	Milburn[1]	Haines[2]	Hancocks[2]	
ckburn	S Matthews	Mortensen	Milburn[1]	Pearson	Finney	
ckburn	Finney[1]	Mortensen	Bentley	J Rowley	Langton	
kinson	Finney[1]	Morris[1]	Mortensen	Mannion	Mullen[1]	†
kinson	Finney	Morris[2]	J Rowley	Mannion	Mullen	
kinson	P Harris	Morris	Pye	Mannion	Finney	
kinson	Finney	Mortensen[1]	Milburn[3]	Shackleton	Hancocks	
Wright*	Finney	Mortensen[2]	J Rowley[4]	Pearson[2]	J Froggatt[1]	
Wright*[1]	Finney	Mortensen	J Rowley[1]	Pearson	J Froggatt	
kinson	Finney	Mannion	Mortensen	Bentley[1]	Langton	
kinson	Milburn	Mortensen[1]	Bentley	Mannion	Finney[4]	
kinson	Milburn	Mortensen[1]	Bentley[1]	Mannion[1]	Finney	Mullen(7)[1]
kinson	Finney	Mannion[1]	Bentley	Mortensen[1]	Mullen	
kinson	Finney	Mannion	Bentley	Mortensen	Mullen	
kinson	S Matthews	Mortensen	Milburn	E Baily	Finney	
kinson	S Matthews	Mannion	J Lee[1]	E Baily[2]	Langton	
kinson	Finney	Mannion[1]	Milburn[1]	E Baily[2]	Medley	
kinson	Hancocks	Mannion	Lofthouse[2]	E Baily	Medley	
Wright*	S Matthews	Mannion	Mortensen	Hassall[1]	Finney[1]	
kburn	Finney	Mortensen[1]	Milburn[1]	Hassall	Metcalfe	
kburn	Finney[1]	Pearson	Milburn[2]	Hassall[1]	Metcalfe	
ckburn	Finney	Mannion	Milburn	Hassall	Medley[1]	†
kinson	Finney	T Thompson	Lofthouse	E Baily[1]	Medley	
kinson	Finney	Sewell	Lofthouse[2]	Phillips	Medley	
kinson	Milton	Broadis	Lofthouse[1]	E Baily	Medley	
kinson	Finney	Broadis	Lofthouse	Pearson[2]	J Rowley	
kinson	Finney	Broadis[1]	Lofthouse	Pearson	Elliott	
kinson	Finney	Sewell[1]	Lofthouse[2]	E Baily	Elliott	

versus	venue	result	1	2	3	4	5
Switzerland	A	3–0	Merrick	Ramsey	Eckersley	W Wright*	J Froggatt
1952–53							
N Ireland	A	2–2	Merrick	Ramsey	Eckersley	W Wright*	J Froggatt
Wales	H	5–2	Merrick	Ramsey	L Smith	W Wright*	J Froggatt
Belgium	H	5–0	Merrick	Ramsey	L Smith	W Wright*	J Froggatt
Scotland	H	2–2	Merrick	Ramsey	L Smith	W Wright*	Barrass
Argentina	A	0–0	Merrick	Ramsey	Eckersley	W Wright*	Johnston
Chile	A	2–1	Merrick	Ramsey	Eckersley	W Wright*	Johnston
Uruguay	A	1–2	Merrick	Ramsey	Eckersley	W Wright*	Johnston
USA	A	6–3	Ditchburn	Ramsey	Eckersley	W Wright*	Johnston
1953–54							
Wales	A	4–1	Merrick	Garrett	Eckersley	W Wright*	Johnston
Rest of Europe	H	4–4	Merrick	Ramsey^1	Eckersley	W Wright*	Ufton
N Ireland	H	3–1	Merrick	Rickaby	Eckersley	W Wright*	Johnston
Hungary	H	3–6	Merrick	Ramsey^1	Eckersley	W Wright*	Johnston
Scotland	A	4–2	Merrick	Staniforth	R Byrne	W Wright*	H Clarke
Yugoslavia	A	0–1	Merrick	Staniforth	R Byrne	W Wright*	Owen
Hungary	A	1–7	Merrick	Staniforth	R Byrne	W Wright*	Owen
Belgium	N	4–4	Merrick	Staniforth	R Byrne	McGarry	W Wright*
Switzerland	N	2–0	Merrick	Staniforth	R Byrne	McGarry	W Wright*
Uruguay	N	2–4	Merrick	Staniforth	R Byrne	McGarry	W Wright*
1954–55							
N Ireland	A	2–0	Wood	Foulkes	R Byrne	Wheeler	W Wright
Wales	H	3–2	Wood	Staniforth	R Byrne	Phillips	W Wright
W Germany	H	3–1	Williams	Staniforth	R Byrne	Phillips	W Wright
Scotland	H	7–2	Williams	Meadows	R Byrne	Armstrong	W Wright
France	A	0–1	Williams	P Sillett	R Byrne	Flowers	W Wright
Spain	A	1–1	Williams	P Sillett	R Byrne	Dickinson	W Wright
Portugal	A	1–3	Williams	P Sillett	R Byrne	Dickinson	W Wright
1955–56							
Denmark	A	5–1	Baynham	Hall	R Byrne	McGarry	W Wright
Wales	A	1–2	Williams	Hall	R Byrne	McGarry	W Wright
N Ireland	H	3–0	Baynham	Hall	R Byrne	Clayton	W Wright
Spain	H	4–1	Baynham	Hall	R Byrne	Clayton	W Wright
Scotland	A	1–1	R Matthews	Hall	R Byrne	Dickinson	W Wright
Brazil	H	4–2	R Matthews	Hall	R Byrne	Clayton	W Wright
Sweden	A	0–0	R Matthews	Hall	R Byrne	Clayton	W Wright
Finland	A	5–1	Wood	Hall	R Byrne	Clayton	W Wright
W Germany	A	3–1	R Matthews	Hall	R Byrne	Clayton	W Wright
1956–57							
N Ireland	A	1–1	R Matthews	Hall	R Byrne	Clayton	W Wright
Wales	H	3–1	Ditchburn	Hall	R Byrne	Clayton	W Wright
Yugoslavia	H	3–0	Ditchburn	Hall	R Byrne	Clayton	W Wright
Denmark	H	5–2	Ditchburn	Hall	R Byrne	Clayton	W Wright
Scotland	H	2–1	Hodgkinson	Hall	R Byrne	Clayton	W Wright
Rep of Ireland	H	5–1	Hodgkinson	Hall	R Byrne	Clayton	W Wright
Denmark	A	4–1	Hodgkinson	Hall	R Byrne	Clayton	W Wright
Rep of Ireland	A	1–1	Hodgkinson	Hall	R Byrne	Clayton	W Wright
1957–58							
Wales	A	4–0	Hopkinson	D Howe	R Byrne	Clayton	W Wright
N Ireland	H	2–3	Hopkinson	D Howe	R Byrne	Clayton	W Wright
France	H	4–0	Hopkinson	D Howe	R Byrne	Clayton	W Wright
Scotland	A	4–0	Hopkinson	D Howe	Langley	Clayton	W Wright
Portugal	H	2–1	Hopkinson	D Howe	Langley	Clayton	W Wright

*captain   †own goal   *Small numerals goals scored*   *Numbers after sub player replaced*

	7	8	9	10	11	substitutes
kinson	R Allen	Sewell[1]	Lofthouse[2]	E Baily	Finney	
kinson	Finney	Sewell	Lofthouse[1]	E Baily	Elliott[1]	
kinson	Finney[1]	R Froggatt	Lofthouse[2]	Bentley[1]	Elliott	
kinson	Finney	Bentley	Lofthouse[2]	R Froggatt	Elliott[2]	
kinson	Finney	Broadis[2]	Lofthouse	R Froggatt	J Froggatt	
kinson	Finney	Broadis	Lofthouse	T Taylor	Berry	
kinson	Finney	Broadis	Lofthouse[1]	T Taylor	Berry	
kinson	Finney	Broadis	Lofthouse	T Taylor[1]	Berry	
kinson	Finney[2]	Broadis[1]	Lofthouse[2]	R Froggatt[1]	J Froggatt	
kinson	Finney	Quixall	Lofthouse[2]	Wilshaw[2]	Mullen	
kinson	S Matthews	Mortensen[1]	Lofthouse	Quixall	Mullen[2]	
kinson	S Matthews	Quixall	Lofthouse[1]	Hassall[2]	Mullen	
kinson	S Matthews	E Taylor	Mortensen[1]	Sewell[1]	Robb	
kinson	Finney	Broadis[1]	R Allen[1]	Nicholls[1]	Mullen[1]	
kinson	Finney	Broadis	R Allen	Nicholls	Mullen	
kinson	P Harris	Sewell	Jezzard	Broadis[1]	Finney	
kinson	S Matthews	Broadis[2]	Lofthouse[2]	T Taylor	Finney	
kinson	Finney	Broadis	T Taylor	Wilshaw[1]	Mullen[1]	
kinson	S Matthews	Broadis	Lofthouse[1]	Wilshaw	Finney[1]	
low	S Matthews	Revie[1]	Lofthouse	Haynes[1]	Pilkington	
er	S Matthews	Bentley[3]	R Allen	Shackleton	Blunstone	
er	S Matthews	Bentley[1]	R Allen[1]	Shackleton[1]	Finney	
vards	S Matthews	Revie[1]	Lofthouse[2]	Wilshaw[4]	Blunstone	
vards	S Matthews	Revie	Lofthouse	Wilshaw	Blunstone	
vards	S Matthews	Bentley[1]	Lofthouse	Quixall	Wilshaw	
vards	S Matthews	Bentley	Lofthouse	Wilshaw	Blunstone	Quixall(9)
kinson	Milburn	Revie[2]	Lofthouse[2]	Bradford[1]	Finney	
kinson	S Matthews	Revie	Lofthouse	Wilshaw	Finney	†
kinson	Finney[1]	Haynes	Jezzard	Wilshaw[2]	Perry	
kinson	Finney[1]	Atyeo[1]	Lofthouse	Haynes	Perry[2]	
vards	Finney	T Taylor	Lofthouse	Haynes[1]	Perry	
vards	S Matthews	Atyeo	T Taylor[2]	Haynes	Grainger[2]	
vards	Berry	Atyeo	T Taylor	Haynes	Grainger	
vards	Astall[1]	Haynes[1]	T Taylor	Wilshaw[1]	Grainger	Lofthouse(9)[2]
vards[1]	Astall	Haynes[1]	T Taylor	Wilshaw	Grainger[1]	
vards	S Matthews[1]	Revie	T Taylor	Wilshaw	Grainger	
kinson	S Matthews	Brooks[1]	Finney[1]	Haynes[1]	Grainger	
kinson	S Matthews	Brooks[1]	Finney	Haynes	Blunstone	T Taylor(10)[2]
kinson[1]	S Matthews	Brooks	T Taylor[3]	Edwards[2]	Finney	
vards[1]	S Matthews	T Thompson	Finney	Kevan[1]	Grainger	
vards	S Matthews	Atyeo[2]	T Taylor[3]	Haynes	Finney	
vards	S Matthews	Atyeo[1]	T Taylor[2]	Haynes[1]	Finney	
vards	Finney	Atyeo[1]	T Taylor	Haynes	Pegg	
vards	Douglas	Kevan	T Taylor	Haynes[2]	Finney[1]	†
vards[1]	Douglas	Kevan	T Taylor	Haynes	A'Court[1]	
vards	Douglas	R Robson[2]	T Taylor[2]	Haynes	Finney	
ter	Douglas[1]	R Charlton[1]	Kevan[2]	Haynes	Finney	
ter	Douglas	R Charlton[2]	Kevan	Haynes	Finney	

versus	venue	result	1	2	3	4	5
Yugoslavia	A	0–5	Hopkinson	D Howe	Langley	Clayton	W Wright
USSR	A	1–1	McDonald	D Howe	T Banks	Clamp	W Wright
USSR	N	2–2	McDonald	D Howe	T Banks	Clamp	W Wright
Brazil	N	0–0	McDonald	D Howe	T Banks	Clamp	W Wright
Austria	N	2–2	McDonald	D Howe	T Banks	Clamp	W Wright
USSR	N	0–1	McDonald	D Howe	T Banks	Clamp	W Wright
1958–59							
N Ireland	A	3–3	McDonald	D Howe	T Banks	Clayton	W Wright
USSR	H	5–0	McDonald	D Howe	G Shaw	Clayton	W Wright
Wales	H	2–2	McDonald	D Howe	G Shaw	Clayton	W Wright
Scotland	H	1–0	Hopkinson	D Howe	G Shaw	Clayton	W Wright
Italy	H	2–2	Hopkinson	D Howe	G Shaw	Clayton	W Wright
Brazil	A	0–2	Hopkinson	D Howe	Armfield	Clayton	W Wright
Peru	A	1–4	Hopkinson	D Howe	Armfield	Clayton	W Wright
Mexico	A	1–2	Hopkinson	D Howe	Armfield	Clayton	W Wright
USA	A	8–1	Hopkinson	D Howe	Armfield	Clayton	W Wright
1959–60							
Wales	A	1–1	Hopkinson	D Howe	A Allen	Clayton*	T Smith
Sweden	H	2–3	Hopkinson	D Howe	A Allen	Clayton*	T Smith
N Ireland	H	2–1	R Springett	D Howe	A Allen	Clayton*	Brown
Scotland	A	1–1	R Springett	Armfield	Wilson	Clayton*	Slater
Yugoslavia	H	3–3	R Springett	Armfield	Wilson	Clayton*	Swan
Spain	A	0–3	R Springett	Armfield	Wilson	R Robson	Swan
Hungary	A	0–2	R Springett	Armfield	Wilson	R Robson	Swan
1960–61							
N Ireland	A	5–2	R Springett	Armfield	McNeil	R Robson	Swan
Luxembourg	A	9–0	R Springett	Armfield	McNeil	R Robson	Swan
Spain	H	4–2	R Springett	Armfield	McNeil	R Robson	Swan
Wales	H	5–1	Hodgkinson	Armfield	McNeil	R Robson	Swan
Scotland	H	9–3	R Springett	Armfield	McNeil	R Robson[1]	Swan
Mexico	H	8–0	R Springett	Armfield	McNeil	R Robson[1]	Swan
Portugal	A	1–1	R Springett	Armfield	McNeil	R Robson	Swan
Italy	A	3–2	R Springett	Armfield	McNeil	R Robson	Swan
Austria	A	1–3	R Springett	Armfield	Angus	Miller	Swan
1961–62							
Luxembourg	H	4–1	R Springett	Armfield*	McNeil	R Robson	Swan
Wales	A	1–1	R Springett	Armfield	Wilson	R Robson	Swan
Portugal	H	2–0	R Springett	Armfield	Wilson	R Robson	Swan
N Ireland	H	1–1	R Springett	Armfield	Wilson	R Robson	Swan
Austria	H	3–1	R Springett	Armfield	Wilson	Anderson	Swan
Scotland	A	0–2	R Springett	Armfield	Wilson	Anderson	Swan
Switzerland	H	3–1	R Springett	Armfield	Wilson	R Robson	Swan
Peru	A	4–0	R Springett	Armfield	Wilson	Moore	Norman
Hungary	N	1–2	R Springett	Armfield	Wilson	Moore	Norman
Argentina	N	3–1	R Springett	Armfield	Wilson	Moore	Norman
Bulgaria	N	0–0	R Springett	Armfield	Wilson	Moore	Norman
Brazil	N	1–3	R Springett	Armfield	Wilson	Moore	Norman
1962–63							
France	H	1–1	R Springett	Armfield*	Wilson	Moore	Norman
N Ireland	A	3–1	R Springett	Armfield*	Wilson	Moore	Labone
Wales	H	4–0	R Springett	Armfield*	G Shaw	Moore	Labone
France	A	2–5	R Springett	Armfield*	Henry	Moore	Labone
Scotland	H	1–2	G Banks	Armfield*	G Byrne	Moore	Norman
Brazil	H	1–1	G Banks	Armfield*	Wilson	Milne	Norman

*captain †own goal Small numerals goals scored Numbers after sub player replaced

	7	8	9	10	11	substitutes
er	Douglas	R Charlton	Kevan[1]	Haynes	Finney	
er	Douglas	R Robson	Kevan[1]	Haynes	Finney	
er	Douglas	R Robson	Kevan[1]	Haynes	Finney[1]	
er	Douglas	R Robson	Kevan	Haynes	A'Court	
er	Douglas	R Robson	Kevan[1]	Haynes[1]	A'Court	
er	Brabrook	Broadbent	Kevan	Haynes	A'Court	
Guinness	Brabrook	Broadbent	R Charlton[2]	Haynes	Finney[1]	
er	Douglas	R Charlton[1]	Lofthouse[1]	Haynes[3]	Finney	
vers	Clapton	Broadbent[2]	Lofthouse	Haynes	A'Court	
vers	Douglas[1]	Broadbent	R Charlton[1]	Haynes	Holden	
vers	Bradley[1]	Broadbent	R Charlton[1]	Haynes	Holden	
vers	Deeley	Broadbent	R Charlton	Haynes	Holden	
vers	Deeley	Greaves[1]	R Charlton	Haynes	Holden	
Guinness	Holden	Greaves	Kevan[1]	Haynes	R Charlton	Flowers(6) Bradley(7)
vers[2]	Bradley[1]	Greaves	Kevan[1]	Haynes[1]	R Charlton[3]	
vers	Connelly	Greaves[1]	Clough	R Charlton	Holliday	
vers	Connelly[1]	Greaves	Clough	R Charlton[1]	Holliday	
vers	Connelly	Haynes	Baker[1]	Parry[1]	Holliday	
vers	Connelly	Broadbent	Baker	Parry	R Charlton[1]	
vers	Douglas[1]	Haynes[1]	Baker	Greaves[1]	R Charlton	
vers	Brabrook	Haynes*	Baker	Greaves	R Charlton	
vers	Douglas	Haynes*	Baker	Viollet	R Charlton	
vers	Douglas[1]	Greaves[2]	R Smith[1]	Haynes*	R Charlton[1]	
vers	Douglas[1]	Greaves[3]	R Smith[2]	Haynes*[1]	R Charlton[3]	
vers	Douglas[1]	Greaves[1]	R Smith[2]	Haynes*	R Charlton[1]	
vers	Douglas[1]	Greaves[2]	R Smith[1]	Haynes*[1]	R Charlton[1]	
vers	Douglas[1]	Greaves[3]	R Smith[2]	Haynes*[2]	R Charlton	
vers[1]	Douglas[2]	Kevan	Hitchens[1]	Haynes*	R Charlton[3]	
vers[1]	Douglas	Greaves	R Smith	Haynes*	R Charlton	
vers	Douglas	Greaves[1]	Hitchens[2]	Haynes*	R Charlton	
vers	Douglas	Greaves[1]	Hitchens	Haynes*	R Charlton	
vers	Douglas	Fantham	Pointer[1]	Viollet[1]	R Charlton[2]	
vers	Connelly	Douglas[1]	Pointer	Haynes*	R Charlton	
vers	Connelly[1]	Douglas	Pointer[1]	Haynes*	R Charlton	
vers	Douglas	J Byrne	Crawford	Haynes*	R Charlton[1]	
vers[1]	Connelly	Hunt[1]	Crawford[1]	Haynes*	R Charlton	
vers	Douglas	Greaves	R Smith	Haynes*	R Charlton	
vers[1]	Connelly[1]	Greaves	Hitchens	Haynes*	R Charlton	
vers[1]	Douglas	Greaves[3]	Hitchens	Haynes*	R Charlton	
vers[1]	Douglas	Greaves	Hitchens	Haynes*	R Charlton	
vers[1]	Douglas	Greaves[1]	Peacock	Haynes*	R Charlton[1]	
vers	Douglas	Greaves	Peacock	Haynes*	R Charlton	
vers	Douglas	Greaves	Hitchens[1]	Haynes*	R Charlton	
vers[1]	Hellawell	Crowe	Charnley	Greaves	A Hinton	
vers	Hellawell	F Hill	Peacock	Greaves[1]	O'Grady[2]	
vers	Connelly[1]	F Hill	Peacock[2]	Greaves[1]	Tambling	
vers	Connelly	Tambling[1]	R Smith[1]	Greaves	R Charlton	
vers	Douglas[1]	Greaves	R Smith	Melia	R Charlton	
ore	Douglas[1]	Greaves	R Smith	Eastham	R Charlton	

versus	venue	result	1	2	3	4	5
Czechoslovakia	A	4–2	G Banks	Shellito	Wilson	Milne	Norman
E Germany	A	2–1	G Banks	Armfield*	Wilson	Milne	Norman
Switzerland	A	8–1	R Springett	Armfield*	Wilson	Kay[1]	Moore
1963–64							
Wales	A	4–0	G Banks	Armfield*	Wilson	Milne	Norman
Rest of World	H	2–1	G Banks	Armfield*	Wilson	Milne	Norman
N Ireland	H	8–3	G Banks	Armfield*	R Thomson	Milne	Norman
Scotland	A	0–1	G Banks	Armfield*	Wilson	Milne	Norman
Uruguay	H	2–1	G Banks	Cohen	Wilson	Milne	Norman
Portugal	A	4–3	G Banks	Cohen	Wilson	Milne	Norman
Rep of Ireland	A	3–1	Waiters	Cohen	Wilson	Milne	Flowers
USA	A	10–0	G Banks	Cohen	R Thomson	M Bailey	Norman
Brazil	A	1–5	Waiters	Cohen	Wilson	Milne	Norman
Portugal	N	1–1	G Banks	R Thomson	Wilson	Flowers	Norman
Argentina	N	0–1	G Banks	R Thomson	Wilson	Milne	Norman
1964–65							
N Ireland	A	4–3	G Banks	Cohen	R Thomson	Milne	Norman
Belgium	H	2–2	Waiters	Cohen	R Thomson	Milne	Norman
Wales	H	2–1	Waiters	Cohen	R Thomson	M Bailey	Flowers*
Holland	A	1–1	Waiters	Cohen	R Thomson	Mullery	Norman
Scotland	H	2–2	G Banks	Cohen	Wilson	Stiles	J Charlton
Hungary	H	1–0	G Banks	Cohen	Wilson	Stiles	J Charlton
Yugoslavia	A	1–1	G Banks	Cohen	Wilson	Stiles	J Charlton
W Germany	A	1–0	G Banks	Cohen	Wilson	Flowers	J Charlton
Sweden	A	2–1	G Banks	Cohen	Wilson	Stiles	J Charlton
1965–66							
Wales	A	0–0	R Springett	Cohen	Wilson	Stiles	J Charlton
Austria	H	2–3	R Springett	Cohen	Wilson	Stiles	J Charlton
N Ireland	H	2–1	G Banks	Cohen	Wilson	Stiles	J Charlton
Spain	A	2–0	G Banks	Cohen	Wilson	Stiles	J Charlton
Poland	H	1–1	G Banks	Cohen	Wilson	Stiles	J Charlton
W Germany	H	1–0	G Banks	Cohen	K Newton	Moore*	J Charlton
Scotland	A	4–3	G Banks	Cohen	K Newton	Stiles	J Charlton
Yugoslavia	H	2–0	G Banks	Armfield*	Wilson	Peters	J Charlton
Finland	A	3–0	G Banks	Armfield*	Wilson	Peters[1]	J Charlton
Norway	A	6–1	R Springett	Cohen	G Byrne	Stiles	Flowers
Denmark	A	2–0	Bonetti	Cohen	Wilson	Stiles	J Charlton
Poland	A	1–0	G Banks	Cohen	Wilson	Stiles	J Charlton
Uruguay	H	0–0	G Banks	Cohen	Wilson	Stiles	J Charlton
Mexico	H	2–0	G Banks	Cohen	Wilson	Stiles	J Charlton
France	H	2–0	G Banks	Cohen	Wilson	Stiles	J Charlton
Argentina	H	1–0	G Banks	Cohen	Wilson	Stiles	J Charlton
Portugal	H	2–1	G Banks	Cohen	Wilson	Stiles	J Charlton
W Germany	H	4–2	G Banks	Cohen	Wilson	Stiles	J Charlton
1966–67							
N Ireland	A	2–0	G Banks	Cohen	Wilson	Stiles	J Charlton
Czechoslovakia	H	0–0	G Banks	Cohen	Wilson	Stiles	J Charlton
Wales	H	5–1	G Banks	Cohen	Wilson	Stiles	J Charlton
Scotland	H	2–3	G Banks	Cohen	Wilson	Stiles	J Charlton
Spain	H	2–0	Bonetti	Cohen	K Newton	Mullery	Labone
Austria	A	1–0	Bonetti	K Newton	Wilson	Mullery	Labone
1967–68							
Wales	A	3–0	G Banks	Cohen	K Newton	Mullery	J Charlton
N Ireland	H	2–0	G Banks	Cohen	Wilson	Mullery	Sadler
USSR	H	2–2	G Banks	C Knowles	Wilson	Mullery	Sadler

*captain   †own goal   *Small numerals goals scored*   *Numbers after sub player replaced*

	7	8	9	10	11	substitutes
ore*	Paine	Greaves[2]	R Smith[1]	Eastham	R Charlton[1]	
ore	Paine	Hunt[1]	R Smith	Eastham	R Charlton[1]	
vers	Douglas[1]	Greaves	J Byrne[2]	Melia[1]	R Charlton[3]	
ore	Paine	Greaves[1]	R Smith[2]	Eastham	R Charlton[1]	
ore	Paine[1]	Greaves[1]	R Smith	Eastham	R Charlton	
ore	Paine[3]	Greaves[4]	R Smith[1]	Eastham	R Charlton	
ore	Paine	Hunt	J Byrne	Eastham	R Charlton	
ore*	Paine	Greaves	J Byrne[2]	Eastham	R Charlton	
ore*	P Thompson	Greaves	J Byrne[3]	Eastham	R Charlton[1]	
ore*	P Thompson	Greaves[1]	J Byrne[1]	Eastham[1]	R Charlton	
vers*	Paine[2]	Hunt[4]	Pickering[3]	Eastham	P Thompson	R Charlton(10)[1]
ore*	P Thompson	Greaves[1]	J Byrne	Eastham	R Charlton	
ore*	Paine	Greaves	J Byrne	Hunt[1]	P Thompson	
ore*	P Thompson	Greaves	J Byrne	Eastham	R Charlton	
ore*	Paine	Greaves[3]	Pickering[1]	R Charlton	P Thompson	
ore*	P Thompson	Greaves	Pickering[1]	Venables	A Hinton	
ing	P Thompson	Hunt	Wignall[2]	J Byrne	A Hinton	
vers*	P Thompson	Greaves[1]	Wignall	Venables	R Charlton	
ore*	P Thompson	Greaves[1]	Bridges	J Byrne	R Charlton[1]	
ore*	Paine	Greaves[1]	Bridges	Eastham	Connelly	
ore*	Paine	Greaves	Bridges[1]	Ball	Connelly	
ore*	Paine	Ball[1]	M Jones	Eastham	Temple	
ore*	Paine	Ball[1]	M Jones	Eastham	Connelly[1]	
ore*	Paine	Greaves	Peacock	R Charlton	Connelly	
ore*	Paine	Greaves	Bridges	R Charlton[1]	Connelly[1]	
ore*	P Thompson	Baker[1]	Peacock[1]	R Charlton	Connelly	
ore*	Ball	Hunt[1]	Baker[1]	Eastham	R Charlton	Hunter(9)
ore*[1]	Ball	Hunt	Baker	Eastham	G Harris	
nter	Ball	Hunt	Stiles[1]	G Hurst[1]	R Charlton	Wilson(3)
ore*	Ball	Hunt[2]	R Charlton[1]	G Hurst[1]	Connelly	
nter	Paine	Greaves[1]	R Charlton[1]	G Hurst	Tambling	
nter	Callaghan	Hunt[1]	R Charlton	G Hurst	Ball	
ore*[1]	Paine	Greaves[4]	R Charlton	Hunt	Connelly[1]	
ore*	Ball	Greaves	G Hurst	Eastham[1]	Connelly	
ore*	Ball	Greaves	R Charlton	Hunt[1]	Peters	
ore*	Ball	Greaves	R Charlton	Hunt	Connelly	
ore*	Paine	Greaves	R Charlton[1]	Hunt[1]	Peters	
ore*	Callaghan	Greaves	R Charlton	Hunt[2]	Peters	
ore*	Ball	G Hurst[1]	R Charlton	Hunt	Peters	
ore*	Ball	G Hurst	R Charlton[2]	Hunt	Peters	
ore*	Ball	G Hurst[3]	R Charlton	Hunt	Peters[1]	
ore*	Ball	G Hurst	R Charlton	Hunt[1]	Peters[1]	
ore*	Ball	G Hurst	R Charlton	Hunt	Peters	
ore*	Ball	G Hurst[2]	R Charlton[1]	Hunt	Peters	†
ore*	Ball	Greaves	R Charlton	G Hurst[1]	Peters	
ore*	Ball	Greaves[1]	G Hurst	Hunt[1]	Hollins	
ore*	Ball[1]	Greaves	G Hurst	Hunt	Hunter	
ore*	Ball[1]	Hunt	R Charlton[1]	G Hurst	Peters[1]	
ore*	P Thompson	Hunt	R Charlton[1]	G Hurst[1]	Peters	
ore*	Ball[1]	Hunt	R Charlton	G Hurst	Peters[1]	

versus	venue	result	1	2	3	4	5
Scotland	A	1–1	G Banks	K Newton	Wilson	Mullery	Labone
Spain	H	1–0	G Banks	C Knowles	Wilson	Mullery	J Charlton
Spain	A	2–1	Bonetti	K Newton	Wilson	Mullery	Labone
Sweden	H	3–1	Stepney	K Newton	C Knowles	Mullery	Labone
W Germany	A	0–1	G Banks	K Newton	C Knowles	Hunter	Labone
Yugoslavia	N	0–1	G Banks	K Newton	Wilson	Mullery	Labone
USSR	N	2–0	G Banks	T Wright	Wilson	Stiles	Labone
1968–69							
Romania	A	0–0	G Banks	T Wright	K Newton	Mullery	Labone
Bulgaria	H	1–1	West	K Newton	McNab	Mullery	Labone
Romania	H	1–1	G Banks	T Wright	McNab	Stiles	J Charlton
France	H	5–0	G Banks	K Newton	Cooper	Mullery	J Charlton
N Ireland	A	3–1	G Banks	K Newton	McNab	Mullery	Labone
Wales	H	2–1	West	K Newton	Cooper	Moore*	J Charlton
Scotland	H	4–1	G Banks	K Newton	Cooper	Mullery	Labone
Mexico	A	0–0	West	K Newton	Cooper	Mullery	Labone
Uruguay	A	2–1	G Banks	T Wright	K Newton	Mullery	Labone
Brazil	A	1–2	G Banks	T Wright	K Newton	Mullery	Labone
1969–70							
Holland	A	1–0	Bonetti	T Wright	E Hughes	Mullery	J Charlton
Portugal	H	1–0	Bonetti	Reaney	E Hughes	Mullery	J Charlton
Holland	H	0–0	G Banks	K Newton	Cooper	Peters	J Charlton
Belgium	A	3–1	G Banks	T Wright	Cooper	Moore*	Labone
Wales	A	1–1	G Banks	T Wright	E Hughes	Mullery	Labone
N Ireland	H	3–1	G Banks	K Newton	E Hughes	Mullery	Moore*
Scotland	A	0–0	G Banks	K Newton	E Hughes	Stiles	Labone
Colombia	A	4–0	G Banks	K Newton	Cooper	Mullery	Labone
Ecuador	A	2–0	G Banks	K Newton	Cooper	Mullery	Labone
Romania	N	1–0	G Banks	K Newton	Cooper	Mullery	Labone
Brazil	N	0–1	G Banks	T Wright	Cooper	Mullery	Labone
Czechoslovakia	N	1–0	G Banks	K Newton	Cooper	Mullery	J Charlton
W Germany	N	2–3	Bonetti	K Newton	Cooper	Mullery[1]	Labone
1970–71							
E Germany	H	3–1	Shilton	E Hughes	Cooper	Mullery	Sadler
Malta	A	1–0	G Banks	Reaney	E Hughes	Mullery*	McFarland
Greece	H	3–0	G Banks	Storey	E Hughes	Mullery	McFarland
Malta	H	5–0	G Banks	Lawler[1]	Cooper	Moore*	McFarland
N Ireland	A	1–0	G Banks	Madeley	Cooper	Storey	McFarland
Wales	H	0–0	Shilton	Lawler	Cooper	T Smith	Lloyd
Scotland	H	3–1	G Banks	Lawler	Cooper	Storey	McFarland
1971–72							
Switzerland	A	3–2	G Banks	Lawler	Cooper	Mullery	McFarland
Switzerland	H	1–1	Shilton	Madeley	Cooper	Storey	Lloyd
Greece	A	2–0	G Banks	Madeley	E Hughes	Bell	McFarland
W Germany	H	1–3	G Banks	Madeley	E Hughes	Bell	Moore*
W Germany	A	0–0	G Banks	Madeley	E Hughes	Storey	McFarland
Wales	A	3–0	G Banks	Madeley	E Hughes[1]	Storey	McFarland
N Ireland	H	0–1	Shilton	Todd	E Hughes	Storey	Lloyd
Scotland	A	1–0	G Banks	Madeley	E Hughes	Storey	McFarland

* *captain*   †*own goal*   *Small numerals goals scored*   *Numbers after sub player replaced*

	7	8	9	10	11	substitutes
re*	Ball	G Hurst	Summerbee	R Charlton	Peters[1]	
re*	Ball	Hunt	Summerbee	R Charlton[1]	Peters	
re*	Ball	Peters[1]	R Charlton	Hunt	Hunter[1]	
re*	Bell	Peters[1]	R Charlton	Hunt[1]	Hunter	G Hurst(9)
re*	Ball	Bell	Summerbee	G Hurst	P Thompson	
re*	Ball	Peters	R Charlton	Hunt	Hunter	
re*	Hunter	Hunt	R Charlton[1]	G Hurst[1]	Peters	
re*	Ball	Hunt	R Charlton	G Hurst	Peters	McNab(2)
re*	F Lee	Bell	R Charlton	G Hurst[1]	Peters	Reaney(2)
ter	Radford	Hunt	R Charlton*	G Hurst	Ball	
re*	F Lee[1]	Bell	G Hurst[3]	Peters	O`Grady[1]	
re*	Ball	F Lee[1]	R Charlton	G Hurst[1]	Peters[1]	
ter	F Lee[1]	Bell	Astle	R Charlton[1]	Ball	
re*	F Lee	Ball	R Charlton	G Hurst[2]	Peters[2]	
re*	F Lee	Ball	R Charlton	G Hurst	Peters	T Wright(2)
re*	F Lee[1]	Bell	G Hurst[1]	Ball	Peters	
re*	Ball	Bell[1]	R Charlton	G Hurst	Peters	
re*	F Lee	Bell[1]	R Charlton	G Hurst	Peters	P Thompson(7)
re*	F Lee	Bell	Astle	R Charlton	Ball	Peters(8)
ter	F Lee	Bell	M Jones	R Charlton*	I Moore	Mullery(7) G Hurst(9)
ghes	F Lee	Ball[2]	Osgood	G Hurst[1]	Peters	
re*	F Lee[1]	Ball	R Charlton	G Hurst	Peters	
s	Coates	Kidd	R Charlton[1]	G Hurst[1]	Peters[1]	Bell(2)
re*	P Thompson	Ball	Astle	G Hurst	Peters[2]	Mullery(7)
re*	F Lee	Ball[1]	R Charlton[1]	G Hurst	Peters[2]	
re*	F Lee[1]	Ball	R Charlton	G Hurst	Peters	Kidd(7)[1] Sadler(9)
re*	F Lee	Ball	R Charlton	G Hurst[1]	Peters	T Wright(2) Osgood(7)
re*	F Lee	Ball	R Charlton	G Hurst	Peters	Astle(7) Bell(9)
re*	Bell	R Charlton	Astle	A Clarke[1]	Peters	Ball(8) Osgood(9)
re*	F Lee	Ball	R Charlton	G Hurst	Peters[1]	Bell(9) Hunter(11)
re*	F Lee[1]	Ball	G Hurst	A Clarke[1]	Peters[1]	
ter	Ball	Chivers	Royle	Harvey	Peters[1]	
re*	F Lee[1]	Ball	Chivers[1]	G Hurst[1]	Peters	Coates(8)
ghes	F Lee[1]	Coates	Chivers[2]	A Clarke[1]	Peters	Ball(11)
re*	F Lee	Ball	Chivers	A Clarke[1]	Peters	
ghes	F Lee	Coates	G Hurst	A Brown	Peters*	A Clarke(8)
re*	F Lee	Ball	Chivers[2]	G Hurst	Peters[1]	A Clarke(7)
re*	F Lee	Madeley	Chivers[1]	G Hurst[1]	Peters	† Radford(10)
re*	Summerbee[1]	Ball	G Hurst	F Lee	E Hughes	Chivers(7) Marsh(10)
re*	F Lee	Ball	Chivers[1]	G Hurst[1]	Peters	
ter	F Lee[1]	Ball	Chivers	G Hurst	Peters	Marsh(10)
re*	Ball	Bell	Chivers	Marsh	Hunter	Summerbee(10) Peters(11)
re*	Summerbee	Bell[1]	Macdonald	Marsh[1]	Hunter	
ter	Summerbee	Bell*	Macdonald	Marsh	Currie	Chivers(9) Peters(11)
re*	Ball[1]	Bell	Chivers	Marsh	Hunter	Macdonald(10)

versus	venue	result	1	2	3	4	5
1972–73							
Yugoslavia	H	1–1	Shilton	Mills	Lampard	Storey	Blockley
Wales	A	1–0	Clemence	Storey	E Hughes	Hunter	McFarla
Wales	H	1–1	Clemence	Storey	E Hughes	Hunter[1]	McFarla
Scotland	A	5–0	Shilton	Storey	E Hughes	Bell	Madeley
N Ireland	A	2–1	Shilton	Storey	Nish	Bell	McFarla
Wales	H	3–0	Shilton	Storey	E Hughes	Bell	McFarla
Scotland	H	1–0	Shilton	Storey	E Hughes	Bell	McFarla
Czechoslovakia	A	1–1	Shilton	Madeley	Storey	Bell	McFarla
Poland	A	0–2	Shilton	Madeley	E Hughes	Storey	McFarla
USSR	A	2–1	Shilton	Madeley	E Hughes	Storey	McFarla
Italy	A	0–2	Shilton	Madeley	E Hughes	Storey	McFarla
1973–74							
Austria	H	7–0	Shilton	Madeley	E Hughes	Bell[1]	McFarla
Poland	H	1–1	Shilton	Madeley	E Hughes	Bell	McFarla
Italy	H	0–1	Shilton	Madeley	E Hughes	Bell	McFarla
Portugal	A	0–0	Parkes	Nish	Pejic	Dobson	Watson
Wales	A	2–0	Shilton	Nish	Pejic	E Hughes*	McFarla
N Ireland	H	1–0	Shilton	Nish	Pejic	E Hughes*	McFarla
Scotland	A	0–2	Shilton	Nish	Pejic	E Hughes*	Hunter
Argentina	H	2–2	Shilton	E Hughes*	Lindsay	Todd	Watson
E Germany	A	1–1	Clemence	E Hughes*	Lindsay	Todd	Watson
Bulgaria	A	1–0	Clemence	E Hughes*	Todd	Watson	Lindsay
Yugoslavia	A	2–2	Clemence	E Hughes*	Lindsay	Todd	Watson
1974–75							
Czechoslovakia	H	3–0	Clemence	Madeley	E Hughes*	Dobson	Watson
Portugal	H	0–0	Clemence	Madeley	Watson	E Hughes*	Cooper
W Germany	H	2–0	Clemence	Whitworth	Gillard	Bell[1]	Watson
Cyprus	H	5–0	Shilton	Madeley	Watson	Todd	Beattie
Cyprus	A	1–0	Clemence	Whitworth	Beattie	Watson	Todd
N Ireland	A	0–0	Clemence	Whitworth	E Hughes	Bell	Watson
Wales	H	2–2	Clemence	Whitworth	Gillard	G Francis	Watson
Scotland	H	5–1	Clemence	Whitworth	Beattie[1]	Bell[1]	Watson
1975–76							
Switzerland	A	2–1	Clemence	Whitworth	Todd	Watson	Beattie
Czechoslovakia	A	1–2	Clemence	Madeley	Gillard	G Francis*	McFarla
Portugal	A	1–1	Clemence	Whitworth	Beattie	G Francis*	Watson
Wales	A	2–1	Clemence	Cherry	Mills	Neal	P Thomp
Wales	A	1–0	Clemence	Clement	Mills	Towers	Greenho
N Ireland	H	4–0	Clemence	Todd	Mills	P Thompson	Greenho
Scotland	A	1–2	Clemence	Todd	Mills	P Thompson	McFarla
Brazil	N	0–1	Clemence	Todd	Doyle	P Thompson	Mills
Italy	N	3–2	Rimmer	Clement	Neal	P Thompson[1]	Doyle

*captain   †own goal   Small numerals goals scored   Numbers after sub player replaced

	7	8	9	10	11	substitutes
re*	Ball	Channon	Royle[1]	Bell	Marsh	
re*	Keegan	Chivers	Marsh	Bell[1]	Ball	
re*	Keegan	Bell	Chivers	Marsh	Ball	
re*	Ball	Channon[1]	Chivers[1]	A Clarke[2]	Peters	†
re*	Ball	Channon	Chivers[2]	Richards	Peters	
re*	Ball	Channon[1]	Chivers[1]	A Clarke	Peters[1]	
re*	Ball	Channon	Chivers	A Clarke	Peters[1]	
re*	Ball	Channon	Chivers	A Clarke[1]	Peters	
re*	Ball	Bell	Chivers	A Clarke	Peters	
re*	Currie	Channon	Chivers[1]	A Clarke	Peters	† Summerbee(8) Macdonald(10) Hunter(11)
re*	Currie	Channon	Chivers	A Clarke	Peters	
ter	Currie[1]	Channon[2]	Chivers[1]	A Clarke[2]	Peters*	
ter	Currie	Channon	Chivers	A Clarke[1]	Peters*	Hector(9)
re*	Currie	Channon	Osgood	A Clarke	Peters	Hector(10)
d	Bowles	Channon	Macdonald	Brooking	Peters*	Ball(9)
d	Keegan[1]	Bell	Channon	Weller	Bowles[1]	
d	Keegan	Weller[1]	Channon	Bell	Bowles	Hunter(5) Worthington(11)
d	Channon	Bell	Worthington	Weller	Peters	Watson(5) Macdonald(9)
	Keegan	Channon[1]	Worthington[1]	Weller	Brooking	
son	Keegan	Channon[1]	Worthington	Bell	Brooking	
son	Brooking	Bell	Keegan	Channon	Worthington[1]	
son	Keegan[1]	Channon[1]	Worthington	Bell	Brooking	Macdonald(9)
ter	Bell[2]	G Francis	Worthington	Channon[1]	Keegan	Brooking(4) Thomas(9)
king	G Francis	Bell	Thomas	Channon	A Clarke	Todd(5) Worthington(11)
d	Ball*	Macdonald[1]	Channon	Hudson	Keegan	
	Ball*	Hudson	Channon	Macdonald[5]	Keegan	Thomas(9)
	Thomas	Ball*	Channon	Macdonald	Keegan[1]	E Hughes(3) Tueart(11)
d	Ball*	Viljoen	Macdonald	Keegan	Tueart	Channon(9)
d	Ball*	Channon	Johnson[2]	Viljoen	Thomas	Little(8)
d	Ball*	Channon	Johnson[1]	G Francis[2]	Keegan	Thomas(11)
	Currie	G Francis*	Channon[1]	Johnson	Keegan[1]	Macdonald(10)
	Keegan	Channon[1]	Macdonald	A Clarke	Bell	Watson(5) Thomas(8)
	Keegan	Channon[1]	Macdonald	Brooking	Madeley	Thomas(9) A Clarke(11)
e	Keegan*	Channon	Boyer	Brooking	Kennedy[1]	Clement(2) P Taylor(8)[1]
ompson	Keegan	G Francis*	Pearson	Kennedy	P Taylor[1]	
edy	Keegan	G Francis*[1]	Pearson[1]	Channon[2]	P Taylor	Royle(7) Towers(11)
edy	Keegan	G Francis*	Pearson	Channon[1]	P Taylor	Doyle(5) Cherry(9)
ancis*	Cherry	Brooking	Keegan	Pearson	Channon	
ers	Wilkins	Brooking	Royle	Channon*[2]	Hill	Corrigan(1) Mills(3)

versus	venue	result	1	2	3	4	5
Finland	A	4–1	Clemence	Todd	Mills	P Thompson	Madeley
1976–77							
Rep of Ireland	H	1–1	Clemence	Todd	Madeley	Cherry	McFarla
Finland	H	2–1	Clemence	Todd	Beattie	P Thompson	Greenho
Italy	A	0–2	Clemence	Clement	Mills	Greenhoff	McFarla
Holland	H	0–2	Clemence	Clement	Beattie	Doyle	Watson
Luxembourg	H	5–0	Clemence	Gidman	Cherry	Kennedy[1]	Watson
N Ireland	A	2–1	Shilton	Cherry	Mills	Greenhoff	Watson
Wales	H	0–1	Shilton	Neal	Mills	Greenhoff	Watson
Scotland	H	1–2	Clemence	Neal	Mills	Greenhoff	Watson
Brazil	A	0–0	Clemence	Neal	Cherry	Greenhoff	Watson
Argentina	A	1–1	Clemence	Neal	Cherry	Greenhoff	Watson
Uruguay	A	0–0	Clemence	Neal	Cherry	Greenhoff	Watson
1977–78							
Switzerland	H	0–0	Clemence	Neal	Cherry	McDermott	Watson
Luxembourg	A	2–0	Clemence	Cherry	Watson	E Hughes*	Kennedy
Italy	H	2–0	Clemence	Neal	Cherry	Wilkins	Watson
W Germany	A	1–2	Clemence	Neal	Mills	Wilkins	Watson
Brazil	H	1–1	Corrigan	Mills	Cherry	Greenhoff	Watson
Wales	A	3–1	Shilton	Mills*	Cherry	Greenhoff	Watson
N Ireland	H	1–0	Clemence	Neal[1]	Mills	Wilkins	Watson
Scotland	A	1–0	Clemence	Neal	Mills	Currie	Watson
Hungary	H	4–1	Shilton	Neal[1]	Mills	Wilkins	Watson
1978–79							
Denmark	A	4–3	Clemence	Neal[1]	Mills	Wilkins	Watson
Rep of Ireland	A	1–1	Clemence	Neal	Mills	Wilkins	Watson
Czechoslovakia	H	1–0	Shilton	Anderson	Cherry	P Thompson	Watson
N Ireland	H	4–0	Clemence	Neal	Mills	Currie	Watson[1]
N Ireland	A	2–0	Clemence	Neal	Mills*	P Thompson	Watson[1]
Wales	H	0–0	Corrigan	Cherry	Sansom	Wilkins	Watson
Scotland	H	3–1	Clemence	Neal	Mills	P Thompson	Watson[1]
Bulgaria	A	3–0	Clemence	Neal	Mills	P Thompson	Watson[1]
Sweden	A	0–0	Shilton	Anderson	Cherry	McDermott	Watson
Austria	A	3–4	Shilton	Neal	Mills	P Thompson	Watson
1979–80							
Denmark	H	1–0	Clemence	Neal	Mills	P Thompson	Watson
N Ireland	A	5–1	Shilton	Neal	Mills	P Thompson	Watson[1]
Bulgaria	H	2–0	Clemence	Anderson	Sansom	P Thompson*	Watson[1]
Rep of Ireland	H	2–0	Clemence	Cherry	Sansom	P Thompson	Watson
Spain	A	2–0	Shilton	Neal	Mills	P Thompson	Watson

*captain †own goal *Small numerals goals scored* *Numbers after sub player replaced*

	7	8	9	10	11	substitutes
	Keegan[2]	Channon[1]	Pearson[1]	Brooking	G Francis*	
hoff	Keegan*	Wilkins	Pearson[1]	Brooking	George	Hill(11)
as	Keegan*	Channon	Royle[1]	Brooking	Tueart[1]	Mills(10) Hill(11)
hes	Keegan*	Channon	Bowles	Cherry	Brooking	Beattie(2)
ey	Keegan*	Greenhoff	T Francis	Bowles	Brooking	Pearson(6) Todd(8)
hes	Keegan*[1]	Channon[2]	Royle	T Francis[1]	Hill	Mariner(9)
	Wilkins	Channon*[1]	Mariner	Brooking	Tueart[1]	Talbot(7)
hes	Keegan*	Channon	Pearson	Brooking	Kennedy	Tueart(10)
hes*	T Francis	Channon[1]	Pearson	Talbot	Kennedy	Cherry(4) Tueart(11)
hes	Keegan*	T Francis	Pearson	Wilkins	Talbot	Channon(9) Kennedy(10)
hes	Keegan*	Channon	Pearson[1]	Wilkins	Talbot	Kennedy(4)
hes	Keegan*	Channon	Pearson	Wilkins	Talbot	
hes*	Keegan	Channon	T Francis	Kennedy	Callaghan	Hill(8) Wilkins(11)
han	McDermott	Wilkins	T Francis	Mariner[1]	Hill	Beattie(3) Whymark(7)
hes*	Keegan[1]	Coppell	Latchford	Brooking[1]	P Barnes	T Francis(7) Pearson(9)
hes*	Keegan	Coppell	Pearson[1]	Brooking	P Barnes	T Francis(7)
	Keegan*[1]	Coppell	Latchford	T Francis	P Barnes	
s	Coppell	T Francis	Latchford[1]	Brooking	P Barnes[1]	Currie(3)[1] Mariner(9)
hes*	Currie	Coppell	Pearson	Woodcock	Greenhoff	
hes*	Wilkins	Coppell[1]	Mariner	T Francis	P Barnes	Greenhoff(6) Brooking(9)
hes*	Keegan	Coppell	T Francis[1]	Brooking	P Barnes[1]	Greenhoff(5) Currie(8)[1]
hes*	Keegan[2]	Coppell	Latchford[1]	Brooking	P Barnes	
hes*	Keegan	Coppell	Latchford[1]	Brooking	P Barnes	P Thompson(5) Woodcock(11) Latchford(9)
s	Keegan*	Coppell[1]	Woodcock	Currie	P Barnes	
hes*	Keegan[1]	Coppell	Latchford[2]	Brooking	P Barnes	
s	Coppell[1]	McDermott	Latchford	Currie	P Barnes	
hes*	Keegan	Currie	Latchford	McDermott	Cunningham	Brooking(4) Coppell(7)
s	Keegan*[1]	Coppell[1]	Latchford	Brooking	P Barnes[1]	
s	Keegan*[1]	Coppell	Latchford	Brooking	P Barnes[1]	T Francis(9) Woodcock(11) Wilkins(4)
hes*	Keegan	Currie	T Francis	Woodcock	Cunningham	Brooking(8)
s[1]	Keegan*[1]	Coppell[1]	Latchford	Brooking	P Barnes	Clemence(1) T Francis(9) Cunningham(11)
s	Coppell	McDermott	Keegan*[1]	Brooking	P Barnes	
s	Keegan*	Coppell	T Francis[2]	Brooking	Woodcock[2]	† McDermott(10)
s	Reeves	Hoddle[1]	T Francis	Kennedy	Woodcock	
u	Keegan*[2]	McDermott	Johnson	Woodcock	Cunningham	Coppell(9)
s	Keegan*	Coppell	T Francis[1]	Kennedy	Woodcock	E Hughes(2) Cunningham(9)

versus	venue	result	1	2	3	4	5
Argentina	H	3–1	Clemence	Neal	Sansom	P Thompson	Watson
Wales	A	1–4	Clemence	Neal	Cherry	P Thompson*	Lloyd
N Ireland	H	1–1	Corrigan	Cherry	Sansom	E Hughes*	Watson
Scotland	A	2–0	Clemence	Cherry	Sansom	P Thompson*	Watson
Australia	A	2–1	Corrigan	Cherry*	Lampard	Talbot	Osman
Belgium	N	1–1	Clemence	Neal	Sansom	P Thompson	Watson
Italy	A	0–1	Shilton	Neal	Sansom	P Thompson	Watson
Spain	N	2–1	Clemence	Anderson	Mills	P Thompson	Watson
1980–81							
Norway	H	4–0	Shilton	Anderson	Sansom	P Thompson*	Watson
Romania	A	1–2	Clemence	Neal	Sansom	P Thompson*	Watson
Switzerland	H	2–1	Shilton	Neal	Sansom	Robson	Watson
Spain	H	1–2	Clemence	Neal	Sansom	Robson	Butcher
Romania	H	0–0	Shilton	Anderson	Sansom	Robson	Watson
Brazil	H	0–1	Clemence*	Neal	Sansom	Robson	Martin
Wales	H	0–0	Corrigan	Anderson	Sansom	Robson	Watson
Scotland	H	0–1	Corrigan	Anderson	Sansom	Wilkins	Watson
Switzerland	A	1–2	Clemence	Mills	Sansom	Wilkins	Watson
Hungary	A	3–1	Clemence	Neal	Mills	P Thompson	Watson
1981–82							
Norway	A	1–2	Clemence	Neal	Mills	P Thompson	Osman
Hungary	H	1–0	Shilton	Neal	Mills	P Thompson	Martin
N Ireland	H	4–0	Clemence	Anderson	Sansom	Wilkins	Watson
Wales	A	1–0	Corrigan	Neal	Sansom	P Thompson*	Butcher
Holland	H	2–0	Shilton*	Neal	Sansom	P Thompson	Foster
Scotland	A	1–0	Shilton	Mills	Sansom	P Thompson	Butcher
Iceland	A	1–1	Corrigan	Anderson	Neal*	Watson	Osman
Finland	A	4–1	Clemence	Mills	Sansom	P Thompson	Martin
France	N	3–1	Shilton	Mills*	Sansom	P Thompson	Butcher
Czechoslovakia	N	2–0	Shilton	Mills*	Sansom	P Thompson	Butcher
Kuwait	N	1–0	Shilton	Neal	Mills*	P Thompson	Foster
W Germany	N	0–0	Shilton	Mills*	Sansom	P Thompson	Butcher
Spain	A	0–0	Shilton	Mills*	Sansom	P Thompson	Butcher
1982–83							
Denmark	A	2–2	Shilton	Neal	Sansom	Wilkins*	Osman
W Germany	H	1–2	Shilton	Mabbutt	Sansom	P Thompson	Butcher

* captain   †own goal   Small numerals goals scored   Numbers after sub player replaced

	7	8	9	10	11	substitutes
as	Keegan*[1]	Coppell	Johnson[2]	Woodcock	Kennedy	Cherry(2) Birtles(9) Brooking(11)
dy	Coppell	Hoddle	Mariner[1]	Brooking	P Barnes	Sansom(2) Wilkins(5)
as	Reeves	McDermott	Johnson[1]	Brooking	Devonshire	Mariner(7)
as	Coppell[1]	McDermott	Johnson	Mariner	Brooking[1]	Hughes(10)
er	Robson	Sunderland	Mariner[1]	Hoddle[1]	Armstrong	Greenhoff(7) Ward(8) Devonshire(11)
as[1]	Keegan*	Coppell	Johnson	Woodcock	Brooking	McDermott(8) Kennedy(9)
as	Keegan*	Coppell	Birtles	Kennedy	Woodcock	Mariner(9)
as	McDermott	Hoddle	Keegan*	Woodcock[1]	Brooking[1]	Cherry(3) Mariner(8)
in	Gates	McDermott[2]	Mariner[1]	Woodcock[1]	Rix	
in	Rix	McDermott	Birtles	Woodcock[1]	Gates	Cunningham(9) Coppell(11)
a	Coppell	McDermott	Mariner[1]	Brooking	Woodcock	† Rix(10)
a	Keegan*	T Francis	Mariner	Brooking	Hoddle[1]	P Barnes(8) Wilkins(10)
a	Wilkins	Brooking	Coppell	T Francis	Woodcock	McDermott(8)
as	Coppell	McDermott	Withe	Rix	P Barnes	
s	Coppell	Hoddle	Withe	Rix	P Barnes	Woodcock(9)
in	Coppell	Hoddle	Withe	Rix	Woodcock	Martin(5) T Francis(11)
a	Coppell	Robson	Keegan*	Mariner	T Francis	P Barnes(5) McDermott(11)[1]
n	Coppell	McDermott	Mariner	Brooking[2]	Keegan*[1]	Wilkins(10)
in[1]	Keegan*	T Francis	Mariner	Hoddle	McDermott	Withe(9) P Barnes(10)
in	Keegan*	Coppell[1]	Mariner[1]	Brooking	McDermott	Morley(8)
	Keegan*[1]	Robson[1]	T Francis	Hoddle[1]	Morley	Regis(9) Woodcock(11)
in	Wilkins	T Francis[1]	Withe	Hoddle	Morley	McDermott(8) Regis(10)
in	Wilkins	Devonshire	Mariner[1]	McDermott	Woodcock[1]	Rix(8) P Barnes(9)
in	Keegan*	Coppell	Mariner[1]	Brooking	Wilkins	McDermott(7) T Francis(9)
mott	Hoddle	Devonshire	Withe	Regis	Morley	Perryman(8) Goddard(10)[1]
n[2]	Keegan*	Coppell	Mariner[2]	Brooking	Wilkins	Rix(6) T Francis(8) Woodcock(10)
n[2]	Coppell	T Francis[1]	Mariner[1]	Rix	Wilkins	Neal(3)
n	Coppell	T Francis[1]	Mariner	Rix	Wilkins	† Hoddle(6)
e	Coppell	T Francis[1]	Mariner	Rix	Wilkins	
n	Coppell	T Francis	Mariner	Rix	Wilkins	Woodcock(8)
n	Rix	T Francis	Mariner	Woodcock	Wilkins	Brooking(7) Keegan(10)
r	Morley	Robson	Mariner	T Francis[2]	Rix	R Hill(7)
s*	R Hill	Regis	Mariner	Armstrong	Devonshire	Woodcock(8)[1] Blissett(9) Rix(10)

versus	venue	result	1	2	3	4	5
Greece	A	3–0	Shilton	Neal	Sansom	P Thompson	Martin
Luxembourg	H	9–0	Clemence	Neal[1]	Sansom	Robson*	Martin
Wales	H	2–1	Shilton*	Neal[1]	Statham	S Lee	Martin
Greece	H	0–0	Shilton*	Neal	Sansom	S Lee	Martin
Hungary	H	2–0	Shilton*	Neal	Sansom	S Lee	Martin
N Ireland	A	0–0	Shilton*	Neal	Sansom	Hoddle	Roberts
Scotland	H	2–0	Shilton	Neal	Sansom	S Lee	Roberts
Australia	A	0–0	Shilton*	Thomas	Statham	Williams	Osman
Australia	A	1–0	Shilton*	Neal	Statham	Barham	Osman
Australia	A	1–1	Shilton*	Neal	Pickering	S Lee	Osman
1983–84							
Denmark	H	0–1	Shilton	Neal	Sansom	S Lee	Osman
Hungary	A	3–0	Shilton	Gregory	Sansom	S Lee[1]	Martin
Luxembourg	A	4–0	Clemence	Duxbury	Sansom	S Lee	Martin
France	A	0–2	Shilton	Duxbury	Sansom	S Lee	Roberts
N Ireland	H	1–0	Shilton	Anderson	A Kennedy	S Lee	Roberts
Wales	A	0–1	Shilton	Duxbury	A Kennedy	S Lee	Martin
Scotland	A	1–1	Shilton	Duxbury	Sansom	Wilkins	Roberts
USSR	H	0–2	Shilton	Duxbury	Sansom	Wilkins	Roberts
Brazil	A	2–0	Shilton	Duxbury	Sansom	Wilkins	Watson
Uruguay	A	0–2	Shilton	Duxbury	Sansom	Wilkins	Watson
Chile	A	0–0	Shilton	Duxbury	Sansom	Wilkins	Watson
1984–85							
E Germany	H	1–0	Shilton	Duxbury	Sansom	Williams	Wright
Finland	H	5–0	Shilton	Duxbury	Sansom[1]	Williams	Wright
Turkey	A	8–0	Shilton	Anderson[1]	Sansom	Williams	Wright
N Ireland	A	1–0	Shilton	Anderson	Sansom	Steven	Martin
Rep of Ireland	H	2–1	Bailey	Anderson	Sansom	Steven[1]	Wright
Romania	A	0–0	Shilton	Anderson	Sansom	Steven	Wright
Finland	A	1–1	Shilton	Anderson	Sansom	Steven	Fenwick
Scotland	A	0–1	Shilton	Anderson	Sansom	Hoddle	Fenwick
Italy	N	1–2	Shilton	Stevens	Sansom	Steven	Wright
Mexico	A	0–1	Bailey	Anderson	Sansom	Hoddle	Fenwick
W Germany	N	3–0	Shilton	Stevens	Sansom	Hoddle	Wright

* captain   †own goal   *Small numerals goals scored*   *Numbers after sub player replaced*

	7	8	9	10	11	substitutes
on*	S Lee[1]	Mabbutt	Mariner	Woodcock[2]	Morley	
er	Coppell[1]	S Lee	Woodcock[1]	Blissett[3]	Mabbutt	† Chamberlain(7)[1] Hoddle(11)[1]
er[1]	Mabbutt	Blissett	Mariner	Cowans	Devonshire	
er	Coppell	Mabbutt	T Francis	Woodcock	Devonshire	Blissett(10) Rix(11)
er	Mabbutt	T Francis[1]	Withe[1]	Blissett	Cowans	
er	Mabbutt	T Francis	Withe	Blissett	Cowans	J Barnes(10)
er	Robson*[1]	T Francis	Withe	Hoddle	Cowans[1]	Mabbutt(7) Blissett(9)
er	Barham	Gregory	Blissett	T Francis	Cowans	J Barnes(3) Walsh(9)
er	Gregory	T Francis	Walsh[1]	Cowans	J Barnes	Williams(3)
er	Gregory	T Francis[1]	Walsh	Cowans	J Barnes	Spink(1) Thomas(2) Blissett(9)
er	Wilkins*	Gregory	Mariner	T Francis	J Barnes	Blissett(4) Chamberlain(11)
er	Robson*	Hoddle[1]	Mariner[1]	Blissett	Mabbutt	Withe(10)
er[1]	Robson*[2]	Hoddle	Mariner[1]	Woodcock	Devonshire	J Barnes(10)
er	Robson*	Stein	Walsh	Hoddle	Willams	J Barnes(4) Woodcock(8)
er	Robson*	Wilkins	Woodcock[1]	T Francis	Rix	
t	Wilkins*	Gregory	Walsh	Woodcock	Armstrong	Fenwick(5) Blissett(11)
ck	Chamberlain	Robson*	Woodcock[1]	Blissett	J Barnes	Hunt(7) Lineker(9)
ck	Chamberlain	Robson*	T Francis ·	Blissett	J Barnes	Hateley(9) Hunt(11)
ck	Robson*	Chamberlain	Hateley[1]	Woodcock	J Barnes[1]	Allen(10)
ck	Robson*	Chamberlain	Hateley	Allen	J Barnes	Woodcock(10)
ck	Robson*	Chamberlain	Hateley	Allen	J Barnes	S Lee(8)
r	Robson*[1]	Wilkins	Mariner	Woodcock	J Barnes	Hateley(9) T Francis(10)
er	Robson*[1]	Wilkins	Hateley[2]	Woodcock[1]	J Barnes	G A Stevens(2) Chamberlain(7)
er	Robson*[3]	Wilkins	Withe	Woodcock[2]	J Barnes[2]	G A Stevens(4) T Francis(10)
er	Stevens	Wilkins*	Hateley[1]	Woodcock	J Barnes	T Francis(10)
er	Robson*	Wilkins	Hateley	Lineker[1]	Waddle	Hoddle(7) Davenport(9)
er	Robson*	Wilkins	Mariner	T Francis	J Barnes	Lineker(9) Waddle(11)
er	Robson*	Wilkins	Hateley[1]	T Francis	J Barnes	Waddle(4)
er	Robson*	Wilkins	Hateley	T Francis	J Barnes	Lineker(4) Waddle(11)
er	Robson*	Wilkins	Hateley[1]	T Francis	Waddle	Hoddle(4) Lineker(10) J Barnes(11)
n	Robson*	Wilkins	Hateley	T Francis	J Barnes	K Dixon(4) Reid(8) Waddle(11)
er	Robson*[1]	Reid	K Dixon[2]	Lineker	Waddle	Bracewell(7) J Barnes(10)

versus	venue	result	1	2	3	4	5
USA	A	5–0	Woods	Anderson	Sansom	Hoddle	Fenwick
1985–86							
Romania	H	1–1	Shilton	Stevens	Sansom	Reid	Wright
Turkey	H	5–0	Shilton	Stevens	Sansom	Hoddle	Wright
N Ireland	H	0–0	Shilton	G A Stevens	Sansom	Hoddle	Wright
Egypt	A	4–0	Shilton	Stevens	Sansom	Cowans[1]	Wright
Israel	A	2–1	Shilton	Stevens	Sansom	Hoddle	Martin
USSR	A	1–0	Shilton	Anderson	Sansom	Hoddle	Wright
Scotland	H	2–1	Shilton	Stevens	Sansom	Hoddle[1]	Watson
Mexico	N	3–0	Shilton	Anderson	Sansom	Hoddle	Fenwick
Canada	A	1–0	Shilton	Stevens	Sansom	Hoddle	Martin
Portugal	N	0–1	Shilton	Stevens	Sansom	Hoddle	Fenwick
Morocco	N	0–0	Shilton	Stevens	Sansom	Hoddle	Fenwick
Poland	N	3–0	Shilton*	Stevens	Sansom	Hoddle	Fenwick
Paraguay	N	3–0	Shilton*	Stevens	Sansom	Hoddle	Martin
Argentina	N	1–2	Shilton*	Stevens	Sansom	Hoddle	Fenwick
1986–87							
Sweden	A	0–1	Shilton*	Anderson	Sansom	Hoddle	Martin
N Ireland	H	3–0	Shilton	Anderson	Sansom	Hoddle	Watson
Yugoslavia	H	2–0	Woods	Anderson[1]	Sansom	Hoddle	Wright
Spain	A	4–2	Shilton	Anderson	Sansom	Hoddle	Adams
N Ireland	A	2–0	Shilton	Anderson	Sansom	Mabbutt	Wright
Turkey	A	0–0	Woods	Anderson	Sansom	Hoddle	Adams
Brazil	H	1–1	Shilton	Stevens	Pearce	Reid	Adams
Scotland	A	0–0	Woods	Stevens	Pearce	Hoddle	Wright
1987–88							
W Germany	A	1–3	Shilton*	Anderson	Sansom	Hoddle	Adams
Turkey	H	8–0	Shilton	Stevens	Sansom	Steven	Adams
Yugoslavia	A	4–1	Shilton	Stevens	Sansom	Steven	Adams[1]
Israel	A	0–0	Woods	Stevens	Pearce	Webb	Watson
Holland	H	2–2	Shilton*	Stevens	Sansom	Steven	Adams[1]

* captain   †own goal   Small numerals goals scored   Numbers after sub player replaced

	7	8	9	10	11	substitutes
ner	Robson*	Bracewell	K Dixon[2]	Lineker[2]	Waddle	Watson(3) Steven(4)[1] Reid(7) J Barnes(11)
ick	Robson*	Hoddle[1]	Hateley	Lineker	Waddle	Woodcock(10) J Barnes(11)
ick	Robson*[1]	Wilkins	Hateley	Lineker[3]	Waddle[1]	Steven(7) Woodcock(9)
ick	Bracewell	Wilkins*	K Dixon	Lineker	Waddle	
ick	Steven[1]	Wilkins*	Hateley	Lineker	Wallace[1]	† Woods(1) R Hill(7) Beardsley(10)
ner	Robson*[2]	Wilkins	K Dixon	Beardsley	Waddle	Woods(1) Woodcock(9) J Barnes(11)
ner	Cowans	Wilkins*	Beardsley	Lineker	Waddle[1]	Hodge(7) Steven(11)
ner[1]	Wilkins*	T Francis	Hateley	Hodge	Waddle	Reid(7) G A Stevens(10)
аer	Robson*	Wilkins	Hateley[2]	Beardsley[1]	Waddle	G A Stevens(7) Steven(8) K Dixon(9)
аer	Hodge	Wilkins*	Hateley[1]	Lineker	Waddle	Woods(1) Reid(8) Beardsley(10) J Barnes(11)
аer	Robson*	Wilkins	Hateley	Lineker	Waddle	Hodge(7) Beardsley(11)
аer	Robson*	Wilkins	Hateley	Lineker	Waddle	Hodge(7) G A Stevens(9)
аer	Hodge	Reid	Beardsley	Lineker[3]	Steven	Waddle(9)
аer	Hodge	Reid	Beardsley[1]	Lineker[2]	Steven	G A Stevens(8) Hateley(9)
аer	Hodge	Reid	Beardsley	Lineker[1]	Steven	Waddle(8) J Barnes(11)
аer	Steven	Wilkins	K Dixon	Hodge	J Barnes	Cottee(7) Waddle(11)
аer	Robson*	Hodge	Beardsley	Lineker[2]	Waddle[1]	Cottee(9)
аer*	Mabbutt[1]	Hodge	Beardsley	Lineker	Waddle	Wilkins(8) Steven(11)
аer	Robson*	Hodge	Beardsley	Lineker[4]	Waddle	Woods(1) Steven(11)
аer	Robson*[1]	Hodge	Beardsley	Lineker	Waddle[1]	Woods(1)
оutt	Robson*	Hodge	Allen	Lineker	Waddle	J Barnes(8) Hateley(9)
аer	Robson*	J Barnes	Beardsley	Lineker[1]	Waddle	Hateley(10)
аer	Robson*	Hodge	Beardsley	Hateley	Waddle	
оutt	Reid	J Barnes	Beardsley	Lineker[1]	Waddle	Pearce(3) Webb(4) Hateley(11)
аer	Robson*[1]	Webb[1]	Beardsley[1]	Lineker[3]	J Barnes[2]	Hoddle(4) Regis(9)
аer	Robson*[1]	Webb	Beardsley[1]	Lineker	J Barnes[1]	Reid(7) Hoddle(8)
nt	Allen	McMahon	Beardsley*	J Barnes	Waddle	Fenwick(6) Harford(7)
оn	Robson	Webb	Beardsley	Lineker[1]	J Barnes	Wright(6) Hoddle(8) Hateley(9)

versus	venue	result	1	2	3	4	5
Hungary	A	0–0	Woods	Anderson	Pearce	Steven	Adams
Scotland	H	1–0	Shilton	Stevens	Sansom	Webb	Watson
Colombia	H	1–1	Shilton	Anderson	Sansom	McMahon	Wright
Switzerland	A	1–0	Shilton	Stevens	Sansom	Webb	Wright
Rep of Ireland	N	0–1	Shilton	Stevens	Sansom	Webb	Wright
Holland	N	1–3	Shilton	Stevens	Sansom	Hoddle	Wright
USSR	N	1–3	Woods	Stevens	Sansom	Hoddle	Watson
1988–89							
Denmark	H	1–0	Shilton	Stevens	Pearce	Rocastle	Adams
Sweden	H	0–0	Shilton	Stevens	Pearce	Webb	Adams
Saudi Arabia	A	1–1	Seaman	Sterland	Pearce	M Thomas	Adams[1]
Greece	A	2–1	Shilton	Stevens	Pearce	Webb	Walker
Albania	A	2–0	Shilton	Stevens	Pearce	Webb	Walker
Albania	H	5–0	Shilton	Stevens	Pearce	Webb	Walker
Chile	H	0–0	Shilton	Parker	Pearce	Webb	Walker
Scotland	A	2–0	Shilton	Stevens	Pearce	Webb	Walker
Poland	H	3–0	Shilton	Stevens	Pearce	Webb[1]	Walker
Denmark	A	1–1	Shilton	Parker	Pearce	Webb	Walker
1989–90							
Sweden	A	0–0	Shilton	Stevens	Pearce	Webb	Walker
Poland	A	0–0	Shilton	Stevens	Pearce	McMahon	Walker
Italy	H	0–0	Shilton	Stevens	Pearce	McMahon	Walker
Yugoslavia	H	2–1	Shilton	Parker	Pearce	M Thomas	Walker
Brazil	H	1–0	Shilton	Stevens	Pearce	McMahon	Walker

*captain   †own goal   *Small numerals goals scored*   *Numbers after sub player replaced*

	7	8	9	10	11	substitutes
ter	Robson*	McMahon	Beardsley	Lineker	Waddle	Stevens(3) Hateley(9) Cottee(10) Hoddle(11)
us	Robson*	Steven	Beardsley[1]	Lineker	J Barnes	Waddle(8)
us	Robson*	Waddle	Beardsley	Lineker[1]	J Barnes	Hoddle(8) Hateley(9)
us	Robson*	Steven	Beardsley	Lineker[1]	J Barnes	Woods(1) Watson(6) Reid(7) Waddle(8)
us	Robson*	Waddle	Beardsley	Lineker	J Barnes	Hoddle(4) Hateley(9)
us	Robson*[1]	Steven	Beardsley	Lineker	J Barnes	Waddle(8) Hateley(9)
us[1]	Robson*	Steven	McMahon	Lineker	J Barnes	Webb(9) Hateley(10)
er	Robson*	Webb[1]	Harford	Beardsley	Hodge	Woods(1) Walker(5) Cottee(9) Gascoigne(10)
er	Robson*	Beardsley	Waddle	Lineker	J Barnes	Walker(5) Cottee(11)
ter	Robson*	Rocastle	Beardsley	Lineker	Waddle	Gascoigne(4) A Smith(9) Marwood(11)
er	Robson*[1]	Rocastle	A Smith	Lineker	J Barnes[1]	Beardsley(9)
er	Robson*[1]	Rocastle	Waddle	Lineker	J Barnes[1]	Beardsley(9) A Smith(10)
er	Robson*	Rocastle	Beardsley[2]	Lineker[1]	Waddle[1]	Parker(2) Gascoigne(8)[1]
er	Robson*	Gascoigne	Clough	Fashanu	Waddle	Cottee(10)
er	Robson*	Steven	Fashanu	Cottee	Waddle[1]	Bull(9)[1] Gascoigne(10)
er	Robson*	Waddle	Beardsley	Lineker[1]	J Barnes[1]	Rocastle(8) A Smith(9)
er	Robson*	Rocastle	Beardsley	Lineker[1]	J Barnes	Seaman(1) McMahon(4) Bull(9) Waddle(11)
er*	Beardsley	McMahon	Waddle	Lineker	J Barnes	Gascoigne(4) Rocastle(11)
er	Robson*	Rocastle	Beardsley	Lineker	Waddle	
er	Robson*	Waddle	Beardsley	Lineker	J Barnes	Beasant(1) Winterburn(3) Hodge(4) Phelan(7) Platt(9)
er*	Robson[2]	Rocastle	Bull	Lineker	Waddle	Beasant(1) Dorigo(3) Platt(4) McMahon(7) Hodge(8)
er*	Platt	Waddle	Beardsley	Lineker[1]	J Barnes	Woods(1) Gascoigne(9)

versus	venue	result	1	2	3	4	5
Czechoslovakia	H	4–2	Shilton	Dixon	Pearce[1]	Steven	Walker
Denmark	H	1–0	Shilton	Stevens	Pearce	McMahon	Walker
Uruguay	H	1–2	Shilton	Parker	Pearce	Hodge	Walker
Tunisia	A	1–1	Shilton	Stevens	Pearce	Hodge	Walker
Rep of Ireland	N	1–1	Shilton	Stevens	Pearce	Gascoigne	Walker
Holland	N	0–0	Shilton	Parker	Pearce	Wright	Walker
Egypt	N	1–0	Shilton*	Parker	Pearce	Gascoigne	Walker
Belgium	N	1–0	Shilton	Parker	Pearce	Wright	Walker
Cameroon	N	3–2	Shilton	Parker	Pearce	Wright	Walker
W Germany	N	1–1‡	Shilton	Parker	Pearce	Wright	Walker
Italy	A	1–2	Shilton*	Stevens	Dorigo	Parker	Walker
1990–91							
Hungary	H	1–0	Woods	Dixon	Pearce	Parker	Walker
Poland	H	2–0	Woods	Dixon	Pearce	Parker	Walker
Rep of Ireland	A	1–1	Woods	Dixon	Pearce	Adams	Walker
Cameroon	H	2–0	Seaman	Dixon	Pearce	Steven	Walker
Rep of Ireland	H	1–1	Seaman	Dixon[1]	Pearce	Adams	Walker
Turkey	A	1–0	Seaman	Dixon	Pearce	Wise[1]	Walker
USSR	H	3–1	Woods	Stevens	Dorigo	Wise	Parker
Argentina	H	2–2	Seaman	Dixon	Pearce	Batty	Walker
Australia	A	1–0	Woods	Parker	Pearce	Batty	Walker
New Zealand	A	1–0	Woods	Parker	Pearce	Batty	Walker
New Zealand	A	2–0	Woods	Charles	Pearce*[1]	Wise	Walker
Malaysia	A	4–2	Woods	Charles	Pearce	Batty	Walker
1991–92							
Germany	H	0–1	Woods	Dixon	Dorigo	Batty	Pallister
Turkey	H	1–0	Woods	Dixon	Pearce	Batty	Walker
Poland	A	1–1	Woods	Dixon	Pearce	Gray	Walker
France	H	2–0	Woods	R Jones	Pearce*	Keown	Walker
Czechoslovakia	A	2–2	Seaman	Keown[1]	Pearce*	Rocastle	Walker

*captain   †own goal   *Small numerals goals scored*   *Numbers after sub player replaced*   ‡W Germany

	7	8	9	10	11	substitutes
:her	Robson*	Gascoigne[1]	Bull[2]	Lineker	Hodge	Seaman(1) Dorigo(3) Wright(5) McMahon(7)
:her*	Hodge	Gascoigne	Waddle	Lineker[1]	J Barnes	Woods(1) Dorigo(3) Platt(4) Rocastle(9) Bull(10)
:her	Robson*	Gascoigne	Waddle	Lineker	J Barnes[1]	Beardsley(4) Bull(10)
:her	Robson*	Waddle	Gascoigne	Lineker	J Barnes	Beardsley(4) Wright(6) Platt(8) Bull(10)[1]
:her	Waddle	Robson*	Beardsley	Lineker[1]	J Barnes	McMahon(9) Bull(10)
:her	Robson*	Waddle	Gascoigne	Lineker	J Barnes	Platt(7) Bull(8)
ght[1]	McMahon	Waddle	Bull	Lineker	J Barnes	Platt(8) Beardsley(9)
:her*	McMahon	Waddle	Gascoigne	Lineker	J Barnes	Platt(7)[1] Bull(11)
:her*	Platt[1]	Waddle	Gascoigne	Lineker[2]	J Barnes	Steven(6) Beardsley(11)
:her*	Platt[1]	Waddle	Gascoigne	Lineker[1]	Beardsley	Steven(6)
ght	Platt[1]	Steven	McMahon	Lineker	Beardsley	Waddle(6) Webb(9)
ght	Platt	Gascoigne	Bull	Lineker*[1]	J Barnes	Dorigo(3) Waddle(9)
ght	Platt	Gascoigne	Bull	Lineker*[1]	J Barnes	Beardsley(9)[1] Waddle(10)
ght	Platt[1]	Cowans	Beardsley	Lineker*	McMahon	
ght	Robson	Gascoigne	I Wright	Lineker*[2]	J Barnes	Pallister(7) Hodge(8)
ght	Robson	Platt	Beardsley	Lineker*	J Barnes	Sharpe(4) I Wright(10)
ister	Platt	G Thomas	A Smith	Lineker*	J Barnes	Hodge(8)
ght*	Platt[2]	G Thomas	A Smith[1]	I Wright	J Barnes	Batty(4) Beardsley(10)
ght	Platt[1]	G Thomas	A Smith	Lineker*[1]	J Barnes	Clough(11)
ght	Platt	G Thomas	Clough	Lineker*	Hirst	† Wise(10) Salako(11)
rett	Platt	G Thomas	Wise	Lineker*[1]	Walters	Deane(4) Salako(11)
ght	Platt	G Thomas	Deane	I Wright	Salako	Hirst(9)[1]
ght	Platt	G Thomas	Clough	Lineker*[4]	Salako	
:ker	Platt	Steven	A Smith	Lineker*	Salako	Stewart(8) Merson(11)
bbutt	Robson	Platt	A Smith[1]	Lineker*	Waddle	A Smith(4) Daley(11)
bbutt	Platt	G Thomas	Rocastle	Lineker*	Sinton	Lineker(11)[1]
ght	Webb	G Thomas	Clough	Shearer[1]	Hirst	Dixon(4) Lineker(6) Stewart(9) Dorigo(11)
bbutt	Platt	Merson[1]	Clough	Hateley	J Barnes	

versus	venue	result	1	2	3	4	5
CIS	A	2–2	Woods	Stevens	Sinton	Palmer	Walker
Hungary	A	1–0	Martyn	Stevens	Dorigo	Curle	Walker
Brazil	H	1–1	Woods	Stevens	Dorigo	Palmer	Walker
Finland	A	2–1	Woods	Stevens	Pearce	Keown	Walker
Denmark	N	0–0	Woods	Curle	Pearce	Palmer	Walker
France	N	0–0	Woods	Batty	Pearce	Palmer	Walker
Sweden	A	1–2	Woods	Batty	Pearce	Keown	Walker
1992–93							
Spain	A	0–1	Woods	Dixon	Pearce*	Ince	Walker
Norway	H	1–1	Woods	Dixon	Pearce*	Batty	Walker
Turkey	H	4–0	Woods	Dixon	Pearce*[1]	Palmer	Walker
San Marino	H	6–0	Woods	Dixon	Dorigo	Palmer[1]	Walker
Turkey	A	2–0	Woods	Dixon	Sinton	Palmer	Walker
Holland	H	2–2	Woods	Dixon	Keown	Palmer	Walker
Poland	A	1–1	Woods	Bardsley	Dorigo	Palmer	Walker
Norway	A	0–2	Woods	Dixon	Pallister	Palmer	Walker
United States	A	0–2	Woods	Dixon	Dorigo	Palmer	Pallister
Brazil	N	1–1	Flowers	Barrett	Dorigo	Walker	Pallister
Germany	N	1–2	Martyn	Barrett	Sinton	Walker	Pallister

*captain   †own goal   *Small numerals goals scored*   *Numbers after sub player replaced*

	7	8	9	10	11	substitutes
›wn	Platt	Steven[1]	Shearer	Lineker*[1]	Daley	Martyn(1) Curle(3) Stewart(8) Clough(9)
›wn	Webb[1]	Palmer	Merson	Lineker*	Daley	Seaman(1) Sinton(4) Batty(7) A Smith(9) I Wright(10)
›wn	Daley	Steven	Platt[1]	Lineker*	Sinton	Pearce(3) Merson(7) Webb(8) Rocastle(11)
ight	Platt[2]	Steven	Webb	Lineker*	J Barnes	Palmer(2) Daley(8) Merson(11)
›wn	Platt	Steven	A Smith	Lineker*	Merson	Daley(2) Webb(11)
›wn	Platt	Steven	Shearer	Lineker*	Palmer	
mer	Platt[1]	Webb	Sinton	Lineker*	Daley	Merson(9) A Smith(10)
ight	White	Platt	Clough	Shearer	Sinton	Bardsley(2) Palmer(2) Merson(7) Deane(11)
ams	Platt[1]	Gascoigne	Shearer	I Wright	Ince	Palmer(2) Merson(10)
ams	Platt	Gascoigne[2]	Shearer[1]	I Wright	Ince	
ams	Platt*[4]	Gascoigne	Ferdinand[1]	J Barnes	Batty	
ams	Platt*[1]	Gascoigne[1]	J Barnes	I Wright	Ince	Clough(2) Sharpe(10)
ams	Platt*[1]	Gascoigne	Ferdinand	J Barnes[1]	Ince	Merson(8)
ams	Platt*	Gascoigne	Sheringham	J Barnes	Ince	I Wright(4)[1] Clough(8)
ams	Platt*	Gascoigne	Ferdinand	Sheringham	Sharpe	Clough(5) I Wright(10)
ty	Ince*	Clough	Sharpe	Ferdinand	J Barnes	Walker(4) I Wright(10)
ty	Ince*	Clough	I Wright	Sinton	Sharpe	Platt(6)[1] Palmer(7) Merson(8)
e	Platt*[1]	Clough	Sharpe	J Barnes	Merson	Keown(5) I Wright(8) Winterburn(9)

PRE-WAR INTERNATIONAL PLAYERS

ABBOTT, WALTER Centre half
Club: Everton *Caps:* 1 *Goals:* 0
ADCOCK, HUGH Outside Right
Club: Leicester City *Caps:* 5 *Goals:* 1
ALCOCK, CHARLES Forward
Club: Wanderers *Caps:* 1 *Goals:* 1
Captain: 1
ALDERSON, JACK Goalkeeper
Club: Crystal Palace *Caps:* 1
Goals conceded: 1
ALDRIDGE, ALBERT Full back
Clubs: West Bromwich Albion (1), Walsall
Town Swifts (1) *Caps:* 2 *Goals:* 0
ALLEN, ALBERT Inside left
Club: Aston Villa *Caps:* 1 *Goals:* 3
ALLEN, HENRY Centre half
Club: Wolves *Caps:* 5 *Goals:* 0
ALLEN, JIM Centre half
Club: Portsmouth *Caps:* 2 *Goals:* 0
ALSFORD, WALTER Left half
Club: Tottenham Hotspur *Caps:* 1 *Goals:* 0
AMOS, ANDREW Left half
Club: Old Carthusians *Caps:* 2 *Goals:* 1
ANDERSON, RUPERT Goalkeeper
Club: Old Etonians *Caps:* 1 *Goals
conceded:* 0
ARMITAGE, GEORGE Centre half
Club: Charlton Athletic *Caps:* 1 *Goals:* 0
ARNOLD, JOHN Outside left
Club: Fulham *Caps:* 1 *Goals:* 0
ARTHUR, HERBERT Goalkeeper
Club: Blackburn Rovers *Caps:* 7
Goals conceded: 4
ASHCROFT, JIMMY Goalkeeper
Club: Woolwich Arsenal *Caps:* 3
Goals conceded: 2
ASHMORE, GEORGE Goalkeeper
Club: West Bromwich Albion *Caps:* 1
Goals conceded: 3
ASHTON, CLAUDE Centre forward
Club: Corinthians *Caps:* 1 *Goals:* 0
Captain: 1
ASHURST, BILL Right back
Club: Notts County *Caps:* 5 *Goals:* 0
ATHERSMITH, CHARLIE Outside right
Club: Aston Villa *Caps:* 12 *Goals:* 3
AUSTIN, SID Outside right
Club: Manchester City *Caps:* 1 *Goals:* 0
BACH, PHIL Full back
Club: Sunderland *Caps:* 1 *Goals:* 0

BACHE, JOE Inside left
Club: Aston Villa *Caps:* 7 *Goals:* 4
BADDELEY, TOM Goalkeeper
Club: Wolves *Caps:* 5 *Goals conceded:* 5
BAGSHAW, JIMMY Right half
Club: Derby County *Caps:* 1 *Goals:* 0
BAILEY, HORACE Goalkeeper
Club: Leicester Fosse *Caps:* 5
Goals conceded: 3
BAILEY, NORMAN Half back
Club: Clapham Rovers *Caps:* 19 *Goals:* 2
Captain: 15
BAIN, JOHN Forward
Club: Oxford University *Caps:* 1 *Goals:* 0
BAKER, ALFRED Right half
Club: Arsenal *Caps:* 1 *Goals:* 0
BALL, JOHN Goalkeeper
Club: Bury *Caps:* 1 *Goals conceded:* 1
BALMER, WILLIAM Right back
Club: Everton *Caps:* 1 *Goals:* 0
BAMBER, JOHN Right half
Club: Liverpool *Caps:* 1 *Goals:* 0
BAMBRIDGE, ARTHUR Left back/Forward
Club: Swifts *Caps:* 3 *Goals:* 1
BAMBRIDGE, CHARLES Outside left
Clubs: Swifts (13), Swifts & Corinthians
(5) *Caps:* 18 *Goals:* 11 *Captain:* 2
BAMBRIDGE, ERNEST Forward
Club: Swifts & Corinthians *Caps:* 1
Goals: 0
BANKS, HERBERT Inside left
Club: Millwall Athletic *Caps:* 1 *Goals:* 0
BANNISTER, WILLIAM Centre half
Clubs: Burnley (1), Bolton Wanderers (1)
Caps: 2 *Goals:* 0
BARCLAY, BOBBY Inside right
Club: Sheffield United *Caps:* 3 *Goals:* 2
BARKAS, SAM Inside right/Left back
Club: Manchester City *Caps:* 5 *Goals:* 0
Captain: 3
BARKER, JOHN Centre half
Club: Derby County *Caps:* 11 *Goals:* 0
Captain: 1
BARKER, ROBERT Goalkeeper
Club: Hertfordshire Rangers *Caps:* 1
Goals conceded: 0
BARKER, RICHARD Half back
Club: Casuals *Caps:* 1 *Goals:* 0
BARNET, HORACE Forward
Club: Royal Engineers *Caps:* 1 *Goals:* 0

BARRETT, ALBERT Left half
Club: Fulham *Caps:* 1 *Goals:* 0
BARRETT, JIMMY Centre half
Club: West Ham United *Caps:* 1 *Goals:* 0
BARRY, LEN Outside left
Club: Leicester City *Caps:* 5 *Goals:* 0
BARSON, FRANK Centre half
Club: Aston Villa *Caps:* 1 *Goals:* 0
BARTON, JOHN Right half
Club: Blackburn Rovers *Caps:* 1 *Goals:* 1
BARTON, PERCY Left half
Club: Birmingham FC *Caps:* 7 *Goals:* 0
BASSETT, BILL Outside right
Club: West Bromwich Albion *Caps:* 16
Goals: 7
BASTARD, SEGAL RICHARD Outside right
Club: Upton Park *Caps:* 1 *Goals:* 0
BASTIN, CLIFF Outside/Inside left
Club: Arsenal *Caps:* 21 *Goals:* 12
BAUGH, DICK Right back
Clubs: Stafford Road (1), Wolves (1)
Caps: 2 *Goals:* 0
BAYLISS, JEM Right half
Club: West Bromwich Albion *Caps:* 1
Goals: 0
BEASLEY, ALBERT Outside left
Club: Huddersfield *Caps:* 1 *Goals:* 1
BEATS, BILLY Centre forward
Club: Wolves *Caps:* 2 *Goals:* 0
BECTON, FRANK Inside left
Clubs: Preston NE (1), Liverpool (1)
Caps: 2 *Goals:* 2
BEDFORD, HENRY Centre forward
Club: Blackpool *Caps:* 2 *Goals:* 1
BENNETT, WALTER Outside right
Club: Sheffield United *Caps:* 2 *Goals:* 0
BENSON, BOBBY Left back
Club: Sheffield United *Caps:* 1 *Goals:* 0
BERESFORD, JOE Inside right
Club: Aston Villa *Caps:* 1 *Goals:* 0
BERRY, ARTHUR Outside right
Club: Oxford University *Caps:* 1 *Goals:* 0
BESTALL, JOHN Inside right
Club: Grimsby Town *Caps:* 1 *Goals:* 0
BETMEAD, HARRY Centre half
Club: Grimsby Town *Caps:* 1 *Goals:* 0
BETTS, MORTON Goalkeeper
Club: Old Harrovians *Caps:* 1 *Goals conceded:* 3
BETTS, BILLY Left half
Club: Sheffield Wednesday *Caps:* 1 *Goals:* 0
BEVERLEY, JOE Full back

Club: Blackburn Rovers *Caps:* 3 *Goals:* 0
BIRKETT, RALPH Outside right
Club: Middlesbrough *Caps:* 1 *Goals:* 1
BIRKETT, REG Goalkeeper
Club: Clapham Rovers *Caps:* 1
Goals conceded: 4
BIRLEY, FRANCIS Half back
Clubs: Oxford University (1), Wanderers
(1) *Caps:* 2 *Goals:* 0
BISHOP, SID Left half
Club: Leicester City *Caps:* 4 *Goals:* 1
BLACKBURN, FRED Outside left
Club: Blackburn Rovers *Caps:* 3 *Goals:* 1
BLACKBURN, GEORGE Left half
Club: Aston Villa *Caps:* 1 *Goals:* 0
BLENKINSOP, ERNEST Left back
Club: Sheffield Wednesday *Caps:* 26
Goals: 0 *Captain* 4
BLISS, HERBERT Inside left
Club: Tottenham Hotspur *Caps:* 1 *Goals:* 0
BLOOMER, STEVE Inside right
Clubs: Derby County (21), Middlesbrough
(2) *Caps:* 23 *Goals:* 28 *Captain:* 1
BOND, DICKY Outside right
Clubs: Preston NE (5), Bradford City (3)
Caps: 8 *Goals:* 2
BONSOR, ALEX Forward/Goalkeeper
Club: Wanderers *Caps:* 2 *Goals:* 1
Goals conceded: 0
BOOTH, FRANK Outside left
Club: Manchester City *Caps:* 1 *Goals:* 0
BOOTH, TOM Centre half
Clubs: Blackburn Rovers (1), Everton (1)
Caps: 2 *Goals:* 0
BOWDEN, RAY Inside right
Club: Arsenal *Caps:* 6 *Goals:* 1
BOWER, ALFRED 'BAISHE' Right/Left back
Club: Corinthians *Caps:* 5 *Goals:* 0
Captain: 3
BOWERS, JOHN Centre forward
Club: Derby County *Caps:* 3 *Goals:* 2
BOWSER, SID Centre half
Club: West Bromwich Albion *Caps:* 1
Goals: 0
BOYES, WALTER Outside left
Clubs: West Bromwich Albion (1),
Everton (2) *Caps:* 3 *Goals:* 0
BOYLE, TOMMY Centre half
Club: Burnley *Caps:* 1 *Goals:* 0
BRADFORD, JOE Centre forward
Club: Birmingham FC *Caps:* 12 *Goals:* 7
BRADSHAW, BILL Left half

Club: Blackburn Rovers *Caps:* 4 *Goals:* 0
BRADSHAW, FRANK Centre forward
Club: Sheffield Wednesday *Caps:* 1
Goals: 3
BRADSHAW, T. HARRY Outside left
Club: Liverpool *Caps:* 1 *Goals:* 0
BRANN, GEORGE Outside left/Inside
forward
Club: Swifts *Caps:* 3 *Goals:* 1
BRAWN, BILLY Outside right
Club: Aston Villa *Caps:* 2 *Goals:* 0
BRAY, JOHN Left half
Club: Manchester City *Caps:* 6 *Goals:* 0
BRAYSHAW, EDWARD Centre half
Club: Sheffield Wednesday *Caps:* 1
Goals: 0
BRIDGETT, ARTHUR Outside left
Club: Sunderland *Caps:* 11 *Goals:* 3
BRINDLE, THOMAS Right/Left back
Club: Darwen *Caps:* 2 *Goals:* 1
BRITTLETON, TOMMY Right half
Club: Sheffield Wednesday *Caps:* 5
Goals: 0
BRITTON, CLIFF Inside right
Club: Everton *Caps:* 9 *Goals:* 1
BROCKBANK, JOHN Forward
Club: Cambridge University *Caps:* 1
Goals: 0
BRODIE, JOHN Centre forward
Club: Wolves *Caps:* 3 *Goals:* 1
Captain: 1
BROMILOW, TOM Left half
Club: Liverpool *Caps:* 5 *Goals:* 0
BROMLEY-DAVENPORT, WILLIAM E.
Centre forward
Club: Oxford University *Caps:* 2 *Goals:* 2
BROOK, ERIC Outside left
Club: Manchester City *Caps:* 18
Goals: 10
BROOME, FRANK Centre forward/Winger
Club: Aston Villa *Caps:* 7 *Goals:* 3
BROWN, ARTHUR Inside right
Club: Aston Villa *Caps:* 3 *Goals:* 4
BROWN, ARTHUR S. Centre forward
Club: Sheffield United *Caps:* 2 *Goals:* 1
BROWN, GEORGE Inside right/Centre
forward
Clubs: Huddersfield Town (8), Aston Villa
(1) *Caps:* 9 *Goals:* 5
BROWN, JAMES Centre forward
Club: Blackburn Rovers *Caps:* 5 *Goals:* 3
BROWN, JOHN Goalkeeper

Club: Sheffield Wednesday *Caps:* 6
Goals conceded: 7
BROWN, BILL Inside right
Club: West Ham United *Caps:* 1 *Goals:* 1
BRUTON, JOHN Outside right
Club: Burnley *Caps:* 3 *Goals:* 0
BRYANT, BILLY Centre half
Club: Clapton *Caps:* 1 *Goals:* 0
BUCHAN, CHARLIE Inside right/Centre
forward
Club: Sunderland *Caps:* 6 *Goals:* 4
Captain: 2
BUCHANAN, WALTER Forward
Club: Clapham Rovers *Caps:* 1 *Goals:* 0
BUCKLEY, FRANK Centre half
Club: Derby County *Caps:* 1 *Goals:* 0
BULLOCK, FRED Left back
Club: Huddersfield Town *Caps:* 1 *Goals:* 0
BULLOCK, NORMAN Centre forward
Club: Bury *Caps:* 3 *Goals:* 2
BURGESS, HARRY Inside left
Club: Sheffield Wednesday *Caps:* 4
Goals: 2
BURGESS, HERBERT Left back
Club: Manchester City *Caps:* 4 *Goals:* 0
BURNUP, CUTHBERT JAMES Outside left
Club: Cambridge University *Caps:* 1
Goals: 0
BURROWS, HORACE Left half
Club: Sheffield Wednesday *Caps:* 3
Goals: 0
BURTON, FRANK Forward
Club: Nottingham Forest *Caps:* 1 *Goals:* 0
BURY, LINDSAY Full back
Clubs: Cambridge University (1), Old
Etonians (1) *Caps:* 2 *Goals:* 0
BUTLER, JOHN Centre half
Club: Arsenal *Caps:* 1 *Goals:* 0
BUTLER, BILL Outside right
Club: Bolton Wanderers *Caps:* 1 *Goals:* 0
CALVEY, JOHN Centre forward
Club: Nottingham Forest *Caps:* 1 *Goals:* 0
CAMPBELL, AUSTEN Left half
Clubs: Blackburn Rovers (2), Huddersfield
Town (6) *Caps:* 8 *Goals:* 0
CAMSELL, GEORGE Centre forward
Club: Middlesbrough *Caps:* 9 *Goals:* 18
CARR, JOHN Left back
Club: Newcastle United *Caps:* 2 *Goals:* 0
CARR, JOHN Inside/Outside right
Club: Middlesbrough *Caps:* 2 *Goals:* 0
CARR, BILL Goalkeeper

Club: Owlerton (Sheffield) *Caps:* 1
Goals conceded: 2

CARTER, JOE Inside right/left
Club: West Bromwich Albion *Caps:* 3
Goals: 4

CARTER, RAICH Inside right
Clubs: Sunderland (6), Derby County (7)
Caps: 13 *Goals:* 7

CATLIN, TED Left back
Club: Sheffield Wednesday *Caps:* 5
Goals: 0

CHADWICK, ARTHUR Centre half
Club: Southampton *Caps:* 2 *Goals:* 0

CHADWICK, EDGAR Inside left
Club: Everton *Caps:* 7 *Goals:* 3

CHAMBERS, HENRY Inside left/Centre
forward
Club: Liverpool *Caps:* 8 *Goals:* 5

CHAPPELL, FREDERICK Forward
Club: Oxford University *Caps:* 1 *Goals:* 0

CHARSLEY, CHARLES Goalkeeper
Club: Small Heath *Caps:* 1
Goals conceded: 1

CHEDGZOY, SAM Outside right
Club: Everton *Caps:* 8 *Goals:* 0

CHENERY, CHARLES Forward
Club: Crystal Palace *Caps:* 3 *Goals:* 1

CHIPPENDALE, HENRY Outside right
Club: Blackburn Rovers *Caps:* 1 *Goals:* 0

CHRISTIAN, EDWARD Full back
Club: Old Etonians *Caps:* 1 *Goals:* 0

CLARE, TOMMY Right back
Club: Stoke FC *Caps:* 4 *Goals:* 0

CLAY, TOMMY Right back
Club: Tottenham Hotspur *Caps:* 4 *Goals:* 0

CLEGG, CHARLES Forward
Club: Sheffield Wednesday *Caps:* 1
Goals: 0

CLEGG, WILLIAM Forward
Clubs: Sheffield Wednesday (1), Sheffield
Albion (1) *Caps:* 2 *Goals:* 0

COBBOLD, NEVILL Inside/Outside forward
Clubs: Cambridge University (6), Old
Carthusians (3) *Caps:* 9 *Goals:* 6

COCK, JOHN Centre forward
Clubs: Huddersfield Town (1), Chelsea (1)
Caps: 2 *Goals:* 2

COLCLOUGH, HORACE Left back
Club: Crystal Palace *Caps:* 1 *Goals:* 0

COLEMAN, ERNEST Goalkeeper
Club: Dulwich Hamlet *Caps:* 1
Goals conceded: 0

COLEMAN, TIM Inside right
Club: Woolwich Arsenal *Caps:* 1 *Goals:* 0

COMMON, ALFRED Inside/Centre forward
Clubs: Sheffield United (2), Middlesbrough
(1) *Caps:* 3 *Goals:* 3

CONLIN, JAMES Outside left
Club: Bradford City *Caps:* 1 *Goals:* 0

COOK, TOMMY Centre forward
Club: Brighton and Hove Albion *Caps:* 1
Goals: 0

COOPER, NORMAN Half back
Club: Cambridge University *Caps:* 1
Goals: 0

COOPER, TOMMY Right back
Club: Derby County *Caps:* 15 *Goals:* 0
Captain: 4

COPPING, WILF Left half
Clubs: Leeds United (8), Arsenal (12)
Caps: 20 *Goals:* 0

CORBETT, BERTIE Outside left
Club: Corinthians *Caps:* 1 *Goals:* 0

CORBETT, REGINALD Outside left
Club: Old Malvernians *Caps:* 1 *Goals:* 0

CORBETT, WALTER Left back
Club: Birmingham FC *Caps:* 3 *Goals:* 0

COTTERILL, GEORGE Centre forward
Clubs: Cambridge University (1); Old
Brightonians (3) *Caps:* 4 *Goals:* 2
Captain: 2

COTTLE, JOSEPH RICHARD Left back
Club: Bristol City *Caps:* 1 *Goals:* 0

COWAN, SAMUEL Centre/Left half
Club: Manchester City *Caps:* 3 *Goals:* 0

COWELL, ARTHUR Left back
Club: Blackburn Rovers *Caps:* 1 *Goals:* 0

COX, JOHN Outside left
Club: Liverpool *Caps:* 3 *Goals:* 0

COX, JOHN D. Right half
Club: Derby County *Caps:* 1 *Goals:* 0

CRAWFORD, JACK Outside left
Club: Chelsea *Caps:* 1 *Goals:* 0

CRAWSHAW, TOMMY Centre half
Club: Sheffield Wednesday *Caps:* 10
Goals: 1

CRAYSTON, JACK Right half
Club: Arsenal *Caps:* 8 *Goals:* 1

CREEK, NORMAN Centre forward
Club: Corinthians *Caps:* 1 *Goals:* 1
Captain: 1

CRESSWELL, WARNEY Right back
Clubs: South Shields (1), Sunderland (5),
Everton (1) *Caps:* 7 *Goals:* 0

CROMPTON, BOB Right back
Club: Blackburn Rovers *Caps:* 41 *Goals:* 0
Captain: 23

CROOKS, SAMMY Outside right
Club: Derby County *Caps:* 26 Goals: 7

CUGGY, FRANK Right half
Club: Sunderland *Caps:* 2 *Goals:* 0

CULLIS, STAN Centre half
Club: Wolves *Caps:* 12 *Goals:* 0
Captain: 1

CUNLIFFE, ARTHUR Outside left
Club: Blackburn Rovers *Caps:* 2 *Goals:* 0

CUNLIFFE, DANIEL Inside right
Club: Portsmouth *Caps:* 1 *Goals:* 0

CUNLIFFE, JIMMY Inside left
Club: Everton *Caps:* 1 *Goals:* 0

CURREY, EDMUND Inside forward
Club: Oxford University *Caps:* 2 *Goals:* 2

CURSHAM, ARTHUR Forward
Club: Notts County *Caps:* 6 *Goals:* 2
Captain: 2

CURSHAM, HARRY Outside left/right
Club: Notts County *Caps:* 8 *Goals:* 5

DAFT, HARRY Left-sided forward
Club: Notts County *Caps:* 5 *Goals:* 3

DANKS, TOM Forward
Club: Nottingham Forest *Caps:* 1 *Goals:* 0

DAVENPORT, KENNY Inside/Outside right
Club: Bolton Wanderers *Caps:* 2 *Goals:* 2

DAVIS, GEORGE Outside left
Club: Derby County *Caps:* 2 *Goals:* 0

DAVIS, HENRY Outside right
Club: Sheffield Wednesday *Caps:* 3
Goals: 1

DAVISON, TEDDY Goalkeeper
Club: Sheffield Wednesday *Caps:* 1
Goals conceded: 0

DAWSON, JERRY Goalkeeper
Club: Burnley *Caps:* 2 *Goals conceded:* 2

DAY, SAMMY Inside foward
Club: Old Malvernians *Caps:* 3 *Goals:* 2

DEAN, WILLIAM 'DIXIE' Centre forward
Club: Everton *Caps:* 16 *Goals:* 18

DE PARAVICINI, PERCY Right back
Club: Cambridge University *Caps:* 3
Goals: 0

DEVEY, JACK Forward
Club: Aston Villa *Caps:* 2 *Goals:* 1

DEWHURST, FRED Inside right/left
Club: Preston NE *Caps:* 9 *Goals:* 12

DEWHURST, GERALD Inside foward
Club: Liverpool Ramblers *Caps:* 1 *Goals:* 0

DIMMOCK, JIMMY Outside left
Club: Tottenham Hotspur *Caps:* 3 *Goals:* 0

DIX, RONNIE Inside left
Club: Derby County *Caps:* 1 *Goals:* 1

DIXON, JOHN Left-sided forward
Club: Notts County *Caps:* 1 *Goals:* 0

DOBSON, ALF Right back
Club: Notts County *Caps:* 4 *Goals:* 0

DOBSON, CHARLEY Half back
Club: Notts County *Caps:* 1 *Goals:* 0

DOGGART, A. GRAHAM Inside left
Club: Corinthians *Caps:* 1 *Goals:* 0
Captain: 1

DORRELL, ARTHUR Outside left
Club: Aston Villa *Caps:* 4 *Goals:* 1

DOWNS, JOHN Right back
Club: Everton *Caps:* 1 *Goals:* 0

DRAKE, TED Centre forward
Club: Arsenal *Caps:* 5 *Goals:* 6

DUCAT, ANDY Right half
Clubs: Woolwich Arsenal (3), Aston Villa
(3) *Caps:* 6 *Goals:* 1

DUNN, ARTHUR Centre forward/Right back
Clubs: Cambridge University (2), Old
Etonians (2) *Caps:* 4 *Goals:* 2 *Captain:* 2

EARLE, STAN Inside right
Clubs: Clapton (1), West Ham United (1)
Caps: 2 *Goals:* 0

EASTHAM, GEORGE Inside right
Club: Bolton Wanderers *Caps:* 1 *Goals:* 0

EDWARDS, WILLIS Right half
Club: Leeds United *Caps:* 16 *Goals:* 0
Captain: 5

ELLIOTT, GEORGE Centre forward
Club: Middlesbrough *Caps:* 3 *Goals:* 0

EVANS, BOBBY Outside left
Club: Sheffield United *Caps:* 4 *Goals:* 1

EWER, FREDDIE Right/Left half
Club: Casuals *Caps:* 2 *Goals:* 0

FAIRCLOUGH, PERCY Forward
Club: Old Foresters *Caps:* 1 *Goals:* 0

FAIRHURST, DAVID Left back
Club: Newcastle United *Caps:* 1 *Goals:* 0

FELTON, BILLY Left back
Club: Sheffield Wednesday *Caps:* 1
Goals: 0

FENTON, MICHAEL Centre forward
Club: Middlesbrough *Caps:* 1 *Goals:* 0

FIELD, EDGAR Full back
Club: Clapham Rovers *Caps:* 2 *Goals:* 0

FLEMING, HAROLD J. Inside right
Club: Swindon Town *Caps:* 11 *Goals:* 9

FLETCHER, ALBERT T. Right half
Club: Wolves *Caps:* 2 *Goals:* 0
FORMAN, FRANK Half back
Club: Nottingham Forest *Caps:* 9
Goals: 1
FORMAN, FREDERICK Outside left
Club: Nottingham Forest *Caps:* 3 *Goals:* 3
FORREST, JIMMY Left half/Centre half
Club: Blackburn Rovers *Caps:* 11 *Goals:* 0
FORT, JOHN Right back
Club: Millwall *Caps:* 1 *Goals:* 0
FOSTER, REGINALD Inside forward
Clubs: Oxford University (1), Corinthians
(4) *Caps:* 5 *Goals:* 3 *Captain:* 1
FOULKE, WILLIE H. Goalkeeper
Club: Sheffield United *Caps:* 1
Goals conceded: 0
FOX, FRED S. Goalkeeper
Club: Millwall *Caps:* 1 *Goals conceded:* 2
FREEMAN, BERT Centre forward
Clubs: Everton (2), Burnley (3) *Caps:* 5
Goals: 3
FRY, CHARLES (CB) Right back
Club: Corinthians *Caps:* 1 *Goals:* 0
FURNESS, BILL Inside left
Club: Leeds United *Caps:* 1 *Goals:* 0
GALLEY, THOMAS Inside right
Club: Wolves *Caps:* 2 *Goals:* 1
GARDNER, TOM Right half
Club: Aston Villa *Caps:* 2 *Goals:* 0
GARFIELD, BEN Outside left
Club: West Bromwich Albion *Caps:* 1
Goals: 0
GARRATTY, BILLY Inside right
Club: Aston Villa *Caps:* 1 *Goals:* 0
GAY, LESLIE Goalkeeper
Clubs: Cambridge University (1), Old
Brightonians (2) *Caps:* 3
Goals conceded: 5
GEARY, FRED Centre forward
Club: Everton *Caps:* 2 *Goals:* 3
GEAVES, RICHARD Outside left
Club: Clapham Rovers *Caps:* 1 *Goals:* 0
GEE, CHARLIE Centre half
Club: Everton *Caps:* 3 *Goals:* 0
GELDARD, ALBERT Outside right
Club: Everton *Caps:* 4 *Goals:* 0
GEORGE, BILL Goalkeeper
Club: Aston Villa *Caps:* 3
Goals conceded: 2
GIBBINS, VIV Centre forward
Club: Clapton *Caps:* 2 *Goals:* 3

GILLIAT, WALTER Inside forward
Club: Old Carthusians *Caps:* 1 *Goals:* 3
GOODALL, JOHN Inside forward/Centre
forward
Clubs: Preston NE (4), Derby County (10)
Caps: 14 *Goals:* 11 *Captain:* 2
GOODALL, ROY Right back
Club: Huddersfield Town *Caps:* 25
Goals: 0 *Captain:* 11
GOODHART, HARRY Forward
Club: Old Etonians *Caps:* 3 *Goals:* 0
GOODWYN, ALF Half back
Club: Royal Engineers *Caps:* 1 *Goals:* 0
GOODYER, ARTHUR Outside right
Club: Nottingham Forest *Caps:* 1 *Goals:* 1
GOSLING, CUNLIFFE Outside/Inside forward
Club: Old Etonians *Caps:* 5 *Goals:* 2
Captain: 1
GOSNELL, ALBERT Outside left
Club: Newcastle United *Caps:* 1 *Goals:* 0
GOUGH, HAROLD Goalkeeper
Club: Sheffield United *Caps:* 1
Goals conceded: 3
GOULDEN, LEN Inside left/right
Club: West Ham United *Caps:* 14 *Goals:* 4
GRAHAM, LEN Left half
Club: Millwall *Caps:* 2 *Goals:* 0
GRAHAM, TOMMY Centre half
Club: Nottingham Forest *Caps:* 2 *Goals:* 2
GREEN, FRED Full back
Club: Wanderers *Caps:* 1 *Goals:* 0
GREEN, GEORGE Left half
Club: Sheffield United *Caps:* 8 *Goals:* 0
GREENHALGH, ERNIE Defender
Club: Notts County *Caps:* 2 *Goals:* 0
GREENWOOD, DOC Right/left back
Club: Blackburn Rovers *Caps:* 2 *Goals:* 0
GRIMSDELL, ARTHUR Left half
Club: Tottenham Hotspur *Caps:* 6 *Goals:* 0
Captain: 3
GROSVENOR, TOM Inside right
Club: Birmingham FC *Caps:* 3 *Goals:* 2
GUNN, BILLY Forward
Club: Notts County *Caps:* 2 *Goals:* 1
GURNEY, BOB Centre forward
Club: Sunderland *Caps:* 1 *Goals:* 0
HACKING, JOHN Goalkeeper
Club: Oldham Athletic *Caps:* 3
Goals conceded: 4
HADLEY, HAROLD Left half
Club: West Bromwich Albion *Caps:* 1
Goals: 0

HALL, ALBERT Outside left
Club: Aston Villa *Caps:* 1 *Goals:* 0
HALL, WILLIE Inside left/right
Club: Tottenham Hotspur *Caps:* 10
Goals: 9
HALSE, HAROLD Inside right
Club: Manchester United *Caps:* 1 *Goals:* 2
HAMMOND, HENRY Half back
Club: Oxford University *Caps:* 1 *Goals:* 0
HAMPSON, JIMMY Centre forward
Club: Blackpool *Caps:* 3 *Goals:* 5
HAMPTON, HARRY Centre forward
Clubs: Aston Villa *Caps:* 4 *Goals:* 2
HAPGOOD, EDDIE Left back
Club: Arsenal *Caps:* 30 *Goals:* 0
Captain: 21
HARDINGE, HAROLD 'WALLY' Inside left
Club: Sheffield United *Caps:* 1 *Goals:* 0
HARDMAN, HAROLD Outside left
Club: Everton *Caps:* 4 *Goals:* 1
HARDY, HENRY Goalkeeper
Club: Stockport County *Caps:* 1
Goals conceded: 0
HARDY, SAM Goalkeeper
Clubs: Liverpool (14), Aston Villa (7)
Caps: 21 *Goals conceded:* 25
HARGREAVES, FRED Half back
Club: Blackburn Rovers *Caps:* 3 *Goals:* 0
HARGREAVES, JOHN Outside right/left
Club: Blackburn Rovers *Caps:* 2 *Goals:* 0
HARPER, TED Centre forward
Club: Blackburn Rovers *Caps:* 1 *Goals:* 0
HARRIS, STANLEY Inside forward
Clubs: Cambridge University (1), Old
Westminsters (5) *Caps:* 6 *Goals:* 2
Captain: 4
HARRISON, ALBAN Right back
Club: Old Westminsters *Caps:* 2 *Goals:* 0
HARRISON, GEORGE Outside left
Club: Everton *Caps:* 2 *Goals:* 0
HARROW, JACK Left back
Club: Chelsea *Caps:* 2 *Goals:* 0
HART, ERNIE Centre half
Club: Leed United *Caps:* 8 *Goals:* 0
HARTLEY, FRANK Inside left
Club: Oxford City *Caps:* 1 *Goals:* 0
HARVEY, ALF Full back
Club: Wednesbury Strollers *Caps:* 1
Goals: 0
HAWKES, BOB Left half
Club: Luton Town *Caps:* 5 *Goals:* 0
HAWLEY EDWARDS, JOHN Forward

Club: Shropshire Wanderers *Caps:* 1
Goals: 0
HAWORTH, GEORGE Half back
Club: Accrington FC *Caps:* 5 *Goals:* 0
HAWTREY, JOHN PURVIS Goalkeeper
Club: Old Etonians *Caps:* 2
Goals conceded: 7
HAYGARTH, EDWARD Full back
Club: Swifts *Caps:* 1 *Goals:* 0
HEALLESS, HENRY Centre/Left half
Club: Blackburn Rovers *Caps:* 2 *Goals:* 0
HEDLEY, GEORGE Centre forward
Club: Sheffield United *Caps:* 1 *Goals:* 0
HEGAN, KENNETH Outside left/right
Club: Corinthians *Caps:* 4 *Goals:* 4
HENFREY, ARTHUR Half back/Forward
Clubs: Cambridge University (1),
Corinthians (4) *Caps:* 5 *Goals:* 2
HERON, FRANK Forward
Club: Wanderers *Caps:* 1 *Goals:* 0
HERON, HUBERT Forward
Clubs: Uxbridge (2), Wanderers (3)
Caps: 5 *Goals:* 0 *Captain:* 1
HIBBERT, WILLIAM Inside right
Club: Bury *Caps:* 1 *Goals:* 0
HIBBS, HARRY Goalkeeper
Club: Birmingham FC *Caps:* 25
Goals conceded: 26
HILL, JACK Right/Centre half
Clubs: Burnley (8), Newcastle United (3)
Caps: 11 *Goals:* 0 *Captain:* 8
HILL, RICHARD Left back
Club: Millwall *Caps:* 1 *Goals:* 0
HILLMAN, JOHN Goalkeeper
Club: Burnley *Caps:* 1 *Goals conceded:* 2
HILLS, ARNOLD Forward
Club: Old Harrovians *Caps:* 1 *Goals:* 0
HILSDON, GEORGE Centre forward
Club: Chelsea *Caps:* 8 *Goals:* 14
HINE, ERNIE Inside right/left
Club: Leicester City *Caps:* 6 *Goals:* 4
HOBBIS, HAROLD Outside left
Club: Charlton Athletic *Caps:* 2 *Goals:* 1
HODGETTS, DENNIS Inside/Outside left
Club: Aston Villa *Caps:* 6 *Goals:* 1
HODGSON, GORDON Inside right
Club: Liverpool *Caps:* 3 *Goals:* 1
HODKINSON, JOE Outside left
Club: Blackburn Rovers *Caps:* 3
Goals: 0
HOGG, WILLIAM Outside right
Club: Sunderland *Caps:* 3 *Goals:* 0

HOLDCROFT, HARRY Goalkeeper
Club: Preston NE *Caps:* 2
Goals conceded: 3
HOLDEN, GEORGE Outside right
Club: Wednesbury Old Athletic *Caps:* 4
Goals: 0
HOLDEN-WHITE, CECIL Left half
Club: Corinthians *Caps:* 2 *Goals:* 0
HOLFORD, THOMAS Centre half
Club: Stoke FC *Caps:* 1 *Goals:* 0
HOLLEY, GEORGE Inside foward
Club: Sunderland *Caps:* 10 *Goals:* 8
HOLMES, ROBERT Full back/Half back
Club: Preston NE *Caps:* 7 *Goals:* 0
Captain: 3
HOLT, JOHN Centre half
Clubs: Everton (9), Reading (1) *Caps:* 10
Goals: 0
HOSSACK, TONY Right half
Club: Corinthians *Caps:* 2 *Goals:* 0
HOUGHTON, ERIC Outside left
Club: Aston Villa *Caps:* 7 *Goals:* 5
HOULKER, ALBERT ('KELLY') Left half
Clubs: Blackburn Rovers (1), Portsmouth
(2) Southampton (2) *Caps:* 5 *Goals:* 0
HOWARD BAKER, BEN Goalkeeper
Clubs: Everton (1), Chelsea (1) *Caps:* 2
Goals conceded: 0
HOWARTH, ROBERT Right back
Clubs: Preston NE (4), Everton (1)
Caps: 5 *Goals:* 0
HOWELL, LEONARD Defender
Club: Wanderers *Caps:* 1 *Goals:* 0
HOWELL, RABBI Right half
Clubs: Sheffield United (1), Liverpool (1)
Caps: 2 *Goals:* 1
HUDSON, JOHN Half back
Club: Sheffield Wednesday *Caps:* 1
Goals: 0 *Captain:* 1
HUDSPETH, FRANCIS Left back
Club: Newcastle United *Caps:* 1 *Goals:* 0
HUFTON, EDWARD Goalkeeper
Club: West Ham United *Caps:* 6
Goals conceded: 14
HULME, JOE Outside right
Club: Arsenal *Caps:* 9 *Goals:* 4
HUMPHREYS, PERCY Inside right
Club: Notts County *Caps:* 1 *Goals:* 0
HUNT, GEORGE Centre forward
Club: Tottenham Hotspur *Caps:* 3 *Goals:* 1
HUNT, KENNETH Left half
Club: Leyton *Caps:* 2 *Goals:* 0

HUNTER, JOHN Half back
Club: Sheffield Heeley *Caps:* 7 *Goals:* 0
Captain: 1
IREMONGER, JAMES Full back
Club: Nottingham Forest *Caps:* 2 *Goals:* 0
JACK, DAVID Inside right
Clubs: Bolton Wanderers (4), Arsenal (5)
Caps: 9 *Goals:* 3 *Captain:* 4
JACKSON, ELPHINSTONE Full back
Club: Oxford University *Caps:* 1 *Goals:* 0
JARRETT, BEAUMONT GRIFFITH Half back
Club: Cambridge University *Caps:* 3
Goals: 0
JEFFERIS, FRANK Inside right
Club: Everton *Caps:* 2 *Goals:* 0
JOHNSON, EDWARD Outside right
Clubs: Saltley College (1), Stoke FC (1)
Caps: 2 *Goals:* 2
JOHNSON, JOSEPH Outside left
Club: Stoke City *Caps:* 5 *Goals:* 2
JOHNSON, HARRY Half back
Club: Sheffield United *Caps:* 6 *Goals:* 1
JOHNSON, THOMAS Inside left
Clubs: Manchester City (2), Everton (3)
Caps: 5 *Goals:* 5
JONES, ALFRED Right/Left back
Clubs: Walsall Town Swifts (2), Great
Lever (1) *Caps:* 3 *Goals:* 0
JONES, HARRY Left back
Club: Nottingham Forest *Caps:* 1 *Goals:* 0
JONES, HERBERT Left back
Club: Blackburn Rovers *Caps:* 6 *Goals:* 0
JONES, WILLIAM Half back
Club: Bristol City *Caps:* 1 *Goals:* 0
JOY, BERNARD Centre half
Club: Casuals *Caps:* 1 *Goals:* 0
KAIL, EDGAR Inside right
Club: Dulwich Hamlet *Caps:* 3 *Goals:* 2
KEAN, FREDERICK Right/Centre half
Clubs: Sheffield Wednesday (7), Bolton
Wanderers (2) *Caps:* 9 *Goals:* 0 *Captain:* 1
KEEN, ERRINGTON Left half
Club: Derby County *Caps:* 4 *Goals:* 0
KELLY, ROBERT Inside/Outside right
Clubs: Burnley (11), Sunderland (1),
Huddersfield Town (2) *Caps:* 14 *Goals:* 8
KENYON SLANEY, WILLIAM Forward
Club: Wanderers *Caps:* 1 *Goals:* 2
KING, ROBERT Half back
Club: Oxford University *Caps:* 1 *Goals:* 0
KINGSFORD, ROBERT Forward
Club: Wanderers *Caps:* 1 *Goals:* 1

KINGSLEY, MATTHEW Goalkeeper
Club: Newcastle United *Caps:* 1
Goals conceded: 0
KINSEY, GEORGE Left half
Clubs: Wolves (2), Derby County (2)
Caps: 4 *Goals:* 0
KIRCHEN, ALFRED Outside right
Club: Arsenal *Caps:* 3 *Goals:* 2
KIRKE SMITH, ARNOLD Forward
Club: Oxford University *Caps:* 1 *Goals:* 0
KIRTON, WILLIAM Inside right
Club: Aston Villa *Caps:* 1 *Goals:* 1
KNIGHT, ARTHUR Left back
Club: Portsmouth *Caps:* 1 *Goals:* 0
Captain: 1
LATHERON, EDWIN Inside left
Club: Blackburn Rovers *Caps:* 2 *Goals:* 1
LAWTON, TOMMY Centre forward
Clubs: Everton (8), Chelsea (11), Notts
County (4) *Caps:* 23 *Goals:* 22
LEACH, THOMAS Centre half
Club: Sheffield Wednesday *Caps:* 2
Goals: 0
LEAKE, ALEXANDER Left half
Club: Aston Villa *Caps:* 5 *Goals:* 0
LEE, ALBERT Right half
Club: Southampton *Caps:* 1 *Goals:* 0
LEIGHTON, JOHN EDWARD Outside right
Club: Nottingham Forest *Caps:* 1
Goals: 0
LILLEY, HENRY Left back
Club: Sheffield United *Caps:* 1 *Goals:* 0
LINACRE, HENRY Goalkeeper
Club: Nottingham Forest *Caps:* 2
Goals conceded: 1
LINDLEY, TINSLEY Centre forward
Clubs: Cambridge University (9),
Nottingham Forest (4) *Caps:* 13
Goals: 14 *Captain:* 4 at least
LINDSAY, WILLIAM Full back
Club: Wanderers *Caps:* 1 *Goals:* 0
LINTOTT, EVELYN Left half
Clubs: QPR (3), Bradford City (4) *Caps:* 7
Goals: 0
LIPSHAM, HERBERT Outside left
Club: Sheffield United *Caps:* 1 *Goals:* 0
LOCKETT, ARTHUR Outside left
Club: Stoke FC *Caps:* 1 *Goals:* 0
LODGE, L. VAUGHAN Full back
Club: Cambridge University *Caps:* 5
Goals: 0
LOFTHOUSE, JOSEPH Outside right

Clubs: Blackburn Rovers (6), Accrington
FC (1) *Caps:* 7 *Goals:* 2
LONGWORTH, EPHRAIM Right back
Club: Liverpool *Caps:* 5 *Goals:* 0
Captain: 1
LOWDER, ARTHUR Half back
Club: Wolves *Caps:* 1 *Goals:* 0
LUCAS, THOMAS Left/Right back
Club: Liverpool *Caps:* 3 *Goals:* 0
Captain: 1
LUNTLEY, EDWIN Right back
Club: Nottingham Forest *Caps:* 2 *Goals:* 0
LYTTELTON, ALFRED Forward
Club: Cambridge University *Caps:* 1
Goals: 1
LYTTELTON, EDWARD Full back
Club: Cambridge University *Caps:* 1
Goals: 0
MACAULAY, REGINALD Centre forward
Club: Cambridge University *Caps:* 1
Goals: 0
McCALL, JOSEPH Centre half
Club: Preston NE *Caps:* 5
Goals: 1 *Captain:* 1
McINROY, ALBERT Goalkeeper
Club: Sunderland *Caps:* 1
Goals conceded: 3
McNEAL, ROBERT Left half
Club: West Bromwich Albion *Caps:* 2
Goals: 0
MACRAE, STUART Half back
Club: Notts County *Caps:* 6 *Goals:* 0
MAGEE, THOMAS Right half
Club: West Bromwich Albion *Caps:* 5
Goals: 0
MAKEPEACE, HENRY Half back
Club: Everton *Caps:* 4 *Goals:* 0
MALE, GEORGE Right back
Club: Arsenal *Caps:* 19 *Goals:* 0
Captain: 6
MARSDEN, JOSEPH Right back
Club: Darwen *Caps:* 1 *Goals:* 0
MARSDEN, WILLIAM Left half
Club: Sheffield Wednesday *Caps:* 3
Goals: 0
MARSHALL, THOMAS Outside right
Club: Darwen *Caps:* 2 *Goals:* 0
MARTIN, HENRY Outside left
Club: Sunderland *Caps:* 1 *Goals:* 0
MASKREY, HARRY Goalkeeper
Club: Derby County *Caps:* 1
Goals conceded: 1

MASON, CHARLES Left back
Club: Wolves *Caps:* 3 *Goals:* 0
MATTHEWS, STANLEY Outside right
Clubs: Stoke City (18), Blackpool (36)
Caps: 54 *Goals:* 11 (including post-war
appearances and goals)
MATTHEWS, VINCENT Centre half
Club: Sheffield United *Caps:* 2 *Goals:* 1
MAYNARD, WILLIAM Forward/Goalkeeper
Club: 1st Surrey Rifles *Caps:* 2 *Goals:* 0
Goals conceded: 3
MEEHAN, THOMAS Left half
Club: Chelsea *Caps:* 1 *Goals:* 0
MERCER, DAVID Outside right
Club: Sheffield Wednesday *Caps:* 2 *Goals:* 1
MERCER, JOSEPH Left half
Club: Everton *Caps:* 5 *Goals:* 0
MEW, JOHN Goalkeeper
Club: Manchester United *Caps:* 1
Goals conceded: 0
MIDDLEDITCH, BERNARD Right half
Club: Corinthians *Caps:* 1 *Goals:* 0
MILLER, HAROLD Inside left
Club: Charlton Athletic *Caps:* 1 *Goals:* 1
MILLS, GEORGE Centre forward
Club: Chelsea *Caps:* 3 *Goals:* 3
MILWARD, ALFRED Outside left
Club: Everton *Caps:* 4 *Goals:* 3
MITCHELL, CLEMENT Centre forward
Club: Upton Park *Caps:* 5 *Goals:* 5
MITCHELL, JAMES Goalkeeper
Club: Manchester City *Caps:* 1
Goals conceded: 1
MOFFAT, HUGH Right half
Club: Oldham Athletic *Caps:* 1 *Goals:* 0
MOLYNEUX, GEORGE Left back
Club: Southampton *Caps:* 4 *Goals:* 0
MOON, WILLIAM Goalkeeper
Club: Old Westminsters *Caps:* 7
Goals conceded: 8 *Captain:* 1
MOORE, HENRY Full back
Club: Notts County *Caps:* 2 *Goals:* 0
MOORE, JAMES Inside right
Club: Derby County *Caps:* 1 *Goals:* 1
MOORE, WILLIAM Inside right
Club: West Ham United *Caps:* 1 *Goals:* 2
MORDUE, JOHN Outside left/right
Club: Sunderland *Caps:* 2 *Goals:* 0
MORICE, CHARLES Forward
Club: Barnes *Caps:* 1 *Goals:* 0
MORLEY, HERBERT Right back
Club: Notts County *Caps:* 1 *Goals:* 0

MORREN, THOMAS Centre half
Club: Sheffield United *Caps:* 1 *Goals:* 1
MORRIS, FRED Inside left
Club: West Bromwich Albion *Caps:* 2
Goals: 1
MORRIS, WILLIAM Left back
Club: Wolves *Caps:* 3 *Goals:* 0
MORSE, HAROLD Left back
Club: Notts County *Caps:* 1 *Goals:* 0
MORT, THOMAS Left back
Club: Aston Villa *Caps:* 3 *Goals:* 0
MORTEN, ALEXANDER Goalkeeper
Club: Crystal Palace *Caps:* 1
Goals conceded: 2 *Captain:* 1
MORTON, JOHN Outside left
Club: West Ham United *Caps:* 1 *Goals:* 1
MOSFORTH, WILLIAM Outside left
Clubs: Sheffield Albion (5), Sheffield
Wednesday (4) *Caps:* 9 *Goals:* 3
MOSS, FRANK Half back
Club: Aston Villa *Caps:* 5 *Goals:* 0
Captain: 1
MOSS, FRANK Goalkeeper
Club: Arsenal *Caps:* 4 *Goals conceded:* 6
MOSSCROP, EDWIN Outside left
Club: Burnley *Caps:* 2 *Goals:* 0
NEEDHAM, ERNEST Left half
Club: Sheffield United *Caps:* 16 *Goals:* 3
Captain: 1
NUTTALL, HENRY Right/left half
Club: Bolton Wanderers *Caps:* 3 *Goals:* 0
OAKLEY, WILLIAM Full back
Clubs: Oxford University (4), Corinthians
(12) *Caps:* 16 *Goals:* 0 *Captain:* 1
O'DOWD, PETER Centre half
Club: Chelsea *Caps:* 3 *Goals:* 0
OGILVIE, ROBERT Full back
Club: Clapham Rovers *Caps:* 1 *Goals:* 0
OLIVER, LEONARD FREDERICK Right half
Club: Fulham *Caps:* 1 *Goals:* 0
OLNEY, BENJAMIN Goalkeeper
Club: Aston Villa *Caps:* 2 *Goals
conceded:* 2
OSBORNE, FRANK Centre forward/Outside
right
Clubs: Fulham (2), Tottenham Hotspur (2)
Caps: 4 *Goals:* 3
OSBORNE, REGINALD Left back
Club: Leicester City *Caps:* 1 *Goals:* 0
OTTAWAY, CUTHBERT Forward
Club: Oxford University *Caps:* 2 *Goals:* 0
Captain: 2

OWEN, JOHN Forward
Club: Sheffield Club *Caps:* 1 *Goals:* 0
PAGE, LOUIS Outside left
Club: Burnley *Caps:* 7 *Goals:* 1
PANTLING, HARRY Right half
Club: Sheffield United *Caps:* 1 *Goals:* 0
PARKER, THOMAS Right back
Club: Southampton *Caps:* 1 *Goals:* 0
PARKINSON, JOHN Centre forward
Club: Liverpool *Caps:* 2 *Goals:* 0
PARR, PERCIVAL Inside forward
Club: Oxford University *Caps:* 1 *Goals:* 0
PARRY, EDWARD Forward
Club: Old Carthusians *Caps:* 3 *Goals:* 1
PATCHITT, BASIL Right/Left half
Club: Corinthians *Caps:* 2 *Goals:* 0
Captain: 2
PAWSON, FRANK Outside right/Centre
forward
Clubs: Cambridge University (1), Swifts (1)
Caps: 2 *Goals:* 1
PAYNE, JOSEPH Centre forward
Club: Luton Town *Caps:* 1 *Goals:* 2
PEACOCK, JOHN Left half
Club: Middlesbrough *Caps:* 3 *Goals:* 0
PEARSON, HAROLD Goalkeeper
Club: West Bromwich Albion *Caps:* 1
Goals conceded: 0
PEARSON, JACK Inside right
Club: Crewe Alexandra *Caps:* 1 *Goals:* 0
PEASE, WILLIAM Outside right
Club: Middlesbrough *Caps:* 1 *Goals:* 0
PELLY, FREDERICK Left back
Club: Old Foresters *Caps:* 3 *Goals:* 0
PENNINGTON, JESSE Left back
Club: West Bromwich Albion *Caps:* 25
Goals: 0 *Captain:* 2
PENTLAND, FREDERICK Outside right
Club: Middlesbrough *Caps:* 5 *Goals:* 0
PERRY, CHARLES Centre half
Club: West Bromwich Albion *Caps:* 3
Goals: 0
PERRY, THOMAS Right half
Club: West Bromwich Albion *Caps:* 1
Goals: 0
PICKERING, JOHN Inside left
Club: Sheffield United *Caps:* 1 *Goals:* 0
PIKE, THELWELL Outside left
Club: Brentwood *Caps:* 1 *Goals:* 0
PLANT, JOHN Outside left
Club: Bury *Caps:* 1 *Goals:* 0
PLUM, SETH Right half

Club: Charlton Athletic *Caps:* 1 *Goals:* 0
PORTEOUS, THOMAS Right back
Club: Sunderland *Caps:* 1 *Goals:* 0
PRIEST, ALFRED Left-sided forward
Club: Sheffield United *Caps:* 1 *Goals:* 0
PRINSEP, JAMES Half back
Club: Clapham Rovers *Caps:* 1 *Goals:* 0
PUDDEFOOT, SYDNEY Inside right
Club: Blackburn Rovers *Caps:* 2 *Goals:* 0
PYM, RICHARD Goalkeeper
Club: Bolton Wanderers *Caps:* 3
Goals conceded: 6
QUANTRILL, ALFRED Outside left
Club: Derby County *Caps:* 4 *Goals:* 1
RAIKES, GEORGE Goalkeeper
Club: Oxford University *Caps:* 4
Goals conceded: 4
RAWLINGS, ARCHIBALD Outside right
Club: Preston NE *Caps:* 1 *Goals:* 0
RAWLINGS, WILLIAM Centre forward
Club: Southampton *Caps:* 2 *Goals:* 0
RAWLINSON, JOHN Goalkeeper
Club: Cambridge University *Caps:* 1
Goals conceded: 0
RAWSON, HERBERT Forward
Club: Royal Engineers *Caps:* 1 *Goals:* 0
RAWSON, WILLIAM Full back
Club: Oxford University *Caps:* 2 *Goals:* 0
Captain: 1
READ, ALBERT Right half
Club: Tufnell Park *Caps:* 1 *Goals:* 0
READER, JOSEPH Goalkeeper
Club: West Bromwich Albion *Caps:* 1
Goals conceded: 2
REYNOLDS, JOHN Right half
Clubs: West Bromwich Albion (3), Aston
Villa (5) *Caps:* 8 *Goals:* 3
RICHARDS, CHARLES Inside forward
Club: Nottingham Forest *Caps:* 1
Goals: 0
RICHARDS, GEORGE Left half
Club: Derby County *Caps:* 1 *Goals:* 0
RICHARDSON, JAMES Inside right
Club: Newcastle United *Caps:* 2 *Goals:* 2
RICHARDSON, WILLIAM Centre forward
Club: West Bromwich Albion *Caps:* 1
Goals: 0
RIGBY, ARTHUR Inside left
Club: Blackburn Rovers *Caps:* 5 *Goals:* 3
RIMMER, ELLIS Outside left
Club: Sheffield Wednesday *Caps:* 4
Goals: 2

ROBERTS, CHARLES Centre half
Club: Manchester United *Caps:* 3 *Goals:* 0
ROBERTS, FRANK Inside right/Centre forward
Club: Manchester City *Caps:* 4 *Goals:* 2
ROBERTS, HENRY Inside right
Club: Millwall *Caps:* 1 *Goals:* 1
ROBERTS, HERBERT Centre forward
Club: Arsenal *Caps:* 1 *Goals:* 0
ROBERTS, ROBERT Goalkeeper
Club: West Bromwich Albion *Caps:* 3
Goals conceded: 2
ROBERTS, THOMAS Centre forward
Club: Preston NE *Caps:* 2 *Goals:* 2
ROBINSON, JOHN Inside right
Club: Sheffield Wednesday *Caps:* 4
Goals: 3
ROBINSON, JOHN Goalkeeper
Clubs: Derby County (2), New Brighton Tower (3), Southampton (6) *Caps:* 11
Goals conceded: 11
ROSE, WILLIAM Goalkeeper
Clubs: Swifts (3), Preston NE (1), Wolves (1) *Caps:* 5 *Goals conceded:* 4
ROSTRON, THURSTON Forward
Club: Darwen *Caps:* 2 *Goals:* 0
ROWE, ARTHUR Centre half
Club: Tottenham Hotspur *Caps:* 1 *Goals:* 0
ROWLEY, WILLIAM Goalkeeper
Club: Stoke FC *Caps:* 2 *Goals conceded:* 1
RUDDLESDIN, HEROD Half back
Club: Sheffield Wednesday *Caps:* 3
Goals: 0
RUFFELL, JAMES Outside left
Club: West Ham United *Caps:* 6 *Goals:* 0
RUSSELL, BRUCE Left back
Club: Royal Engineers *Caps:* 1 *Goals:* 0
RUTHERFORD, JOHN Outside right
Club: Newcastle United *Caps:* 11 *Goals:* 3
SAGAR, CHARLES Inside left/Centre forward
Club: Bury *Caps:* 2 *Goals:* 1
SAGAR, EDWARD Goalkeeper
Club: Everton *Caps:* 4 *Goals conceded:* 7
SANDFORD, EDWARD Inside left
Club: West Bromwich Albion *Caps:* 1
Goals: 0
SANDILANDS, RUPERT Outside left
Club: Old Westminsters *Caps:* 5 *Goals:* 3
SANDS, JOHN Goalkeeper
Club: Nottingham Forest *Caps:* 1
Goals conceded: 2

SAUNDERS, FRANK Half back
Club: Swifts *Caps:* 1 *Goals:* 0
SAVAGE, A.H. Goalkeeper
Club: Crystal Palace *Caps:* 1
Goals conceded: 3
SAYER, JAMES Outside right
Club: Stoke FC *Caps:* 1 *Goals:* 0
SCATTERGOOD, ERNALD Goalkeeper
Club: Derby County *Caps:* 1
Goals conceded: 3
SCHOFIELD, JOSEPH Left-sided forward
Club: Stoke FC *Caps:* 3 *Goals:* 1
SCOTT, WILLIAM Inside right
Club: Brentford *Caps:* 1 *Goals:* 0
SEDDON, JAMES Centre half
Club: Bolton Wanderers *Caps:* 6 *Goals:* 0
SEED, JAMES Inside right
Club: Tottenham Hotspur *Caps:* 5 *Goals:* 1
SETTLE, JAMES Inside left
Clubs: Bury (3), Everton (3) *Caps:* 6
Goals: 6
SEWELL, RONALD Goalkeeper
Club: Blackburn Rovers *Caps:* 1
Goals conceded: 2
SHARP, JOHN Inside/outside right
Club: Everton *Caps:* 2 *Goals:* 1
SHAW, GEORGE Right back
Club: West Bromwich Albion *Caps:* 1
Goals: 0
SHEA, DANIEL Inside right
Club: Blackburn Rovers *Caps:* 2 *Goals:* 0
SHELTON, ALFRED Half back
Club: Notts County *Caps:* 6 *Goals:* 1
SHELTON, CHARLES Half back
Club: Notts Rangers *Caps:* 1 *Goals:* 0
SHEPHERD, ALBERT Centre forward
Clubs: Bolton Wanderers (1), Newcastle United (1) *Caps:* 2 *Goals:* 2
SHUTT, GEORGE Half back
Club: Stoke FC *Caps:* 1 *Goals:* 0
SILCOCK, JOHN Left back
Club: Manchester United *Caps:* 3 *Goals:* 0
SIMMS, ERNEST Centre forward
Club: Luton Town *Caps:* 1 *Goals:* 0
SIMPSON, JOHN Outside right
Club: Blackburn Rovers *Caps:* 8 *Goals:* 1
SMALLEY, TOM Right half
Club: Wolves *Caps:* 1 *Goals:* 0
SMART, THOMAS Right back
Club: Aston Villa *Caps:* 5 *Goals:* 0
SMITH, ALBERT Right half
Club: Nottingham Forest *Caps:* 3 *Goals:* 0

SMITH, BERT Right half
Club: Tottenham Hotspur *Caps:* 2 *Goals:* 0
SMITH, CHARLES Forward
Club: Crystal Palace *Caps:* 1 *Goals:* 0
SMITH, GILBERT Centre forward
Clubs: Oxford University (7), Old
Carthusians (6), Corinthians (7) *Caps:* 20
Goals: 11 *Captain:* 14
SMITH, HERBERT Left back
Club: Reading *Caps:* 4 *Goals:* 0
SMITH, JOHN Inside right
Club: Portsmouth *Caps:* 3 *Goals:* 4
SMITH, JOSEPH Inside left
Club: Bolton Wanderers *Caps:* 5 *Goals:* 1
SMITH, JOSEPH Right back
Club: West Bromwich Albion *Caps:* 2
Goals: 2
SMITH, LESLIE Outside left
Club: Brentford *Caps:* 1 *Goals:* 0
SMITH, REGINALD Outside left
Club: Millwall *Caps:* 2 *Goals:* 2
SMITH, SEPTIMUS Right half
Club: Leicester City *Caps:* 1 *Goals:* 0
SMITH, STEPHEN Outside left
Club: Aston Villa *Caps:* 1 *Goals:* 1
SMITH, WILLIAM Outside left
Club: Huddersfield Town *Caps:* 3 *Goals:* 0
SORBY, THOMAS HEATHCOTE Forward
Club: Thursday Wanderers (Sheffield)
Caps: 1 *Goals:* 1
SOUTHWORTH, JOHN Centre forward
Club: Blackburn Rovers *Caps:* 3 *Goals:* 3
SPARKS, FRANCIS Forward
Clubs: Hertfordshire Rangers (1), Clapham
Rovers (2) *Caps:* 3 *Goals:* 3 *Captain:* 1
SPENCE, JOSEPH Outside right
Club: Manchester United *Caps:* 2 *Goals:* 1
SPENCE, RICHARD Outside right
Club: Chelsea *Caps:* 2 *Goals:* 0
SPENCER, CHARLES Centre half
Club: Newcastle United *Caps:* 2 *Goals:* 0
SPENCER, HOWARD Left/Right back
Club: Aston Villa *Caps:* 6 *Goals:* 0
Captain: 3
SPIKSLEY, FREDERICK Outside left
Club: Sheffield Wednesday *Caps:* 7
Goals: 5
SPILSBURY, BENJAMIN Inside/Outside right
Club: Cambridge University *Caps:* 3
Goals: 5
SPOUNCER, ALF Outside left
Club: Nottingham Forest *Caps:* 1 *Goals:* 0

SPROSTON, BERT Right back
Clubs: Leeds United (8), Tottenham
Hotspur (2), Manchester City (1) *Caps:* 11
Goals: 0
SQUIRE, RALPH Half back/Right back
Club: Cambridge University *Caps:* 3
Goals: 0
STANBROUGH, HUGH Outside left
Club: Old Carthusians *Caps:* 1 *Goals:* 0
STARLING, RONALD Inside right/left
Clubs: Sheffield Wednesday (1), Aston
Villa (1) *Caps:* 2 *Goals:* 0
STEELE, FREDERICK Striker
Club: Stoke City *Caps:* 6 *Goals:* 8
STEPHENSON, CLEMENT Inside left
Club: Huddersfield Town *Caps:* 1 *Goals:* 0
STEPHENSON, ERIC Inside left
Club: Leeds United *Caps:* 2 *Goals:* 0
STEPHENSON, GEORGE Inside left/right
Clubs: Derby County (2), Sheffield
Wednesday (1) *Caps:* 3 *Goals:* 2
STEWART, JAMES Inside left
Clubs: Sheffield Wednesday (2), Newcastle
United (1) *Caps:* 3 *Goals:* 2
STOKER, LEWIS Right half
Club: Birmingham FC *Caps:* 3 *Goals:* 0
STORER, HARRY Inside left/Left half
Club: Derby County *Caps:* 2 *Goals:* 0
STRANGE, ALFRED Right half
Club: Sheffield Wednesday *Caps:* 20
Goals: 0 *Captain:* 3
STRATFORD, ALFRED Full back
Club: Wanderers *Caps:* 1 *Goals:* 0
STURGESS, ALBERT Left half/Right half
Club: Sheffield United *Caps:* 2 *Goals:* 0
SUTCLIFFE, JOHN Goalkeeper
Clubs: Bolton Wanderers (4), Millwall
Athletic (1) *Caps:* 5 *Goals conceded:* 3
SWEPSTONE, HARRY Goalkeeper
Club: Pilgrims *Caps:* 6
Goals conceded: 18
TAIT, GEORGE Centre forward
Club: Birmingham Excelsior *Caps:* 1
Goals: 0
TATE, JOSEPH Left half
Club: Aston Villa *Caps:* 3 *Goals:* 0
TAYLOR, EDWARD Goalkeeper
Club: Huddersfield Town *Caps:* 8
Goals conceded: 10
THICKETT, HENRY Right back
Club: Sheffield United *Caps:* 2 *Goals:* 0
THORNEWELL, GEORGE Outside right

Club: Derby County *Caps:* 4 *Goals:* 0
THORNLEY, IRVINE Centre forward
Club: Manchester City *Caps:* 1 *Goals:* 0
TILSON, FREDERICK Centre forward
Club: Manchester City *Caps:* 4 *Goals:* 5
TITMUSS, FRED Left back
Club: Southampton *Caps:* 2 *Goals:* 0
TOONE, GEORGE Goalkeeper
Club: Notts County *Caps:* 2
Goals conceded: 1
TOPHAM, ARTHUR Half back
Club: Casuals *Caps:* 1 *Goals:* 0
TOPHAM, ROBERT Outside right
Club: Wolves *Caps:* 2 *Goals:* 0
TOWNLEY, WILLIAM J. Outside left
Club: Blackburn Rovers *Caps:* 2 *Goals:* 2
TOWNROW, JOHN Centre half
Club: Clapton Orient *Caps:* 2 *Goals:* 0
TREMELLING, DANIEL Goalkeeper
Club: Birmingham FC *Caps:* 1
Goals conceded: 2
TRESADERN, JOHN Left half
Club: West Ham United *Caps:* 2 *Goals:* 0
TUNSTALL, FREDERICK Outside left
Club: Sheffield United *Caps:* 7 *Goals:* 0
TURNBULL, ROBERT Outside right
Club: Bradford FC *Caps:* 1 *Goals:* 0
TURNER, ARTHUR Outside right
Club: Southampton *Caps:* 2 *Goals:* 0
TURNER, HUGH Goalkeeper
Club: Huddersfield Town *Caps:* 2
Goals conceded: 6
TWEEDY, GEORGE Goalkeeper
Club: Grimsby Town *Caps:* 1
Goals conceded: 2
UNDERWOOD, ALFRED Left/right back
Club: Stoke FC *Caps:* 2 *Goals:* 0
URWIN, THOMAS Outside left/right
Clubs: Middlesbrough (2), Newcastle
United (2) *Caps:* 4 *Goals:* 0
UTLEY, GEORGE Left half
Club: Barnsley *Caps:* 1 *Goals:* 0
VAUGHTON, HOWARD Foward
Club: Aston Villa *Caps:* 5 *Goals:* 6
VEITCH, COLIN Half back
Club: Newcastle United *Caps:* 6 *Goals:* 0
VEITCH, JOHN G. Forward
Club: Old Westminsters *Caps:* 1 *Goals:* 3
VIDAL, ROBERT Foward
Club: Oxford University *Caps:* 1 *Goals:* 0
VON DONOP, GEORGE Forward
Club: Royal Engineers *Caps:* 2 *Goals:* 0

WACE, HENRY Forward
Club: Wanderers *Caps:* 3 *Goals:* 0
Captain: 2
WADSWORTH, SAMUEL Left back
Club: Huddersfield Town *Caps:* 9
Goals: 0 *Captain:* 4
WAINSCOAT, RUSSELL Inside left
Club: Leeds United *Caps:* 1 *Goals:* 0
WALDEN, FREDERICK INGRAM
Outside right
Club: Tottenham Hotspur *Caps:* 2 *Goals:* 0
WALKER, WILLIAM Inside left
Club: Aston Villa *Caps:* 18 *Goals:* 9
Captain: 3
WALLACE, CHARLES Outside right
Club: Aston Villa *Caps:* 3 *Goals:* 0
WALTERS, ARTHUR Full back
Clubs: Cambridge University (5), Old
Carthusians (4) *Caps:* 9 *Goals:* 0
Captain: 1
WALTERS, PERCY Left/right back
Clubs: Oxford University (2), Old
Carthusians (11) *Caps:* 13 *Goals:* 0
Captain: 4
WALTON, NATHANIEL Forward
Club: Blackburn Rovers *Caps:* 1 *Goals:* 0
WARD, JAMES THOMAS Left back
Club: Blackburn Olympic *Caps:* 1 *Goals:* 0
WARING, THOMAS Centre forward
Club: Aston Villa *Caps:* 5 *Goals:* 4
WARNER, CONRAD Goalkeeper
Club: Upton Park *Caps:* 1
Goals conceded: 7
WARREN, BENJAMIN Right half
Clubs: Derby County (13), Chelsea (9)
Caps: 22 *Goals:* 2
WATERFIELD, GEORGE SMITH Left back
Club: Burnley *Caps:* 1 *Goals:* 0
WATSON, VICTOR Centre forward
Club: West Ham United *Caps:* 5 *Goals:* 4
WATSON, WILLIAM Left half
Club: Burnley *Caps:* 3 *Goals:* 0
WEAVER, SAMUEL Left half
Club: Newcastle United *Caps:* 3 *Goals:* 0
WEBB, GEORGE Centre forward
Club: West Ham United *Caps:* 2 *Goals:* 1
WEBSTER, MAURICE Centre half
Club: Middlesbrough *Caps:* 3 *Goals:* 0
WEDLOCK, WILLIAM Centre half
Club: Bristol City *Caps:* 26 *Goals:* 2
WEIR, DAVID Centre half/Inside left
Club: Bolton Wanderers *Caps:* 2 *Goals:* 1

WELCH, REGINALD Defender/Goalkeeper
Club: Harrow Chequers *Caps:* 2 *Goals:* 0
Goals conceded: 2
WELSH, DONALD Left half/Inside left
Club: Charlton Athletic *Caps:* 3 *Goals:* 1
WESTWOOD, RAYMOND Inside left
Club: Bolton Wanderers *Caps:* 6 *Goals:* 0
WHATELEY, OLIVER Inside right/left
Club: Aston Villa *Caps:* 2 *Goals:* 2
WHEELER, JOHN Right half
Club: Bolton Wanderers *Caps:* 1 *Goals:* 0
WHELDON, FREDERICK Inside forward
Club: Aston Villa *Caps:* 4 *Goals:* 6
WHITE, THOMAS Centre half
Club: Everton *Caps:* 1 *Goals:* 0
WHITEHEAD, JAMES Inside right
Clubs: Accrington FC (1), Blackburn
Rovers (1) *Caps:* 2 *Goals:* 0
WHITFIELD, HERBERT Forward
Club: Old Etonians *Caps:* 1 *Goals:* 1
WHITHAM, MICHAEL Left half
Club: Sheffield United *Caps:* 1 *Goals:* 0
WIDDOWSON, SAM Centre forward
Club: Nottingham Forest *Caps:* 1 *Goals:* 0
WILKES, ALBERT Half back
Club: Aston Villa *Caps:* 5 *Goals:* 1
WILKINSON, BERNARD Centre half
Club: Sheffield United *Caps:* 1 *Goals:* 0
WILKINSON, LEONARD Goalkeeper
Club: Oxford University *Caps:* 1
Goals conceded: 1
WILLIAMS, OWEN Outside left
Club: Clapton Orient *Caps:* 2 *Goals:* 0
WILLIAMS, WILLIAM Full back
Club: West Bromwich Albion *Caps:* 6
Goals: 0
WILLIAMSON, ERNEST Goalkeeper
Club: Arsenal *Caps:* 2 *Goals conceded:* 3
WILLIAMSON, REGINALD Goalkeeper
Club: Middlesbrough *Caps:* 7
Goals conceded: 6
WILLINGHAM, KENNETH Right half
Club: Huddersfield Town *Caps:* 12
Goals: 1
WILSON, CHARLES Half back
Club: Hendon *Caps:* 2 *Goals:* 0
WILSON, CLAUDE Full back
Club: Oxford University *Caps:* 2 *Goals:* 0
WILSON, GEOFFREY PLUMPTON Inside left
Club: Corinthians *Caps:* 2 *Goals:* 1
WILSON, GEORGE Centre half

Club: Sheffield Wednesday *Caps:* 12
Goals: 0 *Captain:* 7
WILSON, THOMAS Centre half
Club: Huddersfield Town *Caps:* 1 *Goals:* 0
WINCKWORTH, NORMAN Centre half
Club: Old Westminsters *Caps:* 2 *Goals:* 1
WINDRIDGE, JAMES Inside left
Club: Chelsea *Caps:* 8 *Goals:* 7
WINFIELD-STRATFORD, CECIL VERNON
Outside left
Club: Royal Engineers *Caps:* 1 *Goals:* 0
WOLLASTON, CHARLES Forward
Club: Wanderers *Caps:* 4 *Goals:* 1
Captain: 1
WOLSTENHOLME, SAMUEL Right half
Clubs: Everton (1), Blackburn Rovers (2)
Caps: 3 *Goals:* 0
WOOD, HARRY Inside forward
Club: Wolves *Caps:* 3 *Goals:* 1
WOODGER, GEORGE Outside left
Club: Oldham Athletic *Caps:* 1 *Goals:* 0
WOODHALL, GEORGE Outside right
Club: West Bromwich Albion *Caps:* 2
Goals: 1
WOODLEY, VICTOR Goalkeeper
Club: Chelsea *Caps:* 19 *Goals conceded:* 26
WOODWARD, VIVIAN Centre forward
Clubs: Tottenham Hotspur (21), Chelsea
(2) *Caps:* 23 *Goals:* 29 *Captain:* 13
WOOSNAM, MAXWELL Centre half
Club: Manchester City *Caps:* 1 *Goals:* 0
Captain: 1
WORRALL, FREDERICK Outside right
Club: Portsmouth *Caps:* 2 *Goals:* 2
WREFORD-BROWN, CHARLES Half back
Clubs: Oxford University (1), Old
Carthusians (3) *Caps:* 4 *Goals:* 0
Captain: 1
WRIGHT, DOUGLAS Left half
Club: Newcastle United *Caps:* 1 *Goals:* 0
WRIGHT, GORDON Outside left
Club: Cambridge University *Caps:* 1
Goals: 0
WYLIE, JOHN Forward
Club: Wanderers *Caps:* 1 *Goals:* 1
YATES, JOHN Outside left
Club: Burnley *Caps:* 1 *Goals:* 3
YORK, RICHARD Outside right
Club: Aston Villa *Caps:* 2 *Goals:* 0
YOUNG, ALFRED Centre half
Club: Huddersfield Town *Caps:* 9 *Goals:* 0